CAMBRIDGE TEXTS IN THE
HISTORY OF POLITICAL THOUGHT

——

Utopias of the British Enlightenment

DATE DUE

GAYLORD			PRINTED IN U.S.A.

CAMBRIDGE TEXTS IN THE HISTORY OF POLITICAL THOUGHT

Series editors

RAYMOND GEUSS

Reader *in Social and Political Sciences, University of Cambridge*

QUENTIN SKINNER

Professor of Political Science in the University of Cambridge

Cambridge Texts in the History of Political Thought is now firmly established as the major student textbook series in political theory. It aims to make available to students all the most important texts in the history of western political thought, from ancient Greece to the early twentieth century. All the familiar classic texts will be included but the series does at the same time seek to enlarge the conventional canon by incorporating an extensive range of less well-known works, many of them never before available in a modern English edition. Wherever possible, texts are published in complete and unabridged form, and translations are specially commissioned for the series. Each volume contains a critical introduction together with chronologies, biographical sketches, a guide to further reading and any necessary glossaries and textual apparatus. When completed, the series will aim to offer an outline of the entire evolution of western political thought.

For a list of titles published in the series, please see end of book.

Utopias of the British Enlightenment

EDITED BY

GREGORY CLAEYS

University of London

CAMBRIDGE
UNIVERSITY PRESS

PUBLISHED BY THE PRESS SYNDICATE OF THE UNIVERSITY OF CAMBRIDGE
The Pitt Building, Trumpington Street, Cambridge, United Kingdom

CAMBRIDGE UNIVERSITY PRESS
The Edinburgh Building, Cambridge, CB2 2RU, UK
40 West 20th Street, New York, NY 10011-4211, USA
477 Williamstown Road, Port Melbourne, VIC 3207, Australia
Ruiz de Alarcón 13, 28014 Madrid, Spain
Dock House, The Waterfront, Cape Town 8001, South Africa

http://www.cambridge.org

First published 1994
Reprinted 2003

Printed in the United Kingdom at the University Press, Cambridge

A catalogue record for this book is available from the British Library

Library of Congress Cataloguing in Publication data
Utopias of the British Enlightenment / edited by Gregory Claeys.
p. cm. – (Cambridge texts in the history of political thought)
Includes bibliographical references and index.
ISBN 0 521 43084 4. (hc)
1. Utopias 2. Utopian socialism – Great Britain – History – 18th century
1. Claeys, Gregory II. Series.
HX810.U798 1994
335'.02 – c20 93-26683 CIP

ISBN 0 521 43084 4 hardback
ISBN 0 521 45590 1 paperback

Contents

For Anna

Introduction

Literally and figuratively, the domain of eighteenth-century British utopianism is largely *terra incognita*. The subject itself, indeed, was once thought hardly to exist. For the age called Augustan is often supposed to have been singularly hard-headed and worldly, its speculative energies prematurely squandered by the constitutional experiments of the mid-seventeenth century, its intellectual fancies modest beside the spuriously 'enlightened' musings beloved of the French *philosophes*. Britain's only contemporary literary masterpieces which adopted the utopian genre, this view presumes, were typically sceptical satires like *Gulliver's Travels*. None the less, this is in itself a fanciful portrait. There were, indeed, many satires upon the notions of primitive innocence and of terrestrial moral perfectibility in this era, as well as the widespread use of the utopian format primarily to lampoon existing social imperfections, rather than to recommend a superior regime. But these are not solely characteristic of an age which, after all, swarmed with projectors, adventurers, moralists and improvers of all sorts. Much enamoured of the idea of progressing somewhere, if only back to a more virtuous epoch, eighteenth-century Britain could not but imagine a variety of fictional ideal societies and (the genres are closely related) model commonwealths. These often distinctively portray well-ordered and virtuous if normally still imperfect regimes, where property is held in common or limited by agrarian laws. The diversity of such works, however, is considerable. Several authors mix satire and reform proposal so intimately that their real intent remains obscure. Some utopias are political tracts or constitutional proposals only scantily clad in utopian disguise. Others, more literary, leap imaginatively into the lived personal experience of the ideal, concretizing hopes and aspirations as drier tracts of propaganda rarely can.

The more satirical, the constitutional, and the more idealistic literary texts can none the less be conceived as forming a single genre which retailed – or in the case of the satires, discounted – similar images of purportedly superior societies. In this period the anti-utopian satires and the ideal societies and model commonwealths together comprise some fifty texts. These include fictional critiques of utopian primitivism and perfectionism as well as Robinsonades, detailed constitutions in utopian form in the mould of James Harrington's *Oceana* (1656), and ideal societies of various types. With the exception of Defoe, Swift and their imitators, few of these texts have been studied carefully. They do, however, clearly form a genre, identified partly by form but also often, and more importantly, by content. Collectively, both utopias and anti-utopias focus primarily upon the idea of a community defined centrally by virtue and its absence, corruption. Not all such tracts, of course, focus *centrally* on the problem of corruption. A few do so only very marginally (e.g. [John Witherspoon], *The History of a Corporation of Servants*, Glasgow, 1765, which satirizes various developments in post-Reformation Protestantism). That such concerns were prominent in this literature is none the less unsurprising. For this theme was crucial to the prolonged debates about morals, manners and national survival in this period, which focussed on the immoderate increase in vice many contemporaries complained of. A few, like Bernard Mandeville in *The Fable of the Bees: or, Private Vices, Publick Benefits* (1714), ridiculed such concerns. But many more lamented that the era was dissolute in the extreme. Often they blamed increasing access to luxury goods by the lower orders for a seeming breakdown in deference and self-control which was potentially corrosive of the entire social order. It was also widely evident that few periods had tolerated such political corruption, notably under the 'Robinocracy' or patronage system of Sir Robert Walpole, Prime Minister from 1721 to 1742. Given this broader debate about 'corruption', utopianism is clearly less marginal to our understanding of the period than has been assumed. But we still need to ascertain what is distinctive about its response to these issues.

In general, the utopian literary genre has been adopted primarily to imagine societies of greater virtue and equality, both as a means of criticizing existing inadequacies, and of proposing more seriously ideas of or plans for greatly superior societies. In its negative, dystopian variety, the literary device also serves to ridicule as foolish, futile and whimsical efforts to institutionalize such qualities, at least in such an idealized form. The unique, extremely imaginative form of the genre permits normal social restrictions to be dissolved more readily than in other, more realistic, types of fiction. Among other things, this allows the expression of more extreme or implausible principles of social reform felt none the less to be practicable or desirable at some time and in some place. What might be seen as an embarrassing fantasy inadmissible in polite company when presented as a straightforward proposal becomes, in utopian disguise, with intentions masked, more circumspect, perhaps only an affable jest, but perhaps also an ardent wish. Frequently satirical to some degree, utopian authors have not always necessarily wished to see their plans materialize, at least in their own societies. Some, however, have been dedicated unswervingly to their legislative programmes. (Much ink has been spilt on how serious Thomas More, for example, was in this regard.) When seriously intended, their ideals, moreover, have altered somewhat from one era to the next. Utopias are hence not timeless in the sense of addressing only an hermetically sealed 'tradition', though a canon of texts clearly existed by 1700. Plato, More, Bacon, Harrington and others are thus customary reference points for the writers who concern us.[1]

But while they pay homage to this canon, utopias also confront the social and political transformations of their own time, and often propose more dramatic solutions than the mainstream political literature. This, in turn, is often how the form of a utopia or model common-

---

[1] James Burgh, for example, mentions More in *An Account of the . . . Cessares*, reprinted here (below, p. 73), as well as the ancient Jewish polity and Sparta under Lycurgus (p. 8.) The Scottish–American tract, *Equality – A Political Romance*, refers to Utopia and Lilliput, p. 1. *Bruce's Voyage to Naples*, also in this volume, turns to Lycurgus and Rome, while Robert Wallace invokes Plato, More, Harrington and Hume, in *Various Prospects of Mankind, Nature and Providence*, p. 36.

Where no precise reference is given in the original, I have tried to cite editions likely to have been used by the authors. The place of publication is London unless otherwise noted. Thanks for assistance with the texts is due to Lyman Tower Sargent, John Barrell, and Jack Clarke; to Rosalind Thomas for help with various classical quotations; and to the staffs of the following libraries: the British Library; the John Rylands University Library, Manchester; the Goldsmith's Library, University of London; the Library of the House of Lords, Westminster; Olin Library of Washington University; the Library of Congress; the Huntington Library; the Bodleian Library, Oxford; the Houghton Library, Harvard University; and Cambridge University Library.

wealth reveals a distinctive content. David Hume's 'Idea of a Perfect Commonwealth', for example, is his most adventurous, speculative and radical piece of writing, and places him uncomfortably close to Harrington compared to his other works (his *History of England* dismisses fantasies like *Oceana* as 'as chimerical as that of a perfect and immortal man', 1763 edn, 8 vols., vol. VII, p. 355). Similarly, Burgh's *Cessares* extends dramatically as a practical piece of social engineering the historical critique of manners of his much better-known *Political Disquisitions* (see, e.g., vol. III, pp. 1–97). Utopias thus can provide special insights into the history of social and political thought. As works of fiction which easily capture the imagination, moreover, they were often more successful at popularizing certain principles than constitutional or polemical tracts. Defoe and Swift, most notably, inspired many imitators, and within the utopian canon created the best-known sub-genres (the Robinsonade, Gulliveriana). Defining these literary genres thus remains of abiding interest, even it is not my main purpose here.

What, then, was the chief contribution of utopian writing to wider eighteenth-century social and political debates? And what can it tell us, looking forward to the explosion of practical utopianism which occurred after 1815, about the roots of early socialism? As we have seen, the growth of commerce, poverty, social inequality and moral and political corruption evoked considerable protest in this period. Responding to these problems, the less satirical utopian texts often called for greater egalitarianism, community of goods or limits on landed property, and the reformation of manners. Such proposals often went well beyond the speculations of even radical political pamphleteers. Both utopian writers and their critics were centrally concerned with how far civic and personal virtue could be institutionalized or sheltered against the ravages of time and the moral frailty of humanity. Both were keenly aware that the ancient republics, Christian monasticism, Cromwell's commonwealth and other models provided quite different responses to this question. In an admittedly sceptical age, what the more serious utopian proposals in particular helped to preserve, in light of these concerns, was a mixture of radical republicanism and Christian primitivism which provided an alternate ideal of sociability, moral economy and community against the growing individualism of the wider society. Utopian writers often reacted to the expansion of commercial society by resurrecting earlier ideals of moral and economic regulation. Some concocted schemes for community of goods and agrarian laws which were more radical than most were willing to contemplate. But these became increasingly popular early in the following century, when poverty and social dislocation suddenly became far more widespread. In some instances, too, utopian tracts led liberal and humanitarian thinking about individual rights, at least a century and sometimes two in advance of their times. In order to reconstruct this alternative view of the economy and social relations, we need to look first at some of the sources of utopian thinking in this period, and then at its leading principles.

Sources of utopian and anti-utopian thought in eighteenth-century Britain

Six factors underpinned most eighteenth-century writing about imaginary societies: (1) a burgeoning travel literature, which in utopian form included fantastic voyages to the moon (an established sub-genre since the early seventeenth century); Crusoe-like shipwrecks in imaginary lands; and projected experimental colonies in the new world, where social reforms unlikely in Britain were both more imaginable and had sometimes been attempted, for instance in the Jesuit colony in Paraguay; (2) the increasing importance of science and technology, of Francis Bacon's 'the effecting of all things possible' (*New Atlantis*, 1629 (1659 edn), p. 28), which sometimes embraced an interest in prolonging life as well as in Hermetic efforts to turn base metals into gold; (3) the growing popularity of the secular idea of progress, which was applied to science and technology, to the notion of a succession of social stages towards opulence and refinement, and to human knowledge and the species' potential for greater spiritual and physical perfection (this did not replace, but operated beside, older ideas of the millennium and golden age); (4) the threat of poverty and social dislocation (crucial to More's *Utopia* in the sixteenth century as well as Winstanley's *Law of Freedom* in the seventeenth), with economic organization and greater productivity becoming more prominent themes in utopias from the seventeenth through the twentieth centuries; (5) the age-old perception that commercial expansion and political corruption encouraged greed, vice and religious scepticism; and (6) the growing tendency, culminating in a partial fusion of utopianism and constitutionalist political theory in the French revolution, for political reform proposals, especially by republicans, to be connected to more ambitious, even perfectibilist, utopian forms and aims.

Most British utopias in this period were indebted to two quite different approaches to the question of a superior society which lay outside the utopian canon proper. Those sceptical of the possibility of much greater social improvement expressed their doubts satirically, as utopias themselves often did in reference to existing vices. (The distance between satire and programme is sometimes curiously close. Indeed, the tradition itself thrives precisely on such ambiguity, with utopias feeding on their negation, and vice versa.) Jonathan Swift's Toryish *Gulliver's Travels* (1726), most notably, brilliantly lambasted political corruption (in the voyages to Lilliput and Brobdingnag); projectors and inventors (the voyage to Laputa); and finally, moralists who urged government by reason and a return to simplicity (the voyage to the Houyhnhnms). But Swift himself clearly aimed at a degree of moral and political reform, and there is enough ambiguity in Gulliver's fourth voyage to the Houhnyhmns, in particular, to dismiss the work confidently as wholly anti-utopian. (Some thought the Houyhnhnms good classical republicans: see Dr Bantley, *Critical Remarks on Gulliver's Travels*, 1735, p. 5.) Similarly, and very successfully, Edmund Burke's *Vindication of Natural Society* (1756) satirically contrasted primitive innocence to the dissipation of 'artificial' or 'political' society, but was itself sometimes misread as a straightforward utopian treatise. The second influential but non-traditional model for fantastic literature in this period, however, lay not in satire, but in the 'individualist utopia' of Daniel Defoe's *Robinson Crusoe* (1719). Here the ideal of the well-ordered society is lived out mostly in solitude, partly taking the form of a fantasy of power (Crusoe becomes governor of his island), and a rumination on the development of conscience and the idea of returning to a state of nature. The latter, however, is rendered idyllic only by the most arduous labour, which helps to inspire Crusoe's religious conversion and hence salvation (*Robinson Crusoe*, 1719, p. 133). For many, too, the work is a discourse on *homo oeconomicus* which idealizes ambitious projectors, the middle station, and the Providential direction of the world.

In the sub-genres spawned by Swift and Defoe, and most of the other forms of utopian satire in this period, the dangers of luxury, the idleness of rich and poor alike, and moral and political corruption are frequently advertised.[2] Those utopias and model commonwealths which contained serious designs for improved societies often linked these themes to republican theories of good government. The latter in this period were much indebted to Harrington's *Oceana* in particular, and reflections on it by men like Henry Neville, John Toland and Andrew Fletcher of Saltoun. (None the less there were certainly also political radicals, especially those highly favourable to commerce, like the Dissenter Joseph Priestley, who denied that More's *Utopia* or Harrington's *Oceana* could ever be reduced to practice; 'Lectures on History and General Policy', *The Theological and Miscellaneous Works of Joseph Priestley*, vol. XXIV, 1803, p. 34.) Against the threat of executive tyranny, most republicans emphasized the benefits of rotation of office; the primacy of retaining popular control over government by, for example, voting by ballot to inhibit corruption (but Burgh still favoured an hereditary executive (below, p. 94); the value of public virtue or patriotism as the moral underpinning of wise polities; and the advantages of an agrarian law to limit property. They also condemned the use of a standing army instead of a citizens' militia, and, by the end of the century, were increasingly critical of economic specialization. (This issue would become crucial to socialists after 1815.) 'Independence' was the term which most encapsulated these ideals. 'Corruption' was its antithesis.

Some model constitutions grounded on such ideas were quite moderate: David Hume's essay, 'Idea of a Perfect Commonwealth' (1752; reprinted here), has a chiefly Harringtonian if also 'deliberately utopian' aim (John Plamenatz, *Man and Society*, Longman, 1971, vol. I, p. 331) to balance the gentry and aristocracy in order to neutralize faction. But it places no limits on property, and, while republican, hardly welcomes the political participation of the lower orders. But

---

[2] See *Memoirs of the Court of Lilliput* (2nd edn, 1727), p. 11; [Charles Johnstone], *The Reverie; or, A Flight to the Paradise of Fools* (Dublin, 1762), e.g., vol. I, p. 17; 'Sir Humphrey Lunatic', *A Trip to the Moon. Containing an Account of the Island of Noibla* (York, 1764), pp. 26–39; *The Modern Atalantis, or, the Devil in an Air Balloon* (1784), largely a satire on the nobility; *The Adventures of Sig. Gaudentia di Lucca* (1776), criticizes the perversion of the legal process by the rich (p. 154), praises a patriarchal, anti-partisan form of government (p. 160), and enjoins sharing goods in common and trading 'as one brother would do with another' (p. 162); and John Kirkby, *The Capacity and Extent of the Human Understanding; Exemplified in the Extraordinary Case of Automathes* (1745), which imagines a Christian island considerably more virtuous than England (pp. 16, 22).

others of Harrington's admirers, like Andrew Fletcher, extended such ideas further into the direction of what has been called 'an evidently utopian project' (J.G.A. Pocock, 'Clergy and Commerce. The Conservative Enlightenment in England', in *L'Eta dei Lumi*, Jovene, 1985, vol. I, p. 544). To limit wars, this proposed dividing all Europe into regions governed by twelve cities possessing their own militia and governing assembly (see 'An Account of a Conversation Concerning the Right Regulation of Governments for the Common Good of Mankind', 1704, in *The Political Works of Andrew Fletcher*, 1732, p. 432). And beyond these, stretching over the horizon towards undiluted fantasy, were various considerably more egalitarian schemes, some inspired by Sparta under Lycurgus, others a pre-Norman, Anglo-Saxon ancient constitution, or various images of the Christian community.

Not all critics of corruption who adopted the utopian form were republican, however. The 'Country party', sometimes Tory and sometimes Jacobite opposition to Walpole and the later Whig oligarchy also inveighed against mercantile greed and political knavery in defence of the landed gentry and monarchy. Swift did so, and, in a similar vein, *The Voyages, Travels & Wonderful Discoveries of Capt. John Holmesby* (1757) portrays a venal Whig oligarchy 'warmly opposed by those who possess the lands of this island', whose efforts are however foiled by 'an interest in opposition, which we called the Paper-interest' (the new financiers and government fund-holders). Like radical Whigs and republicans, Country writers cautioned that 'luxury, vice, and slavery, crept in under the terms of elegance, politeness, and civility'. They too reiterated that Britain's liberty was anchored 'in the virtue of the people', who were growing all too 'corrupt and profligate'. Often inspired by Bolingbroke, the Country remedy was a patriot-king who banished luxury and decadence, healed social divisions, and patronized science and learning.[3]

Some of the improvements proposed in eighteenth-century utopias, however, are inspired less by partisan politics than the prospect of a far-reaching reformation of morals suitable to most forms of

---

[3] E.g., *The Voyages . . . of Capt. John Holmesby* (1757), pp. 41, 88, 162–3, 171–2. See also *The Reign of George IV 1900–1925* (1763), where a virtuous monarch is prominent (e.g., p. xxviii). Similarly, the *Island of Content* (1709), reprinted here, retains an hereditary monarchy whose power, moreover, is unlimited, and underscores the people's obligations towards it (below, pp. 18–21).

polity. This is true, for example, with respect to pleas for women's rights. At a time when the issue was not widely discussed, the position of women and their rights in marriage was frequently addressed in British utopian works, as it was in French utopias of this period, like Saint-Jory's *Les Femmes Militaires* (1736). In *The Island of Content*, for instance, the most beautiful women are privileged and, while men still rule within the family, all women aged fifteen and over are granted their freedom, and divorce is simple (and is held to reinforce marital virtue) (below, pp. 12–14). *The Travels of Hildebrand Bowman* (1778), recognizes three grounds for divorce and, though women cannot inherit, they are granted an annuity on the death of their parents in order to limit marriages based on financial interest (pp. 223–5). In Sarah Scott's proto-feminist novel, *Millennium Hall* (1762), a charitable community for women alone is described in detail. By the 1790s, the problem of relations between the sexes was perceived as increasingly urgent. *An Essay on Civil Government, or Society Restored* (1793), for example, written shortly after Mary Wollstonecraft's *Vindication of the Rights of Woman* (1792), states that 'Perhaps nothing else shews clearer the infancy of the human race, than the yet domineering spirit of the male over the female sex' (p. 175). And William Hodgson, the author of *The Commonwealth of Reason*, termed despotism over women a 'scandalous remnant of feudal barbarism and gothic ignorance' (*Proposals, for Publishing by Subscription, A Treatise Called the Female Citizen: or, A Historical, Political, and Philosophical Enquiry into the Rights of Women*, ?1796).

Besides feminism, there were also other issues prominent in utopias which transcended partisan boundaries and reflected a wider concern with manners in general. Many texts condemn the century's notorious callousness towards animals, with some advocating vegetarianism (see *Bruce's Voyage to Naples*, below, p. 271. Proposals to banish gambling, bawdy houses and the like are common (*Memoirs of Planetes*, below, p. 195), as are pleas that public amusements become 'rational and instructive' (A.E., *Libellus*, 1798, p. 39). The benefits of religious toleration are stressed in many works (e.g., *The Travels of Hildebrand Bowman*, 1778, p. 200), as is elevating the lax moral standards of the clergy (e.g., *Private Letters from an American*, 1769, pp. 58–63; *A Journey . . . through the Air*, 1784, p. 29). Some utopias praise 'natural religion' or deism against the perversions of supposed Biblical revelation and false mysteries of clericalism. Slavery is frequently denounced (e.g., *A Voyage to Cacklogallinia*, 1727, pp. 6–8). Legal reforms like the abolition of capital punishment and the game laws are widely mooted. So are the humane treatment of colonized peoples, and improvements in education and the poor law system. Such proposals are often interwoven with political concerns. But they as often project a more humane, just and deeply Christian society compatible with nearly any mild form of government.

This pervasive desire for moral reform reveals one of the great tensions in the utopian genre. Many such texts can be read as part of the early history of radical and liberal humanitarianism, and of the extension of rights from propertied white males to women, slaves, labourers, foreigners, children, and, very commonly, animals of all kinds, but especially beasts of burden. Yet there are also profoundly illiberal elements in many utopias which jar uneasily beside such libertarian and individualist concerns. These stem chiefly from a puritanical approach to morality, from the biases of a Protestant state, and from republican emphases on public virtue. Burgh's *Cessares*, for instance, disenfranchises Catholics, and prohibits gambling, lewd books and the theatre (below, pp. 100, 115, 118). *The Island of Content* rejects all learning beyond reading and writing as hostile to public order (but 'New Athens' to the contrary insists that national security requires increased popular education: below, p. 42). 'Innocent amusements' alone are condoned, while improper books, words and actions are suppressed in *The Travels of Hildebrand Bowman* (1778, p. 217). Similar forms of utopian regimentation, enforcing for example a uniformity of dress and housing, have consequently been seen as indicative more of the early history of totalitarianism than of liberalism. Some have indeed identified such constraints with the tradition *per se*, More's *Utopia* having set the precedent by prohibiting travel without leave or a passport, as well as idleness and alehouses, and regulating trades, clothing and much else (Cambridge University Press, 1989, pp. 44–60). In this view, utopias essentially embody an ideology of order rather than of freedom, and of paternal protection rather than increasing individual independence and responsibility. Underscoring such concerns is the political role assigned to elders. These arbitrate minor disputes in 'New Athens' (below, p. 46) and virtually rule in Lithgow's *Equality*. In *Bruce's Voyage*, the oldest person is the reigning prince (below, p. 273). This patriarchalism divulges once again the price paid in democratic coin for measures designed to enhance social harmony.

This approach to politics was clearly indebted to conceptions of a pristine state of nature or 'golden age' which many imagined had followed the Fall of Adam and Eve. Taking their cue from classical, Biblical and natural law texts, utopian writers generally characterized natural society as primitive but relatively peaceful. It had been renounced for political society (usually monarchy), they thought, because of various inconveniences, such as no common judge of disputes. In a few utopias, natural society is conceived counterfactually as having evolved into something like More's Utopia, with community of goods and all labouring for the public good. Most trace the corruption of mankind to the origins of government and the foundation of private property, when envy, love of ease and ambition came to dominate. They often insist, in turn, that abolishing private ownership might help to restore primitive innocence, though some immorality might remain (e.g., Robert Wallace, *Various Prospects of Mankind, Nature and Providence*, 1761, pp. 38–42, 60–5, 74–8, 101–3). Jean-Jacques Rousseau's immensely influential *Discourse on the Origins of Inequality* (1754) was the prototype for many subsequent discussions of the theme. It popularized the view that depravity originated with private property and the abandonment of the state of nature, and did much to ensure that the idea of returning to nature, fuelled by nostalgia for a fast-disappearing village life, was prominent well before the Romantic era. Fascination with 'freaks of nature' like Peter the Wild Boy, captured near Hanover in mid-century, also overlapped with the myth of the noble savage and the rejection of ideas of the Fall and Original Sin. Natural society rediscovered was consequently a popular theme in eighteenth-century imaginary voyages in particular. *The Adventures & Surprizing Deliverances of James Dubourdieu* (1719), for example, recounts the discovery of a land of 'children of love', where animals are tame and never eaten by people, the inhabitants are unashamed of their nakedness, and gain and riches are unthinkable. There is no government or magistrates, property or contention, and rule is patriarchal, by the eldest men as heads of families (pp. 70, 77, 80–1, 92, 99). These ideals could also be adapted to other political purposes. In the anti-slavery satire, *A Voyage to the New Island Fonseca* (1708), for instance, the natives of a West Indian island subsist happily in their natural state before the British 'civilize 'em to misery' (pp. 35–6).

A third major component of the positive ideals of eighteenth-century utopianism was a Christian tradition supportive of what was to most believers an heretical doctrine, community of goods. As in France, where the ideal formed an important part of such famous utopias as Morelly's *Code de la Nature* (1755), this was sometimes linked to millennarianism, as well as to ideas of primitive apostolic Christianity, paradise, heaven, and the Garden of Eden. These concepts overlapped with notions of the state of nature as well as republican thought in various ways. Here we can distinguish two strands. One is more primitivist, and is typified early in this period in two works by the same author, *An Essay Concerning Adepts* (1698) and *Annus Sophiae Jubilaeus. The Sophick Constitution: or, the Evil Customs of the World Reformed* (1700). These plead for the equality of mankind and universal charity, for the Christian imitation of Sparta under Lycurgus, with iron money alone permitted, and for common living in 'colleges'. A uniformity of attire for all of the same age is recommended, as well as plain but wholesome food. Painting, engraving, adornment with ribbons or other frivolous articles, and songs about love or drinking, are all proscribed. Streets are to be identical, without lanes or alleys, with each house cleaning its respective section thereof. Equality is here proclaimed to be the law of God, which would have endured had Adam not sinned. The chief injunction is for Christians to be 'plainer than Quakers'. Luxury is the great temptation to sin, and throughout this period the Quakers indeed provide a crucial moral example, though one increasingly distant from reality (*An Essay Concerning Adepts*, pp. 10–12, 20, 22, 27; *The Sophick Constitution*, pp. 17–18, 55). Similarly, in 'A Description of New Athens in Terra Australis Incognita' (1720), reprinted here, Christianity is incorporated into law, with charity the fount of religion. Oppression of the poor is unknown, wages and prices are fixed, no coaches are tolerated in the city (all walk instead), and there are no lawyers or apothecaries and only twelve physicians. In addition, all places of trust and profit are rotated annually (below, pp. 43–4, 46–7).

A variation on such proposals advanced the case that model communities could help provide additional employment. Here injunctions to charity, prohibitions on idleness, and measures to augment Britain's comparative economic advantage were united. In the Quaker John Bellers' *Proposals for Raising a Colledge of Industry* (1695), reprinted by the early socialist Robert Owen in 1818, for example, community of goods encourages both economic efficiency and virtue, useless labour is proscribed, money is denounced as the root of all evil, and private interest is merged in the public (pp. 7, 13). We still encounter sumptuary restraints on luxury here. But an expanding, production-oriented economy is accepted, rather than the more common utopian assumption of simplified needs.

The idea that satisfying needs was a crucial problem in such proposals was also central to many anti-utopian satires. These generally accepted commerce as a means of meeting seemingly limitless desires, and conceded at least some of the moral consequences thought to ensue, while dismissing more primitivist alternatives. By the mid-nineteenth century, indeed, perfecting the means of satisfying expanding needs, mainly through centralized planning, was to become a goal for most socialists, notably Marx and Engels, though a substitution of free time for expanded production is evident in, for example, William Morris's *News From Nowhere* (1890). This helps us to see that both utopian and anti-utopian writings were united by a single discourse or set of assumptions about the compatibility of trade and protracted enthusiasm for the public good. Many utopias opposed increased trade because they feared it would foster civic disunity by placing private gain above public welfare. Defenders of commerce, however, usually contended that the fervent patriotism demanded by republicanism, especially in conjunction with Protestantism, and often present *in extremis* in utopias, was both impracticable in modern society and equally unnecessary. Selfishness, they confessed, was bound to increase in the most commercially minded society the world had ever seen. But trade could also bond interests together, and forge a sense of common enterprise. And the more peaceable, sociable manners of the new towns, they insisted, would help foster a more humane and 'polite' culture which would unite individuals every bit as effectively as the more intensive patriotism required by the republican ideal. The latter was in turn condemned, for example by Hume, as now unnecessary given the civilizing tendency of commerce; as overly militaristic; and as moreover reminiscent, in its allegiance with some kinds of Protestantism, of the sort of fanaticism which had erupted during the English Civil War (*The History of England*, 1763, vol. VII, p. 18).

Linked to this theory of civilization was a new analysis of the progression of society from barbarism to opulence. Historians like Hume and William Robertson replaced notions of an originally harmonious, propertyless state of nature intended by God with a more secular account of social evolution. This stressed the natural emergence of private property as society moved from hunting and gathering to the pastoral, the agricultural, and eventually the commercial stage. Property, it was conceded, might once have been held in common *negatively*, that is, for all to make the best use they could of it. But God had never intended it to remain common, as some misguided readers of 'Genesis' supposed. Instead, private ownership had arisen by common consent as the most commodious arrangement (see, e.g., Hugo Grotius, *The Rights of War and Peace*, 1625; 1738 edn, p. 145). Social inequality had admittedly grown as trade advanced. But even the least advantaged benefited as greater specialization reduced unit costs and increased production. This meant that the great bugbear of most utopians, luxury, was now seen principally as simply a useful means of dispersing income by inducing farmers to produce more food in order to acquire the baubles newly manufactured in the towns. With notable exceptions, such as Adam Ferguson, William Ogilvie and Robert Wallace, the proponents of this view thus repudiated republican appeals for much greater equality or limits on property. Nor would they concede that a narrow division of labour fatally impaired a nation's ability to fight for, or its citizens' willingness to understand, the common good.

Those who regarded commercial society as immeasurably superior to previous stages still retained some conception of the state of nature, for it helped to explain the genesis of government through an original social contract (the preferred Whig interpretation), as well as to assert the divine origins if not right of monarchy (the Tory view). John Locke, for example, whose views remained popular through the early nineteenth century, had portrayed a golden age before vain ambition depraved men's minds (*Two Treatises of Government*, 1690, Cambridge University Press, 1988, p. 360). But, despite occasional appeals to the nobility of savage life, the state of nature was increasingly seen as merely the earliest stage of society, rather than a condition of pristine innocence. Community of goods, in turn, was now identified chiefly with primitivism, barbarism and poverty, or with a degree of moral restraint attainable only by small communities of religious believers. To most modernists, thus, the North American natives, widely thought to lack landownership, were merely poor, and not especially virtuous. Republicans who criticized existing inequalities could thus easily be damned as would-be cave-dwellers in consequence, as Thomas Paine's followers found to their chagrin during the heated debates of the early 1790s (see the satirical *A Trip to the Island of Equality*, 1792, discussed with similar works in my *Thomas Paine: Social and Political Thought*, Unwin Hyman, 1989, pp. 153–64). And the reputation of classical Greek and Roman ideals of virtue also suffered. Hume, for instance, asserted that his own era was both the happiest in human history and the most virtuous, luxury being injurious only when it annihilated all social duties. By comparison, ancient Rome had been an 'ill-modelled government' tainted by an 'unlimited extent of conquests'. And these, not 'luxury and the arts', accounted for its demise ('Of Luxury', 1742, *Essays and Treatises on Several Subjects*, 1768, p. 161).

This new commercial humanism underpinned the undoubtedly practical character of the age, and consequently looms large in its anti-utopian satires. These typically resisted the idea that primitive communities had surpassed the moderns in either virtue or plenitude. In Burke's parody of Bolingbroke, *A Vindication of Natural Society*, for example, artificial wants are absent from the state of nature. Life is simple, and 'therefore it is happy'. This is superficially appealing. But a closer reading indicates that the many inconveniences of natural society enumerated (for example the lack of a common arbitrator, a limited diet, and a craving after artificial wants) make returning to such a state undesirable (pp. 10–11, 62). Similarly, if rather more obviously, Oliver Goldsmith's satirical 'The Proceedings of Providence Vindicated' (1759) depicts a world without vice, but one where – perhaps to counter the claims of animal rights proponents – the inhabitants have renounced violence against the beasts, and consequently are pursued by squirrels and dogs. 'Ancient simplicity' meant no houses, statues, or even wisdom, with all reduced to the barest subsistence (*Works*, 1806, vol. IV, pp. 315–23). None the less such caricatures were themselves sometimes sources for positive utopias: Burke's *Vindication* was admired by Godwin, and reprinted in

1858 in aid of Josiah Warren's individualist anarchism, while Swift's depiction of the Houyhnhnms helped inspire the simple society commended in Godwin's *Enquiry concerning Political Justice.*

Some eighteenth-century British utopias and model republics

Over twenty primarily non-satirical utopias portraying more or less ideal societies appeared in Britain during the eighteenth century, reaching an apogee during the revolutionary debates of the 1790s. The sub-genres of utopian literature published included several arcadias, or pastoral visions. Some of these, in J.C. Davis's terms, were also perfect moral commonwealths, where complete social harmony results from moral renewal. In *The Island of Content* (1709), for example, the earth disgorges food without labour, no animals are eaten (they too consume only fruit and nuts), wine flows without drunkenness, and piety reigns supreme. Commerce is only with the Dutch, who are extolled for lacking the 'Frenchified foppery' of overbreeding (below, pp. 5–7, 16–18, 22–4). In their politics, these works were often republican, and usually described a more regulated, virtuous and equal society. They denounced the steady advance of commercial greed and of inequality of property, the effects of ministerial manipulation of the Commons and electoral system, and the explosion of the national debt. Mocking the nation for too blithely conceding its declining moral fibre as the price of opulence, they assailed the government's willingness to deploy a standing army, which many feared could be wielded against a domestic opposition, and even to hire mercenaries, whose loyalty was only to their paymaster. These strands of criticism were fused, as we have seen, in the charge of 'corruption', perhaps 'the single most important political issue of the eighteenth century' (Paul Langford, *A Polite and Commercial People. England 1727–83*, Oxford University Press, 1989, p. 716). To William Hodgson, writing in 1795, corruption was 'the most dreadful evil that can possibly affect either public or private life', and originated in the monopolization of wealth by a few (*The Commonwealth of Reason*, below, p. 201). In *A Voyage to the Moon Strongly Recommended to All Lovers of Real Freedom* (1793), similarly, the 'opium wand' (gold) holds the nation in subjection (p. 8), while in *The Father of the City of Eutopia* (1757), gold and wine compete to lull the conscience of politicians (p. 13). For James Burgh, it is luxury, synonymous with city life and London in particular, which chiefly induces modern depravity (*An Account . . . of the Cessares*, below, p. 117). In *A Voyage to Cacklogallinia* (1727), avarice, envy, folly, and the luxury of courtiers hasten national decay. (p. 53).

For most of these writers, such degeneration had accelerated only recently. The *Memoirs Concerning . . . Capt. Mackheath* (1728), for example, relates that in the early eighteenth century 'there arose among us a general and uncommon desire for money, and after this an extraordinary appetite for power; the two great fundamentals of every evil'. The people soon became weak, enervated, and dissolute, the middle ranks mimicking the wealthy and becoming 'enfeebled by luxury', and the lower ranks slavishly aping their affections in turn. Here, as elsewhere, the South Sea Bubble epitomized the collapse of public morals when financial speculation ran wild (pp. 10–11; see also [Daniel Defoe], *The Consolidator*, 1705, p. 260). In some works, Britain has already sunk under the weight of such debauchery. Lamenting 'all this decay of virtue for near a century past', *Private Letters from an American in England to His Friends in America* (1769), for example, recounts how universal luxury and dissipation forced the transfer of government to the United States at the end of the eighteenth century. In Britain, every village overflows with vanity and idleness, every twenty houses boasts a French friseur, and servants take up Italian and fencing. The Stock Exchange is a college for repentant prostitutes, and the vaults of St Paul's Cathedral house a wine cellar. Public life is debased by raging partisanship, political despotism, a standing army, and a veritable plague of plundering lawyers. Loss of economic competitiveness through self-indulgence has impoverished the country (pp. 11, 25, 27, 45–6, 56, 79, 84, 89–96, 129). Similarly, in *The Travels of Hildebrand Bowman* (1778), the narrator visits five countries at different stages of social evolution. In the ideal 'Bonhommica', guided by Queen Tudorina (Elizabeth I), plain cooking satisfies, good wines are imbibed only in moderation, lawyers and physicians return fees when proven wrong, and the people exude bravery and virtue. But in Luxo-Volupto, presided over by King Gorgeris (George III), prosperity from trade and manufactures has refined tastes and loosened morals. Even tailors must be seen in their own carriages, and there is frenzied gambling and intense partisan fervour (pp. 173, 190–2, 255–7, 278, 281).

To forestall such nightmares, reminiscent foremost of the fate of ancient Rome, political corruption was to be tackled by rotating leading offices more frequently (Hodgson, *The Commonwealth of Reason*, below, p. 20; [Thomas Northmore], *Memoirs of Planetes*, 1795, reprinted here, below, p. 178; Macaulay, 'Short Sketch', 1767, p. 33). We also find pleas for more frequent elections (sometimes annually, by universal male suffrage, e.g. [Daniel Alexander], *The Thirty-Nine Articles*, 1785, pp. 7–8); a citizens' militia; and the rewarding of public service by reasonable rather than inflated salaries (Hodgson, *The Commonwealth of Reason*, below, p. 204). The most extreme republican utopias and model commonwealths, however, went well beyond the critique of corruption the opposition was agreed upon to what they regarded as the core of the problem, inequality of property. Instead of merely declaiming against primogeniture and the laws of entail, they recommended that agrarian laws regulate landownership.[4] Such restrictions were occasionally propounded in more academic discussions of property rights (e.g., Frances Hutcheson, *A System of Moral Philosophy*, 1755, vol. I, p. 327). But the most detailed proposals for republican agrarian laws in this period appear in utopian form, and this is one of the most distinctive aspects of the utopian 'programme', to the extent that one existed. The government in Burgh's *Cessares*, for example, proscribes gold and silver mining and luxury generally, advocates sumptuary laws reminiscent of medieval order, like prohibiting dressing above one's rank, controls the prices of food and labour, builds all houses alike, and curtails trade (below, pp. 108, 115, 117–18). William Ogilvie's *Essay on the Right of Property in Land* limits manufactures and suggests sumptuary laws, though aiming at a 'progressive agrarian' rather than equality of fortune (p. 41). *Bruce's Voyage to Naples* (1802) visits a world inside the globe where only age and wisdom are venerated. Luxury is banned and all, hardy and healthy, live three hundred years. Here Sparta is also extolled for having realized that gold made men 'luxurious, corrupt, factious, and effeminate' (below, pp. 226–7, 280). In the chief such regulatory model republic included in this edition, Hodgson's *Commonwealth of Reason*, committees of agriculture, trades and provisions

---

[4] E.g., Charles Lee, 'A Sketch of a Plan for the Formation of a Military Colony' (1792), p. 75; William Ogilvie, *An Essay on the Right of Property in Land* (1781), p. 37; Catherine Macaulay, 'Short Sketch' (1767), p. 34; Burgh, *An Account . . . of the Cessares*, below, p. 122; A.E., *Libellus* (1798), pp. 40–1.

ensure adequate food supplies, the minimum wage is set at one bushel of wheat daily, and national manufactories offer employment when needed (below, pp. 231–3, 245). In 'New Athens', the prices of labour and goods are fixed (below, p. 43). In most such works, unproductive or useless professions are abolished; Lee's 'Plan' imposes the 'effeminate and vile occupations' of tailors, barbers, etc., on women alone (p. 75). The bane of any utopia, lawyers, are banned in virtually all.

Some works, moreover, going well beyond the boundaries of most established republican thought towards what we might term Platonic or utopian republicanism, counselled the most extreme solution of all, communal property holding. This, in fact, was the single most important doctrine implied by the more technical use of the label 'utopian', which was sometimes simply contrasted to 'the system of private property' (e.g., Thomas Reid, *Practical Ethics*, ed. Knud Haakonssen, Princeton University Press, 1990, p. 284). In the agrarian radical Thomas Spence's *Supplement to the History of Robinson Crusoe* (1782), all land is owned by the nation and managed by parishes (pp. 9, 27–8). The Godwinian *An Essay on Civil Government* (1793) concluded of the debate raging around it that 'the principle of the original and political equality of man, now so much insisted upon, is inapplicable and impossible, without a community of property' (p. 86). In the émigré John Lithgow's Scottish-American utopia, *Equality – A Political Romance* (1802) (first published in Philadelphia but clearly written against a background of British debates), all property is common, labour is restricted to four hours daily, and money is disparaged as the root of all evil (p. 2). By the early 1830s, such proposals were increasingly known as 'socialism', and were associated with the desire to cure poverty and the corrosive effects of social inequality once and for all. Their influence surged with rapid European industrialization in the following decades, until the 'utopian' programme became the chief modern alternative to the liberal 'system of private property'.

Even by the mid-eighteenth century, however, relatively moderate utopian proposals still varied widely from current European practices. Deflecting the charge that renewed political virtue was inconceivable amidst such decay no matter how property arrangements were altered, many ideal polities were situated in new colonies in safely distant lands. Burgh's *Cessares* is set in little-known South America.

General Charles Lee's 'Plan for the Formation of a Military Colony' (probably written in colonial America, though first published in Britain) tolerated external trade only at one annual fair, warning that it 'corrupts every true republican and manly principle' and obliterated 'all sensibility for real pleasure and happiness' (p. 83). Nor were such expectations as unrealistic as we might expect: in the colony of Georgia, a 1739 resolution sought to limit landholdings to 500 acres (Hugh Anderson *et al.*, *A True and Historical Narrative of the Colony of Georgia in America*, Charles Town, 1741, p. 57). Parallel proposals for Sierra Leone recommended restricting wants (C.B. Wadstrom, *An Essay on Colonization*, 1784, p. 119) and establishing an agrarian law ([Granville Sharp], *A Short Sketch of Temporary Regulations . . . for the Intended Settlement . . . Near Sierre Leone*, 1786, pp. 32–53). And the Jesuits' 150-year-long experiment with community of property at Paraguay was often cited as the most extensive effort of this type since early Christianity (e.g., very approvingly, by Thomas Reid: *Practical Ethics*, ed. Knud Haakonssen, Princeton University Press, 1990, p. 284). For similar reasons, many republican constitutions were also devised for poor, sparsely settled lands: both Rousseau's *Social Contract* and Macaulay's 'democratical republic' were aimed at Corsica, not France or Britain.

Conclusion

The coming of the French revolution fundamentally altered the terms in which utopian writing took place. Heavenly and lunar worlds now descended to earth, while plans for virtuous republics once envisioned for distant islands were now deemed applicable to the long-civilized monarchies of Europe. America's victorious republican institutions had seemingly avoided extreme luxury, and secured both moral regeneration and greater social simplicity. The French revolution, at least in its early, innocent years, held out a similar promise, and utopias now often included accounts of revolution and the establishment of a new regime (e.g., [Thomas Northmore], *Memoirs of Planetes*, 1795, below, p. 172).[5] Replicating America in Europe, however, thought many radicals, required at least some limits on property ownership, if not (as far fewer thought) rendering it common. Here

[5] It might be added that the problem of transition from a monarchy to a republic was recognized in some earlier republican utopias, e.g., *The Free State of Noland* (1696), p. 16.

the utopian canon could be of some assistance. In France, Babeuf and Buonarroti took up themes from Morelly. In Britain, Spence, Godwin and others ransacked utopias for ideas suitable to a coming, rather than a past, golden age.

Like their predecessors, utopias of the revolutionary period were divided over the question of commerce. The most popular radical proposals of the 1790s, largely American in inspiration, dismissed a 'utopian' model republic as now too distant to be recreated, and instead sought to combine republican equality with some of the advantages of commerce. Paine did not care 'how affluent some may be, provided none be miserable in consequence' (*Agrarian Justice*, 1797, p. 11). His widely mooted taxation scheme in the *Rights of Man*, part two (1792), the best-known reform programme of the period, is a modified agrarian law operating within a commercial society and tolerating very considerable social inequality (ed. G. Claeys, Hackett Publishing Company, 1992, pp. 195–216). Much indebted to Paine, Hodgson's *Commonwealth of Reason*, too, though firmly attached to a Harringtonian rotation scheme (below, p. 223), advances no agrarian law. Their enemies said the radicals aspired to seize property: in 1800, 140 men were rumoured to belong to a 'Levelling Society' seeking an equal division of land, some of whom became highwaymen when their political efforts faltered (*Anti-Jacobin Review*, Vol. 6, 1800, 355). But most reformers insisted that they were '*perfectly satisfied* with ... an equal representation' (*Universal Society of the Friends of the People*, n.p., n.d.). And most, by the 1790s, in fact appear to have accepted a refined, modern economy, and defined the overcoming of corruption more in terms of political rights and constitutional mechanisms than the perils of luxury and the degradation of manners. And this was at least partially a response to the widespread and apparently convincing identification of primitivism with republicanism in contemporary loyalist, or anti-reformist, propaganda (which was itself indebted, as we have seen, to a tradition of anti-utopian satire).

The older vision of republican utopianism which commended a much simpler economy and was far more hostile to commerce was by no means entirely defeated, however. The primitive social model advocated in Godwin's *Political Justice* was praised by many of his followers, like Thomas Northmore. Similar themes were reinforced after the turn of the new century by the physician Charles Hall (*The*

Civilization of the People in European States, 1805). Thomas Spence's agrarian radicalism continued to excite interest until well into the 1840s. Most influentially, Robert Owen's experimental communitarianism wedded the Christian tradition of monastic communism to an ideal of the ultimate benefits of machinery, though some Owenites favoured little more than the reproduction of basic needs. Radical but sometimes still Toryish agrarian ideals were also recrafted in the early nineteenth century radicalism of William Cobbett, Richard Oastler and Feargus O'Connor.

Two roads thus emerged from the utopianism of the 1790s. The first led from a new democratic form of commercial republicanism towards the more welfare-oriented forms of liberal democracy. The second, scouted by Godwin and Spence, pointed towards socialist proposals for a complete community of goods in order to abolish vice and poverty, and to efforts to eliminate political conflict altogether. In both cases, utopias helped to flesh out tentative visions of the ideal modern future, and to project imaginatively what would often later become programme, dogma and even reality.

Chronology of main eighteenth-century British utopian and anti-utopian texts

1700   *Annus Sophiae Jubilaeus. The Sophick Constitution: or, the Evil Customs of the World Reformed*

1703   David Russen, *Iter Lunare* (repr. 1707)

1704   George Psalmanaazaar (pseud.), *An Historical and Geographical Description of Formosa* (repr. 1705)

1704   Andrew Fletcher of Saltoun, *An Account of a Conversation Containing a Right Regulation of Governments for the Common Good of Mankind* (repr. 1732, 1737, 1749, 1798)

1705   [Daniel Defoe], *The Consolidator: or, Memoirs of Sundry Transactions from the World in the Moon* (repr. 1741)

1705   Joseph Browne, *The Moon-Calf: or, Accurate Reflections on the Consolidator*

1708   *A Voyage to the New Island Fonseca*

1709   William King, 'A Voyage to the Island of Cajamai in America', in *The Original Works of William King* (3 vols., 1776), pp. 132–78

1709   *The Island of Content; or, A New Paradise Discovered*

1713   [Edmund Stacy], *A New Voyage to the Island of Fools* (repr. 1715)

1719   [Ambrose Evans], *The Adventures and Surprizing Deliverances of James Dubourdieu*

1719   Daniel Defoe, *The Adventures of Robinson Crusoe* (many edns)

1720   'A Voyage to the Mountains of the Moon under the Equator', in *Miscellanea Aurea*, pp. 1–34

*Very likely written in Britain, where extensive 'notes' to the text were supplied, though the title page says 'Translated from the Italian'.

Bibliographical note

Though much has been written on Defoe and Swift, there are few treatments of most eighteenth-century British utopias. A.L. Morton's *The English Utopia* (Lawrence & Wishart, 1952), examines only four works written between 1700 and 1793: Defoe's *Crusoe*, Swift's *Gulliver's Travels*, Simon Berington's *Memoirs of Signor Gaudentio di Lucca*, and Robert Paltock's *The Life and Adventures of Peter Wilkins*. Artur Blaim, *Failed Dynamics. The English Robinsonade of the Eighteenth Century* (Univwersytet Marii Curie-Sklodowskiej, Lublin, 1987) is a good account of its genre. An older study is J.K. Fuz, *Welfare Economics in English Utopias from Francis Bacon to Adam Smith* (M. Nijhoff, 1962). Specialized essays include Vivian Fox, 'Deviance in Some English Utopias, Sixteenth to Eighteenth Centuries', *Humboldt Journal of Social Relations*, 2 (1973), 14–18; Lyman Tower Sargent, 'Utopianism in Colonial America', *History of Political Thought*, 4 (1983), 483–522; and my 'Utopianism and the French Revolution Debate in Britain', in Stephen Bann and Krishan Kumar, eds., *Utopianism and the Millennium* (Reaktion Books, 1993). A general survey of satirical trends is given in Jacob Viner, 'Satire and Economics in the Augustan Age of Satire', in Henry Knight Miller, Eric Rothstein and G.S. Rousseau, eds., *The Augustan Milieu* (Clarendon Press, 1970), pp. 77–101. Economic aspects are also treated in my 'Utopias', in John Eatwell, Murray Milgate and Peter Newman, eds., *The New Palgrave: A Dictionary of Economic Theory and Doctrine* (Macmillan, 1987), vol. IV, pp. 783–6, and in relation to early socialism, in my *Machinery, Money and the Millennium: From Moral Economy to Socialism, 1815–1860* (Princeton University Press, 1987). While not immediately concerned with utopias as such, Franco Venturi's *Utopia and Reform in the Enlightenment* (Cambridge University Press, 1971) illuminates their relation to social theory, as does Girolamo Imbruglia's *The Invention of Paraguay* (Syracuse University Press, 1995). There is also relevant discussion in Philip Gove, *The Imaginary Voyage in Prose Fiction* (Columbia University Press, 1941); Martha Conant, *The Oriental Tale in England in the 18th Century* (Columbia University Press, 1908); Marjorie Nicolson, *Voyages to the Moon* (Macmillan, 1948); Percy G. Adams, *Travellers and Travel Liars 1660–1800* (University of California Press, 1962); Ernest Tuveson, *Millennium and Utopia. A Study in the Background of the Idea of Progress* (University of California Press, 1949), and Colleen McDannell and Bernhard Lang, *Heaven: A History* (Vintage Books, 1988). More general studies include Frank and Fritzie Manuel's *Utopian Thought in the Western World* (Harvard University Press, 1979) and Krishan Kumar, *Utopia and Anti-Utopia in Modern Times* (Blackwell, 1987). For the earlier period as well as its typology of perfect moral communities, arcadias, and utopias, J.C. Davis' pioneering study, *Utopia and the Ideal Society. A Study of English Utopian Writing, 1516–1700* (Cambridge University Press, 1981) is crucial. The standard bibliography is Lyman Tower Sargent, *British and American Utopian Literature, 1516–1985. An Annotated Chronological Bibliography* (Garland, 1988), to which I am much indebted. A collection of parallel French writings is Frank Manuel and Fritzie Manuel, eds., *French Utopias* (Schocken Books, 1971). A good summary of French utopian writing at this time is R.B. Rose, 'Utopias and the Enlightenment', in Eugene Kamenka, ed., *Utopias* (Oxford University Press, 1987), pp. 35–47. The Scottish-American origins of John Lithgow's *Equality: A Political Romance* (1802) are explored in Michael Durey's 'John Lithgow's Lithconia: The Making and Meaning of America's First "Utopian Socialist" Tract', *William and Mary Quarterly* 49 (1992), 675–694.

Historians of political thought have also touched on many themes relevant to the student of utopias. On eighteenth-century British republicanism see especially Caroline Robbins, *The Eighteenth Century Commonwealthman* (Harvard University Press, 1959); J.G.A. Pocock, *The Machiavellian Moment. Florentine Political Thought and the Atlantic Republican Tradition* (Princeton University Press, 1975); Margaret Jacob, *The Radical Enlightenment: Pantheists, Freemasons and Republicans* (George Allen & Unwin, 1981); Jack Fruchtman, Jr, *The Apoca-*

lyptic Politics of Richard Price and Joseph Priestley: A Study in Late Eighteenth Century English Republican Millennialism (American Philosophical Society, 1983); and Alan Craig Houston, *Algernon Sidney and the Republican Heritage in England and America* (Princeton University Press, 1991). See also Myrddin Jones, 'Swift, Harrington and Corruption in England', *Philological Quarterly*, 53 (1974), 59–70. On the state of nature debate, see especially H.V.S. Ogden, 'The State of Nature and the Decline of Lockean Political Theory in England, 1760–1800', *American Historical Review*, 46 (1940–1), 21–44; Lois Whitney, *Primitivism and the Idea of Progress* (Johns Hopkins University Press, 1934); Chauncey Tinker, *Nature's Simple Plan* (Oxford University Press, 1922); Stelio Cro, *The Noble Savage: Allegory of Freedom* (Wilfred Laurier University Press, 1990); Arthur Lovejoy, 'The First Gothic Revival and the Return to Nature', *Modern Language Notes*, 48 (1932), 419–46; Michael Kraus, 'America and the Utopian Ideal in the Eighteenth Century', *Mississippi Valley Historical Review*, 21 (1936), 487–504; Vincent Geoghegan, 'A Golden Age: From the Reign of Knossos to the Realm of Freedom', *History of Political Thought*, 12 (1991), 189–208; and P.J. Marshall and Glyndwr Williams, *The Great Map of Mankind. British Perceptions of the World in the Age of Enlightenment* (Dent, 1982), ch. 7: 'Savages Noble and Ignoble'. Some of the relations between utopianism and early socialist political ideas are explored in my *Citizens and Saints. Politics and Anti-Politics in Early British Socialism* (Cambridge University Press, 1989). Much of the immense literature on romanticism also touches upon related topics. On theories of progress in the eighteenth century see Ronald Meek, *Social Science and the Ignoble Savage* (Cambridge University Press, 1976); Istvan Hont and Michael Ignatieff, eds., *Wealth and Virtue: The Shaping of Political Economy in the Scottish Enlightenment* (Cambridge University Press, 1982); and David Spadafora, *The Idea of Progress in Eighteenth Century Britain* (Yale University Press, 1990). The aftermath of this period is explored in Judith Shklar's *After Utopia: The Decline of Political Faith* (Princeton University Press, 1957).

Biographical notes

BURGH, James (1714–75): Dissenting schoolmaster and republican. Best known for his *Political Disquisitions* (3 vols., 1774–5), Burgh's Scottish Calvinist background lent additional moral rigour to his politics and sharpened his critique of luxury and corruption. These themes first emerged in his *Britain's Remembrancer* (1746), which ascribed to English degeneracy the considerable successes of the 1745 Jacobite rebellion. Burgh's school at Newington Green occasioned several of his main writings, including *Thoughts on Education* (1747) and *The Dignity of Human Nature* (2 vols., 1754). A member of the club of Honest Whigs from the early 1760s, in the company of Richard Price, Benjamin Franklin and others, Burgh became one of the most widely read reformers of the period. For biography and criticism, see Carla Hay, *James Burgh: Spokesman for Reform in Hanoverian England* (Greenwood Press, 1982) and Isaac Kramnick, *Republicanism and Bourgeois Radicalism. Political Ideology in Late Eighteenth-Century England and America* (Cornell University Press, 1990), pp. 200–59.

HODGSON, William (1745–1851): London physician, political writer and organizer. Tried for sedition in 1793, he was imprisoned in Newgate for two years for comparing the king to a German hog butcher. Active in the radical London Corresponding Society, he later made a living popularizing literature and science, and edited *The Temple of Apollo. Being a Selection of the Best Poems from the Most Esteemed Authors* (1797). Amongst his other works, *The Life of Napoleon Bonaparte* (1845) argued that laws should be few and precise, portrayed the industrious classes as the most valuable part of the community, and, in the midst of the anti-corn law controversy, put the case for cheap food (pp. 3, 9). On Hodgson see Nicholas Hans, 'Franklin, Jefferson, and the English Radicals at the End of the Eighteenth Century', *Proceedings of the American Philosophical Society*, 98 (1954), 406–26, and generally Mary Thale, ed., *Selections from the Papers of the London Corresponding Society 1792–1799* (Cambridge University Press, 1983).

HUME, David (1711–76): philosopher and historian. Best known for his *History of England* (1754–61), which provided his financial independence, Hume established his philosophical reputation with his *Treatise on Human Nature* (1739), the *Philosophical Essays Concerning the Human Understanding* (1748) and the *Enquiry Concerning the Principle of Morals* (1751). His *Dialogues Concerning Natural Religion*, published posthumously, confirmed his reputation as a notorious sceptic. His main political writings are the *Essays, Moral and Political* (2 vols., 1741–2) and the *Political Discourses* (1752). Born at Edinburgh, Hume travelled in France and was for a time attached to the British Embassy at Paris. Long keeper of the Library of the Faculty of Advocates at Edinburgh, he was at his death the leading Enlightenment philosopher in Britain.

NORTHMORE, Thomas (1766–1851): writer and inventor, most of whose life was spent on his Devon estate. Educated at Emmanuel College, Cambridge, where he received his B.A. in 1789, Northmore was an ardent admirer of William Godwin's *Enquiry Concerning Political Justice* (1793). Elected a Fellow of the Society of Antiquaries in 1791, he was interested in gases, fossils, mineralogy, and the early languages of Britain. He also edited Plutarch, produced an edition of Gray's *Tour through England and Wales* (1799), and wrote on education. He ran unsuccessfully for Parliament at Exeter and Barnstaple on several occasions as a radical reformer.

A note on the texts

The Island of Content (1709)

Only one edition is known. The pseudonym, 'Dr Merryman', which appears on the title page, was used by the playwright Henry Playford. The work has also been attributed to John Pomfret (who died in 1702); to Thomas Brown, presumably the poet and satirist from Shifnal, who died in 1704; and to one 'Mr More', possibly James Moore Smith. To complicate matters, the title page says 'By the author of *The Pleasures of a Single Life; or, The Miseries of Matrimony*' (1701). This was first attributed to Sir John Dillon in a London edition, *c.* 1860. Knighted in 1677, he lived at Lismullen, Co. Meath, Ireland, and served as an MP from 1692 to 1711. He divorced his wife in 1701, but later remarried and had three children. David Foxon, however, describes this attribution as 'completely spurious' (*English Verse 1701–1750*, Cambridge University Press, 1975, p. 591). Instead, *The Pleasures of a Single Life* has been ascribed with greater confidence (by *The Eighteenth Century Short-Title Catalogue*) to the poet and anti-Whig satirist Edward Ward (1667–1731). He not only had visited the West Indies, but, unlike Dillon (who wrote nothing else as far as is known), was the author of over seventy works, including *A Trip to Jamaica* (1698), which describes the country as 'as sickly as an hospital, as dangerous as the plague, as hot as hell, and as wicked as the devil' (p. 13). His writings include a 'Pastoral Dialogue ... Concerning the Innocent Pleasures of a Rural Life' (*Works*, 3 vols., 1706–10, vol. III, pp. 263–76), which conforms to the pastoral canon, defined by Theophilus Cibber as concerning the 'manners of the

Golden Age, and the moral formed upon the representation of innocence' (*Lives of the Poets*, 1753, vol. V, p. 125). Stylistic parallels support the probability of his authorship of *The Island of Content*. (None the less Howard Troyer does not include the work even amongst doubtful attributions to Ward: *Ned Ward of Grubstreet*, Harvard University Press, 1946). Born 'of low extraction' in Oxfordshire, and poorly educated, Ward became a publican known for his entertainment of and patronage by the High Church party. Described as a burly, pleasant man, he was twice sentenced in 1705 to the pillory for attacking the government. His satires were widely known, as were his descriptions of London low life, notably prisons, taverns and brothels.

'A Description of New Athens in Terra Australis Incognita' (1720)

The full title of this work in the sole edition known is 'The Fortunate Shipwreck, or a Description of New Athens, Being an Account of the Laws, Manners, Religion, and Customs of That Country; by Morris [elsewhere spelled Maurice] Williams, Gent. who resided there above Twenty Years'. The text is pp. 80–118 of fifty-one short works called *Miscellanea Aurea; or The Golden Medley* (1720), one other utopian chapter of which is called 'A Voyage to the Mountains of the Moon under the Aequator, or Parnassus Reform'd'. The title page describes *Miscellanea Aurea* as 'by Mr. Milton, the Lady W [probably the early feminist Lady Mary Wortley Montagu], Mr. Philips, Mr Killegrew . . . and several others'. Usually termed the main author of the work, though only one section, 'The Fable of Aumillus', is signed by him, Thomas Killegrew the Younger (1657–1719) was a playwright who became gentleman of the bedchamber to the Prince of Wales, later George II. His major production was *Chit-Chat, a Comedy in Five Acts*, which played for eleven nights in 1719. 'A Description of New Athens in Terra Australis Incognita', as the internal title page calls it, has also been attributed to the playwright Charles Gildon. The most likely author, however, is the playwright, pastoral poet, translator of oriental tales and Greek poetry, and political journalist Ambrose Philips (1674/5–1749). Known as a 'zealous Whig' much attached to 'revolution principles', Philips was educated at St John's College, Cambridge, was a close friend of Joseph Addison, at whose home he lived for a time, and secretary during Queen Anne's reign of the Hanover Club. A reputedly vain, talkative man, Philips was noted for his foppery (and mocked by Pope for his red stockings) and skill with a sword. He was friendly with Swift for a time, and later became a Justice of the Peace, judge, and MP for Armagh. His play, *The Distressed Mother*, was first performed in 1711. In 1718–19 he edited *The Freethinker*, which included contributions by Gilbert Burnet and others. The journal warned against the effects of luxury (vol. 1, p. 306), and asserted that, while a commonwealth suited a great city, its application to 'a large extensive country' was 'absurd and impracticable' (vol. 1, pp. 248–9). Such views, while not uncommon, suit the positions taken in 'New Athens'. The latter may have been intended as a continuation of 'A Voyage to the Mountains of the Moon' (pp. 1–34), and is certainly linked thematically to 'On the Love of Our Country' (pp. 70–9). This compares the robust patriotism of the Greeks and Romans to the selfish place-hunting of the modern Whigs and Tories alike (a quest Philips himself was often linked with, not unjustly, by his enemies). It concludes by observing that great heroes emerge only in commonwealths which 'have a pretty large mixture of a Democracy in them, as those of *Greece* and *Rome*'. 'New Athens' begins on the next page.

David Hume, 'Idea of a Perfect Commonwealth' (1752)

First published in the *Political Discourses* (1752). Reprinted after 1754 with the other discourses (3rd edn) in *Essays and Treatises on Several Subjects* (1st edn, 1750), vol. IV.

[James Burgh], *An Account of the First Settlement, Laws, Form of Government, and Police, of the Cessares, A People of South America (1764)*

The inspiration for Burgh's location of the story is drawn from a supposed lost colony of descendants of Spanish sailors settled in a city 'of the Caesars' (de los Cesares) built on an island in the middle of a lake somewhere in the Andes south of Valdivia, and served by Indian converts to Christianity. In 1781 the court of Spain tried to relocate the colony. Nine volumes of evidence from the governor of Chile concluded that the settlement had probably existed. But by 1837 the story was described as 'generally disbelieved' (*Journal of the Royal Geographical Society of London*, 7, 1837, 356–7). The work has been described as wedding 'a Commonwealthman's ideal of 'mixed' government, a Dissenter's idea of religious freedom, and a Calvinist's ideal of moral rectitude, abstemiousness, and industry', and notes that it was ignored by critics (Carla Hay, *James Burgh*, p. 33). Only one edition is known. There is a Spanish translation: *Un Relato de la Colonizacion de las Leyes, Formas de Gobierno y Costumbres de los Césares* (Santiago de Chile, Universidad de Chile, Curiosa Americana, 1963).

[Thomas Northmore], *Memoirs of Planetes, or a Sketch of the Laws and Manners of Makar* (1795)

Only one edition appeared, written under the pseudonym of 'Phileleutherus Devoniensis'. 'Macaria' was the country adjacent to Utopia in More's *Utopia*.

William Hodgson, *The Commonwealth of Reason* (1795)

Two editions appeared in 1795, the second adding a list of errata. The preface, concerning Hodgson's arrest and trial, is omitted in this edition.

Bruce's Voyage to Naples (1802)

This excerpt from the anonymous *A Voyage to the World in the Centre of the Earth* (1755) comprises most of the original, excepting chiefly pp. 119–93. The latter is not part of the main story, but contains 'The History of an Inhabitant of the Air', Mr Thompson, who warns of the dire fate assigned to tyrants, lawyers, priests, courtiers, flatterers, beaux and fops in the afterlife. The hypocrisy and depravity of the contemporary nobility are also contrasted to the great Roman patriots (p. 186). Attribution is uncertain, though William Bingfield is a possibility (see *Monthly Review*, 12, 1755, 395).

The Island of Content: or, A New Paradise Discovered (1709)

[Anon]

The *Island of Content*

Dear Friend,

Since my Golden Pills prov'd so acceptable a Present, and you are very importunate to be made acquainted with the State and Condition of our happy *Island of Content*, where such chearful Physick is alone administer'd in all Distempers; persuent to your Request, I have carefully improv'd some leisure Hours on purpose to oblige you, and have accordingly sent you an exact Account of the Situation of the Place, the Products of the Country, the Constitution of the Government; also the Customs and Manners of the merry Inhabitants of our musical Kingdom, that you may be the better sensible how far the Pleasures of Peace and Dulcitude of Harmony, exceed the noisy Surprizes of uncertain War, and the grinning Malice of domestick Discord. Therefore, that I may not weary out your Patience with a tedious Introduction, I shall treat you as a Friend, and, free of all Partiality to my native Country, let you into the Secret, without farther Preparation, *viz.*

Chap. I.
Of the Situation and Climate.

We are happily seated in a very moderate Climate, but suffering no Man to study the Heathenish Science of Astronomy, I cannot, according to the Rules of Art, pretend to acquaint you with the Degrees of our Latitude: And the Reasons why we think it not safe to suffer a Star-gazer among us, are, that they generally dwindle into Astrological Wiseakers, and by their lying Prophesies, corrupt the Minds of the People, to the Disturbance of the Kingdom; therefore, when ever we catch any Person writing an Almanack, telling Fortunes, or pretending to predict what shall happen hereafter, we tye his Thumbs behind him with Coblers Ends, hang a Shoe-maker's Last about his Neck for a Sygil, and then flog him to Death with a Leathern Strap, without Mercy; for you must know we dread nothing so much as the Subversion of our Government, and the Change of our Constitution; for having a due Sense of our own Happiness, we are well assur'd, from the sad Experience of other Countries, that nothing but Misery would attend a Revolution. However, as to the comfortable Temperature of our happy Climate, we are such absolute Strangers to all manner of Extreams, that we never need Fire, in Winter, to warm our Fingers, or Water, in Summer, to cool our Wines, but enjoy, thro' the Circle of the whole Year, such a peaceful Serenity in all the Elements, that the Distillations of the Clouds are but gentle Dews, that give a lasting Fertility to the fragrant Earth, and only keep the Dust from rising, to the Injury of our Eyes, above its natural Centre; so that we are neither subject to be offended with Dirt, or incommoded with Dust, but always tread upon a verdent Carpet, fresh as a Bowling-Green after a soft Shower in the Month of *April*. As we have no Ice in the coldest of our Weather, to make the Ground deceitful, so have we no destructive Lightning, or surprizing Thunder, in the hottest of our Seasons, to make our Fears terrible; nor will the greatest of our Hurricanes, either in Spring or Autumn, extinguish the Flame of a Farthing Candle, tho' it be stuck lighted, during the whole Storm, upon the Weather-cock of a Steeple.

In short, we are always bless'd with such a comfortable Warmth, that a Man may lie safely between the Heavens and his Wife, and she between her Husband and the bare Ground, without the Danger of catching Cold, tho' it be in Winter: Nor should we have any Occasion for Cloths, not so much as a Fig-leafe, did not Decency oblige us to wear Tiffany Apparel. So that from the Exuberance of Nature, and the Moderation of our Climate, some of our learned Commentators do prophanely assert, that this our Island is the very Paradise that *Adam* lost, but was restor'd lately to our Great Grandfathers, as some deserving Branch of the old Gentleman's Family.

> Old Paradise *is only lost to such*
> *Who search too little, or offend too much,*
> *But easily found by those who can descry*
> *The Heav'nly Being with a righteous Eye.*

Chap. II.

Of our Food and Delicacies

As to our Eatables, Nature is here so lavish of her Plenty, that we abound in Variety of Dainties, without human Labour; nor have we any Occasion to improve our Food by the Art of Cookery, for nothing can be added to make our lusheous Fruits more wholsome, or more palatable.

As to our Bread, the principal Staff of Life, our fertile Ground is so over-run with delicious Potatoes, that we easily dig them up where ever we please, without the Assistance of any other Spade, that our fore Fingers; so that the only Labour we are at, is, to turn them out of the Ground, spread them upon the Surface, and there let them lie but half an Hour in the Sun-shine, and they'll be as well bak'd into crusty half-penny Rolls, as if they had been stopp'd up as long in a well-heated Oven; therefore our Poor here have no Occasion to run to Church for the Sake of the Penny Loaves, nor to dissent from it in Hopes of a better Maintenance, for we have no Bakers to plague them with long Tallies, or oppressive Work-houses to keep 'em to hard Fare, as well as hard Labour, for a parcel of rich Knaves to run away with the Profit of their Earnings, that the Saints in Authority over 'em may say long Graces to large Meals, and thank God for what the Devil has given them.

Pleasant Roots and Herbs are our common Food, from the Lord to the Beggar; by which abstemious sort of Living, we hold our Lusts in such an absolute Subjection, that there is not one Great Magistrate among us, that keeps a Harlot under his Lady's Nose, nor one smock-fac'd Flatterer in all our Dominions, that ever made himself a Great Man by committing Adultery; nor do we ever eat Flesh because we look upon it sinful to destroy one of God's Creatures for the Preservation of another; nor have we any Necessity to prompt us to it, indeed not so much as our own Luxury. As to all sorts of Hortelage, every Man has it in his Backside, as surely as a House of Office; nor can any Inhabitant take a Walk in his Garden, without great Caution, but Clusters of thumping Peaches, and over-grown Nectorals, swinging at the end of stragling Boughs, will be ready at each Step to knock his Teeth down his Throat, as if they were angry with their Owner, that he had not eaten 'em sooner. To be short, we abound with such vast Variety of delicious Products, that our Monkeys and

Squirrels feed upon sweet Almonds, and our wild Hogs upon Mus-
mellons and Pine-apples.

> *If Brutes, thou in our happy Island dwell,*
> *Feed on such dainty Fruits, and live so well,*
> *What Blessings may be found by Human Race,*
> *Who thankfully possess so sweet a Place?*

Chap. III.
Of our Wines and potable Juices.

The outside of every Man's House is here a plentiful Vineyard, for
Vines spring up as naturally under every Body's Windows, as Mush-
rooms from the rotten Stump of an old Horse-black, and creep up
our Walls over the Eves of our Mansions, as commonly as Ivy grows
round an Oak, or Houselick on the top of a Country Bog-house,
insomuch that every Inhabitant, when he wants to drink, may squeeze
his Grapes with his own Teeth, instead of a Wine-press; however,
for Society's Sake, because we cannot be so free in our own Houses,
we allow some Taverns, but to prevent Adulteration, we cut down
all Apple-trees as fast as they spring up, lest the Purity of our Wines
should be debas'd with Cyder; by which Means we keep our Vintners
honest, our Juices wholsome, and the People healthful; yet, tho' our
Liquors are plenty, and in the highest Perfection, we are a sober
Nation, only for want of a large Excise to make it the Interest of our
Government to connive at Drunkenness: So that indeed the Cheapness of our Wines, and the due Execution of our Laws against Vice,
without the least Help of a Society of Reformation, makes Ebriety a
Scandal. Notwithstanding our great Inclinations to Temperance and
Chastity, yet the brightest Rainbow can have no Tincture in her
mottl'd Diversity, but what we can match with some excellent Liquor
of the same Colour, yet we have no Brewers among us; for which
Reason our capital Cities are never govern'd by Lord-Mayors and
Aldermen. But above all other Potables, I have a certain Cordial
Composition of my own, distill'd from the Rays of the Sun, *May*-dew,
Moon-shine, and Honey-drops, that I prepare purposely for the
speedy Suppression of all melancholly Vapours: Which excellent
Cordial, I may say, without Flattery, surpasses all the Nectar in the
Heavens, all the Wines upon Earth, and all the exalted Elements that
mix between both to quench the scorching Drowth of thirsty *Phœbus.*

Therefore, since you inform'd me, in your last Letter, what a pesti-
lential Stupidity had unhappily over-run that flatulent part of the
World wherein you are now resident, I have thought a true Recipe
of so rich a *Nostrum* might be very welcome to a Brother Physician
of your singular Pretensions; but must strictly enjoin you, by all the
Bonds of Friendship, to lock it fast in your own Bosom, as a valuable
Secret. If you happen to find, in your colder Climate, the Ingredients
difficult to come by, or too expensive to turn to Account, then, instead
of *May*-dew, you may use Pump-water; for the Rays of the Sun,
Leaf-Gold; burnt Silver, in the room of Moon-shine; and the want
of Honey-drops, supply with common Sugar; tho', whatever you do,
be sure you observe the true Quantities according to my Recipe; for
it ought to be a Maxim in Physick, *viz. Nulla veritas nulla virtus.*[1]
When you have thus prepar'd it *secundum Artem*, pursuant to Instructions, for its singular Efficacy in all melancholly Distempers, I would
have you call it, *Chear-up*, a Name so applicable to so excellent a
Cordial, that you cannot find a better in the whole *Nomen Clatura*,
for one Thimble-full administer'd in due Season, that is, a little
before the Paroxysm, will certainly cure any dull Fanatick of the
Spirit of Contradiction, or the yawning Evil, and make him as merry
Company for a whole Afternoon, over a Bottle, as a young Player, or
a Mountebank; Merry *Andrew*;[2] also infallibly cures all heavy-hearted
Sinners of the Spleen, Hypo, or Night-mare. Maids of the amorous
Suspiration, Whores of prick'd Consciences, and Wives of the
Vapours; and is so highly in Esteem among the merry Inhabitants of
our peaceful Island, that it is publickly sold here, instead of Brandy,
to make the People laugh.

> *A cordial Dram, with Moderation us'd,*
> *Revives the Heart, but injures when abus'd.*
> *Enough, that happy Quantum, makes us glad;*
> *But with too much, we sottish grow, or mad.*

Chap. IV.

Of our Apparel.

We abound in Spiders of several Sorts and Colours, but all so very
large, that few of 'em appear less than an Ox's Bladder blown to its

---

[1] No virtue is possible without truth.
[2] A humorous physician of the reign of Henry VIII.

full Extension, each carrying in his swelling Bag so much textable
Matter, of a silky Nature, that he will not only spin, but weave as
much Gause in a Day's Time, as would fill a *Scotch*-man's Pack,
every one's Manufacture differing in Strength, Colour, and Substance, according to the Food, Magnitude, Variation, and Agility of
the industrious Insect that happens to be the Weaver, which makes
their excellent Work fit for sundry Uses; so that when any Body has
a Mind to change their Apparel, it is but stepping into their Garden,
and they may furnish themselves with a loose Mantle, (which is the
fashionable Garment here worn) ready spun and wove, either suitable
to their Youth, or agreeable to their Gravity. Therefore we have no
Occasion here for Mercers and Drapers, to dun and plague our
Quality, that they cannot sit easy in their own Parlours for fear of
some Hawk-nos'd Citizen or other, with a long Bill, fifty Scrapes,
and as many humble Beseech ye's, and all to know when he shall
come next to go Home without his Money. Neither is any Person
here distinguish'd by their Dress, because every Body has the Liberty,
without the least Expence, of chusing such Apparel as shall best
humour their own Fancy; for which Reason our very Women here are
wholly innocent of Pride, not at all regarding superficial Ornaments,
endeavouring only to excel each other in Vertue, Modesty, Eloquence, Musick, and such like Female Graces, that are Ornaments
to the Mind, as well as to the Body. We have no Rising by five a
Clock of a Sunday Morning, to get to Church by eleven; no bor-
rowing Jewels upon a Ball-Night, to tempt the Butterflies to attack,
the Honey-pot; no costly Dresses for new Intrigues, to the Wife's
Scandal and the Husband's Ruin; no proud lascivious Lady to cry
Foh at another, when herself is just going to commit Adultery. In
short, our Women of all Degrees, tho' they are commonly beautiful,
yet they are very chast, notwithstanding their Garments, as well as
those of the Men, are so very transparent, that, were not the principal
Covering lin'd with Mulberry-leaves, the Scepter of *Priapus* and the
Mount of Venus would be almost as visible through our Cobweb-Veils,
as any other Indecency, through a pink'd Fan, or a wanton Eye
through the Mask of a Harlot. Yet both Sexes deport themselves with
such awful Modesty, that we behold each others Beauty with an
innocent Admiration, without desiring to unfold the sacred Tiffany,
'till the Laws have granted us a mutual License to enjoy nuptial
Felicity.

8

Bless'd is such Vertue, that can curb Desire,
And free from Lust, sweet Beauty's Charms admire;
Yet, when they're licens'd to enjoy the Same,
Can fan their Love, but never cool their Flame.

Chap. V.
Of the Inhabitants in general, and their Arts, Trades, and Occupations.

Of all Arts and Sciences amongst us, Physick and Musick are held the most venerable, and for these two Reasons: In the first Place, every Body's Life is so extremely happy, and all that conducts to human Felicity, so easily come by, that all Men are equally unwilling to resign so pleasing a Certainty, for a doubtful Futurity; so that if a melancholy Fume does but happen to eclipse the natural Chearfulness of any One's Temper, I am presently sent for, to administer some of my Golden Pills, and a Dose or two of my *Chear-up*, which either recovers them presently to their former Spriteliness, or if the Patient continues but one Hour after in a Fit of the Dumps, we certainly give him over as a dying Victim to the fatal Conqueror. Therefore the Dread of Melancholy, and the Fear of Death, makes them adore their Physicians as their Life's Safe-guard, and so much the more, because they have but three in the whole Island, Dr. *Diet*, Dr. *Quiet*, and Dr. *Merryman*: The first corrects the Patient's Food, and prescribes him Rules to eat by; the second lulls him to sleep by an emphatical Repetition of some drowsy Poetry of his own writing, which he always uses instead of Poppy-water; and when the Patient wakes, then my self administers a Dose of my Golden Pills, and a reviving Thimble-full of my Cordial *Chear-up*; and if these Methods will not raise his Spirits above the Depression of Melancholy, which is the only Distemper we are here subject to, then he must even follow the Steps of his Fore-fathers; for it is not in the Power of human Art to respite him from Eternity.

Secondly, The principal Reason why Musicians are as much wor-shipp'd as Owls among the *Egyptians*, is, that since all the Comforts of Life are handed to us by Nature, without the least Assistance of our own Labour, we have nothing else to do, besides Eating, Drinking, and Sleeping, but to fidle away our Time, sing, dance, laugh, and be merry: So that if a Man has but a tunable Nack upon any Instrument, tho' it be but the *Jews*-trump, he shall be as much respected and admir'd, if he does not want Entreaty, as ever *Tubal Cain* was for playing a Madigral upon his Cockle-shells. So that the only Artists that are valuable among us, next to Physicians, are Fidlers, Pipers, Singers, Dancers, Rimers, and Punsters, tho' the last is forc'd to be a Lacquey to the former, by the Custom of the Country, and to carry the great Crowd, because we are all of an Opinion here, that Punning much better becomes a Fidler's Boy, than it does his Master.

We had a Theatre, and a Company of Comedians for a little Time, but they were always quarrelling about their Mistresses, or who should have most Wages; so we furnish'd 'em with a large Canow, and turn'd 'em out of the Island.

We have very few Handicrafts among us, besides those who make our Musical Instruments, and they grow such lazy Rogues, because they live in Clover, that we are often forc'd to put a Neck and a Bridge to one of my *Chear-up* Runlets, and string it up for a Treble Viol, and to make a homely Shift with a Bow and a Bladder to play our Thorough Bases on; yet, we are always as well pleas'd with our Musick, as you can be with the harmonious Neighings of your *Italian* Geldings; for whoever here finds the least Fault, or shews himself discontented upon any Occasion, immediately forfeits his Residence, and is banish'd the Island.

Our Dancing-masters have more Business among our young Ladies, than they can well turn their Toes to, tho' they never receive any Reward, above Thanks, for their Labour; for every thing here is so plenty without Money, that they need as little Pay as they can possibly deserve; but if any one, by Chance, be catch'd kissing a Scholar, he must patiently suffer his Heels to be par'd, that he may never dance afterwards, or else he must be forc'd in twenty four Hours to depart the Country; for it is wisely consider'd, that nothing can be a greater Interruption to the Content of Parents, than to have their Daughters debauch'd by those very Miscreants, who have the Confidence to undertake to teach them Breeding; nay, some are apt to think it carries along with it such a heinous Piece of Treachery, that a Man deserves to be gelt for.

> *If, in strict Justice, a deceitful Friend*
> *Deserves a Jayl, that tricks me when I lend;*
> *What must be merit, who his Trust betrays,*
> *Deflow'rs my Child, and robs me of my Ease?*

Chap. VI.

Of our Laws, and Methods for the Dispatch of Justice.

We have but one Court of Judicature, no Juries, and but one Judge, who has an absolute Power, without the Circumscription of any Law, to determine all Matters, *Coram Judice*, according to the best of his own Judgment, which he is bound to do upon the first Hearing, without any Delay. *Astrea* like, he is always blindfold when he sits upon the Bench, to prevent Corruption, that he may neither be affected with the Deportment of one Man, or offended with the homely Figure or clownish Behaviour of another, so as to be inclin'd to any manner of Partiality; nor does he ever hear with more than one Ear at a Time; for as soon as the Plaintiff begins to speak, he always stops the other, and reserves it for the Defendant. Every Person here is not only suffer'd, but under an inevitable Necessity of pleading his own Cause, for we have no such Things as old musty Customs, Precedents, or ancient intricate Rules, lock'd up in a barbarous obsolete Language, to puzzle Justice, delay Judgment, and make Right a Difficulty; for which Reason we have no Occasion for those nimble-tongu'd Divers into Querks and Quidities, call'd Lawyers: Tho', some Years since, our Court admitted of two Orators, one for the Plaintiff, and the other for the Defendant, but in a little Time they had like to have set the whole Island by the Ears; so that being found a Nusance, One, who was the greatest Incendiary, was decently tuck'd up upon an o'd Crab-tree, and the other presently after dy'd for Fear; so that ever since the Inhabitants have been restor'd to their ancient Content, and every one has the Liberty in plain Words to exhibit his own Case, and his Witnesses the Priviledge of speaking freely, without being banter'd either out of the Truth, or out of their Senses; and that no Man, in any wise, should have the Advantage of his Adversary, we suffer no Learning above Writing and Reading, to be taught among us; by which Means we preserve our Peace, prevent the Growth of Blockheads, and defend our ancient Constitution from all manner of Innovations: Nor indeed is our Court of Judicature troubled with any Matters of Debt, because all Persons live so plentifully here, that no Man has Occasion to borrow any thing of his Neighbour: Nor have we any Disputes about Titles of Estates, because every Man has more than himself or his Family knows well what to do with; to that most of our Controversies are about the

Disturbance of our Peace, by warm Words between Neighbours, or accidental Contentions between Man and Wife; which, as they happen but seldom, are always punish'd with the utmost Severity, least others should be corrupted by their evil Example, and the Content of our Island be unhappily impair'd. The Loss of the Tongue, or perpetual Banishment, are the usual Sentences pronounc'd by the Judge upon such Offenders; which terrible Dooms are never superseded upon other Terms than an humble Submission, an open Penance, a sincere Repentance, and a publick Recantation: So that notwithstanding Judgment, if the Convict can find Sureties for his due Performance of the aforesaid Articles, he is again restor'd to his former Liberties. From whence you may observe, that our greatest Severity is not without Mercy.

> *He that is truly sad for his Offence,*
> *Merits Compassion by his Penitence;*
> *And want of Mercy, all good Men agree,*
> *Turns human Justice into Tyranny.*

Chap. VII.
Of our Marriages.

As we have but little Occasion for either Money or Huswifry, so the only Gifts, Graces, and Acquirements, that we value in a Woman, are, Beauty, Modesty, and a charming Excellency both in Musick and Dancing; and the higher Perfection she happily enjoys in these amorous Inducements, the greater Fortune we esteem her, and respect her accordingly: And in Regard the Woman was the last most excellent and beautiful Work that crown'd the whole Creation, we give them the Precedency in all Cases, excepting Family-Government: They chuse first, eat first, drink first, go to Bed first, and have a peculiar Liberty in discovering their Affections, without incurring thereby the least Scandal or Reflexion; for which Reason, Men never address 'em as in other Countries, or tire their Ears with impertinent Courtship, but always leave them to their own Choice: which extraordinary Priviledge, no Parent has Power to deny any Daughter, when she is fully arriv'd at the Age of fifteen. And the Method that they use to signify their Liking to the happy Person that they honour with their Love, is in Manner following, *viz.* The enamour'd Damsel, when she has pitch'd upon her Man, knits with her pretty Fingers an artificial Ring of her own Maiden Hair, which she sends wrap'd up in a white Paper, whereon is inscrib'd her own Name very fairly written, and in what Grove she intends to be walking the next Day, with some of her Relations. If the Receiver of the Present be no ways pre-engag'd, and approves her for his Bride, he keeps the Token, and tearing out a Mulberry-Leaf from the Lining of his fore Garment, sends it back to the Lady in another Piece of Paper, wherein he signifies his kind Acceptance, and that he will certainly meet her at the Place appointed; but if he dislikes the Proposal, he returns the Present by the Bearer, which is look'd upon here to be the highest Contempt that can be put upon a Virgin, without he is able to excuse himself by some substantial Reasons. But if they happen to meet, the Match is made up upon their first Conference, and the Time is appointed by the young Lady for their Marriage, which is always thus conditional, *viz.* That if at any Time hereafter, for Reasons known to themselves, they shall both jointly agree upon an absolute Separation, they may both come together, and with one Accord signify their Consent so to part before the Parson that marry'd 'em. The same Priest or his succeeding Incumbent in the same Parish, having a lawful Power, without farther Contest, to pronounce an utter Separation; so that either shall have the Freedom of wedding new Spouses, to their farther Satisfaction; and in Case of Children, who are never here thought burthensome, by Reason of our Plenty, the Boys always go with the Man, and the Girls with the Woman. Without this Liberty, we should never be able to preserve the Content of the Publick, which has ever been esteem'd the highest Blessing of our peaceful Island; for nothing seems more unreasonable here to the wise Conservators of our happy Constitution, than that Man and Wife should be forc'd by a Law to live together, contrary to their Wills, in perpetual Discord, when both might propose to enjoy asunder undisturb'd Felicity, or to match themselves so comfortably a second Time, that neither should hereafter find any Cause of Repentance. Besides, 'tis to this excellent Custom of willing Separation, that we principally owe the Vertue of our marry'd Women, and the Continence of their Husbands; for knowing, that when they are weary of one another, they may part by Consent, makes the matrimonial Shackles fit the easier without galling, and causes both Sides to consider, if they should bring themselves under Scandal by any libidinous Practices, during the first Marriage-Contract, that if ever hereafter they should so far disagree, as to be willing to part, no Body would be so mad to trust either Man or Woman a second Time, who had so infamously broken their former Covenant; so that we have no marry'd women that run one Way with their Gallants, whilst their Husbands steal another with their lip-licking Harlots; no Courtiers at the Tails of our Citizens Wives and Daughters, whilst titular Cousins are revenging the Wrongs done to their finer Ladies. In short, we are a very happy People, not at all addicted to either Pride, Lust, or Avarice; and tho' any Man and his Wife may part at Pleasure, if both are consenting, yet they are generally such mutual Lovers of each other, that its seldom put in Practice.

> *Since Love can only make a nuptial Life*
> *Sweet to the Husband, pleasant to the Wife,*
> *When that's declin'd, 'tis hard they should be forc'd*
> *By Law, against their Wills, to live accurs'd.*

Chap. VIII.
Of our Sports and Recreations.

Those Sports among us, that are most innocent, are always best belov'd, and accounted the most noble; nor are we at all addicted to Hunting, Fowling, or Fishing, because we hold it sinful to make a Pastime of the Life, or to delight in the Blood of any Manner of Creature; nay, some are so conscientious, that they will not venture to play a Game at Push-pin, for fear by Accident they should prick their Neighbour's Fingers, yet we allow of Lawful Sports and Recreations upon the Sabbath-day, but then they are such, that can no Ways be offensive either to God or Man, as Consorts of Musick in our Woods and Groves, floating upon our Rivers in our Canows and Barges, grave Dancing in our Meadows, without Noise or Disorder, and the like; and the main Reason why we grant these Liberties after divine Service, are, *viz.* That we have no Intriguing to divert our Quality, few Taverns, and no Coffee-houses to refresh our Citizens, no Bawdy-houses to entertain our Youth, no Brandy-Bottles and Tobacco for our Ladies Closets, neither Sots Holes or Ale-houses for drunken Porters and Carmen. Therefore we think it but reasonable to

tollerate what's harmless, since our Government gains nothing by the
Sins and Vices of the People. Cards we look upon to be Witchcraft,
and Dice Devilism; for which Reason, the Use of both are very strictly
prohibited, lest Gaming should fill our Island with that hell-born
Retinue which it always draws after it, *viz.* Cursing, Swearing, Cheating, Avarice, and Contention, such diabolical Attendance that would
prove very destructive to our peaceable Constitution. We have no
Horses upon our Island, nor indeed Occasion for any; but instead
thereof, we have a tame pretty black Animal, with a white List down
his Back, that, as to our Pleasure, does us the same Service. He is
very gentle, yet very swift of Foot, about the Bigness of an Ass, but
rather shap'd like a Buck, and is so towardly a Pad, that we ride him
without a Bridle. When we are once mounted, bid him walk and he'll
walk, trot and he'll trot, run and he'll gallop; and is so wonderful a
Creature of that inherent Docibility, that we can bring him to fetch
and carry, jump over a Stick, or swim after a Duck with a Rider upon
his Back, as well as a Spaniel. The common Name of this Animal,
is, an Errandeer, so call'd, I suppose, from his Swiftness, and his
Shape, being somewhat like a Stag in Body, and always employ'd
upon such Business, that requires speedy Dispatch. Upon these serviceable Creatures we often take our Recreation out of our great
Cities, among the distant Villages, sounding our Horns and Trumpets
along the Roads as we pass, with all the chearful Magnificence that
can add Pleasure to our Progress. Thus we ramble round the Country, to visit our Friends and Relations, twice every Year, and when
we have enjoy'd one another in moderate Drinking, Mirth, Musick,
and Dancing, we return Home to our Families, without the Care of
Business, and by the Charms of our Wives, and the Sweetness of
our Children, still continue our Alacrity, and preserve our Content.
Our next Enjoyment, is, a familiar Conversation with our amicable
Neighbours, which we daily renew under the Shade of our own Vines,
and sometimes at the Tavern, but are always careful of these theer
Mischiefs, *viz.* Talking to an Uneasiness, Jesting to Prophaneness,
and Drinking to Excess; so that we have no obscene Discourses, that
begin with Bawdy, run into Blasphemy, and end with Religion; no
wrangling about Government, or Disputes upon Matters which none
of us understand; no factious Cabals, to propagate Sedition, or
undermine the Church; no quarrelling about our Sanctity, to give
our Adversary, the Devil the better End of the Staff; no politick

Projects, to sell our Country's Welfare to the Avarice of our Superiors; no sinister Inventions, to make nineteen Parts of our Kingdom
more Slaves to the twentieth; no Party-Divisions, to occasion our
Fools to contend about Shadows, whilst we lose our Substance. In
short, we are an amicable People, who, together and apart, study our
King's Ease, the publick Safety, and our own Happiness. We never
privately promote intestine Discords, and consecrate the Subtility, by
openly recommending Peace, Love, and Unity; so that indeed our
Sports are innocent, our Recreations delightful, and all our merry
Meetings, which are only upheld for the Advancement of Harmony,
are so well regulated, that nothing passes throughout our whole Conversation, but what is joyful at the Present, and sweet in the Reflexion;
and the principal Reasons why we live so secure in this State of
Felicity, are these, *viz.* We are unanimous in our Devotion, have but
little Preaching, and that orthodox, and are neither plagu'd with either
polemick Pamphlets, or deceitful News-Papers.

> *Where e'ery factious Scribbler is allow'd*
> *To vent his Whimsies, to corrupt the Crowd*
> *And preaching K—s in Alley-Pulpits vend*
> *Their wicked Nonsense, Discords have no End.*

Chap. IX.
Of our Religion and our Clergy.

In Matters of Faith, we have but one entire Opinion, which, without
Scruple, is universal among us; and the nominal Symbol which our
Church bears, is, the Church of Peace, and the general Appellation
by which her Sons are distinguish'd, *viz.* The Brethren of Content.
In Affairs Ecclesiastical, we are under the Government but of one
Bishop, and be a true Friend to the Church, fearing, if we had more,
they should dispute their Seniority, and perplex the Church with
their contentious Wrangles, to the Hurt of her Community; so that
the whole Island, it being but small, is happily resolv'd into one
Bishoprick: Nor is any Man chosen into this sacred Authority, 'till
he has given the whole Nation, by his exemplary Life, sufficient
Testimonials of his extraordinary Wisdom, sincere Piety, and unspot-
ted Integrity; so that whoever is invested with this holy Dignity, is
always reverenc'd by the whole People, as a *Moses* or an *Aaron.* His

highest Care, is, to preserve the Church upon her ancient Foundation, in Love and Unity, and to be watchful and diligent in supplying
the Island with a peaceable, knowing, and discreet Clergy, such as
are qualify'd by their Lives, as well as their Doctrines, to teach the
People their Duty. Nor are they ever suffer'd to adorn their Eloquence with unintelligible Sentences, or abstruse Terms, borrow'd
from the Froth of foreign Languages, but are strictly oblig'd to be as
familiar in their Pulpits, as they are in their Parlours, all of us agree-
ing, it is the Business of our Guides not to puzzle, but instruct their
Congregations; for we are never affected with metaphysical Rodo-
montado's, or apt to admire, like other Nations, what we do not
understand. Our Creed and our Worship are strictly consonant to
the Scriptures, and the Preaching of our Clergy never dissonant to
our Creed. We universally approve of divine Musick in our Churches,
as a sweet and comfortable Means to elevate our Souls in the holy
Service of Almighty God; and should a Man among us but intimate
his Aversion to such heavenly Harmony, he would be look'd upon as
a Brute, without a rational Soul, and unworthy to be admitted into
the House of Prayer. We never enter into the holy Door, but with a
profound Humility, and are all so unanimously sincere in our Devotion, that we think it a Contempt to the divine Majesty, to shew a
roving Eye, or a disettl'd Countenance; so that none come to Church,
but with a sincere Intention to perform their Duty, and in their Looks
and Actions to express that Reverence which is highly becoming of
so solemn an Occasion. We have no ogling between intriguing Ladies
and their amorous Gallants; no study'd Gestures, languishing
Deportments, or bewitching Glances, to excite the Wanton to polute
the Temple with adulterous Inclinations; no coming to Church out
of Pride, instead of Piety, much rather to shew the Fineness of their
new Apparel, than the Sincerity of their Devotion; no hiding of
female Faces with pink'd Fans, in the Interim of Prayer, when all
the Time of their pretended Sanctity, they are peeping thro' the
Holes to examine the Faces of the young Gentlemen; no kneeling
down with a lustful Heart, and an hypocritical Countenance,
squinting one Eye at Heaven, and the other at a Lover; no Assigna-
tions in the Church-Porch, where to meet and be wicked after divine
Service; nor are we ever troubl'd with tender Consciences, who are
for stripping the Priest of his Benefice, as well as his Surplice, the
Church of her Rites and Ceremonies, the Chancel of its Plate, the

Steeple of its Bells, and God's holy House of its Harmony. In short, we are a People that abominate Pride, love Unity, and hate Dissention, and that shew no more Zeal in our Looks, than what is visible in our Practices; we never pray aloud in our Parlours, and cheat the World in our Shops, heap Calumnies upon the Innocent, and protect our guilty Brethren, oppress our Country, to gratify our Ambition, over-power Truth with notorious Falsities, or prefer the windy Froth of proud, illiterate Dunces, to the sound Doctrine of pious, learn'd, and reverend Instructors; nor do we suffer any Man to ascend the Pulpit, but such as are truly worthy of so divine an Office, or ever permit the sacred Function of the Priesthood to be mimick'd in Holes and Corners by Apes, Monkeys, and Baboons, who, like Quacks and Mountebanks, have no Way to gain the good Opinion of Fools, but by railing on their Stages at the true and able Physicians; so that by the extraordinary Care of our Church-Governors, we are always preserv'd in such peaceable Unanimity, that we have not so much as one Fanatick among us, to disturb the Quiet of our Island.

> *Where one Religion is preserv'd entire,*
> *It does the Flock with peaceful Minds inspire;*
> *But where contending Churches are advanc'd,*
> *Destructive Feuds by Zeal countenanc'd.*

Chap. X.
Of our civil Government.

We esteem it our great Happiness, that we are under the Government of an hereditary Monarchy, which, by the Blessing of Providence, has been long preserv'd among us, without any Interruption: Nor have we any Tradition that gives us an Account of either Fraction, Commotion, Rebellion, or Revolution, that ever happen'd since the first Settlement of a King over us, who (according to our best and truest Histories, our old Ballads, which have been sung down from one Generation to another) was a good old Gentleman, who forsook his native Country, with his Children, Friends, and Relations, to save their Lives in a Time of Rebellion and Cruelty, when their Prince was murder'd, the Constitution torn in Pieces, Religion made a Mock of, their Estates sequester'd into the Hands of Traytors, and the whole Kingdom painted of a sanguine Complexion, with the Blood of the Loyal. 'Twas in these Times of Trouble, when there was no other Prospect, but of Misery and Destruction, that our first King and Governor, with his whole Family, put themselves on board a large Vessel they had bought, and rather chose to trust themselves to the Mercy of unbridl'd Winds, and the tempestuous Ocean, than to the ruder Malice and more ungovernable Rage of a poyson'd Rabble, and a fanatick Enemy, who were made the Instruments of God's Justice upon a sinful Nation. When thus embark'd, by the Help of a Pilot, and some few Sea-men, they put out to Sea, where they rov'd for many Weeks under the Protection of Providence, in order to discover some uninhabited Country, wherein they might propose to live secure and free from the Tyranny and Oppression of such inhuman Monsters as they had left behind them. At length, when driven to great Hardships, thro' the Scarcity of Provisions, good Heaven, in Compassion to the distress'd Wanderers, steer'd their Bark in View of this our fruitful Island, who sailing round it, and judging, by the Want of Towns upon the Beech, it was uninhabited, they ventur'd to cast Anchor in a commodious Bay, and hoisting out their Boat, came a-shore, as it happen'd, in the most pleasant Part of the whole Country, where uncultivated Nature was so very exuberant, that upon their first Entrance, they found every Thing needful for the Support of Life in a peaceful State of uncontroulable Felicity; for they soon perceiv'd, by the Wildness of the Woods, the Want of passable Roads, and the rude Appearance of every Thing they met with at their Landing, that they were in no Danger from any prior Inhabitants, except wild Beasts, and against those they were well arm'd and guarded; so that being pleas'd with the Climate, comforted by the Products, and delighted with the Country, they were all highly satisfy'd with what Providence had allotted them, and unanimously resolv'd to thankfully enjoy the peaceable Possession of their new Land of *Canaan*; and for the better securing of their farther Happiness, they thought it necessary to agree upon such a Form of Government, as might preserve hereafter their growing Community from those fatal Troubles and Disorders, which had caus'd them to forsake their native Country. After a short Consultation of the wisest Heads among 'em, an absolute Monarchy, without any Limitation, was determin'd as the best, because they had too lately observ'd the miserable Confusions from whence they had withdrawn, were all undisputably owing to the Pride, Folly, and Madness of a stubborn, hot-headed Senate, who pretended to have Share in the Government. Therefore they were resolv'd to prevent the like Mischiefs arising in their new Kingdom from the like Causes, and thought it much safer to trust to the Mercy, Wisdom, and Conduct of one good Man, than to the Heats, Factions, and Whimsies that might happen to arise among many hundreds. Accordingly the good old Gentleman, who was the Father of the Family he had deliver'd out of Slavery, took upon himself the sovereign Authority; and being anointed King, under God, by his own Chaplain, assum'd the Name of *Philodespot*, from his being a true Lover of his injur'd Master. No sooner was he climb'd into his new regal seat, but he wisely proceeded to settle the Government upon a lasting Foundation, and to order every Thing to the unspeakable Joy and Satisfaction of his Subjects, who were so highly pleas'd with the discreet Management and Princely Conduct of their new King *Philodespot*, that they began to esteem Loyalty as the chiefest Vertue, and greatest Obligation, that ought to be regarded by so happy a People, who found themselves now so absolutely free from all Cruelty and Oppression, and suddenly advanc'd into such a State of Felicity, that they reverenc'd their Royal Patriot as a *Solomon* for his Wisdom, and a *David* for his Goodness, since his only Care and Ambition, were his own just Glory, and his Subjects Happiness. From the Sacred Loins of this venerable Prince, descended that wise and peaceable worthy *Philodespot* the IId, who did not only inherit the Throne, but the Vertues of his Father, under whose Government the Content of the Publick still flourish'd above twenty Years, without the least Interruption, 'till, as he had reign'd in Comfort, he expir'd in Peace, and was happily succeeded by his Royal Son, *Philodespot* the IIId, our present Sovereign, a Prince of that matchless Piety, serene Temper, unspeakable Lenity and Goodness to his People, that he would sooner suffer himself to die a Martyr, than to sacrifice the Peace and Welfare of his Subjects, upon any other Terms, than their own Security; insomuch, that we think our selves, under his excellent Government, the happiest People in the Universe. He has no Flatterers about him, to make their own Markets, by raising and fomenting groundless Fears and Jealousies; no ambitious Upstarts, to swell their own Fortunes by Fraud, Treachery, and Oppression, but guides the Reins with so much Wisdom and Moderation, and is

obey'd in all Things with so much Zeal and Loyalty, that it is impress-
ible to determine which are the most happy, the Prince or the People.

> *Where the King's just, and Loyalty prevails,*
> *No Nation of a happy Union fails:*
> *But, where the People from the Prince divide,*
> *They're always curs'd for their rebellious Pride.*

Chap. XI.

Of our Courtiers and our Quality.

No Person is dignify'd or distinguish'd here upon any other Account,
than for their Wisdom, Piety, and Vertue; and when any of their
Heirs shall be found wanting of these excellent Gifts and Qualities,
their Honour ceases, and their Titles are forfeited: Nor are they
longer reverenc'd by the humbler Crowd, than they can support their
Merits, not by Art, but by Action, far above the Level of the common
People; nor are they ever admitted into publick Authority, 'till they
have given such Evidence of their singular Perfections, that neither
King nor Country have the least Reason, from any vitious Habit, to
doubt of their Integrity; and if ever they are detected in any evil,
Practice between Prince and People, they are presently dipt into a
Fat of Honey, like a Wick into Tallow when you make a Candle,
then ty'd in a Wood with their Back to a Tree, that they may be
tickl'd to Death with Bees, Wasps, and Muschetoes; so that Great
Men here, as well as our Ladies, are wisely careful to be as just as
Astrea, as virtuous as Nuns, and as pious as Bishops, and by the
Strictness of their Lives, are a great Encouragement to the whole
Island to follow their Example. If they are proud, covetous, or imperious, the King despises 'em, and the People laugh at 'em; if they are
wanton, vitious, or immoral, we put them into a Pest-house, for fear
the wicked Contagion should spread itself thro' the Kingdom, and if
they carelessly give the Publick any Testimonies of their Folly, they
are divested of their Honour, degraded with a Fool's Cap, a Muck-
ender, and a Slabbering-Bib, and doom'd to be Merry *Andrews* to
our travelling Mountebanks. Therefore all our Quality are so very
circumspect in their Lives and Practices, and so cautious and exact
in the Management of their Posts, and the Execution of Authority,
that we never hear of the publick Money being told over a Grid-Iron,

or of a crafty Upstart's getting an Estate by cozening our Government, but all Persons here are well content with a bare Sufficiency to support themselves in their Stations, and never seek to improve their own Fortunes, by the Oppression of others: Nor have we any Minions here rais'd above their Merits, for sly Chamber-Practices, officious watching at the Door of Iniquity, or smuggling prohibited Commodities; for our Petticoat Quality are all so wonderful vertuous, that a new-marry'd Lord may go a Progress for twelve Months, and leave his Lady behind him, without the Danger of a Beau-Rival, a spurious Heir, or losing one Jewel out of his Bride's Casket. We have no strong-back'd Sicophants, who set up for Men of Breeding, to play at Cards among our Ladies; no Sir *Foplin Flutters*, to idolize the Charms of a lascivious Countess, or to sublevate her Fringes to administer Titulation to her itching Honour; no Curtizans at Court, to riggle their wanton Tails into the Royal Favour of our King, that they may betray the Secrets which they gain by their Levity, to those who better please 'em, by diving farther into their lustful Embraces; no Stallions at large Stipends, or Concubines in high Keeping; no Bawds of Title, or fawning Pimps in their own lacquer'd Coaches; no looks of Quality to adorn our Churches of a Sunday, that they may gild their Vices with their hypocritical Sanctity, and cover their six Days Shame, with their seventh Day's Devotion. In short, we have no promiscuous Venery among our High and Mighty, but every Great Man puts his little bald Stone-horse into his own Stable, and every Lady takes Care to shut the Stable-door in her Lord's Absence, that no intruding Stallion may rival her *Bucephalus* in his lawful Enjoyments; so that our Ladies live without the Fear of Shame, and our Lords without the Danger of Cuckoldom.

> *In Courts, where Vertue shines among the Great,*
> *It awes the Publick, and adorns the State:*
> *But, where the Guides and Leaders, to their Shame,*
> *Persue their Lusts, the Frape[3] will do the same.*

Chap. XII.

Of our foreign Trade and Commerce.

We are such great Enemies to superfluous Complements, and unnecessary Ceremonies, that we are utter Dissenters to all that trouble-

---

[3] Frape: mob, rabble.

some Cringing and Scraping, which the over *Frenchify'd* Fools of some Nations account the highest Breeding; therefore, to prevent Foppery, instead of Popery, coming in amongst us, our Government will permit us to have no Traffick with any Nation but the *Dutch*, for these two Reasons; first, Because, they are never given to such an Excess of Breeding, as to corrupt our People with over-useful Manners. And secondly, Because they never profess any Religion among us; so that there is no Danger of their introducing a new Worship, or of drawing off Communicants from our establish'd Church; therefore we have no Cause to fear, that their nice Examples will turn our Blockheads into Beaus, or our Zealots into Schismaticks. Our Island is by Nature so well fortify'd, that it is no where accessible, but in two Places, and those by Art are so well secur'd, that none can surprize us, but by our own Treachery; so that the first Time the *Dutch* came to settle a Trade with us, we would not suffer them to set a Foot upon our Island, 'till they had taken a solemn Oath, that whenever they were on Shore, they should keep their Hands in their Pockets, their Knives in their Mouths, and never drink a Drop of any strong Liquor, 'till they return'd to their Ships; which Articles are strictly observ'd to this Day: By this Stratagem, we keep their Fingers from picking and stealing, their Tongues from lying and slandering, the thirsty Brutes from Drunkenness, and the Cowards from quarrelling, only he that negotiates, wears his Knife in his Pocket, and has his Mouth at Liberty; but if ever he be heard to swear *Tonder* and *Blacksom*, he then forfeits his Priviledge. Tho' we always find them a very subtil People, yet we are as cunning as they can be; for we never furnish them with any of our Commodities, but what we can spare without impairing our Plenty, and never take any Thing in Lieu of our Products, but what is useful to the Publick. We are no such Fools to export the best of our Provisions, 'till we want it ourselves, for the Sake of brittle *Dutch* Earth, that's bak'd too hard for our Teeth; we barter not our Bread for a Parcel of *Dutch* Babies, that our Children may have the one to play with, when they want the other to eat; we scorn they should grow rich by our Poverty, proud by our Humility, fat by our Consumption, thrifty by our Extravagance, wise by our Folly, and powerful by our Weakness. In a Word, we are very careful that we lose nothing by 'em, but use them exactly at they would us, and deal with their High and Mightinesses as they do with every Body, or as we would with the Devil; so that in the Main, we only make 'em our Tallow-Chandlers, our Fish-mongers, our

Butter-Boxes, our Brandy-Merchants, and the like; and lastly, our Scavengers to carry our Rubbish off the Island; for we never spare 'em any Thing but what would become a Nusance if we did not get rid of it. Yet their Industry makes all our Superfluities turn to a good Account, because they carry 'em into those foolish Nations, who are so full of Pride and Vanity, that they barter their own staple Commodities, for any foreign Fipperies, that will but adorn a jointed Baby, or a Lady's Lap-dog, or give but a new Flavour to a little warm Water. Thus we keep them at a Bay, tho' we hold a fair Correspondence, and never trust them farther than we are able to manage 'em.

Now I have thus given you a Description of our Island, and told you what a People we are not, as well as what we are, I shall conclude with a Specimen of our Lyrick Poetry, that you may see how far the Muses have honour'd us with their Company; and tho' we cannot boast a learned Retrospection into the profitable Labours of old defunct Worthies, who were the Honour and Ornament of past Ages; yet, by the Assistance of the rhiming Gossips, we are able to conjure up as flourishing a Ballad, as ever you heard sung at the *Porters Block* in *Smithfield*, or purchas'd at *Pye-Corner, viz.*

A SONG.

When fam'd Apollo, God of Light,
   And Monarch of Wilts Throne,
Retires, and leaves old dowdy Night,
   To wear her Starry Crown;
And when Favonius fans our Isle
   With a refreshing Breeze,
And gently cools the fruitful Soil,
   And rocks the lofty Trees;

We then with our Mates to our Bowers remove,
   And with Musick enliven our Hearts,
Sing innocent Sonnets of Friendship and Love,
   Uncorrupted with flattering Arts.

Whilst pulpy Grapes on fertile Vines,
   In juicy Clusters grow
Above our Heads, and with their Wines
   Our chearful Cups o'erflow;
When Turtles murmur out their Love,
   And coo in dusky Shades,

And drooping Boughs, that spread above,
  From Damps defend our Heads;

Then despising all Fraud, we meet with our Friends,
  And chat o'er our jolly full Bowls,
But free from Excess, and all sinister Ends,
  We chear up and quicken our Souls.

Let foreign Kingdoms wast their Store,
  To make their Neighbours yield,
'Till purple Show'rs of wreaking Gore,
  Manure the barren Field;
Let Mothers weep, and Wives lament,
  And wring their Hands and rave,
To see their Sons and Husbands sent
  To feed the gaping Grave;
Whilst we unoppress'd, live in Plenty and Peace,
  In the Good of the Publick agree,
Have no Wolves in Sheeps Clothing to tear off our Fleece,
  But from such Sort of Dangers are free.

We starve no thousands, to enrich
  Or gratify a few,
And, to deceive the Publick, stretch
  The Wonders that they do:
We humour not the Proud and Great,
  To make our selves their Slaves;
Nor draw in Fools, by Tricks of State,
  To be a Prey to Knaves.

We honour our Prince, and take Care of ourselves,
  Trust none that we know would undo us;
But wisely steer wide of those Rocks and those Shelves,
  Where the Danger is visible to us.

FINIS.

A Description of New Athens
in Terra Australis Incognita
(1720)

[Anon]

A Description of *New Athens* in *Terra Australis Incognita*[1]

By one who resided many Years upon the Spot

Letter I.

Sibi convenientia finge

To J – – – – – H – – – – – Esq; at his House near Holborn,
London.

DEAR SIR,

In my former I gave you an Account of our Ship's being cast away
on the Southern Coast, without the Loss of any one Man, or much
of its Cargo; I let you know the Hardships we underwent in an
uninhabited Country, and how, endeavouring to make Discoveries in
our Long Boat, we fell into the Hands of a very hospitable People.
I gave you also an Account of the several Cities, the Manners and
Customs, through which we pass'd, and which were not very different
from our own; the People being actuated by the same Passions of
Avarice, Envy and Malice, which are so common in *Europe*, divided
by the same Factions and Parties, both in Politicks and Religion; and
this, till we arriv'd at the Foot of vast unpassable Mountains, which
Nature seems to have made as the Barrier betwixt these wretched
People, and those happy Men who inhabit the other Side of it. You
must observe, that all those on this Side the Mountain were originally
Exiles banish'd from the other Side for Crimes which would not be
suffer'd among them; such as Avarice, Ingratitude, unchristian
Dealing, Lust, and the like; and they are still the Receptacle of all

---

[1] Sibi convenientia finge: 'Fashion what is consistent' (Horace, *Ars Poetica*, 119).

29

those who are punish'd for such Offences on the other Side of the Mountain, and have Governors in every City sent from them. This was the Substance of my last Letter. Being come to the Foot of these Mountains, which run from North-East to South-West, near fifteen hundred Miles, we were ordered to get ready to pass them; which we did in this very strange Manner: The Place of our Passage was almost a perpendicular Precipice; we enter'd into a sort of a Room or great Coach, which held about fourteen. There when we were seated, with such things as were necessary for us in our Passage, and the little Baggage that each of us had brought with us, we were drawn up by Pullies about threescore Yards to the first landing Place, which was done by a hollow Wheel; Slaves turning it by walking in it like Turn-spits at *Bristol*. Being come to the first landing Place, our Machine was immediately thrust forward into another Pully, and we drawn threescore Yards higher to the next landing Place; and so on, till we came near the Summit of the Mountain; when we left our Machine, and came into a very large fair Plain, from whence we survey'd a most delicious Country, diversify'd with easy Hills, pleasant Vallies, winding Rivers, small Seas, Islands, Towns, Cities and Villages. Two, among the rest, were evidently remarkable for their Largeness; one seem'd to stand in the Sea, which, I was told, was called *Athens*; the other upon the Continent, much larger than the former, upon a very fine River at a little Distance from the Sea; and this was called *Romana*, the Imperial City or Capital of all this Place that we saw; and was full of shining Domes and Spires, which almost dazzled our Eyes at that Distance. About this pleasant Plain, upon the Mountain, were scatter'd several Houses of Entertainment, fit to receive, with all Manner of Convenience, such Passengers as were permitted to come that Way: In the midst was a spacious Hall, or Court of Judicature, where proper Judges were assign'd to examine every particular Person. But before we came to our Examination, we were ordered to refresh ourselves, and wait the Arrival of the rest of our Ship's Crew, who were all brought up by the next Return of the Machine; and who having likewise refresh'd themselves, we were all brought into the Hall, and each Man's Baggage set by him, which, as well as ourselves, were examin'd. Mine consisted chiefly of Books, particularly Poets, such as *Ben Johnson, Shakespear, Beaumont* and *Fletcher, Milton*, and many of the Classicks, both *Greek* and *Latin*. I thought I discover'd a particular Satisfaction in the Judge, at what he saw; and calling me to him, he told me, that he was pleas'd that Fortune had given him an Opportunity of obliging the curious *Athenians*, by sending them a Person that seem'd so agreeable to their Inclinations, and to oblige me by allotting me an Abode in the most Learned and Polite City in the World: For tho' he did not understand great Part of my Books, they being in a strange Language; yet by those that he saw in *Greek* and *Latin*, he concluded me worthy of the Favour he design'd me. This Speech he made to me in tolerable *Latin*, tho' often mix'd with Words that nothing but the Sense of what he said, could make me understand. The Examination of the rest of our Crew took up some time, and I was fain to play the Interpreter with that little *Latin* I had, to expedite their Dispatch; but this being at last all over, there came in an Officer, who mark'd every one of us in the Face with a most lovely and beautiful Flower, which was so far from being a Mark of Infamy, that it was our Security and Honour; for by that every one was oblig'd, wherever we came, to receive and use us with Respect and Hospitality: But another Use of this Mark was to hinder us from ever going out of their Country, lest by the Discovery we had made, we should bring others to invade it. All the Governors therefore of the Frontiers had express Orders to let no one pass who had that Mark, which was made with so subtle a Juice, that no Pains or Wash cou'd ever remove it.

Now the Time was come when we were to be separated, and every one sent to such Town or City as the Judge thought was proper for his Inclinations and Capacity. Of all our Crew, I had but one that was permitted to go with me to *Athens*, and he was an extraordinary *Mathematician*, and very expert in making Draughts necessary for the forming of Maps. We were allow'd some time for our taking Leave of each other; which Ceremony being over, I and my Companion being plac'd with one of the Country, in a little *Coach*, or sort of *Chaise*, set forward in the following Manner.

The Declivity of the Mountain, on the other Side, is not near so steep as that by which we came into the Plain, and yet it is more steep than any Hill I ever pass'd in my Life; tho' I have gone down the *Alps* into *Piedmont*. Tho' this Passage be very swift, yet it is likewise very secure; the Road is no broader than just to contain the Vehicle into which you are put; which being plac'd in two Groofs, runs down with great Rapidity to the Foot of the Hill. Parallel to this Road there is another, by which People ascend to the Plain; for they never ascend and descend by the same Road, and therefore are never in Danger of falling foul upon one another. Being come down the Hill, at an Inn at the Foot of it, we were furnish'd with another Chariot that brought us in a few Hours to a pretty Sea-port, where having refresh'd ourselves for three or four Days, we took Shipping and sail'd directly to *Athens*, and the Wind being fair, we arriv'd there in about eleven or twelve Hours.

This City stands upon a small *Peninsula*, the broadest Part of which is not above four Miles over, and it is considerably rais'd above the Sea, and fortify'd by Nature with a Ridge of little Hills from the very Continent to the End of the *Peninsula*, which is near four and twenty Miles. These little Hills have, by an incredible Application and Labour, for ten Miles together, been work'd into a sort of a Wall, broad enough for three or four Coaches to go on a-breast, and all planted with Rows of shady Trees, which supply the Citizens with a Defence, as well as the most agreeable Prominade in the World. The City is about eight Miles long, and near four over, and is divided into four Parts by four Canals, which pass from the Sea through it, to the little Creek of the Sea that divides the *Peninsula* from the Continent for above twenty Miles, and is about a Mile and half over, and makes a most commodious and safe Harbour for all their Shipping.

Every one of these Canals is about fifty Yards in Breadth; and so far from the Surface of the Streets, that the Sides are fill'd with convenient and capacious Store-houses, where all the Goods and Merchandize brought in by the Shipping, are placed without incumbering the Streets with heavy Carriages; and hence they are brought up by Cranes, and dispers'd as Occasion requires. Over these Canals there are several Bridges, all of one Arch, tho' so very wide, that the *Rialto* of *Venice* is but a Bauble to them. The Town is built of a curious white Stone, and with perfect Regularity; the Streets being in an exact Line from one End of the City to the other. In the Center of the City stands a most noble *Rotondo*, which may be call'd its Cathedral, or Episcopal Church; besides which, there are ten magnificent Churches in each Division of the City, which makes the whole Number one and forty: Each of these Churches stands in the middle of a Square, and has a Coridore supported by fine Pillars, in which the Congregation take a Walk, and pass through them to the Church. All the great Streets are fill'd with the magnificent Houses of the principal Citizens, the *Colleges* and *Schools* of the Students, and *Halls* of Judicature; all the Shops and Places of Trade are in the lesser Streets; but those lesser Streets are of a greater Width than *Cheapside*. One thing is remarkable, That there is no Trade that is offensive to the Nose, the Eyes or Ears, that is permitted to be in the City itself: Thus, Butchers, Poulterers, Smiths, Washer-women, and the like, are confin'd to little Suburbs divided from the City by a small Canal, whose Streets are every Morning washed by Waters from certain Engines, which throw a Stream through every Street, that carries off all the Filth that such Trades produce. There is nothing finer than the High-Street, which, for eight Miles together, leads you up to the Royal Palace, a most magnificent Pile, and worthy so Noble a City. The Gardens and Walks belonging to this Palace, are contriv'd both for Pleasure and Use; for at the same time that the River, which runs from the Continent over the Neck of Land that joins the *Peninsula* to it, is divided into an hundred Channels to supply the Water-works; it is thence convey'd into the City, to furnish fresh Water to all the Inhabitants. The Palace is not only for the Residence of the King, but the Reception of the *Areopagus*, or Chief Council of the Nation, and to lodge all such Ambassadors as come from Friends; those who come from the barbarous Nations in the most Southerly Parts of that Tract of Land, are never permitted to lie in the City, but rather forc'd to remain aboard their own Ships, or to be a sort of Prisoners, during their Negotiations, in the Citadel, which stands upon the *Isthmus.*

Thus I have given you a short Description of the City of *New Athens* itself, which, tho' wonderful in all its Parts, is far less valuable for its Structure, than for the Excellence of its Inhabitants; of which I shall treat in the following Part of my Letter, having first inform'd you of my Reception at my Arrival.

We were no sooner landed, but we were conducted to the Hospital of Strangers, a Pile of Building equally admirable for its Magnificence and Convenience. There are no Inns in this City for the Reception of Strangers, they are always the Care of the Publick, and are provided all Necessaries and Conveniences by Officers, who are answerable for any Indignity or Abuse to any Stranger, either in his Lodging or Diet, which are supplied by the Government at the most easy Rate; but then no one is permitted to stay in this Hospital longer than a Fortnight: So that if their Business require a longer time, they provide themselves with Lodgings in the Houses of some of their Friends or Acquaintance. To this Place my Friend and I were conducted, with all our Baggage, where we remain'd till the King had receiv'd the Letters sent with us, and ordered such to attend us as he thought most fit and capable of giving him a full Account of our Merits and Abilities. Every Morning we were invited to go to Church, and offer up our Prayers after our own Way; for that is a Duty which no one of this City of what Degree, Age or Station soever, is permitted to neglect, unless hinder'd by Sickness.

The first Business that we were set about, was to learn their Language; to the obtaining a Mastery in which, my little Skill in the *Greek* was no small Help; for tho' their Tongue be very much alter'd from the ancient *Greek*, yet it retains not only the Character, but many of the Radical Words of the *Attick* Dialect. The Care of my Instructor, with my own Diligence and Application, made me such a Proficient, that I could, in two Months time, talk it almost as well as a Native; and in two Months more, was able to translate any thing out of *English* into it. But I have forgot to tell you, that as soon as I had Instructors ordered me by the King, I was remov'd from the Hospital of the Strangers, into a very pleasant Apartment in the *College* of the *Muses*, where I enjoy'd all things that were any ways necessary to make my Life easy and pleasant; and as I grew a greater Master of their Language, my Pleasure was heighten'd by the Conversation of the most Polite, as well as the most Humane of all Mankind; and which confirm'd me in a Mastery of their Tongue sooner than I could else have accomplish'd it: They omitted no Means of rendring their Instructions agreeable, as well as useful, watching my Inclinations and Humour with that Care and Nicety, that they would be sure never to make my Lessons tedious or burthensome. But now I was to give some Proof of my Study, by translating some of our *English* Poets into their Language: I chose the *Samson Agonistes* of *Milton* to begin with, as finding his Way of Writing in that, more like their Tragedies than any other of our *English Poets*. They were so pleas'd with this Performance, that it was shew'd to the King, who was a Prince of an admirable Genius himself, and ordered me, upon it, to be admitted into the Number of the *Athenian Poets*, with a handsome Pension for my Maintenance; and Directions were given for the transcribing and acting the Tragedy of *Samson Agonistes*, as soon as the *Chorus's* could be set to Musick, the Actors taught, and the Copy publish'd; for it is a Custom here, that no Play is to be acted, till it is publish'd, and in every body's Hand; that having perus'd it with Sedateness and Judgment in their Closets, they should not be brib'd by the Beauty of Representation, to give an erroneous Judgment of the Poet's Performance; but I found by the Tediousness of the Publication, that how ingenious soever they were, they knew nothing of the Art of Printing. I persuaded my self I could not oblige them more, than by giving them what Insight I could into this Invention: Nor was I mistaken, for they heard me with Rapture; and having acquainted the King with it, I was ordered to discourse the Matter at an Assembly of the *Virtuosi*, where the King himself presided. In order to make my Discourse the clearer, I got several Letters made after my own Model, and a Composing-Stick according to my Directions, and with their Help, made the Matter so plain, that the King ordered me to sit down at the Board, and, with his own Hands, plac'd on my Head a Wreath of Golden Laurel, with this Assurance, That I should always have his Protection.

'Tis an amazing thing to think with how much Speed they arriv'd at a Perfection in it, for they now print with much more Correctness and Delicacy than any Part of *Europe*.

I was not alone in the Favours I receiv'd from the *New Athenians*; my Comrade had his Share; he was a Man of admirable Parts, tho' he had found but little Encouragement in *England*; he was a very good *Mathematician*, and had a great Genius for Building of Ships, and was accordingly received by the Intendant of the Marines, and had his Apartment allotted him in the College of the Admiralty. The Naval Force of these Countries consists in a fort of low-built-Gallies and Galliots; for, knowing nothing of the Use of Guns, those were thought sufficient to cope with the barbarous Nations, who liv'd near the Southern Pole, and with whom only they ever had any Wars.

My Comrade first made them a Model of one of our Men of War, with which they were so well pleased, that they ordered several to be built according to it. In the mean time my Comrade, to make his Service the more compleat, discoursed with them about the Use of *Guns* and *Gunpowder*; but it being a difficult Matter to make them apprehend what he meant, without an Experiment, the Materials for the Composition of Gunpowder being pretty plentiful in that Country, and he being perfectly well skill'd in the making of it, it was not long e'er he had a sufficient Quantity to show them the wonderful

Force of it. They were the more pleas'd with this Invention, because there happen'd then to be a Discourse of a new Invasion from the barbarous Natives, who are a hardy martial People, and delight in War.

By that time the Ships were built, my Comrade had got a pretty Quantity of Gunpowder, and great Guns enough to equip his new *Armada*, and likewise to plant several upon the Walls of the City, on that side which was next to the Sea. But the King, that he might not give any Umbrage to the great Emperor of *Romana*, dispatch'd Ambassadors to him to let him know the wonderful Discoveries this Stranger had made, with Assurances of sending him to him, whenever he should command, that he might not want those Advantages against the common Enemy, which seem'd of that Importance to the publick Safety.

But before any Answer could come to this Embassy, the Barbarians, without ever declaring any War, had fill'd those Seas with their Ships, which made up, by their Number, that Terror, which their Bulk could not give; they were about three hundred Sail, and made directly for *New Athens* to the great Terror of that City. But my Comrade, in the midst of this Consternation, undertook to fight and disperse all this *Barbarian Armada* with only the ships that he had built, and five Hulks of old Vessels, of which he had made Fire-ships, a thing unknown in that Country before. I think the Number of our Fleet, besides the Fire-ships was but seven, the biggest of which came not up to our Third Rates; With these my Comrade sail'd out of the Port, and went to meet the Enemy, who being flush'd with the Success of their sudden Irruption, came up with us, and soon surrounded our little Fleet, but were something surpriz'd at the Largeness of their Make. We soon set our Fireships among them, which they surrounded and grappled with great Expedition, so far, that they could not disengage themselves, when they found them all on Fire, which put them into a very great Confusion; and this was very much encreas'd when we began to give them Broad-sides, which soon put 'em to flight, thinking that the Gods themselves were come down in Thunder to punish their Treachery.

In short, we took, sunk and dispers'd the whole Fleet, scarce twenty of which got home to their own Country, to the no small Satisfaction of our *Athenian* Masters, who were too generous and grateful, not to give a Reward to the Conqueror equal to his Merits: He was immediately made free of that Nation, had a publick Triumph, and was presented with Royal Gifts, being admitted to the King's own Table, who immediately ordered him to prepare to go with the greater Part of his new Fleet to *Romana*, and sent Deputies with him to present him to the Emperor, and give an Account of all that had pass'd, and the great Deliverance the whole Christian Commonwealth in those Parts had receiv'd from him.

It is out of my way to give an Account of the noble Reception he met with, and the Honours that were paid him on his Arrival at *Romana*; it is sufficient to let you know that he was treated like a Sovereign Prince, and a particular Instrument sent by Heaven to check the Insolence of the Barbarians, who by their frequent Irruptions disturb'd that Tranquility which all those Nations otherwise enjoy'd; for you must understand, that all the Countries for above fifteen hundred Miles every way are Christians, and tho' consisting of several Governments, they all hold it an unpardonable Crime for one Christian State to make War with another; to avoid which, there is a general Council compos'd of Deputies from the several Nations, who hear and amicably decide all Disputes that may arise betwixt Nation and Nation. This Overthrow of the Barbarians gave long Peace to this Country, during which my Comrade furnish'd *Romana* and all its Dependencies with Arms according to the Manner of *Europe*, and liv'd in great Splendour and Reputation, in which I shall leave him, to return to my Account of *Athens*.

I told you of my Translation of *Milton's Samson Agonistes*, which being now ready to be acted, it was perform'd at four Theatres in one Day; for you must know, every Quarter of *Athens* has a Theatre for the Representation of Tragedies, in which, some Tragedy or other is perform'd every Night; besides which there is a fifth Theatre in the Royal Palace, which is only made use of for the Entertainment of Foreign Princes when they come to that City, as they do once a Year from all Parts of that Continent, of which Number, the Emperor of *Romana* is always one. To describe them all would be superfluous, I shall only make a short Description of that in the Royal Palace, after the Model of which the rest are built: The Stage is one hundred Foot broad, the Place of the Audience is a Segment of a Circle of above two hundred Foot Diameter, it is divided into what we call a Pit and Boxes, with only one Gallery over; but the Boxes are divided in the Middle from each other by a sort of Throne or Royal Seat, where the King and Regal Family sit to behold a Tragedy. This Throne stretches out about a dozen Foot into the Pit, and is supported on each Side by rich and costly Pillars, either of Silver or Gold, or of precious Stone, much more beautiful than Porphyry; over the Canopy are several Figures of Angels, two of which support an Imperial Crown, all whose precious Stones are compos'd of Lights which illuminate the Place; two larger Angels, who stand more forward to the Pit, support a sort of a Sun, whence issue illustrious Beams that enlighten the whole Theatre, without any Sconces as we have, and by Consequence without all that filthy Smoak which our Candles make. This Sun throws his Beams upwards and downwards as well as directly forward, by which you discover the Beauty of the Ceiling, which is a fine Cupola, form'd by a Master in the Art of Perspective; for tho' the Ceiling be flat, and descends towards the Stage for the convenience of spreading the Sound, yet you would imagine it a lofty Dome. Besides these Illuminations, there come others from two side Pillars upon the Stage, which make the Place of Action very bright and glorious. The Stage here differs from ours, it being broad and shallow, the Depth being made out, when Occasion requires it, by admirable Paintings in Perspective; and indeed the Painting of the Scenes is so admirable, that I dare believe a *London* Audience, as whimsical as it is in that Particular, would not want that ridiculous Variety which they now possess by the Change of Scenes; for they never change here any more than they did in old *Athens*, where such vast Expence was made use of for the Adornment of the Stage, without any such shifting of Scenes, as is now in use in *England*. This is a short and imperfect Account of the principal Theatre in *New Athens*; The other Theatres are equally large, and bear some Proportion to the Beauty and Richness. One thing I had forgot, and that is, an Account of the Seats of the Audience, which are not Benches as in our Theatres, but distinct Seats, by which Means, tho' they are plac'd in a sort of a Semicircle, every one of the Audience sets with his Face to the Stage, and so participates equally both in the Sight and the Hearing. This is enough as to the Place of Representation; but as to the Persons who make this Representation, they are likewise very different from what we have among us. There is none admitted to be an Actor or Actress from out of the Dregs of the People, nor who have the least Stain upon their Reputation; and as they are suppos'd to be born of Parents of Credit, so they must be more than commonly Educated, tho' the common Education here would pass for extraordinary elsewhere. The Men, besides their Learning in History and Poetry, are all taught Painting or Designing, by which they learn not only graceful Postures for themselves, and such as are agreeable to the very Passions, but also how to dispose their Supernumeraries or Mute Persons into such Groupes, as may render them agreeable, if not beautiful to the Audience. To this purpose likewise they are not a Company of Ragamuffins, Old, Young, Tall and Short, Awkward and Clumsey, and Ill-drest as with us; but all proper young handsome Fellows, about six Foot high and well Drest, as well as perfect in Dancing and a graceful Motion, by which the whole Representation becomes Solemn and Touching. The Women are likewise taught History and Poetry, and perfectly instructed in the Action and Gesture, Figure and Motion, proper to every Character and Passion; both the Men and the Women are extreamly careful of observing the Decorum of the Representation, a Neglect in which is here unpardonable, and look'd upon as an insufferable Insolence offer'd to the Audience. With such Actors, and on such a Stage, I was infinitely pleas'd to see old *Milton* perform'd; the Chorus's were compos'd with wonderful Art, the Musical Notes being perfectly adapted to express the Words with the greatest Harmony; and they seem indeed to have retain'd that Genius for Musick of which we hear such Wonders in the Authors of Antiquity. I cannot say, that *Samson Agonistes* was a Tragedy equal to many of their own, and yet thro' the Humanity of the People it was receiv'd with the highest Applause. This having pleas'd 'em so well, I was importun'd to give them some more of the Products of our Nation; but I, who perceiv'd their admirable Taste, would fain have been excus'd from a Task whence I expected so little Applause. However, having *Otway's Orphan*, and *Venice Preserv'd*[2] I translated them, but met not with that Satisfaction which I flatter'd myself they would give my Performance: But at the same time that they acknowledg'd the Poet's Mastery in the Draught of the Passions, especially that of Pity, they assur'd me that his Breach of the Unity of Place had render'd their Stage incapable of representing them.

I thought it was in vain after this, to pretend to give them any thing of *Beaumont* and *Fletcher*, or even of *Shakespear* himself. However, I inform'd *Hermogenes*, one of the Society of Poets, of the Method follow'd by *Shakespear* in all his Plays; and to give him the greater

---

[2] Thomas Otway, *The Orphan* (1680), *Venice Preserved* (1735).

Influence, I translated many of his *Topicks* into their Language, which pleas'd them infinitely; but I told him that this Poet was entirely ignorant of the Rules of the Drama, and therefore that all his Plays were but so many Pieces of History, which by consequence could have no *Moral*, and were of little Use or Importance.

Notwithstanding there are four Theatres in this City, there were no Comedies acted in any of them, upon which I gave them a Version of the *Alchymist* of *Ben Johnson*, expressing my Wonder at their Neglect of that Poem, which yet had its Rise as well as Tragedy in ancient *Greece*. 'Tis true, said *Hermogenes*, that *Greece* gave beginning to Comedy as well as Tragedy; but the former was never so much encourag'd by the wise State of *Old Athens*, as the latter. Comedy, indeed, was born in the Villages amongst the meanest sort of People, and always retain'd something of the Licentiousness and Rusticity of its Original, and was even in those Days look'd on, as a lower and less valuable Entertainment, as being more adapted to the Gusto of the Vulgar, whose Lives, Conversations and Adventures were the general Subject of that Poem. The old Comedy was but a sort of publick Lampoon, which was made use of to set the very Mob against some of the most eminent Citizens. There is an Example of this in the Fate of the Divine *Socrates*, the Cry against whom was first set on foot by *Aristophanes*, the most eminent of all the old Comick Poets, whose Licentiousness at last grew to that height, that the Government was fain to suppress the Chorus, in which the greatest part of the Abuse was generally contain'd. After this arose the new Comedy, in which the Names of the Dramatick Persons were not real, as in the former, but fictitious; and the Subject generally some Adventure of an old Covetous Father, his Son, and some Whore, with the Humours of *Davus*, *Chremes* or some other impertinent Servant, who generally manag'd the old Gentleman for the Advantage of the Son and his Mistrels: *Menander* was the great Master of this new Comedy, and he was followed among the *Romans* by *Terence*, who, like all other Copiers, fell very much short of his Original.

As for this Author of your Country, whose *Alchymist* you have given us, he seems much more excellent than either *Terence* or *Menander*; and yet with all his Excellence, I am very well assur'd he would not be receiv'd in this Country, for the following Reasons: First, because the *Ridicule*, which is essential to this Poem, is what we have the utmost Aversion to, since it is the Nature of that to divert us from thinking seriously of Things; and is, by consequence, a great Enemy to Reason and just Thinking. In the next Place, I thank Heaven we have none of those Vices and Follies among us, which require this sort of Remedy. Beyond the Mountains, indeed, where the irregular Appetites of Mankind prevail too much, Comedy may be of some use, and is therefore allow'd on; while Tragedy is neither desir'd by them, nor permitted to them: It is the finer Spirits only with which this Country is generally blest, that can raise their Souls to so sublime and rational a Pleasure as that of *Tragedy*, and which I am apt to believe we have in the most perfect State of any Nation in the World.

These Reasons were sufficient to satisfy me, that Comedy was a Province not to be attempted in this Place.

One Day *Hermogenes* ask'd me if I had no more Poems of that Author who had written the *Samson Agonistes*. I reply'd, that I had an excellent one call'd *Paradise Lost*, which was in great esteem in our Country, notwithstanding its general ill Taste of good Poetry: I run over the several Arguments of the Books to him extempore, which pleas'd him so well, that he got the King's Order for my applying myself wholly to translate it into their Tongue, and which I had but just finish'd before I lost the Happiness of those fortunate Regions, by an Accident which I shall tell you before I close this Account.

Before I dismiss this Point of Poetry, I must tell you the Method of their accepting or rejecting any Dramatical Piece: The Players, as learned and judicious as they are, have no hand in the determining the Merit of any Tragedy, or whether it shall have the Benefit of a publick Representation or not; that is decided by the Body of Criticks and Poets, who have their principal Residence in the College of the Muses; and that no Favour or Affection, or any Prejudice to the Author may influence them in their Judgment, no Author is to be known till after the Performance of his Piece, under this Penalty, that it shall not be acted if the Author be not kept entirely secret; for tho' the Judges are Men of eminent Candor, as well as Learning and great Genius, yet to remove all possible Prejudice to Merit, this Caution is inviolably observ'd; and that the Judges may not be teaz'd with Plays of little Value, every Author is oblig'd to send in first a Plan of his *Fable*, which if approv'd, publick Notice is given that he may send in the Tragedy itself: And then if the Performance, in the *Manners, Sentiment* and *Diction*, be any ways answerable to the Excellence of the *Fable*, the Play is acted without any more trouble to the Author, without any slavish Solicitation of either the Players or Parties. Whereas in *England* there is nothing less consider'd than the Merits of the Piece, if the Author can make an Interest with the Players, and some leading Men of the Town; that is generally enough to furnish him with the Success he desires, let his Piece be never so indifferent in itself.

The same Method is observ'd in *New Athens*, in regard of all other Poems; for the Author is never known till the Fate of what he has written is decided; by which means the Thing, and not the Name, prevails in the publick Applause.

I have mention'd the College of the Muses: It is a large and noble Pile of Building, and its Apartments extreamly pleasant and convenient; every Member has, at least, four Rooms, and a pretty little private Garden; for the College standing just by the Walls, the Members for larger Walks ascend the Ramparts, which I have told you are set with Rows of shady Trees. In the College there is a publick Hall, in which the Members are oblig'd to dine together, at least, twice a Week; where, after Dinner, which is generally about two a Clock, they spend two or three Hours in learned Discourse, held up by the Benefit of a Bottle of the finest Wine in the World. Besides the Hall, there is likewise a very pretty Chappel, where Prayers are perform'd every Morning and Evening. And thus much for the Poetical Part of *New Athens*.

There are, besides this College of the Muses, several others of a very magnificent Structure, especially that of the Nobles, where not only the Nobility of all this Country are educated, but all such of Quality who come from the other Parts to Study at *Athens*, the Number of which is very great.

Besides all the Colleges, which are too numerous for me to mention, there are in every Parish publick Schools, in which the Children of every Parishioner are oblig'd, till fifteen Years of Age, to be instructed in all manner of Literature, of which their Age is capable; nor are their Instructors such wretched ignorant Fellows, as teach in your Charity-Schools at *London*, but Men of Probity as well as Learning, who are capable of teaching their Pupils what they ought to learn, both in the Duties of Religion and that of the State; tho' in this Country, indeed, they are very nearly related, since all the moral Doctrines of the New Testament are incorporated into the municipal

Laws, which brings me to a short Consideration of the Religion of these People.

They are here all Christians, and may be truly so call'd, since, as I have observ'd, the Precepts of the Gospel are the Laws of the Land, and a Breach of them is punish'd by the Civil Magistrate: Thus, if a Man be found guilty of a Breach of the Precept of doing as you would be done by, he is certainly fin'd or imprison'd; or, upon a frequent Transgression that way, banish'd beyond the Mountains, which is look'd upon to be the greatest Punishment that can be inflicted upon them. The Scripture is in the vulgar Tongue, and read by every one; and yet there is no Dispute about Opinions in Faith, which is avoided chiefly by this Maxim; that no Word or Term be admitted that is not expressly found in the Gospel itself: Thus, tho' there are several who believe the Substance and Matter of the Trinity, yet the Word, as being the Invention of Man, is not suffer'd to be made use of, but every Man left to his own Judgment, to believe or not believe all manner of Speculations, which have or may be drawn from any Expressions in the New Testament; so that these great Grounds of Quarrel, Dissention and Animosity, which rage so much in other Parts of the Christian World, and turn the Gospel of Peace and Love into Confusion and Hatred, are here utterly unknown; for they believe that the principal Business of the Gospel is to regulate, improve, and perfect our Morals, to render us active in the Duties of Brotherly Love, and the Love of the supreme Being: And this, they say, is the Christian Religion; for they find, when our Saviour comes to Judgment, he does not condemn or reward any Man for his speculative Opinions, tho' never so pompous and magnificent towards himself; but for their not doing or doing the Duties of Charity to one another: And this is so fixt in them, that if any Quarrel happen between two Persons, which is very seldom, one does not reproach the other with being of High-Church or Low-Church, or any other Denomination sprung from the difference of Opinion; but they cry, you have not done as you would be done by, you have done that to another, which you would not have another do to you. And indeed, Oppression of the Poor, is a thing that cannot come into this Country; for all working People, of what Trade soever, have certain Prices and Payments fixt to their Labour, as is sufficient to maintain them, their Families and Dependants. And if a great Dealer employs any under Workman, and abate him of his Price, as with us; or if any Workman can prove that he was employ'd by the greatest Man in the City, he can recover his stated Price of him, notwithstanding any Agreement to the contrary.

Their Ecclesiastical Government is divided into Deacons, Elders and Bishops; for they will not allow of the Name of Priest, as being a Word not justified by Scripture, there being no such Order mention'd in the Gospel; the Deacons are a sort of Helpmeets to the Elders, of which there are three in every Parish Church, who officiate in saying of Prayers twice every Day, and Preaching twice every *Sunday*; but it is observable, that they are never permitted to take any Text but out of the four Gospels, by which means all their Sermons run upon the active Duties of Christianity, or upon the Passion and Sufferings of *Jesus Christ*, which they express with that Force and Pathos, for they are excellent Orators, that few of the Audience come away without Tears. Their Pulpits are not like ours, just big enough to contain the Preacher, but more like the *Roman Rostra*, which were large enough to allow room to the Speaker to move some Steps, and give that Action to the Discourse which might make it more touching to the Audience. The Bishop, who is supreme in his own Diocess, exercises his Authority chiefly over his Deacons and Elders, and presides in a Court where all Accusations are brought against them, and they heard in their own Defence; but if cast for any Irregularity of Life, either Avarice, Pride, Revenge, want of Charity, or Drunkenness, they are depriv'd of their Places, and banished beyond the Mountains: But these Condemnations very seldom happen; for the Clergy are maintain'd in so handsome a manner, that there are no scandalous indigent Fellows admitted into their Number for it is such as those, in other Countries, that generally bring that Reproach upon the Clergy, which is so frequently in the Mouths of most Men. If the Elders have any Children, they prove no Incumbrance to 'em, for as soon as they are of fit Age, they are taken from them and put into those Schools, which are settled for both Sexes; and when they grow up, they are provided for by the Publick. The Bishop is oblig'd to hospitable Living, in which he expends the greatest Part of his Revenue, his Children being likewise provided for by the Publick. When a Bishop dies, the King names four, that is, one out of every Quarter of the City; and the Elders meeting in the Cathedral, chuse one of them. As they chuse the Bishop, so each Parish chuses his

Elder; by which means a Man of Merit always gets in; for there is no being chosen by a Number of People, but by being popular; nor any way of being popular but by eminent Parts, and an unblemish'd Life; at least, in a Place where the Majority of the Electors have a large Share of good Sense and Probity.

One Thing I had forgot, and that is, that tho' they have both Vocal and Instrumental Musick in their Churches, it is all great and solemn, and such as naturally raises the Soul to sublime and heavenly Thoughts, and never mingled with those light Airs, which are too frequent in some of our Cathedrals, and of which some of our greatest Masters of Musick have been so preposterously fond, as to force them upon the most terrible Words. Thus in King *Charles* II's Time, these Words were set to a Jig.

The Pangs of Death have encompassed me about.

Which made that pleasant *Monarch* say, that it was the first Time he had ever heard of Death's dancing a Jig. Of this kind also are our *Voluntaries*, as they call 'em, in which the Congregation are merrily entertain'd with the Volubility of the Fingers of the Organist; but how this can contribute any thing to Devotion I know not; but I'm sure there's no such thing in *New Athens*. I might say more of the Religion of this People; but what I have said seems enough to show you their Happiness. However, I cannot omit one thing, which is the Punishment of Adultery; but that is a Vice not so common there, as in most other Parts of the World; and, perhaps, the Punishment very much lessens the Number of Offenders, for when it is discover'd, the Man is banish'd beyond the Mountains; and the Woman has a sort of Composition rub'd over her Face, which immediately infects it with Tumours and Swellings to that degree, that the most beautiful Face is made the most ugly and forbidding, and she herself degraded from her Quality, tho' never so high, and sent into that Quarter of the Town where the Washer-Women are, and under them kept a Slave to hard Work as long as she lives.

It is observable, that there is not in this rich and popular City so much as one Coach; but all, both Male and Female, are oblig'd to walk when they go out, except Women with Child, or such as are sick or lame, or very old, and these are carry'd in a sort of Chair, not very unlike our Sedans; but they are not permitted to go where the People walk, but in a Passage peculiar for all things of Burthen, that are carry'd upon Mens Shoulders; for thus the Streets are divided; the middle part of the Street is pav'd with a Stone about four or five Inches over, and there on that pass all Carts and other Vehicles of Burthen, which are never permitted to be so heavy loaden as the Cars are in *London*; for the People here are merciful to their Beasts, as well as one another. Of each side of this Pavement, there rises another, about a Foot above the Surface of the Street, six Foot over, and of a broader Stone, and upon this Passage or Pavement, all the Chairs and Men of Burthen pass. Above this again, about a Foot and half, is another Pavement, which reaches to the Houses, and which is about twelve Foot broad, that is, in the High-Streets, but narrower in the narrower Streets, and upon this all Passengers on foot go. The Streets are every where kept perfectly clean, which is done by every House, being oblig'd in the Morning early to sweep before their Doors, whilst the Water comes from the Engines plac'd at the End of every Street, and washes away all the Filth into the Common-Shores, which Common-Shores are so large, that one of our Carts may go in it loaden with Hay, and to which, at High-Tide, the Water comes from the Canals, and so keeps them clean and sweet.

I believe you may, by what I have said, conclude that this is one of the happiest Cities in the World; for their Happiness is secured by the Safety of their Peace and Tranquility, as well as their Health, by these following Means; first, there are no Poor, that is, necessitous, wanting Persons, who are deficient in the necessary Subsistance of Life; for it is the Business of the Deacons of every Parish to visit all Families in it, and find out such as Misfortunes may render unhappy; and immediately, as soon as they are known, the free Contribution of the Brethren of that Parish, puts an End to their Unhappiness. Another thing is, that there are no Lawyers here, no Attorneys, Pettifoggers, Solicitors, Bailiffs, and the like; who, in other Countries, have a large hand in the Ruin of Families. Here the Elders of the Parish make up and compose all the lesser Disputes; and every one of the four Quarters of the City have two Orators, who plead pro and con the more difficult Causes before the King himself; but they have no Fees from their Client, but are paid by the Publick a certain stated Salary; so that they have no temptation to embarrass the People in litigious Suits, but are willing to make an end of them all with the utmost Expedition.

That which secures their Health, next to the happy Situation of the Place, is that they have no such thing as an Apothecary in all this Country, and not above a dozen Physicians, who are call'd Ghessers, as knowing very well that the Art of Physick is purely conjectural, the Medicines are few and simple, contriv'd to help Nature, and not to put it upon a double Labour, by Multiplicity of Drugs, when Sickness renders it the least capable of combating with the Evils of the Distemper alone, contrary to the Custom of this Part of the World, where the Physician, to gratify the Apothecary, multiplies the nauseous and loathsome Draughts of Physick to the Patient; so that betwixt the Distemper and them, he perishes, to enrich the Apothecary and Doctor. Specificks, which are here thought ridiculous, are there in great esteem, as being confirm'd by an Historical Practice, and the Experience of many Ages; and this comes to pass by the Fewness of Distempers; for Intemperance, the Source of most of ours, is not known in this fortunate Climate.

I should say something of the King, and several Prerogatives; but it will be sufficient to let you know that this wise People allow him all those Privileges which may render him capable of doing good to his People, without any that may enable him to be injurious to their Liberty and Happiness. Accordingly, there is no Prince in the World, who is attended with greater Pomp, Magnificence and Ceremony, than the King of *New Athens*, and the Territories thereunto belonging; he never is seen in publick, but with the highest Applause and Veneration of the People, who look upon him as the Instrument of God for their Good.

At his Inauguration, the two principal Members of the great Council tell him plainly, that tho' he be greater than any particular one in his Kingdom, yet that all united together are greater than he; that he ought always to remember that that illustrious Office, to which he was now exalted, was instituted for the Good and Happiness of the People he is to reign over, and not to gratify his private Passions and corrupt Inclinations, without regard to the Peace and Quiet of his Subjects; and much more to the same purpose, in which the Encouragement of Virtue, and *Arts* and *Sciences*, and all manner of useful Knowledge, is recommended with great Efficacy; for these People are of Opinion, that a general Knowledge among the People is the best Security of a general Happiness; and that Ignorance is a dangerous Inlet to Novelties, Commotions, and all other Disturbances whatever.

But tho' by this, and other Circumscriptions of the regal Power, they have arm'd themselves pretty well against those Encroachments by which the supreme executive Power has, in other Countries, overthrown Liberty, since it was impossible to have a Kingly Government, without confiding very great Trusts to the King; and that there are Men in all Courts who are apt to flatter the Prince, and industrious to find out Ways and Means to enable him to gratify their own private Aims of Avarice or Ambition, it is an establish'd Law, without any Exception, that every Person shall set his Name to the Advice which he gives; which keeps them in awe, and makes them extreamly careful to give no Advice that can be injurious to the Publick, being sure, if they did, to meet with an exemplary Punishment, it being out of the King's Power to pardon the Offence.

By this means the Miscarriages of Government never fall upon the Crown, as in other Countries, but on the true Authors of them. And to avoid the Inconveniences that often arise by the long Continuance of any one Set of Men in the Administration of publick Affairs, the King's Council, and all Places of Trust and Profit were establish'd by Law to be annual, by which means all grounds of Parties and Faction were remov'd, since no tricking nor sinister Designs could be of any use to perpetuate their Authority: And thus, every Person, capable to serve the Publick, either in Military or Civil Affairs, had their Turns to make their Merit conspicuous. From hence it came to pass, that the State, instead of depending upon a few, had a perpetual Succession of able Heads to support it; and I'm of Opinion, that this annual Succession of Magistrates gave so many illustrious Hero's to the Commonwealths of *Athens* and *Rome*; however, if we may believe the History of this Country, this Method has for one Thousand Years preserv'd the Happiness of *New Athens*.

But I fear I have been so tedious in the Account I have given you of this Place, tho' very short of what it deserves, that I ought to draw towards a Conclusion, without proceeding to a Description of the other Cities of this *New Attica*. However, I cannot make an end, without informing you how these old *Grecians* came into this Part of the World; and I shall give it you, as near as I can, in the Words of the Learned *Socrates*, a Member of the College of History of this City; for every part of Knowledge here has its peculiar College. This *Socrates* was in nothing inferior to that Primitive Martyr of the Unity of the Godhead in *Old Athens* and an equal Lover of Truth and

Honesty; yet with this Advantage, that he was enlighten'd with the Doctrine of the Gospel.

One Morning as we were taking a Walk upon the Ramparts, I mov'd this Question to him, which he answer'd in as few Words as the Matter would bear. I shall not need (said he) to give you any Account of the Misfortunes which befel *Old Athens* till its final Destruction, at least, as far as I can tell, by the Inundations of barbarous Nations. Just before the second Approach of those People, a pannick Fear had seiz'd on all the Inhabitants of *Greece*, and the People of *Athens* and *Attica* had a very large share in it, being terrified by the extreme Cruelties and Devastations committed by the Barbarians in their former Irruption: In the midst of this Consternation, a Man of great Authority and Esteem with the People, and who had been a great Traveller, prevail'd with them to listen to his Advice. His Name was *Demophilus*; and his Advice was; that since they lay so expos'd to the Barbarians, as frequently to feel the Effects of it; and that the *Roman* Empire was ever too weak or too negligent to afford them Protection, they ought in common Prudence to take care of themselves: But since they had by Experience found, that they were unable to do this in the Country where they liv'd; he proffer'd himself to be their Conductor to a more fortunate Climate, where they might be secure against all those Evils, with which they were there daily threaten'd. He confess'd that *Greece* was a very pleasing Country in itself; that Nature had bestow'd upon it so many Blessings, that few Places in the World could equal it; but that all this Happiness vanish'd, if they would but consider that they had no manner of Security of enjoying those Blessings, but must expect either immediate Death upon the Place, or to be transported into insupportable Bondage, by a People that had no Notion of Christianity or Humanity. That it was not the Fertility and Pleasantness of any Soil, that made a Country dear to its Inhabitants, or indeed, that deserv'd the Name of our Country, which was only due to the Laws and Liberties which the People enjoy'd; that those were of such a Nature, that they might transport them with 'em wherever they went. He concluded his Speech, with assuring them, that he was commission'd by Heaven itself to conduct such as would follow him to a Place, where they might enjoy those Laws and Liberties without Fear or Danger: That, indeed, it would cost some Time, and a great deal of Labour and

Fatigue to Travel to this happy Climate; but certainly, that no Pains or Labour could be thought too great to purchase Security and Happiness to themselves and Posterity.

This Speech and the other Applications of himself and Friends, join'd with a fresh Rumour of the Approach of the Barbarians, made about one hundred thousand follow him in this Expedition; carrying with them all that was valuable and useful to them, either in their Journey or future Settlement.

It would be of no purpose to give you the Particulars of his Voyage, the many Difficulties he met with, or the Murmurings of his Followers, in a Journey of three Years Continuance, thro' strange Countries, vast Desarts and the like: having vanquish'd all which, and having pass'd a very large Tract of uninhabited Land, he at last brought his People to a large and deep River, to which he gave the Name of the River of *Hope*; and here they made their last Stand; *Demophilus* assuring them, that they had nothing to do towards the possessing that noble and beautiful Country he told them of, but to set all Hands to work, and cut down Trees, of which there were there a very great Plenty, to build Boats to carry them down that River. The first that were built, *Demophilus* desir'd might be despatch'd with him and the rest of the Heads of his People, to go and bring them further Assistance. Accordingly they departed, with a Promise to return in a Week's Time; rowing with the Stream, they arriv'd in this Continent of *Attica*, and landed in a Harbour, which we now call *Bizantium*, then only a little Village, containing about twenty Houses.

The *Greeks* that came with *Demophilus*, were infinitely pleas'd with the Beauty of the Land; but much more so, when they found the Humanity of the Inhabitants. For this Country was inhabited by about one hundred and fifty thousand Men, Women and Children, before the Arrival of the *Greeks*, and may properly be call'd the Aborigines of the Place; for we have nothing in History that gives us the least Account of their coming hither from any other Part of the World. They were not Idolaters, but believ'd only in one God; they were Affable, Courteous and Docile; in short, they were very much pleas'd with this new Accession of People to their little State: Not to dwell upon Trifles, or every minute Circumstance, Care was taken to convey all the rest from the Desart to this Continent, to the infinite Satisfaction of the weary Travellers, to find this happy Retreat after all their Pains and Fatigue. In short, they soon made the old Inhabitants Christians; and by marrying and intermarrying among them, grew together into one People; and this was the Occasion of the Corrupting, if I may so call it, of the old *Greek* Language, into that which you now find us speak.

We easily prevail'd with our new Brethren to chuse *Demophilus* and *Aristus* the Head of the old Inhabitants, joint Kings of the united People, under whose Government all Things seem'd to prosper; wholesome Laws were made, and Liberty every way secur'd, Towns and Cities were founded, and Arts and Arms improv'd; but this City of *Athens* was not built till some Ages afterwards, when the Country was grown Populous, and wanted as it were a sort of Elbow Room; when *Theophilus*, one of the Successors of the two first Kings, whose Families had been united some time before, look'd upon this Spot of Ground, as a fit Place to build *New Athens* upon; the *Isthmus* and *Peninsula* seeming to be a proper Barrier or Bulwark against the Invasions of the Southern Barbarians, who then began to infest these Coasts. From small Beginnings this City is arriv'd at length to that Magnificence in which you find it; and in which, I believe, scarce any City in the World excels it, except the great City of *Romana*, the Capital of this Part of the Christian World: But to give you an Account of that, its Rise, Progress and History, requires more Time than is now upon our Hands: for now our Hours of Lecture are come, and we must each repair to the Performance of our Duty, leaving the Enquiries of Curiosity to those vacant Times, when we are not employ'd on more important Business. Having said this, we each return'd to our several Colleges; but I shall defer not only my Account of *Romana*, but of all the several Cities of *Attica*. I shall only conclude this Discourse, with a short Account of my unwilling Return to these Parts of the World.

After the Barbarians had receiv'd that great Defeat, which I mention'd before; they lay still for many Years, till the Terror of that Defeat, and the Memory of it were both vanish'd; and new Desire of Plunder, with their Native Hardiness and unquiet Temper, put them again in Arms. I was at that Time in the City of *Romana* with my old Comrade, who was declar'd General in this Expedition against the Barbarians: At his Desire I attended him to the War: which was soon brought pretty near to a Conclusion, by the Force of our Artillery and small Fire-Arms, against which the Enemy could by no means think of standing; so that we having penetrated a great way into their Country, a Treaty was propos'd and agreed to, during which, I and some more ventur'd, out of Curiosity, to go up to the Top of a vast high Mountain, from whence we might discover to the Northward vast Seas, and great Tracts of Lands; but as we came down again, mistaking the Path which led to our Camp, we pursu'd one which brought us into that of the Enemy, where we were soon made Prisoners, notwithstanding the Treaty, for they have little regard to Faith or Honour. There happen'd to be among them one who had been a Prisoner in *New Athens*, and there had seen me frequently; his Knowledge of me, with the Mark in my Face, which I mention'd formerly, convinc'd the Chiefs that I was no Native of those Parts; but one of those from whom the Christians had learn'd those terrible Engines of War; and therefore they assured me I should not give myself any Fears of ill Treatment from them, since by letting them into the Knowledge of the same Advantages, I might hope for all the Honour and Respect their Country could pay me: Whatever I could say of this Breach of Faith was to no manner of Purpose, for we were all hurried away far into their Country, without any Hopes of Deliverance. In short, I was detain'd there for some Months, till I found an Opportunity of making my Escape from my Keepers, by the Help of a young Woman, who furnish'd me with the Habit of the Country, and with sufficient Disguises to pass from Place to Place, if I had known whither to direct my Flight; but wandring Northward as much as I could, I came at last to an Arm of the Sea, with my Female Companion; which forbad us going any further. We had not been long considering there, but we discover'd a small Ship making to the Shore, who manning their Boat, soon seiz'd us and carry'd us on Board. For my Part, I did not much care into whose Hands I fell, so that I could escape the Natives of that Country; but I was as pleas'd as I could be in that Circumstance, to find it a *French* Ship, who being driven into those Parts by stress of Weather, seiz'd us in hopes of knowing what Country it was, and what the Nature of its Inhabitants. I let them know that it was a most barbarous and inhospitable Coast; and that they could not do better than to make all the haste they could from it, begging them to take me with them, which they consented to do; and the Wind coming to the South East, we sail'd North-West with a brisk Gale. But ill Fortune had not yet forsaken me; for after we had sail'd some Days prosperously enough, a new Storm arose, and toss'd us with such Violence, for two or three Days, that at last we despair'd of escaping; but the Storm passing over, the Master assur'd us that we were not very far from Land; and, as he thought, from *Carolina*, whither he would make, because his Ship was very leaky, so that all we could do was to keep her above Water till we made the Shore, at least, so near that none of us perish'd when the Ship sunk. When we got ashore, I was very well pleas'd to find that it was *Carolina* indeed; for since I could find no way of returning to *New Athens*, I was at least pretty secure of finding a Passage to *Old England*, which I did in about two Months time, having buried my Southern Deliveress in *Carolina*.

Thus, Sir, I have given you a short Account of part of my Adventures, during my Absence from *England*. If this find your Acceptance, I don't know but that I may, some time or other, give you the rest; I shall only now add, that I am

> *Your faithful*
> *humble Servant,*
>
> MAURICE WILLIAMS.

Idea of a Perfect Commonwealth (1752)

David Hume

Idea of a Perfect Commonwealth[1]

Of all mankind, there are none so pernicious as political projectors, if they have power, nor so ridiculous, if they want it: as, on the other hand, a wise politician is the most beneficial character in nature, if accompanied with authority, and the most innocent, and not altogether useless, even if deprived of it. It is not with forms of government, as with other artificial contrivances; where an old engine may be rejected, if we can discover another more accurate and commodious, or where trials may safely be made, even though the success be doubtful. An established government has an infinite advantage, by that very circumstance of its being established; the bulk of mankind being governed by authority, not reason, and never attributing authority to any thing that has not the recommendation of antiquity. To tamper, therefore, in this affair, or try experiments merely upon the credit of supposed argument and philosophy, can never be the part of a wise magistrate, who will bear a reverence to what carries the marks of age; and though he may attempt some improvements for the public good, yet will he adjust his innovations as much as possible to the ancient fabric, and preserve entire the chief pillars and supports of the constitution.

The mathematicians in *Europe* have been much divided concerning that figure of a ship which is the most commodious for sailing; and *Huygens*, who at last determined the controversy, is justly thought to have obliged the learned as well as commercial world; though *Columbus* had sailed to *America*, and *Sir Francis Drake* made the tour of the world, without any such discovery. As one form of government must be allowed more perfect than another, independent of the man-

[1] The first sentence of the text was dropped from some editions after Hume's death, and is relegated to a note at the bottom of the page in others.

ners and humours of particular men; why may we not inquire what is the most perfect of all, though the common botched and inaccurate governments seem to serve the purposes of society, and though it be not so easy to establish a new system of government, as to build a vessel upon a new plan? The subject is surely the most worthy of curiosity of any the wit of man can possibly devise. And who knows, if this controversy were fixed by the universal consent of the wise and learned, but, in some future age, an opportunity might be afforded of reducing the theory to practice, either by a dissolution of the old governments, or the combination of men to form a new one, in some distant part of the world? In all cases, it must be advantageous to know what is the most perfect in the kind, that we may be able to bring any real constitution or form of government as near it as possible, by such gentle alterations and innovations as may not give too great disturbance to society.

All I pretend to in the present essay is to revive this subject of speculation; and therefore I shall deliver my sentiments in as few words as possible. A long dissertation on that head would not, I apprehend, be very acceptable to the public, who will be apt to regard such disquisitions both as useless and chimerical.

All plans of government, which suppose great reformation in the manners of mankind, are plainly imaginary. Of this nature, are the *Republic* of *Plato*[2] and the *Utopia* of *Sir Thomas More*[3]. The *Oceana*[4] is the only valuable model of a commonwealth that has yet been offered to the public.

The chief defects of the *Oceana* seem to be these. *First,* Its rotation is inconvenient, by throwing men, of whatever ability, by intervals, out of public employments. *Secondly,* Its *Agrarian* is impracticable. Men will soon learn the art which was practised in ancient *Rome*, of concealing their possessions under other people's name, till at last, the abuse will become so common, that they will throw off even the appearance of restraint. *Thirdly,* The *Oceana* provides not a sufficient security for liberty, or the redress of grievances. The senate must propose, and the people consent, by which means the senate have

---

[2] Plato, *The Republic* (*c.* 375 BC).

[3] Thomas More, *Utopia* (1516).

[4] James Harrington, *Oceana* (1656). Of its chief doctrines, discussed by Hume in the next paragraph, 'rotation' here meant frequency of parliamentary election (annually, or at most triennially). 'Agrarian' refers to Harrington's proposal to limit landholdings to a value of £5,000 annually.

not only a negative upon the people, but, what is of much greater consequence, their negative goes before the votes of the people. Were the king's negative of the same nature in the *English* constitution, and could he prevent any bill from coming into parliament, he would be an absolute monarch. As his negative follows the votes of the houses, it is of little consequence: Such a difference is there in the manner of placing the same thing. When a popular bill has been debated in parliament, is brought to maturity, all its conveniences and inconveniences weighed and balanced; if afterwards it be presented for the royal assent, few princes will venture to reject the unanimous desire of the people. But could the King crush a disagreeable bill in embryo (as was the case for some time in the *Scotch* parliament, by means of the Lords of the Articles), the British government would have no balance, nor would grievances ever be redressed: And it is certain, that exorbitant power proceeds not, in any government, from new laws, so much as from neglecting to remedy the abuses which frequently rise from the old ones. A government, says *Machiavel*, must often be brought back to its original principles.[5] It appears then, that in the *Oceana*, the whole legislature may be said to rest in the senate; which *Harrington* would own to be an inconvenient form of government, especially after the *Agrarian* is abolished.

Here is a form of government, to which I cannot, in theory, discover any considerable objection.

Let *Great Britain* and *Ireland*, or any territory of equal extent, be divided into 100 counties, and each county into 100 parishes, making in all 10,000. If the country proposed to be erected into a commonwealth be of more narrow extent, we may diminish the number of counties; but never bring them below thirty. If it be of greater extent, it were better to enlarge the parishes, or throw more parishes into a county, than increase the number of counties.

Let all the freeholders of twenty pounds a year in the county, and all the householders worth 500 pounds in the town-parishes, meet annually in the parish church, and choose by ballot, some freeholder of the county for their member, whom we shall call the *county representative.*

Let the 100 county representatives, two days after their election, meet in the county-town, and choose by ballot, from their own body,

---

[5] Niccolo Machiavelli, *The Works of the Famous Nicholas Machiavel* (3rd edn, 1720), pp. 377–9 (*Discourses*, Book 3, ch. 1).

ten county *magistrates*, and one *senator*. There are, therefore, in the whole commonwealth, 100 senators, 1100 county magistrates, and 10,000 county representatives; for we shall bestow on all senators the authority of county magistrates, and on all county magistrates the authority of county representatives.

Let the senators meet in the capital, and be endowed with the whole executive power of the commonwealth; the power of peace and war, of giving orders to generals, admirals, and ambassadors; and, in short, all the prerogatives of a *British* king, except his negative.

Let the county representatives meet in their particular counties, and possess the whole legislative power of the commonwealth, the greater number of counties deciding the question; and where these are equal, let the senate have the casting vote.

Every new law must first be debated in the senate; and though rejected by it, if ten senators insist and protest, it must be sent down to the counties. The senate, if they please, may join to the copy of the law their reasons for receiving or rejecting it.

Because it would be troublesome to assemble all the county representatives for every trivial law that may be requisite, the senate have their choice of sending down the law either to the county magistrates or county representatives.

The magistrates, though the law be referred to them, may, if they please, call the representatives, and submit the affair to their determination.

Whether the law be referred by the senate to the county magistrates or representatives, a copy of it, and of the senate's reasons, must be sent to every representative eight days before the day appointed for the assembling, in order to deliberate concerning it. And though the determination be, by the senate, referred to the magistrates, if five representatives of the county order the magistrates to assemble the whole court of representatives, and submit the affair to their determination, they must obey.

Either the county magistrates or representatives may give, to the senator of the county, the copy of a law to be proposed to the senate; and if five counties concur in the same order, the law, though refused by the senate, must come either to the county magistrates or representatives, as is contained in the order of the five counties.

Any twenty counties, by a vote either of their magistrates or representatives, may throw any man out of all public offices for a year. Thirty counties for three years.

The senate has a power of throwing out any member or number of members of its own body, not to be re-elected for that year. The senate cannot throw out twice in a year the senator of the same county.

The power of the old senate continues for three weeks after the annual election of the county representatives. Then all the new senators are shut up in a conclave like the cardinals; and by an intricate ballot, such as that of *Venice* or *Malta*, they choose the following magistrates; a protector, who represents the dignity of the commonwealth, and presides in the senate; two secretaries of state: these six councils, a council of state, a council of religion and learning, a council of trade, a council of laws, a council of war, a council of the admiralty, each council consisting of five persons; together with six commissioners of the treasury, and a first commissioner. All these must be senators. The senate also names all the ambassadors to foreign courts, who may either be senators or not.

The senate may continue any or all of these, but must re-elect them every year.

The protector and two secretaries have session and suffrage in the council of state. The business of that council is all foreign politics. The council of state has session and suffrage in all the other councils.

The council of religion and learning inspects the universities and clergy. That of trade inspects every thing that may affect commerce. That of laws inspects all the abuses of law by the inferior magistrates, and examines what improvements may be made of the municipal law. That of war inspects the militia and its discipline, magazines, stores, &c.; and when the republic is in war, examines into the proper orders for generals. The council of admiralty has the same power with regard to the navy, together with the nomination of the captains and all inferior officers.

None of these councils can give orders themselves, except where they receive such powers from the senate. In other cases, they must communicate every thing to the senate.

When the senate is under adjournment, any of the councils may assemble it before the day appointed for its meeting.

Besides these councils or courts, there is another called the court of *competitors*; which is thus constituted. If any candidates for the office of senator have more votes than a third of the representatives, that candidate who has most votes, next to the senator elected, becomes incapable for one year of all public offices, even of being a magistrate or representative: But he takes his seat in the court of competitors. Here then is a court which may sometimes consist of a hundred members, sometimes have no members at all; and by that means be for a year abolished.

The court of competitors has no power in the commonwealth. It has only the inspection of public accounts, and the accusing of any man before the senate. If the senate acquit him, the court of competitors may, if they please, appeal to the people, either magistrates or representatives. Upon that appeal, the magistrates or representatives meet on the day appointed by the court of competitors, and choose in each county three persons, from which number every senator is excluded. These, to the number of 300, meet in the capital, and bring the person accused to a new trial.

The court of competitors may propose any law to the senate; and if refused, may appeal to the people, that is, to the magistrates or representatives, who examine it in their counties. Every senator, who is thrown out of the senate by a vote of the court, takes his seat in the court of competitors.

The senate possesses all the judicative authority of the House of Lords, that is, all the appeals from the inferior courts. It likewise appoints the Lord Chancellor and all the officers of the law.

Every county is a kind of republic within itself, and the representatives may make by-laws, which have no authority till three months after they are voted. A copy of the law is sent to the senate, and to every other county. The senate, or any single county, may at any time annul any by-law of another county.

The representatives have all the authority of the *British* justices of the peace in trials, commitments, &c.

The magistrates have the appointment of all the officers of the revenue in each county. All causes with regard to the revenue are carried ultimately by appeal before the magistrates. They pass the accounts of all the officers; but must have their own accounts examined and passed at the end of the year by the representatives.

The magistrates name rectors or ministers to all the parishes.

The Presbyterian government is established; and the highest ecclesiastical court is an assembly or synod of all the presbyters of the county. The magistrates may take any cause from this court, and determine it themselves.

The magistrates may try, and depose or suspend any presbyter.

The militia is established in imitation of that of *Swisserland*, which, being well known, we shall not insist upon it. It will only be proper to make this addition, that an army of 20,000 men be annually drawn out by rotation, paid and encamped during six weeks in summer, that the duty of a camp may not be altogether unknown.

The magistrates appoint all the colonels, and downwards. The senate all upwards. During war, the general appoints the colonel and downwards, and his commission is good for a twelvemonth. But after that, it must be confirmed by the magistrates of the county to which the regiment belongs. The magistrates may break any officer in the county regiment; and the senate may do the same to any officer in the service. If the magistrates do not think proper to confirm the general's choice, they may appoint another officer in the place of him they reject.

All crimes are tried within the county by the magistrates and a jury; but the senate can stop any trial, and bring it before themselves.

Any county may indict any man before the senate for any crime.

The protector, the two secretaries, the council of state, with any five or more that the senate appoints, are possessed, on extraordinary emergencies, of *dictatorial* power for six months.

The protector may pardon any person condemned by the inferior courts.

In time of war, no officer of the army that is in the field can have any civil office in the commonwealth.

The capital, which we shall call *London*, may be allowed four members in the senate. It may therefore be divided into four counties. The representatives of each of these choose one senator and ten magistrates. There are therefore in the city four senators, forty-four magistrates, and four hundred representatives. The magistrates have the same authority as in the counties. The representatives also have the same authority; but they never meet in one general court: they give their votes in their particular county or division of hundreds.

When they enact any by-law, the greater number of counties or divisions determines the matter. And where these are equal, the magistrates have the casting vote.

The magistrates choose the mayor, sheriff, recorder, and other officers of the city.

In the commonwealth, no representative, magistrate, or senator as such, has any salary. The protector, secretaries, councils, and ambassadors, have salaries.

The first year in every century is set apart for correcting all inequalities which time may have produced in the representative. This must be done by the legislature.

The following political aphorisms may explain the reason of these orders.

The lower sort of people and small proprietors are good enough judges of one not very distant from them in rank or habitation; and therefore, in their parochial meetings, will probably choose the best, or nearly the best representative: but they are wholly unfit for country meetings, and for electing into the higher offices of the republic. Their ignorance gives the grandees an opportunity of deceiving them.

Ten thousand, even though they were not annually elected, are a basis large enough for any free government. It is true, the nobles in *Poland* are more than 10,000, and yet these oppress the people. But as power always continues there in the same persons and families, this makes them in a manner a different nation from the people. Besides, the nobles are there united under a few heads of families.

All free governments must consist of two councils, a lesser and a greater, or, in other words, of a senate and people. The people, as *Harrington* observes, would want wisdom without the senate: the senate, without the people, would want honesty[6].

A large assembly of 1,000, for instance, to represent the people, if allowed to debate, would fall into disorder. If not allowed to debate, the senate has a negative upon them, and the worst kind of negative, that before resolution.

Here, therefore, is an inconvenience which no government has yet fully remedied, but which is the easiest to be remedied in the world. If the people debate, all is confusion: if they do not debate, they can only resolve; and then the senate carves for them. Divide the people into many separate bodies, and then they may debate with safety, and every inconvenience seems to be prevented.

Cardinal de *Retz* says, that all numerous assemblies, however com-

---

[6] James Harrington, *The Oceana of Harrington, and his Other Works* (1700), p. 47.

posed, are mere mob, and swayed in their debates by the least motive.[7] This we find confirmed by daily experience. When an absurdity strikes a member, he conveys it to his neighbour, and so on till the whole be infected. Separate this great body; and though every member be only of middling sense, it is not probable that any thing but reason can prevail over the whole. Influence and example being removed, good sense will always get the better of bad among a number of people.

There are two things to be guarded against in every *senate*: Its combination and its division. Its combination is most dangerous; and against this inconvenience we have provided the following remedies: 1. The great dependence of the senators on the people by annual elections; and that not by an undistinguished rabble, like the *English* electors, but by men of fortune and education. 2. The small power they are allowed. They have few offices to dispose of. Almost all are given by the magistrates in the counties. 3. The court of competitors, which, being composed of men that are their rivals next to them in interest, and uneasy in their present situation, will be sure to take all advantages against them.

The division of the senate is prevented, 1. By the smallness of their number. 2. As faction supposes a combination in a separate interest, it is prevented by their dependence on the people. 3. They have a power of expelling any factious member. It is true, when another member of the same spirit comes from the county, they have no power of expelling him: Nor is it fit they should, for that shows the humour to be in the people, and may possibly arise from some ill conduct in public affairs. 4. Almost any man, in a senate so regularly chosen by the people, may be supposed fit for any civil office. It would be proper, therefore, for the senate to form some *general* resolutions with regard to the disposing of offices among the members: Which Resolutions would not confine them in critical times, when extraordinary parts on the one hand, or extraordinary stupidity on the other, appears in any senator; but they would be sufficient to prevent intrigue and faction, by making the disposal of the offices a thing of course. For instance, let it be a resolution, That no man shall enjoy any office till he has sat four years in the senate: that,

---

[7] Jean François Paul de Gondi, Cardinal de Retz and Archbishop of Paris, *Memoirs of the Cardinal De Retz* (4 vols., 1723), vol. I, p. 394.

except ambassadors, no man shall be in office two years following: that no man shall attain the higher offices but through the lower: that no man shall be protector twice, &c. The senate of *Venice* govern themselves by such resolutions.

In foreign politics the interest of the senate can scarcely ever be divided from that of the people; and therefore it is fit to make the senate absolute with regard to them, otherwise there could be no secrecy or refined policy. Besides, without money no alliance can be executed, and the senate is still sufficiently dependent. Not to mention, that the legislative power, being always superior to the executive, the magistrates or representatives may interpose whenever they think proper.

The chief support of the *British* government is the opposition of interest: but that, though in the main serviceable, breeds endless factions. In the foregoing plan, it does all the good without any of the harm. The *competitors* have no power of controlling the senate: they have only the power of accusing, and appealing to the people.

It is necessary, likewise, to prevent both combination and division in the thousand magistrates. This is done sufficiently by the separation of places and interests.

But, lest that should not be sufficient, their dependence on the 10,000 for their elections serves to the same purpose.

Nor is that all; for the 10,000 may resume the power whenever they please, and not only when they all please, but when any five of a hundred please, which will happen upon the very first suspicion of a separate interest.

The 10,000 are too large a body either to unite or divide, except when they meet in one place, and fall under the guidance of ambitious leaders. Not to mention their annual election, by the whole body of the people, that are of any consideration.

A small commonwealth is the happiest government in the world within itself, because every thing lies under the eye of the rulers: But it may be subdued by great force from without. This scheme seems to have all the advantages both of a great and a little commonwealth.

Every county-law may be annulled either by the senate or another county, because that shows an opposition of interest: In which case no part ought to decide for itself. The matter must be referred to the whole, which will best determine what agrees with general interest.

As to the clergy and militia, the reasons of these orders are obvious.

Without the dependence of the clergy on the civil magistrates, and without a militia, it is in vain to think that any free government will ever have security or stability.

In many governments, the inferior magistrates have no rewards but what arise from their ambition, vanity, or public spirit. The salaries of the *French* judges amount not to the interest of the sums they pay for their offices. The *Dutch* burgomasters have little more immediate profit than the *English* justices of peace, or the members of the house of commons formerly. But lest any should suspect that this would beget negligence in the administration (which is little to be feared, considering the natural ambition of mankind), let the magistrates have competent salaries. The senators have access to so many hon-ourable and lucrative offices, that their attendance needs not be bought. There is little attendance required of the representatives.

That the foregoing plan of government is practicable, no one can doubt who considers the resemblance that it bears to the common-wealth of the United Provinces, a wise and renowned government. The alterations in the present scheme seem all evidently for the better. 1. The representation is more equal. 2. The unlimited power of the burgomasters in the towns, which forms a perfect aristocracy in the *Dutch* commonwealth, is corrected by a well-tempered demo-cracy, in giving to the people the annual election of the county repres-entatives. 3. The negative, which every province and town has upon the whole body of the *Dutch* Republic, with regard to alliances, peace and war, and the imposition of taxes, is here removed. 4. The coun-ties, in the present plan, are not so independent of each other, nor do they form separate bodies so much as the seven provinces, where the jealousy and envy of the smaller provinces and towns against the greater, particularly *Holland* and *Amsterdam*, have frequently dis-turbed the government. 5. Larger powers, though of the safest kind, are intrusted to the senate than the States-General possess; by which means the former may become more expeditious and secret in their resolutions than it is possible for the latter.

The chief alterations that could be made on the *British* government, in order to bring it to the most perfect model of limited monarchy, seem to be the following. *First*, the plan of *Cromwell*'s parliament ought to be restored, by making the representation equal, and by allowing none to vote in the county elections who possess not a prop-erty of 200*l.* value. *Secondly*, As such a House of Commons would be too weighty for a frail House of Lords, like the present, the Bishops, and *Scotch* Peers, ought to be removed: The number of the upper house ought to be raised to three or four hundred: the seats not hereditary, but during life: they ought to have the election of their own members: and no commoner should be allowed to refuse a seat that was offered him. By this means the house of lords would consist entirely of the men of chief credit, abilities, and interest in the nation; and every turbulent leader in the house of commons might be taken off, and connected by interest with the house of Peers. Such an aristocracy would be an excellent barrier both to the monarchy and against it. At present, the balance of our government depends in some measure on the abilities and behaviour of the sovereign; which are variable and uncertain circumstances.

This plan of limited monarchy, however corrected, seems still liable to three great inconveniences. *First*, It removes not entirely, though it may soften the parties of *court* and *country*. *Secondly*, The king's personal character must still have great influence on the government. *Thirdly*, The sword is in the hands of a single person, who will always neglect to discipline the militia, in order to have a pretence for keeping up a standing army. It is evident that this is a mortal distemper in the British government, of which it must at last inevitably perish. I must, however, confess, that Sweden seems, in some measure, to have remedied this inconvenience, and to have a militia along with its limited monarchy, as well as a standing army, which is less dangerous than the British.

We shall conclude this subject, with observing the falsehood of the common opinion, that no large state, such as *France* or *Great Britain*, could ever be modelled into a commonwealth, but that such a form of government can only take place in a city or small territory. The contrary seems probable. Though it is more difficult to form a republican government in an extensive country than in a city, there is more facility when once it is formed, of preserving it steady and uniform, without tumult and faction. It is not easy for the distant parts of a large state to combine in any plan of free government; but they easily conspire in the esteem and reverence for a single person, who, by means of this popular favour, may seize the power, and forcing the more obstinate to submit, may establish a monarchical government. On the other hand, a city readily concurs in the same notions of government, the natural equality of property favours liberty, and the nearness of habitation enables the citizens mutually to assist each other. Even under absolute princes, the subordinate government of cities is commonly republican; while that of counties and provinces is monarchical. But these same circumstances, which facilitate the erection of commonwealths in cities, render their constitution more frail and uncertain. Democracies are turbulent. For, however the people may be separated or divided into small parties, either in their votes or elections, their near habitation in a city will always make the force of popular tides and currents very sensible. Aristocracies are better adapted for peace and order, and accordingly were most admired by ancient writers; but they are jealous and oppressive. In a large government, which is modelled with masterly skill, there is compass and room enough to refine the democracy, from the lower people who may be admitted into the first elections, or first concoction of the commonwealth, to the higher magistrates who direct all the movements. At the same time, the parts are so distant and remote, that it is very difficult, either by intrigue, prejudice, or passion, to hurry them into any measures against the public interest.

It is needless to inquire, whether such a government would be immortal. I allow the justness of the poet's exclamation on the endless projects of human race, *Man and for ever!* The world itself probably is not immortal. Such consuming plagues may arise as would leave even a perfect government a weak prey to its neighbours. We know not to what length enthusiasm, or other extraordinary movements of the human mind, may transport men to the neglect of all order and public good. Where difference of interest is removed, whimsical unaccountable factions often arise, from personal favour or enmity. Perhaps rust may grow to the springs of the most accurate political machine, and disorder its motions. Lastly, extensive conquests, when pursued, must be the ruin of every free government; and of the more perfect governments sooner than of the imperfect; because of the very advantages which the former possess above the latter. And though such a state ought to establish a fundamental law against conquests, yet republics have ambition as well as individuals, and present interest makes men forgetful of their posterity. It is a sufficient incitement to human endeavours, that such a government would flourish for many ages; without pretending to bestow, on any work of man, that immortality which the Almighty seems to have refused to his own productions.

An Account of the First Settlement, Laws, Form of Government, and Police, of the Cessares, A People of South America:

In Nine Letters, From Mr Vander Neck, one of the Senators of that Nation, to his Friend in *Holland*.

With Notes by the Editor.

There are three things, which regulate States, viz. Necessity, Laws, and Police. Τρα γαρ εςι κ. τ. λ. Menand. in Epitr.[1]

[JAMES BURGH].

1764

---

[1] In fact, not Menander's *Epitrepontes* (*The Arbitration*), but from a minor fragment, 'The Woman who is Set on Fire', reprinted in *Menander. The Principal Fragments*, ed. Francis Allinson (Heinemann, 1921), p. 351.

Preface.

How these Letters of Mr VANDER NECK[2] fell into my hands, it imports the public but little to know. Some of my readers may perhaps view the following account of the CESSARES in much the same light with Sir T. MORE'S UTOPIA, rather as what a good man would wish a nation to be, than the true account of the state of one really existing. I shall leave, for an exercise of the Reader's ingenuity, the determination of this point, after only mentioning, that if he pleases to consult Ovalle's Account of Chili[3] in the third volume of Churchill's Collection of Voyages;[4] Feuillée's Observations on South America;[5] and Martinière's Dictionaire Géographique,[6] he will find, that there is really a people called the Cessares, in a country near the high mountains, Cordilleras de los Andes, between Chili and Patagonia in South America, in the forty-third or forty-fourth degree of south latitude. They are quite different from the Indians of those parts, and seem to be Europeans, according to the accounts which historians of the best credit give us. That their country is very pleasant and fruitful, bounded on the west by a great river, which runs very swift. That the sound of bells has been heard there, and linnen been seen spread out to whiten in their fields, as practised by the Dutch in Holland. But the account which is given of them by those authors, is very imperfect, because they will not permit any Spaniard to come into their territories, lest they should thereby be deprived of their liberties: having made a law, that whoever discovers the passes which lead into their country, shall be put to death as a traytor, even though he were at the head of their republic.

Some have conjectured, that they were originally the crew of three Spanish ships, which were cast away in the streights of Magellan in 1540: but others with more probability take them to be Dutch, who, losing their ships in the same streights, or rather perhaps on the coast of Patagonia, travelled to these parts and settled here. And this last

---

[2] Jacob van Neck (1564–1638): Dutch explorer whose journal of voyages to the East Indies was first translated into English in 1601.
[3] Alonso de Ovalle, *An Historical Relation of the Kingdom of Chile* (1646).
[4] A. and J. Churchill, *A Collection of Voyages and Travels* (1732), vol. III.
[5] Louis Feuillee, *Journal des Observations Physiques, Mathématiques et Botaniques, faites ... sur les côtes Orientales de l'Amérique Méridionale* (2 vols., Paris, 1714).
[6] Antoine Augustin Bruzen de la Martinière, *Le Grand Dictionnaire Géographique et Critique* (9 vols., The Hague, 1726–9).

opinion is confirmed by their form of government, which is a republic; by their speaking a language different from the Spaniards; and by their forbidding any Spaniard to enter their country; which they would scarce have done, had they themselves been originally of the same nation.

However this may be, if the scheme of government, laws, and establishments, described in the following pages, are founded in wisdom and justice, and are such as would promote the happiness of a state regulated according to them, I humbly presume this publication will not be thought unseasonable, at a time, when there may be occasion to settle colonies in the extensive countries, which the Divine blessing on our efforts in the late glorious war, has added to the British empire.

An Account of the Cessares, &c.

To Mr Vander Zee, at Amsterdam.
Letter I.

The reasons which induced the author and his friends to leave Holland, and settle in a distant and uninhabited country. The distresses of many poor families in Europe at that time. How the lands were divided among the Israelites by Joshua; and also among the Lacedemonians by Lycurgus. The author's scheme.

DEAR SIR,   Sept. 28, 1618.

Your Letter from Paris, dated March 3, 1606, I received a few weeks before I left Holland; but the preparations I was then making for a long voyage, prevented me from returning you any answer. To atone for my silence, I shall now give you a full account of every particular you desire: the motives which induced me and my friends to leave our native country, and to make a small settlement in a distant and uninhabited land; the form of government which we have erected; together with a short description of the country; and some account of our laws, customs, employments, and manner of life. Though I am uncertain whether I shall ever have the opportunity of sending my letters to you, not only on account of the wars, which (I suppose) still subsist between Spain and the Seven United Provinces; but also because our laws forbid us to carry on any correspondence with the Spaniards in Chili, through whose territories alone we can send any packet to Europe. And this prohibition cannot but appear wise and just to you, who know their restless ambition, avarice, and bigotry:[a]

[a] It is no wonder the Cessares should be afraid of holding any correspondence with the Spaniards: for Casas one of their own bishops, assures us, that on their first discovery of America, their avarice, ambition, and tyranny were such, that in order

for if we had any commerce with them, they would soon become acquainted with our situation and strength; and would very probably march into our country with a powerful army, subvert our happy constitution, freedom, and independence, and establish the Popish religion with all its cruelties among us.

The fear of these direful calamities from a threaten'd invasion of the Spaniards, under Spinola, in 1606, was one great motive for our leaving Holland, and seeking a peaceful and quiet retreat in some distant region free from the alarms and terrors of war, the fatal effects of which we well knew and dreaded: for when a land becomes the seat of war, the distresses of its inhabitants are often greater than words can express; more especially as our enemies had determined (if they should have proved successful to root out the reform'd religion; whereby all those protestants, who would not have tamely submitted to the arbitrary and tyrannical power usurped by the Romish clergy over the souls and consciences of men, would have been exposed to the greatest tortures and sufferings. Nor were these fears imaginary, but too well founded on the horrid cruelties exercised on the protestants in the Low Countries, not many years before, by the bloody duke of Alva.[b]

to possess themselves of the wealth and country of the Indians, they treated them, during the term of forty years, with the greatest cruelty and barbarity, inflicted upon them all kinds of torments, put above twelve millions of them to death, and made their countries desolate and waste. Nay, according to the account of the abovementioned author, above fifty millions of them died in that space of time. This conduct of the Spaniards must appear detestable and horrid beyond expression, when we consider (as Casas informs us) that the Indians, whom they thus barbarously treated, had never given them any cause to commit such violences upon them, but on the contrary, were naturally simple, artless, tractable, and of a sweet disposition, humble, patient and submissive, even to the Spaniards who enslaved them. *See Casas's relation of the Spanish cruelties in the West Indies*[7], *page 1, 2, 3, 4, 5, and 15.*

[b] The duke of Alva was made governor of the Netherlands by Philip the second, King of Spain in 1567. As soon as he came thither, he imprison'd and tortur'd the protestants of every age, sex and condition; and the gallows, the wheels, and even the trees in the highways, were loaded with the bodies or limbs of those whom he put to death. He told the magistrates of Antwerp, that the king had rather see all his territories deserted and uncultivated, than suffer one heretic to remain in them. – The king having also consulted the Spanish inquisitors about the affairs of the Netherlands; they told him, they were of opinion that the shortest way would be, that all the Netherlanders, except those whose names should be sent from Spain, should be

[7] Bartholomé de las Casas, Bishop of Chiapa, *The Tears of the Indians: Being an Historical Account of the Cruel Massacres and Slaughters of Above Twenty Millions of Innocent People* (1656).

But this was not our only motive for leaving our native country; we had another end in view, noble, generous, and distinterested, in itself; which was the relieving a few honest, sober, and industrious families, who were in great poverty and distress, and the providing for them and their posterity a comfortable subsistance, under such a form of Government, as would be productive of the most beneficial and salutary consequences to every individual. Such a design, every person who is not insensible of the feelings of humanity and benevolence, and lost to every worthy and generous sentiment, must highly applaud. For if it is charitable and praiseworthy, to give only a transient relief to our fellow-creatures, labouring under the wants and difficulties of life; how much more charitable and God-like must it be, to give them a perpetual security from those evils (as far as this changeable and imperfect state will admit of) by putting them in the full possession of all the necessaries of life; by securing to them the delightful enjoyment of their civil and religious liberties, under the government of laws founded upon justice, goodness, wisdom, and equity; and by transmitting all these invaluable blessings to their posterity?

It is a melancholy reflection to a good and humane person, that distress and poverty should be the lot of a great part of the inhabitants of the most civilized and Christian nations. Yet great numbers of sober and industrious persons are to be found in Christian countries,

---

declar'd Heretics, and guilty of high-treason: and particularly those of the nobility, who had presented a petition against erecting an inquisition there. Philip approv'd their advice, and commanded the duke of Alva to execute it. Upon which he proceeded against the whole nation, letting loose his murdering emissaries, to satiate their avarice and cruelty on an oppress'd and miserable people. Multitudes left the country, and above a hundred thousand houses were reckon'd to have been deserted on this account. Besides which, the Duke of Alva boasted, that in the space of the five years, he governed there, he had caus'd above eighteen thousand heretics and rebels to be executed, without reckoning any of those, who fell by the sword in battle, in defence of their religion and liberties. *See Brandt's history of the Reformation in the Low Countries.*[8] Book IX. and X. – This Philip the second of Spain acknowledged in a writing which he gave to his son, that he had sacrificed twenty millions of men to his lust of dominion, and had laid more countries waste, than all those which he possess'd in Europe: which is enough to raise horror in every mind not wholly divested of humanity. *See Sully's Memoirs,*[9] *Vol.* I. p. 496, 497.

[8] Geeraert Brandt the Elder, *The History of the Reformation and Other Ecclesiastical Transactions in, and about, the Low Countries* (1719).

[9] Maximilien de Béthune, Duke de Sully, *Memoirs of Maximilien de Bethune, Duke of Sully* (3 vols., 1756).

in an abject condition, without one foot of land, though many thousands of acres lie waste and uncultivated. How many are there, who are unable to maintain themselves and families by their daily labour or employment, destitute of the necessaries and comforts of life, pinched by want and cold, perhaps labouring under various diseases, or groaning under the infirmities of old age, without help, support or relief, except the poor pittance, which perhaps an overburthened parish allows them? Yet God has a real regard and concern for the good and welfare of every one of the human race, the poor as well as the rich, for both are equally the work of his hands. He has also given to most of those nations such a quantity of ground, as is sufficient to supply the wants of their several inhabitants, and make their lives comfortable. But unhappily some few, attentive only to their own private interest, and unconcerned for the good of others, have engrossed the greatest part of the land, and left but little for the rest: whereas, if there had been a more equal division of it, every one would have had enough for a decent and plentiful maintenance, by easy labour and industry.*

---

* The case of the Poor has long been the object of serious consideration, their evils and sufferings are many, and every good man would wish to alleviate them. Many of them are the most useful members of society, and it is from their labour and industry, that the rich derive their comforts and conveniences. And when age, sickness or infirmities come upon them, and incapacitate them for their daily labour, surely it is but common justice; that they should be provided for. The poor's rate in England and Wales is grown to a most exorbitant height, and some years ago amounted to 1,700,000*l.* a year, according to a calculation made by Sir Joseph Jekyll. And the number of persons who receive the Poor's rate and other alms, is computed to be no less than 400,000. – Dr Grew reckons there are about 46 millions of acres in England and Wales, one sixth part of which are commons, heaths, forests, chases &c. Now if some of these were to be divided among the sober and industrious poor, the poor's rate would be lessened, great numbers of families would be made happy, and marriage would be encourag'd, on which the strength of a nation depends. About 5, 6 or 7 acres of land (according to the goodness and nature of the soil) would be sufficient for every man, and enable him also to pay one or two shillings a year quit rent to those persons, whose right of commoning there, would then be taken away. And as this portion of land would not be enough to employ their whole time, the men would still work at their respective trades and employments, and the women and children spin wool, flax, or cotton for our manufactures. And tho' some of them would prove idle and vicious, and abuse such a grant; yet it is probable that the greatest part of them would be induced to be sober and diligent: for as a man oppress'd with poverty, notwithstanding all his continual labour and care, naturally gives himself up to sloth and despair; so the having an estate which he can call his own, is no small inducement to sobriety, industry, vigour and alacrity. – At the first establishment of the colony of Georgia in America, every poor man had a lot of fifty acres granted to him and his male heirs, which was to be preserv'd for ever separate and undivided, nor could the

Nor is this a visionary scheme never yet executed. For such was the happy constitution of the Israelites, when they were first setled in the land of Canaan by Joshua: every man had an estate of his own, which was hereditary and unalienable.[d] This equal division of the land cut off the means of luxury with its temptations, checked pride and ambition, and established the habits of industry and diligence among them. And therefore God highly exclaims against those selfish and covetous persons, who, afterwards broke through this wise regulation, and engrossed their neighbours estates.[e]

We are also assured by historians of the best credit, that even in a Heathen nation, the general good was preferred by the rich to every private view. For when the greatest part of the Lacedemonians were reduced to extreme poverty, while a small number only of particular persons were possessed of the whole country: Lycurgus prevailed upon the rich to give up all their estates, and to have an equal division made of them. Accordingly he divided the whole country into 39,000 equal parts, and gave only one to every citizen. This was such an extraordinary instance of zeal for the good of others, as is not to be equalled in the history of any other nation.[f]

Such a generous and disinterested conduct, and so sure and solid a foundation laid for the happiness of every one, justly excited our

---

owner sell it, or even let it to another person, without a license for that purpose: that every one might be oblig'd to cultivate his own lands, and that no one might have more than one lot. See *Moore's voyage to Georgia*,[10] *p. 7, 8.*

[d] Every man's share was above 16 acres. See *Lowman on the civil government of the Hebrews*,[11] *p. 39.* – This was a sufficient estate for any family in that climate, and in those ages, when they were happily ignorant of the luxury of our times, and were contented with a plain and simple life. Nay, we find among the ancient Romans, so late as 462 years after the foundation of Rome, that seven Roman acres, which are not above four and a half English acres (the Roman acre being but 240 Roman feet long, and 120 broad) were thought to be enough for any Roman citizen: for Manius Curius, who had been thrice honour'd with a triumph, and was the glory of the age he liv'd in, publickly declar'd, that the Roman, who was not contented with that quantity of land, was a pernicious Citizen. See *Pliny's Natural History*,[12] B. XVIII. *ch. 3.*

[e] *Isaiah* v. 8.

[f] Every share yielded about 82 medimni or bushels of corn yearly, besides wine, oil, and fruits. It maintain'd also the Helotes who cultivated their lands; and I make no doubt but it also afforded sufficient pasture for their cattle. See *Plutarch's life of Lycurgus.*[13]

[10] Francis Moore, *A Voyage to Georgia Begun in the Year 1735* (1744).

[11] Moses Lowman, *A Dissertation on the Civil Government of the Hebrews* (1740).

[12] Caius Plinius Secundus, *The History of the World* (1601).

[13] *Plutarch's Lives* (5 vols., 1702–9).

admiration, and animated us to settle a new colony on nearly the same plan. But that our posterity might enjoy the same advantages with ourselves, we determined to allow no one any more land, than would be sufficient to answer every necessary and useful purpose, and to reserve the rest for our descendants, as their numbers should increase. We further agreed, that every one should have an equal share, that so we might check every proud, ambitious, and destructive passion, and banish riches as well as poverty from us. And the more effectually to preserve that innocency, simplicity, and regularity of life, which we hoped to establish among us, we fixt upon a distant and retired country, out of the common course of trade: for though some commerce with other nations would be attended with several advantages to us, yet we were afraid it would be productive of some unhappy consequences, and bring in luxury, and customs injurious to the welfare of our state. Besides, sailors, as well as soldiers, are too apt to introduce drunkenness, debauchery, and irreligion, which destroy every good and excellent disposition, and that sober, modest, and decent behaviour, which is so amiable and praise-worthy, and on which the happiness of society depends.

I am, &c.

Letter II.

The author's and his friend's prudent choice of proper persons to go with them. They lay before them the difficulties and hardships they must expect to meet with, which has a happy effect. They fix upon their form of government and laws: and choose their governors and magistrates. They conceal the name of the country they are going to. A general list of the things they carried with them. They set sail from Holland in two ships, but lose one of them on the coast of Patagonia, which obliges them to settle on the western side of that country.

DEAR SIR,   Nov. 9, 1618.
Having in my first Letter acquainted you with our design, I shall now give you some account of our proceedings in it.

Mr Alphen and myself, who first formed the scheme, and furnished the necessary expences, judged it of the utmost importance, that all the first settlers of our colony should be such as sincerely approved of our design, and were sober, peaceable and industrious, as its success would greatly depend upon their dispositions: for if our proposal had been made public, and we had accepted of all that offered themselves indiscriminately, without any regard to their temper or conduct, some of them would soon have become impatient of the restraint of wholesome laws, proved factious and turbulent, and endeavoured to destroy our form of government, and set up a different one of their own, which at last would have ended in anarchy and utter ruin.[g]

We therefore privately proposed our design to about 150 poor, laborious, and industrious families, into whose tempers and conduct we had previously enquired. Some few rejected it, but the far greater number approved of and chearfully embraced our scheme. Among these last there were some husbandmen, bricklayers, carpenters, and blacksmiths, together with persons of other different occupations, who were of a quiet and peaceable disposition, and were masters of their respective employments. We should have been glad also, if persons of several other trades had fallen in with our proposal: but as they did not readily agree to our plan, we thought it best to be without them, and to labour at first under some inconveniences: not doubting but that care and industry, with the assistance of proper books, would in time make us masters of every necessary and useful business; which in the event has happily proved true.

We further chose about 200 orphans of both sexes, and different ages, whose parents had left them in a poor and wretched condition, exposed to the snares and evils of life. These we distributed among us, in the cultivation of our lands and other employments, till they either married, or arrived at the age of one and twenty years, at which time they would be entitled to the same privileges, and an estate of their own equal to ours. And to promote marriage and make incontinency inexcusable, we took care that the numbers of the unmarried of each sex in our whole society should be equal.

We also engaged two ministers to embrace our scheme. They were persons of great piety, and extensive virtue, affable and humble, of

---

[g] This was a wise conduct and it was for want of such a prudent choice, that a few discontented and self-conceited persons made the town of Savanna in Georgia very unhappy at its first settlement, while there was perfect peace and tranquility at Frederica, owing to the better temper and disposition of its inhabitants. *See Stephens's Journal of the Proceedings in Georgia,*[14] *Vol. I. p. 14, 15, 46, 53, 77, 98.*

[14] Col. William Stephens, *A Journal of the Proceedings in Georgia* (1737–41).

universal charity and benevolence: they understood the Scriptures well, had a plain but agreeable delivery, and a persuasive manner of recommending the great duties of religion: and what was of the greatest importance, their behaviour and lives were agreeable to their precepts.[h]

Having thus engaged a sufficient number of persons to embark with us in our undertaking, we laid before them all, (particularly such who we had reason to think were too sanguine in their expectations) the difficulties which they must expect to encounter with, both from a long and perhaps a dangerous voyage, as well as after their arrival at the wish'd for port. For as the land was not inhabited, we told them, that we should want at first many of the conveniences of life, and must use great labour and industry before we could obtain them; and must be contented for some time with such provisions as we carried with us, or could readily find there; and that the clearing the lands,[i] building the houses, preparing the ground for planting and sowing, and making some necessary fortifications to secure us from the assaults of enemies, would require much time, labour and patience. We therefore desired them to take some time, to weigh all these difficulties deliberately in their own minds, lest they should repent, when it would be too late, and blame us for leading them into dangers and hardships which they did not foresee.

This fair and candid procedure, instead of discouraging any of our little society, had a contrary effect. It confirmed and strengthened their resolutions, and they all declared, that being fully sensible of the goodness of our design, and the uprightness and disinterestedness of our intentions, they were firmly resolved to run the risk of the undertaking, and leave the event to Providence: and that if they should struggle with hardships and difficulties, instead of murmuring or repining, they would endure them with patience and chearfulness.

We then held a general assembly, in which the form of government,

---

[h] This reminds me of a couple of lines I have somewhere met with, justly describing a truly good Minister.
> Behold a man, sincere in word and thought,
> Liv'd as he preach'd, and practis'd what he taught.[15]

[i] A machine might be invented to tear up the strongest and best rooted trees, with the assistance of a few men; *See Wilkins's Mathematical Magic*[16], p. 92 & c. This would be of great use in all such new colonies, as have too many woods.

15 'Behold a man . . . taught': Oft paraphrased, by John Armstrong, among others.
16 John Wilkins, Bishop of Chester, *Mathematicall Magick; or, The Wonders That May Be Performed by Mechanicall Geometry* (1648).

and all the laws of our state, (drawn up some time before by Mr Alphen and myself) were read and carefully considered: and having made such alterations as were judged proper, the whole assembly expressed their approbation of them and all who were above 21 years of age sign'd them; expressing thereby their submission to them, and by that means became entitled to all the privileges of citizenship. Then to prevent any disputes on our arrival at the desired country, all the citizens proceeded to the election of the magistrates, and unanimously fixed upon Mr Alphen to be our governor, and myself and three others to be senators: they also chose six inspectors, and ratified the choice of the two ministers above-mentioned. And give me leave to add, that all these (my own weaknesses excepted) were persons of a friendly and benevolent temper, who had a great command over their passions, had prudence and discretion to bear with any little failings and imperfections in others, and yet had sufficient firmness to keep them steady to the original plan.[k]

[k] The Passions and affections are implanted in us by God, to answer the wisest intentions. A man without them, would be indolent and inactive, like a Ship in a calm: whereas he who allows them to govern, resembles a Ship with it's sails full spread and without a rudder, which is toss'd about by every sudden gust, and drove by every stormy and tempestuous wind. But he that is truly wise, can restrain or exert them with judgment and prudence, direct them by just and right principles, and govern them by the rules of reason and religion – An easy thing in theory, but very difficult to practice – *Milton in the first book of his Paradise Regain'd, has beautifully express'd himself on this subject.*

> "Hard are the ways of truth, and rough to walk,
> Smooth on the tongue discours'd, pleasing to th' ear,
> And tuneable as silvan pipe or song
> What wonder then, if I delight to hear
> Her dictates from thy mouth most men admire
> Virtue, who follow not her love."

And again in the second book,

> –"A crown
> Brings dangers, troubles, cares and sleepless nights
> To him who wears the regal diadem,
> When on his shoulders each man's burden lies;
> For therein stands the office of a king,
> His honour, virtue, merit and chief praise,
> That for the public all this weight he bears,
> Yet he who reigns within himself, and rules
> Passions, desires, and fears, is more a king,
> Which every wise and virtuous man attains,
> And who attains not, ill aspires to rule
> Cities of men, or headstrong multitudes;
> Subject himself to anarchy within,
> Or lawless passions in him, which he serves."[17]

[17] John Milton, *Paradise Regained. A Poem* (1763), pp. 16–17, 34.

Mr Alphen and myself had already carefully considered the situation and circumstances of the country, where we had designed to settle. But we had disclosed the particular place to very few of our associates, lest it should be publickly known, and our enemies should be acquainted with it, who would not fail to lay wait for us in our voyage, or to attack us immediately on our arrival there, before we could possibly fortify ourselves.[l] But we assured our society, that in general the climate was temperate, the air healthy, the soil good, and that the place was naturally secure, being difficult of access, and easily fortified: circumstances of the greatest importance to us, who were few in number, not enured to great hardships, nor able to resist, in an open and exposed place, an enemy superior in number, and skilful in the destructive arts of war.

The next point was to consider what things were necessary to carry with us. This required great thought and foresight; and notwithstanding all our prudence and precaution, we afterwards found that we had forgot several things, which would have been very useful to us.

The things we provided were as follows:

First, a sufficient quantity of provisions to serve our colony for two years, to prevent the danger which a bad harvest, the first year, might expose us to.[m]

Secondly, cloaths of all sorts for several years, that we might not be interrupted in our more necessary employments.

Thirdly, the household goods for every family; the proper tools for every trade, and a sufficient quantity of iron, tin, and other useful metals, to serve us for some years.

Fourthly, the seeds of various kinds of plants, for food and physic, for timber and beauty.[n]

---

[l] The late duke of Montagu's intended settlement of the island of St Lucia in the West Indies in 1722 was prevented, by it's being publickly known before hand; for the French came upon the English settlers with a large body of troops, a few days after they had landed there, and obliged them to quit the island. *See Uring's*[18] *relation of this affair.*

[m] New settlers should carry the small maiz or Indian corn with them, for it rises very fast, and ripens in so short a time; that from the same field they may have two crops of it in one year. Besides which, it is more agreeable to the taste than the larger kind. *See Du Pratz's history of Louisiana,*[19] *Vol. II, p. 3.*

[n] The seeds of plants are very apt to be spoiled in long voyages: but Linnaeus the celebrated Swedish botanist assures us that the following method will preserve them.

[18] Nathaniel Uring, *A History of the Voyages and Travels of Nathaniel Uring* (1725–7).
[19] A. S. Le Page Du Pratz, *The History of Louisiana* (2 vols., 1763).

Fifthly, some of the most useful drugs and medicines; and also poison to destroy rats, with which most of the uninhabited places abound, where ships have formerly touched.*

Sixthly, the necessary animals for food and labour.

Seventhly, guns, and such other instruments of war, as were necessary to defend ourselves from enemies.

Eighthly, the best books of all sorts, particularly such as relate to every useful trade, art, and science.

Ninthly, as houses or even huts cannot be immediately built, and the lying under tents is generally found to be unwholesome; we had ten wooden houses framed in such a manner, that they could be taken to pieces for the conveniency of carriage, and easily put together again and erected for use on our landing; two were for the men, four for the women and children, 'and the rest for our provisions and stores.' And further, as the grinding of corn,' and the sawing of timber are very laborious works, we took with us several little corn and saw mills.*

Put the seeds into a cylindrical glass bottle, and fill the interstices with dry sand, to prevent their lying too close together; then cork it, or tie a bladder over it. Put this bottle into another glass bottle, so much larger than that which contains the seeds, that, when it is suspended in it, there may be left a vacant place on all sides of about two inches between the two glasses, to be filled with the following powder. Take four parts of salt-petre, and one fifth part, of equal parts of common salt, and sal. ammoniac; these must be well pounded and mixt together. This saline mass (which should be rather moist than dry) will always be so cold, that the seeds in the inner glass will never suffer during the voyage, from the heat of the air. Chesnuts and the like large fruits may be preserved, by dipping them in bees wax made soft by warmth, and inclosing them in a thick coat of it. *See the Philosophical Transactions,*[20] *Vol.* LI. *part I, page 209 etc.*

* This was a very good thought: for rats greatly abound in many of the uninhabited islands, and on the sea coasts, where ships have touched but more especially where any ships have been wrecked. The first settlers of St Helena and Bermudas were so infested by them, that their corn and many of their plants and fruits were devoured by them.

* Small houses stand in the market-place at Moskow in Russia by hundreds ready made, and put up for sale; and when one of them is sold, it is taken to pieces, and being carried to the place where it is to be set up, it is erected there in a very short time. *See the Present State of Russia,*[21] *Vol.* I. p. 126 – But if tents were made double, and the inner ones were made of oil cloth, or of painted cloth, they would be much drier and warmer than common tents are; nor would the sun be able to crack or injure the inner ones, nor the rain or dews to soak through them.

* There, I suppose, were worked by the wind. In New England they have saw mills of a cheap and slight work, which generally stand upon small streams. And though they

[20] Royal Society, *Philosophical Transactions,* 51, pt 1 for 1759 (1760), 206–15.
[21] [F. C. Weber], *The Present State of Russia* (2 vols., 1722–3).

Having thus endeavoured to provide every thing which was necessary or useful, in the best manner we could, we hired two ships, and agreed with the Captains to carry us to whatever part of the world we should chuse. We then put on board each ship, the half of every sort of our provisions and stores; that if one of our ships should be wrecked, the other might not be destitute of any one article. We then set sail from our native country, humbly recommending ourselves to the protection and blessing of God: being fully sensible, that it was he alone, who could preserve us from every unfortunate accident, give us health and strength, inspire us with wisdom and prudence, and prosper our undertaking: at the same time we determined to submit patiently to his wise providence, if it should please him to disappoint any of our designs. And though we were prevented from going to the place we had proposed,ʳ by one of our ships running ashore on the coast of Patagonia; yet, as our lives and cargo were preserved, things turned out in the end extremely well, and perhaps to our advantage. For, being unable to proceed on our voyage by the loss of this ship, we sent out several of our people to examine the country about us, who at length discovered a retired and uninhabited place on the western side of Patagonia, where we soon settled, in a country fertile, healthy, and pleasant, fortified by nature: so that we enjoy all the blessings, which we can reasonably expect or even wish

often carry only one saw, yet a man and a boy attending upon one of them, can in 24 hours saw 4000 feet, or about 160 boards of the white Pine; those boards are generally one inch thick, and from 15 to 25 feet long, and 1 or 2 feet broad. *See Douglas's State of the British Colonies in North America*[22], *Vol.* II. *p. 54* – They have also in Scotland, and in the Isle of Man, both corn and saw mills of an easy and cheap construction.

ʳ It seems probable, that they had designed to settle in some island of the Great South Sea, perhaps that of John Fernandes, which is a most agreeable place, and in a temperate climate. And it is worthy our observation, that all those small islands, which lie at a considerable distance from the continent, enjoy a more equable and temperate air, and are both warmer in winter, and cooler in summer, than the continent is, in the same latitude. The reason is, because the sea is never so much heated or cooled as the land is, and therefore the sea asswages the heat of the summer, and moderates the cold of the winter: the saline quality also, with which the sea air is generally thought to be impregnated, makes it more healthy. And hence it is, that the Madera and Bermudas islands in about 32 degrees of latitude enjoy a kind of perpetual spring: and that the air of the island of St Helena, though it lies in the 16th degree of latitude, is always temperate and healthy.

[22] William Douglass, *A Summary, Historical and Political of the First Planting, Progressive Improvements and Present State of the British Settlements in North America* (2 vols., 1747–50).

for in this life. But our laws forbid me to disclose the particular place of our abode, or the passages which lead to it; lest any nation should be tempted by the lust of power and dominion to make a conquest of us, to destroy our constitution, and rob us of those inestimable privileges, our civil and religious liberties. We live secluded from the rest of the world, unmixt with any of the nations around us, have no ambitious views of enlarging our dominions, nor any wicked designs of enslaving others: but we know the princes of this world too well ever to trust them.

I am, &c.

Letter III

The form of government they established, consisting of a governor, who is hereditary, and of senators, who are chosen by the citizens. The author's objections to an aristocracy, and democracy, and monarchy. Yet he gives three instances of excellent kings who were possessed of abilities, integrity and zeal for the public good, and shews, the great happiness their subjects enjoyed under them, and adds that, if all kings were such, monarchy would be the most desirable form. He then warmly expatiates against bad Kings, especially such as are called heroes, who delight in wars, and the destruction of mankind and gives some good advice to historians, who write the lives of Princes. And concludes with an account of several excellent laws established by the inca's of Peru.

DEAR SIR,   Febr. 1, 1619.

I shall now give you some account of that particular form of government which we have erected here, with the reasons which induced us to fix upon it.

As the safety and happiness of the whole nation ought to be the great end and design of every government, so we have endeavoured to keep this grand object always in view, and not to aggrandize one man, or set of men, to the prejudice and detriment of the rest. All men are here considered as brethren, united together in one band, to promote the common good. But as civil dissensions, turbulent factions, and precipitate determinations, are found by experience to be the constant effects of a popular government, we agreed that the citizens should chuse, out of their own body, a certain number of persons, called senators, who, in conjunction with the governor, should be invested with the supreme and legislative power. But as many inconveniencies are also found to arise from the execution of the laws by a number of persons, in whose hand the supreme power is lodged; it was agreed to commit the executive power to one man only, whom we call the governor. But as the governor may not always be possessed of proper abilities to conduct the reins of government, or may be disposed to execute such schemes, as may be destructive to the public good: his power is limited, and his authority carefully restrained by our laws.

Such in general is the form which we have established, as the best and wisest we could frame; and in which we endeavoured to guard against the evils and inconveniencies which attend the other forms. For history clearly shews us, that the absolute rule of one man only, if wholly independent of the rest, introduces tyranny and oppression: that where the supreme power is lodged in several persons, jealousies and factions are too apt to arise about precedence and superiority: and that a popular government is giddy and inconstant, rash and tumultuous, full of discord and confusion, and at last often ends in slavery to some eloquent and ambitious man, who puts himself at the head of the lower people, and erects a monarchy on the ruins of the popular government. But by the mixt form which we have settled, we have endeavour'd to secure our rights and liberties, to preserve a due balance, and keep a happy medium between the tyranny of arbitrary monarchy, the factions of aristocracy, and the anarchy, licentiousness, and wild tumults of a democracy.[^5]

I am indeed very sensible, that a monarchy would be the best form of government, if kings were always possest both of abilities suited to their exalted station, and of that uprightness and benevolence of heart, as to be always attentive to, and disposed to make the good of their subjects the sole and ultimate end of their administration.

---

[^5]: Licentiousness must be the ruin of every state, as it consists in doing whatever the will, appetites, and passions suggest. But true liberty desires only the freedom of doing what is agreeable to the dictates of reason; and the rules of religion: and steddily submits to, and chearfully obeys just laws, enjoined by proper authority; and is fully convinced that the preserving peace and good order, with proper reverence to persons in authority, are absolutely necessary for the happiness of every nation. – A certain person having advised Lycurgus to establish a democracy or popular government at Sparta, he wisely answered: Begin it first in your own house, and let every one there be as great a lord and master as another. *See Plutarch's Banquet of the Seven Sages.*[23]

[23]: Plutarch, *Septem Sapientum Convivium* (1711).

Two instances of this kind we have in Gelo and Hiero, kings of Syracuse in Sicily; who, though they first obtained their dominion by violent and unjust methods, yet afterwards became excellent kings. Gelo in particular seems to have reigned with no other view than to do good, from a zeal for the public welfare, and to make thousands of his fellow creatures happy. He established liberty without allowing licentiousness, and banished from his kingdom, luxury, pomp, and ostentation. He set his subjects an amiable pattern of piety and modesty, of a plain, industrious, and regular life. He contented himself with making the laws rule, and not his own will, was possest of a spirit superior to all tyranny and oppression, and carefully taught his subjects, that both himself and they ought to be governed by reason and wisdom. Such an excellent conduct and administration brought the highest reputation and glory to himself, and the greatest happiness to his people, by whom he was greatly admired and beloved.

Hiero, the second of that name and King of the same City, behaved with the greatest wisdom and justice for near fifty years, applied himself to root out idleness and luxury, the parents of many vices; to encourage frugality and industry, to bring agriculture into just reputation and honour, and to make his subjects universally happy. By his prudent conduct he secured to them the blessings of peace and a perfect tranquility for many years, while his neighbours were cruelly ravaging and destroying one another: and he shewed by all his actions, that his principal aim was to gain the love and esteem of his people; and that he considered himself in no other light, than as the protector and father of his country.

Add to these, Alfred king of England, justly surnamed the Great: who exhibited to his subjects an amiable example of a wise and regular self-government, of piety and steddy virtue. Under his auspicious reign learning was encouraged, vice and licentiousness were suppressed, corruption and venality discouraged, and tyranny and oppression banished. He was, in the truest sense, the father of his people, the defender of their property, the assertor of their privileges, and the founder and guardian of their liberties. In his wars, which were undertaken only in the defence of the nation, he was brave; in conquest humane; in council calm and deliberate; and in peace he consulted in the most effectual manner the good of his subjects, by enacting and strictly executing the most salutary laws; which will remain for ever, standing monuments of his eminent abilities, the integrity of his heart, and his ardent zeal for the common good.

Now, if all kings were possessed of abilities, integrity, and zeal for the public good equal to these: monarchy undoubtedly would be the most eligible form of government, and most conducive to the happiness of a nation. But how few of these are to be found? Search the histories of all nations, how seldom do they appear? Trace in your mind the characters of most kings, and you will find that covetousness, or the love of pomp and grandeur, or luxury and an unbounded indulgence of sensual pleasure, or else the lust of power and dominion, have been their predominant principles. The result of which has been, that arbitrary monarchs have frequently proved to be the plagues of the world. Who, without any just provocation, have invaded their neighbours territories, broke down the barriers of public faith and treaties, and trampled upon law, justice, equality, and every thing that is held sacred and venerable by God and man, to accomplish their tyrannical and ambitious views. Such were Alexander, Julius Caesar, and others of both ancient and modern fame; who by fawning flatterers have been styled heroes – heroes! rather the butchers of the human race, and the enslavers of the world! But unhappily these plagues of mankind, instead of being mentioned by historians with that Infamy, horror, and detestation which they deserve; have had their crimes palliated, softened and varnished over, been set up as objects of admiration and delight, and as the glory of human nature, meerly on account of their courage, and skill in destroying their fellow creatures, and in overwhelming whole kingdoms in desolation and ruin. Such are the illustrious worthies, who have been too often made the subject of Panegyric![']

But it were greatly to be wished, that historians were not only men of abilities and extensive knowledge, but also friends to liberty and

---

['] The number of men which Alexander murdered in his wars, is not given us in history. *Pliny in his Natural History*,[24] *B*. vii *ch*. 25. informs us, that Julius Caesar destroyed near one million, two hundred thousand of the Gauls, &c, besides those Romans that were slain in the civil wars, which perhaps were half that number: and without mentioning the millions of widows, orphans &c. which were made miserable by these destructions. Yet after all the misery, desolation, and ruin he brought upon his fellow creatures, only to raise himself to the imperial power, he was in quiet possession of it not above five months, when he was killed for his tyranny and usurpation. *See Vell. Patercul.*[25] B II. ch. 56.

[24] C. Plinius Secundas, *The History of the World* (1635), p. 168.
[25] Marcus Velleius Paterculus, *Historiae Romanae* (1730).

virtue: who would strip the tyrant of all his gaudy plumes, and display him as (what he really is) the enemy of God, and the curse of man, and with peculiar marks of infamy and abhorrence. Whereas on the contrary, those Kings who were a blessing to the world, and whose labours were consecrated to promote religion, peace, and virtue, and to make their subjects free and happy, ought to be painted in the most animating and lively colours, as the ornaments of mankind, and the glory of the human race. For the great end and design of history, is not meerly to serve for amusement, curiosity, or trifling discourse, but to give a just representation of facts, to free virtue from that mist and darkness, which the passions, prejudices, and follies of mankind have thrown around it, and display it in it's own intrinsic beauty and excellence: and likewise to shew vice (though dignified by great abilities, and blended with many shining qualities) in its own detestable colours, divested of that fictitious glare, which recommends it to the admiration of the vain and inconsiderate. And therefore such only as have just ideas of liberty, and understand wherein the true happiness of a nation consists, are rightly qualified to place the actions of kings in a just light, and, by their wise and judicious remarks, to improve our understanding, and direct our conduct."

" It is for want of such principles as these, that Voltaire, in his history of *Lewis the Fourteenth* of France,[26] calls it one of the four happy ages of the world, because plays and poetry, painting, sculpture and architecture, with an external civility and politeness, were encouraged and flourished. He also endeavours to represent him as a truly great king: and yet he acknowledges that he was a lover of the grossest flattery, fond of grandeur, pomp and ostentation, and an encourager of the greatest luxury, profuseness, and extravagance, all which sink and debase the human mind. – And *Keysler*[27] *(Vol. I. p.* 130) tells us, that he was so infatuated by flattery, that at opera's, and the prologues of plays, he would join in singing the most extravagant rants made in his own praise. – Instead of considering himself as invested with sovereign power, only to be the father of his people, and to make them happy; he tyrannised over them with unbounded licentiousness, making his own will and pleasure the sole rule of his government, without any regard to their happiness, or to their natural rights and liberties. Instead of giving them the blessings of peace, which is the foundation of all happiness and felicity, he forced great numbers of them from their houses and families, and all that was dear to them, to enter into his armies: and thus depopulated his dominions and destroyed many myriads of his subjects in unjust wars against other nations, only to promote, what he called his own glory. He broke through his most solemn treaties, employed his great wealth, and made use of every mean art, to set the neighbouring states at variance with each other, that he might the more effectually

[26] François Marie Arouet de Voltaire, *The Age of Lewis XIV* (2 vols., 1752).
[27] Johann Georg Keysler, *Travels through Germany, Bohemia, Hungary, Switzerland, Italy, and Lorrain* (4 vols., 1756).

Give me leave to conclude this letter with an account of some very remarkable and most excellent laws established by the first inca's or kings of Peru, of the truth of which some of our neighbouring Indians (who fled from thence when the Spaniards ravaged their country) have frequently assured us.

All the families of this empire were divided into tens, one of whom was appointed head over the other nine; and in every five divisions, one was made chief of the fifty; another of every hundred; another of every five hundred; and another of every thousand families: and in each province, he was made the chief, who was most able and willing to promote the public good. The head of every ten was obliged to give notice to his superior officer of any faults or irregularities committed by those who were under his inspection; and also to inform him of such as were in want, or had any accident or misfortune, that they might be immediately relieved. If any officer, either

avail himself of any opportunity which should offer, to gratify his ambition, and enlarge his dominions. And to support his unrighteous wars, and his extravagant pleasures, he raised immense taxes upon his people: for Voltaire assures us, that during his reign of 72 years, he spent, one year with another, no less than 330 millions of French livres of the present money; which, at ten pence farthing per livre, comes to about 14 millions of English pounds sterling: and amounts in 72 years to about 1014 millions of English pounds sterling. Moreover, he tormented thousands of his Protestant subjects in the most inhuman, cruel, and barbarous manner by his dragoons, and murdered or drove out of his dominions near half a million of them, because they would not implicitly subject their consciences to the tyranny of the papal power. – Now what idea can we form of such a king, but that of a bloody and oppressive tyrant, who was a curse to his own people, as well as to his neighbours, and who ought to be regarded with the greatest detestation and abhorrence? For shall that man be reckoned wicked and unjust, and be judged unworthy of life, who only robs another of a little money: and shall that king be called great, and be stiled a hero, who takes away immense sums from his own subjects, only to consume them upon his extravagant pleasures and unrighteous wars, who murders and destroys thousands of his own people; who unjustly seizes upon whole provinces belonging to his neighbours, and fills the earth with misery, slaughter and desolation? – How different from Lewis the XIV, is the excellent character of Gustavus Ericson, a king of Sweden; who never attempted to extend his successful arms beyond the deliverance of his own country: who carefully studied how to make his power beneficial to his people, compassionating their necessities, redressing their grievances, rectifying their dispositions, and correcting their vices, with the indulgent hand of a tender parent! And though he softened their rough tempers into humanity, by the innocent pleasures of life; he took care that they should not corrupt their manners, constantly restraining them from every abuse and excess, by the example of an irreproachable virtue in his own conduct. *See Raymond's History of Gustavus Ericson,*[28] *p.* 345, 346, *and* 398 *to the End.*

[28] Henry Augustus Raymond (i.e., Sarah Scott), *The History of Gustavus Ericson, King of Sweden* (1761).

of high or low degree, was remiss in his duty, he was punished for it: and if he neglected to indict an offender without producing a lawful excuse, he was not only liable to answer for his own default, but also to receive the punishment, which was due to the offender. And as every one of the lower officers had a superintendant over him, they were all diligent in discharging their several duties, by which means idleness, fraud, oppression, and every kind of vice was discouraged; and every one who suffered through losses was relieved. To prevent tedious and expensive law suits, every cause was tried and determined in five days, except in difficult and obscure cases. If any one of the superior officers was guilty of a crime, his punishment was greater than another's; it being an established maxim with them, that no crime was to be tolerated in magistrates, whose duty and business it was to set good examples, and to root out vice in others. And hence it came to pass, that in all that great empire, consisting of many nations and languages, and extending itself at last about 1300 leagues in length, and 100 in breadth, they had sometimes hardly one person executed in the space of a whole year.

They had such a veneration for the supreme God, that they never mentioned his name, but with the greatest reverence. They were taught to speak the truth justly and religiously; and if any one gave a false testimony in any affair of importance, he was punished with death. Every one had such a portion of land given him, as was sufficient to support himself and family: and such as were blind, old, or incapable of work, were maintained by the public: the lands also belonging to widows and orphans, and to such as were sick, &c. were tilled, sowed, and reaped by the joint labour of the inhabitants of that district. Yet none were allowed to be idle or exempt from labour; even the lame and infirm were not intirely excused; and children of five years of age were employed according to their strength and capacities, and were brought up to be obedient, modest and of an obliging behaviour; for not only their parents, but the heads of every ten, were answerable for their ill manners or bad conduct.

They were not allowed to change their habits or fashions, so that they wondered to see the Spaniards so often change theirs, and justly attributed it to pride and wantonness of humour. All profusion in banquets, and delicacies of diet were prohibited among them. They had a law in force among them, which they called the law of brotherhood: it obliged them to assist one another in plowing, sowing and reaping the land, and in building of houses, without any pay or reward. In short, most of their laws and customs were dictated by the rules of right reason and equity, and by the principles of goodness and benevolence. The sons of the Inca, and of all the chief men were brought up and enured to labour, were carefully formed to habits of piety and clemency, were taught to be impartial in administring justice, and to practise righteousness and virtue.[x]

I am, &c.

Letter IV.

The laws relating to the governor. This office is made hereditary in the male issue of Mr. Alphen: but an unjust and tyrannical governor may be deposed. His authority limited; has the power of mitigating the punishment due to offenders: may appoint a deputy to assist him: and is obliged every new year to deliver a public speech, with a copy of that which was delivered last.

DEAR SIR,   Feb. 22, 1619.

I have already told you, that Mr. Alphen was unanimously chosen our governor before we set out from our native country, to prevent any disputes which might otherwise have arisen among us on that head, upon our arrival at the destined place. And as elective kingdoms are subject to great tumults and disorders on the death of every king, before the nobles or people can agree in the choice of another, whereby the peace and happiness of the nation is greatly disturbed, and the kingdom often brought to the brink of destruction: we agreed that, in our state, the government should be hereditary for ever in the male issue of Mr. Alphen: and that on his decease, his eldest son should succeed him: or if his eldest son should be then dead, and had left any male issue, that then the eldest of them should succeed his grand-father.

It is difficult exactly to determine how a nation should treat a wicked governor: but as the happiness of the people, and the security of their rights and liberties, are the sole foundation and end of all government; it is certainly lawful for subjects to deprive him of his authority, when he uses his power in a manner which is plainly

---

[x] See this account confirmed in *De la Vega's Royal Commentaries of Peru.*[29]

[29] Garcia Lasso de la Vega, *The Royal Commentaries of Peru* (2 pts, 1688).

destructive to the public good, and becomes manifestly unjust, oppressive, and tyrannical. If therefore any of our governors should endeavour to become arbitrary and to enslave us; a majority of the citizens are allowed to present a petition to the senators, by which they are empowered and obliged to bring the governor to a public trial, to answer to the charges which are brought against him; and, if he is found guilty, to deprive him of his power, and then his next heir is immediately to assume his office.

The governor has no power to make any new law, or to abolish any old one; to lay any tax upon the people, or employ any one in any public service, without the concurrence of the senators. But his power consists in putting in execution those laws which are already made, in obliging all persons to conform to them, and in punishing those who violate them, in the manner which the laws direct.

As no good government can delight to punish offenders, meerly for the sake of punishing; and as a person may fall under the sentence of the law, who from the nature of the circumstances attending the commission of the offence, might justly claim a mitigation of the punishment, which would otherwise be due to such a crime: the governor has the power of reprieving any offender, or of lessening his punishment, agreeable to the rules hereafter laid down for that purpose.

The governor may appoint any one of the senators to be his deputy, and to act for him, in case of sickness or any other just cause: whose assent is equally valid with that of the governor himself, in making of new laws, and in everything else, to which the governor's authority extends. And the governor may change his deputy, when and as often as he pleases.

If at any time the next heir be under age, the governor is to appoint in his last will, one of the senators to be the deputy; who, in case of the governor's death, is to assume the same power, till the heir apparent attains to the age of twenty one years. But if there happens to be no deputy governor appointed, then as soon as the governor is dead, the senators are immediately to assemble, and chuse one of their own body into that office, till the heir is of age.

The governor is obliged to deliver a speech before the whole assembly at our quarterly meeting, at the beginning of every year. The design of which is to set forth the excellency of our constitution, to remind the magistrates and people of their several duties, and to point out the happy effects which must necessarily result to the community, from unanimity and a steady obedience to the laws. That which Mr. Alphen delivered to us the last new year, was as follows.

"My countrymen,
When we first determined to settle this colony, we endeavoured to establish it on the best of principles, liberty and the common good. To this end we took the most effectual methods in our power, to prevent tyranny and oppression, anarchy and confusion, by a wise, equitable and well balanced form of government. And to promote the happiness of every one, and encourage a simple, plain and industrious life, we assigned an equal portion of land to every householder.

Since then you now experience, and gratefully acknowledge the great blessings and advantages which have sprung from these regulations, let me intreat you to preserve your present happy constitution, to revere and obey its laws, which equally guard against the wretchedness and miseries of poverty, and the pride and insolence of riches. May neither the lust of power and dominion, the sordid love of wealth, the parade of grandeur, or the softness and effeminacy of luxury, be ever known among you: but may righteousness, goodness, industry and temperance adorn your lives and manners.

I, the governor of this land do publickly acknowledge, that I am not advanced to this station to acquire riches, to revel in pleasure, or to gratify any pride or ambition of my own; but to promote the public welfare of the state. And therefore I will endeavour, with the assistance of God, to discharge the trust reposed in me, by executing the laws with impartial justice and equity, and by endeavouring to make you happy, by as wise and prudent an administration, as lies in my power.

But as my endeavours alone can be but of little force and efficacy; unless you also in your several stations concur with me, I must intreat you who are the senators to assist me, by enacting wise and good laws, and by promoting a due obedience to them, without which the best system of laws, and form of government will be of no use.

Let me also call upon you, who are the Guardians of this state, the inspectors into the public lives and manners of the people, to consider the important trust which is committed to you. You are to watch over the whole community, to take notice of the first beginnings of vice and every irregularity, and to take care that the virtue and innocency of the nation be not corrupted. Remember that vice always creeps in by imperceptible degrees, and that if it's progress be not timely stoped, it will taint the principles and manners of a people to such a degree, as to render them licentious, and impatient of the restraint of wise and wholesome laws, which at last will end in the ruin of the state.

May every magistrate behave with wisdom, moderation, and goodness; guard against all pride, imperiousness, the love of power and precedence; and chearfully obey those laws which he enjoins others. May every one of us be careful to keep his own passions and desires under a proper regulation and government, without which we shall be very unfit to govern others: and avoiding all strife and contentions among ourselves, let it be our only study and emulation, who shall promote, in the most effectual manner, the good and welfare of the nation.

Permit me also to recommend it to you, who are the ministers of the gospel of Jesus Christ, to instruct your congregations in the great and substantial duties of the Christian religion, and to animate them to a constant and steady practice of all the private and social virtues. Inculcate upon them the greatest reverence and veneration of the Divine Being, which is the only solid foundation of every moral excellency, and of every worthy disposition. And take care that your own lives, your behaviour and conversation be truly worthy of your sacred character, wise and regular, sober and unblameable, that you may edify the people under your care by your good examples as well as by your instructions: and let the constant and uniform tenor of your conduct shew, that you truly believe what you preach and recommend to others.

I must also intreat you who are the masters of families, to bring up your children to be tractable and orderly, to behave with modesty, civility, and courteousness: and to enure them at home to such labour and industry as their ages will admit of, that they may not acquire a habit of sloth and idleness. Guard against a false love and foolish fondness on one hand, as well as too great severity on the other. Remember that if bad dispositions be not checked at their first rise, or subdued in the earliest parts of life; it will be found a work of great difficulty to root them out afterwards: and that the impressions which you give them early, and the habits which they then acquire, will greatly influence their future conduct. Teach them to be ashamed of every mean and base action, inspire them with a generous and ardent desire to do whatever is excellent and praiseworthy: and shew them that the right government of their appetites and passions, and the practice of piety, virtue, humanity and benevolence, are the noblest employments of their rational and moral powers, and the true source of happiness both here and hereafter.

Lastly, let us all remember, that the strength and welfare of every state, depend upon the harmony and union, the goodness and virtue of the individuals. May every one of us therefore seek after those things which are pure, honest, just and amiable; may we cultivate peace and friendship with one another, and unite together as brethren for the common good; and then, with the blessing of God, we shall always be a happy and a flourishing people".

I am, &c.

Letter V.

Every parish is a square of four miles on each side, and every twenty five parishes make a county. The choice of senators by the citizens: every senator must be above forty years of age, their times of meeting, &c. They are chosen for life, but may be expelled the senate for bad conduct. Every citizen must be a married man, a protestant, and not less than twenty-one years of age. No papist is allowed any share in the government, and why. Inspectors are chosen by the householders to watch the public manners and conduct of the people: must be citizens, and at least thirty years of age: their duty and power, &c. Rules observed in the trials of civil and criminal causes: they are tryed by a jury. No tortures nor cruel punishments allowed of; but such chiefly as tend to the good of the state, and the reformation of the offender. Under what restrictions the governor is permitted to mitigate the punishment due to offenders.

DEAR SIR,   Nov. 15, 1619.

The senate has divided the land into parishes, each of them being a square of four miles on every side:^y and twenty five parishes, or a square of twenty miles every way, makes a county; in the middle of which the county town is to be built.

---

^y In the original, it is one mile: now a Dutch or Rhineland mile is not quite three English miles and a half.

During the first century, the citizens in every parish chuse one senator, but after the expiration of that time, as our numbers will be greatly increased, two or more parishes are to join together in the choice of one senator, as the senate then in being shall determine. Every town also, which has above one hundred citizens dwelling in it, is to elect a senator. The choice is made by a majority of the citizens, dwelling in that town or parish: but no one can vote for two different places, nor can those who vote for a town, give their votes for the parish.

There shall not be at one and the same time, more than three senators, of any one family, so nearly related as first cousins, during the space of one hundred years from the commencement of the state: lest any family should acquire too great an influence in the national council.

No one is capable of being chosen a senator, who is not a citizen, and above forty years of age: that he may be a person of some knowledge and experience, and that we may not fall under the power and direction of rash and unexperienced young men.

The senate meets at the chief town, on the first Monday in January, April, July and October, and sits as many days as they please, not exceeding thirteen, lest we should degenerate into an aristocracy. The governor may also assemble the senators at any other time, upon giving them timely notice before-hand. And whenever a governor dies, they are to meet together as soon as possible to proclaim the new one.

The senate consists of the governor and the senators. The governor is always allowed two votes, and every senator only one; but if the votes should be equal, he is further allowed the casting vote. But no law or determination of the senate is of any force, unless the governor (or his deputy) together with a majority of the whole number of senators are actually present.

Every person once chosen a senator, continues so for life, or as long as he continues to be a citizen: but if he should become incapacitated for this station by old age, &c. or if his conduct should prove dissolute, oppressive, and unjust, then the senate can deprive him of this office, and order the town or parish which elected him, to chuse another in his stead. But to prevent any injustice in the two last cases, he may present a petition to the governor, to appeal to the citizens of the place, for which he is a representative: and then the governor (or his deputy) is to assemble the citizens of that place, and take their votes, whose determination is final. And further the more effectually to prevent all tyranny, oppression, and ill behaviour in any of the senators; the major part of the citizens in the town or parish, which chose him, may at any time present a complaint to the governor against him, and then the senate is publickly to try him, and determine whether there is sufficient reason to deprive him of his dignity or not.

No one can be made a citizen, till he is 21 years of age: he must also be a protestant, and to encourage marriage, he must be either a married man or a widower. And to discourage all manner of vice and ill manners, he must also first bring sufficient proof to the senate, on the testimony of several citizens, that he is sober, industrious and peaceable. If the evidence is satisfactory, he is then permitted to subscribe the laws of the land, and from thence forward is entitled to all the privileges of a citizen.

The senate has power to deprive any one of his citizenship, either for life or for any number of years, for great and flagrant crimes. And as every one's conduct is in a great measure influenced by his religious principles, we have excluded all papists from having any share in the administration; for the nature, genius and tendency of their religion is such, that it sanctifies all manner of oppression and cruelty to protestants, and therefore must naturally prove destructive to every protestant state, whenever it is in the power of the papists to overturn it; as universal history and experience shew. If therefore any of that sect should ever arise among us, a toleration is fully sufficient for them, without allowing them to enjoy any public office. And if either the governor, any of the senators, inspectors or other magistrates should embrace the popish religion, he immediately forfeits his citizenship, and consequently his public post and station, whatever it be.[z]

Though it is impossible to keep every one within the due bounds of order and decency: yet it is of the greatest importance to the well

---

[z] So in England we allow no Papist to enjoy any public office – What numbers of Papists there are in England, we may easily judge by this, that there were reckoned to be 100,000 of them in London and Westminster, in 1745: since which time they are much increased, if reports are to be relied on. *See Harris's Life of Oliver Cromwell,*[30] p. 304.

[30] William Harris, *An Historical and Critical Account of Oliver Cromwell* (1762). Modern accounts offer a figure of *c.* 115,000 for all Britain in 1720, and *c.* 70,000 in 1780.

being of every state to prevent disorders as much as possible, rather than to punish them when committed. We have therefore decreed, that persons should be chosen to inspect into the public manners and conduct of all the people, none excepted. These we call inspectors: they are obliged to inform against all offenders, that they may be brought to justice, and no crime escape it's proper punishment. They are also empowered to hear and reconcile any little civil disputes and differences: but any one may appeal from their judgement to the higher courts. Neither have they any power to try criminal causes, or to punish an offender: and if an inspector behaves ill or oppresses any one, the person injured may freely complain to the senate, who shall reprove or punish the inspector, according to the nature of the offence, and give full satisfaction to the injured.

Every inspector must be a citizen of a good reputation and character, and at least thirty years of age, and is to continue in this office for three years. In the country, the householders of every parish chuse six inspectors; but in the towns, their number is settled by the senate in proportion to the number of the inhabitants. One third part of them is chosen every year, and consequently as many go out of the office every year: thus the new ones are joined with such as have already had some experience in the office, are acquainted with it's duties, and have acquired a knowledge of the characters of the people whose conduct they are to inspect. And whoever has once discharged this office well for three years, is freed from any obligation of serving it a second time, unless it is his own choice.

Every inspector must, at the four quarterly meetings at the chief town, give the senate an account of the state and behaviour of the people under his care, and whether the publick roads, bridges &c. are in good condition. The senate at the same time examines into their conduct, that so none may be injured by them. And at the expiration of their office, the senate publickly approves such as have discharged their duty well, and punishes those who have been remiss and negligent, or tyrannical and oppressive. Thus though the inspectors are such only as the people themselves make choice of; yet since they are answerable for their conduct to the senate, they are obliged to be diligent and faithful in their office: and while we give them power to preserve the virtue of the nation, and to prevent vice from springing up among us; we carefully guard against their using it to the hurt or injury of any one.

To make the office of inspector the more honourable, no one (since the land has been inhabited ten years) can be chosen a senator, who has not served the office of an inspector for three years, and obtained the approbation of the senate.

I shall conclude this letter with some account of the regulations which relate to our trials and punishments.

All trials and law suits are public, and without any charge or expence: and every law is to be understood in its plain, natural, and obvious meaning. Every one may plead his own cause himself, or by a friend; but it must be done with plainness and sincerity; and whoever does it with artful evasions, and with a manifest design to deceive, is punishable for it: but no one is allowed to plead another's cause for money or reward of any kind, lest he should thereby be tempted to pervert justice, and conceal or disguise the truth. We also disallow of all nice and trifling disputes about words, and that eloquence which is often used to screen malefactors from their due punishment, and to palliate falshood: on the contrary we use the utmost diligence to find out the truth stripped of all disguise and borrowed ornaments, and determine causes with all the equity and dispatch that is in our power.[a]

The governor, or a senator appointed by him, presides at every trial: and eighteen persons are annually chosen out of every county by the senate, to be the jurymen to try the civil and criminal causes in that county for one year. They must be citizens and above forty years of age, capable of judging in all these affairs, and of uncorrupted honesty and integrity. The names of the whole eighteen are written on so many different papers, then folded up and put into a box, and

---

[a] How happy would it be for thousands, if these laws of the Cessares were universally adopted: for in some countries, the expences attending a law-suit through the several courts of judicature, especially in the chancery, are so enormous, and the causes are protracted for so many years, that many families are ruined by it: nay, one would think that law was designed there only to enrich the lawyers, and without any view of administring cheap, speedy, and impartial justice. – The king of Prussia has made a great reformation of such abuses in his country; and it were greatly to be wished that every king would follow so good an example. – At Naples, there is a weekly meeting of the heads of a society, consisting of two hundred gentlemen of the law, to examine the private grievances of the poor: and if any such is found to be oppressed, and his complaint to be well founded, a member of this society is nominated to undertake his cause; the expences of which are defrayed by the Theatine Convent, which has large endowments for this purpose. This is an institution, which must give pleasure to every humane and benevolent person. *See Keysler's travels, vol. II. p. 383.*

then nine of them are publickly drawn by a little child; these are to try the cause, and the verdict of the major part of them determines the case. But if it should happen that any of the jury should have an intimate and close connexion either by ties of blood or otherwise; or has conceived any enmity against either of the parties concerned: upon their being objected to, the president is to forbid his name being put into the box. And further, if any one thinks himself injured by the verdict of the jury, he may petition the governor for another trial by the senate; provided twenty citizens sign his petition, to shew that the appeal is not without just cause.

As the end of every good government is to promote the good of every individual, so far as is consistent with the good of the whole; every kind of punishment that is not calculated to answer this end, is barbarous and cruel: therefore racks and tortures of any sort to force confession are absolutely forbidden to be used among us, especially as confessions made by the force of them are well known to be no certain proof of guilt. So far also as the authority of the laws can be supported, and persons be deterred from the commission of the like offences, the reformation of the offender is always consulted by us. He must also make full reparation to the person he has injured:[b] and his punishment is such, as is of use and advantage to the state, such as fines for the public use, or the employing him in some difficult, laborious and necessary work.[c] The particular punishment of

[b] This is a just and equitable manner of proceeding; whereas in some countries, the injured person has in many cases no reparation made him, but must be contented with the punishment of the offender only, and even that is sometimes attended with a considerable expence. And in some cases the fines go to the king or sheriffs, &c. instead of giving any recompence first to the injured person. A most strange method of executing justice! – Neither is the reformation of the offenders consulted, but, instead of their being confined each in a separate cell, fed only with bread and water, and obliged to hard labour, that they might acquire the habits of sobriety and industry, they are generally permitted to be idle and slothful, and to drink as much strong liquors as they can pay for: and the least offenders are often confined in one common room with the greatest and most hardened criminals; by which methods those who would otherwise be reformed, generally come out of prison worse, than when they first went in. They are also absurdly removed from one part of the British territories to another; for what advantage can the state gain by transporting a felon from England or Scotland to the plantations in America. It is only infesting one part for the ease of another.

[c] This reminds me of a method used by the monks of the convent at Mount Sinai in Arabia. This mountain is very steep, and the steps are bad, and whenever a monk has committed any fault, he is obliged to mend some of the steps of the rock, according to the nature and degree of his offence. So also the culture of the lands round the

every crime is not always expressed in our laws, because it is very difficult to proportion them to every species of offence; nay there ought to be a great distinction made in the punishment inflicted on the same crimes, in different cases and circumstances: for such offenders as are obstinate and hardened ought to be punished with more severity, than those who are guilty through indiscretion and inadvertence: and a cool deliberate resolution to do evil, attended with an artful evasion to keep out of the reach of the laws, far exceeds the enormity of many crimes which are committed in the heat of passion, as they shew the heart to be more thoroughly corrupted. Therefore such offenders as seem to have a due sense of their crimes, and promise amendment, and can procure several citizens to sign their petition, and to be in some measure sureties for their future good behaviour, are allowed to present a petition to the governor, to desire a mitigation of their punishment, who in such cases has a full power to grant it, if he thinks it proper so to do. But no pardon is ever to be granted, without making some attonement for the crime; for lenity and compassion should always be regulated by justice and equity; and no nation can be happy, unless the wicked be restrained: nay, in some cases it is even necessary for the public good and safety, that they should be intirely cut off.

I am, &c.

Letter VI.

The ministers of every parish how chosen: No subscriptions to any human articles of faith required of them: No persecution for religious opinions permitted: A pastor or bishop of a church must be above thirty years of age, and ought to be a married man: Great care taken that they are of good and unblemished characters: Their salaries how raised, as no tithes are allowed of here. Of marriages and divorces. No one is allowed more than one share of land, from thirty-five to fifty acres, according to the goodness of the ground. Of widows and orphans. A law relating to the settlement of foreign protestants. Useful mines of coals, iron, &c. belong to the public. Some land

convent of Belment near Tripoli in Asia, is the penance for any misbehaviour in the monks. See *Van Egmont and Heyman's travels*,[31] *Vol.* II. *p.* 164 *and* 291.

[31] Joannes Aegidius van Egmond van der Nijenburg, and Jan Heyman, *Travels through Parts of Europe, Asia Minor, the Islands of the Archipelago* ... (1759).

is set apart in every parish, and is cultivated by the parishioners to defray the public expences. Of the education of children, and of public schools. Of the militia.

DEAR SIR,   Nov. 29, 1619.

It will now be proper to say something of our religious establishment, which shall be the subject of the first part of this letter.

Since we are dependent beings, receive our existence from God, and are indebted to him for every degree of happiness which we here enjoy, and can hope for hereafter: it is our indispensable duty to worship and adore him, to seek his favour, and to learn and obey his laws. We have therefore built a church in the middle of every inhabited parish, and also a house near it for the minister who officiates there, and who is chosen by the major part of the protestant members of that parish, who are above twenty one years of age.

The bible is our only rule of faith, and therefore no subscription to any human articles of faith, made by any nation, council or synod whatever, is required of any minister. He is only obliged to make a public declaration of his belief in God, and in Jesus Christ, and to promise that he will sincerely endeavour to conform his public preaching, and his life and practice, to the doctrines and precepts of our blessed Lord and Saviour as revealed to us in the New Testament.

No persecution is allowed of for religious opinions; and if any one reproaches another meerly on account of his religious sentiments, he is punishable for it. If any Protestants should dissent from the form of religious worship established among us, they have full liberty to chuse and maintain their own ministers, and to assemble themselves either in our churches at different hours, or to build new ones for themselves.

No one can be elected a pastor of a church till he is above thirty years of age, that he may have gained some knowledge and experience, though he may be chosen an assistant sooner. An assistant is chosen by the pastor, but must be approved by a majority of the members of the church, who are above twenty-one years old. No minister can have any civil or military employment. And every pastor or bishop of a church should also be a married man, according to the apostle's injunctions.[d]

---

[d] A bishop must be the husband of one wife. See I *Timothy III. 2.*

As every one naturally expects a great degree of purity, virtue, and sobriety from those, who take upon them to be the instructors of others; so it is of the greatest importance to religion, that ministers should be of good and unblemished characters, and live agreeably to their own exhortations; for otherwise their precepts (though ever so good) can have little or no influence upon others. Therefore the inspectors are enjoined to enquire into the moral character and behaviour of all the ministers of the established church, and of those who dissent from it. And where any are found faulty, they are to reprove them in private; but if that reproof should not produce the desired effect, they are then to lay the case before the senate; that thereby pride and imperiousness, hypocrisy, vice, and irreligion, may be represt or punished, and not be sheltered under the cloak of religion. And every minister who behaves ill, may be deprived of his office by a majority of the electors. But every one who behaves well, is treated with great respect, and held in high esteem among us, and is maintained out of the public stock; for no tithes are paid, nor are any revenues permitted to be given, to any church. And if such worthy ministers become aged, infirm, and incapacitated for their duty, they are nevertheless still maintained by the public, as long as they live.

With regard to marriages: the parties must appear publickly at the town-house with some of their relations and friends, before the governor, or a senator appointed by him; and there declare their desire to take one another for husband and wife, and then sign their names in a proper book kept for that purpose, and from that time they become man and wife. But no marriage is permitted, till the magistrate is fully satisfied that it is with the free consent of both the parties, and that neither of them are forced to it by their parents or guardians, as their future happiness must greatly depend upon their mutual love and esteem. And if either of them is under twenty-one years of age, they cannot be married without the consent of the parents or guardians. And when there is so great a difference of age between the two parties as twenty-five years, our laws will not admit of such an union, because the sentiments, taste, dispositions and tempers of youth and age are so widely different, that there can be no foundation for happiness.

No marriage settlement is allowed to be made upon a wife or any child, because every widow and orphan is provided for, by the laws of our land. And to prevent all domestic contentions, no wife has any property of her own, separate and distinct from her husband, but he is entitled to whatever money, goods or inheritance falls to her possession. But if a wife has any just reason to complain of her husband, or any child of it's parent or guardian, the senate is then empowered to redress their grievances, and to settle affairs as circumstances require.

The senate has power also to grant a divorce, with liberty to marry another, upon a just and substantial reasons being produced, such as adultery, or of five years absence from home, without being heard of during that space of time, &c.

I come next to the laws which relate to our estates.

I have already observed that one great design in establishing this colony, was to give every man a sufficient quantity of land for the maintenance of himself and family, but not to allow him to engross more: and therefore our laws strictly forbid any one to possess in his own right more than one share. Only the governor, the senators, and such other persons, who by their public office are obliged frequently to absent from their own estates, and to reside elsewhere, are further allowed a small spot of ground for a house and garden in the town where their public business lies; and which each of them enjoys so long only, as he continues in that office, and then it goes to his successor.

Every parish (which consists of four miles square) is divided into sixteen divisions, of a mile square. Every division is again divided into shares. A share contains about thirty-five English acres, if it is good ground, but never exceeds fifty acres, be the soil ever so indifferent.

Every married man is entitled to a share, but no person who has not been married, can have more than half a one. Any married person may succeed to another share left to him by another person, or which descends to him by inheritance: but in these and all other cases, he must, within the space of one year, surrender up his own share to the senate, or give it to some other person (whomsoever he pleases) who is lawfully qualified to receive it. Every share is numbered, and as soon as the senate has registered the owner's name in a book kept for that purpose, his title to it can never be disputed: so that estates are firmly secured to every person in this country.

Every one may chuse his share where-ever he pleases, with the consent of the senate: and when he dies, his widow possesses it as long as she lives, even though she should marry again, that marriage may not be discouraged: but she can have only one share, namely that of her first husband. And if he has left any child or children by her or by a former wife, she must maintain them, till they become qualified to receive estates elsewhere. And when she dies, the eldest son succeeds to the inheritance, but if he refuses to accept of it, it is offered to the second son, &c. But if a man dies without leaving any issue, he may by his last will dispose of his share, after the death of his wife, to any person he pleases who is lawfully qualified to possess it.

Every widow is entitled to her first husband's stock of corn, poultry, sheep, and cattle, and the necessary instruments for agriculture: also to half of his household goods and moveables: and the other half is equally divided among his children. But no widow, who has been married more than once, is allowed any part of the above-mentioned particulars, belonging to any of her other husbands, unless it is left her by any of their wills.

If at any time a number of foreign protestants should be desirous of settling among us, they shall not be allowed to live all together in one place; but shall be dispersed in different parishes and divisions, that they may be the sooner incorporated with us, and not continue a separate and distinct people.

All mines of coal, of iron, or any other useful mineral &c. also all medicinal waters, and whatever else is of public use and benefit, though they should be discovered in any person's share, belong to the public, for the use of every person, according to the rules established by the senate for that purpose. But a full satisfaction is given to every one, on whose estate they are found. But no gold or silver mines (if any such should ever be discovered) are allowed to be worked, lest they should excite some nation to invade us.

The senate has also a power to lay a yearly tax on every one's estate, payable in corn, cattle &c. to defray the expences of the public. But they have thought it more eligible at present, to set apart a quantity of land in every parish for public uses, which is cultivated by the joint labour of the inhabitants of each parish.

I now come to an affair which is of the greatest importance to the public welfare, I mean the education of children. This is a subject which has been discuss'd by many learned men, both ancient and modern. It has been frequently observed, that when the education of children is intrusted to their parents only, instead of instilling just and good principles into their tender minds, they have, either through ignorance, or blind indulgence, rendered them untractable, stubborn, and conceited, or indolent and effeminate, lovers of ease and pleasure, and impatient of labour. And when these habits have taken deep root, in early life, experience shews how very difficult it is to eradicate them. And when these vices become the characteristics of a nation, one may easily prognosticate the approaching dissolution of that state. Therefore our laws enjoin the senate to build a public school in every parish, and to appoint proper masters and mistresses for them, whither all Parents and guardians are obliged to send their children at such ages, and for so long a time as the senate directs. These schools are put under the care, not only of the senate, but also of the inspectors, who are directed to have a constant eye upon them, and to see that the masters and mistresses do their duty with fidelity; that good order and discipline be carefully established, that their diversions as well as exercises be well regulated, and that an equal regard be had to their moral character and behaviour, as to their health, and proficiency in learning. Here they are instructed in the principles of religion and virtue, justice and goodness, temperance and moderation, self government, modesty, a decent and obliging behaviour, with due respect and obedience to their superiors, and are early accustomed to labour and industry:[c] for half the day is spent in learning useful trades and employments, and the other half in reading, writing, and understanding accounts, with other branches of knowledge, suitable to their genius and inclination, and to their age and sex.

War is certainly the greatest evil on the earth, and productive of the greatest distresses, misery, and ruin: yet the ambition and wickedness of men make it necessary, that a number of persons in

---

[c] Xenophon in his institution of Cyrus,[32] has given us an account of the method of education used among the ancient Persians: by which they endeavoured not only to make them good and virtuous, but even to prevent their having the least inclination to do any thing that was base or dishonourable. They were educated in public schools under the tuition of such elders, as were thought to be the fittest for that purpose. They employed their time in learning the principles of justice and equity, were taught to be temperate and sober, to be obedient to the magistrates, to hate all animosities and disputes, and especially ingratitude: they were also instructed in the use of the bow, and exercised in shooting.

[32] Xenophon, *Cyropaedia; or, The Institutions and Life of Cyrus the Great* (1685).

every state should be qualified to oppose the enemies of their country, and to be the bulwark of liberty and property against the encroachments of rapacious invaders.⸍ Therefore every male from eighteen to sixty years of age (except those who are lame, blind and infirm) is enrolled among the militia, and trained up to the use of arms: they are frequently exercised in every parish, and four times in a year they all exercise together at the chief town, where they also shoot at marks, and rewards are publickly bestowed upon those, who shew the greatest dexterity and skill.

The governor has the supreme command, or can appoint another person to act for him. He also chuses the officers, fixes the times of their meeting together for exercise, summons them together in time of danger, and has full power to direct and order all their proceedings. We have also beacons erected in proper places, ready to be lighted at once on the approach of an enemy; that so the whole militia may immediately assemble.

The senate has power to employ the militia to erect fortifications, and to do whatever else is judged to be necessary for the safety and

---

⸍ Wars which are occasioned by pride, ambition, and a thirst after conquest or false glory, make a shining figure in history: the writer records with pleasure, and his readers too often peruse with admiration, those scenes of blood and cruelty, which depopulate countries, and make great numbers miserable nay, which even distress the subjects of the conqueror, by the great taxes levied upon them to defray the expences, and by the loss of the lives of thousands of his own people, to raise his fame. But sober reason is sensible of the miseries which spring from an ambitious king and lover of war, and looks upon the sufferings of his people, as a punishment inflicted upon them by God for their sins, when he gives them an heroic Prince. Yet such a one considers his victories and conquests as great and illustrious actions, meerly from an ignorance of what is truly great and excellent, those peaceful virtues of a king which dispense happiness to all his subjects, secure to them the quiet enjoyment of all their possessions, and make him the friend and father of his country. *See Raymond's history of Gustavus Ericson*, p. 375, 376, 380, *and* 381. – In how amiable a light does the little state of Geneva appear? A republic founded in wisdom and virtue: where we meet with no ambitious man making thousands wretched and augmenting the miseries of life: no legions of armed men, ravaging the world, and with the thunders of war disturbing the peace of mankind. But a people happy and free, who have defended themselves with bravery, against the various encroachments of tyrants and oppressors: a people who make temperance the guardian of their health; who endeavour by their laws to bar up every avenue to the blandishments of luxury; who carefully promote religion and virtue, infuse into all a tincture of learning, and form the character of a good citizen upon that of a good christian: who preserve the utmost harmony, and live together like one great family. *See Keate's Account of Geneva*,[33] 4, 5, 6, *and* 7.

[33] George Keate, *A Short Account of the Ancient History, Present Government and Laws of Geneva* (1761).

security of the nation. And if at any time we should have an engagement with an enemy; the senate is afterwards carefully to examine into the conduct of the officers and soldiers, and reprove, punish or reward them according to their behaviour. And all plunder taken from the enemy, is to be brought into the public treasury, to be disposed of as the senate sees fit.

We have as yet had no enemy to fight with, and consequently cannot say how we should behave in a time of battle: but if we may judge from appearances, it is very probable, that a body of men enured to labour, accustomed to discipline, and animated with the most ardent zeal for their families and liberties, would sell their lives very dear.

I am, &c.

Letter VII.

Every apprenticeship is dissolved at twenty-one Years of age. No cruelty to any animals permitted. None buried in churches. What crimes are punished with death. Of Debtors. Of Duels. Every head of a family answerable for the ill-behaviour of his dependents, and also every town or parish for the misconduct of those who live there. Of fish and game. Whoever injures another must make a proper satisfaction. No usury allowed of. Whoever unjustly injures another's character &c. is punishable for it. No immodesty, nor obscene books or pictures permitted. Of bad magistrates. Administration of Oaths. Of profane swearing or cursing. None can hold two civil or military offices; or two livings. The prices of food and labour fixed by the senate. Every person that is put into prison must work for the public good. Of the roads and carriages. Of slavery. Of stealing. Of sumptuary laws. Of gaming and plays. The office of the public Treasurer. Towns how to be built &c. Of trees and hedges on every one's estate. Every one gives his vote by ballot at all elections and trials. A stock of wheat is always kept for two or three years beforehand.

DEAR SIR, Jan. 10, 1620.

I shall now give you some of our laws upon several subjects, which I could not well reduce to any of the former general heads. But I would first observe, that all fines are applied to the public use, except such as are otherwise directed: and though we keep a book in which all these public fines are entered; yet at the death of every one, who has been thus punished for his offences, we blot his name out of the book, that it may be no longer publickly remembered, nor be a reproach to his children or relations.

When any persons attain to the age of twenty-one years, their service or apprenticeship is dissolved.

The same freedom extends also to every married person, though under that age, provided the marriage is with the consent of the master or mistress.

No cock-fighting nor horse-races, nor any thing that is contrary to the rules of humanity and decency of manners is allowed of among us, or that has the least tendency to render the mind cruel. And whoever treats his beast with cruelty or barbarity, forfeits that animal to the public, and is further fined according to the nature of the crime; for to treat the creatures (which are in our power) with kindness; and while we make them subservient to our use, to be pleased with adding to their felicity; shews a truly good and divine temper.[g]

[g] There is something very amiable in this compassion shewn to animals: whereas the English are remarkable for their ill treatment of many of them, particularly horses and cocks. They have an annual custom of throwing sticks at the cocks only for their diversion; while the poor innocent and domestic animal sends out his shrieks and mournful cries, as so many calls upon his tormentors for pity: till his toes being battered, his legs or wings broken, and his beak dropping blood, he sinks at last through pain and bitter anguish to the ground: a custom so cruel, as cannot be reflected upon by any humane person without horror. The fishermen also drive a wooden peg into the tender flesh of the claws of lobsters, while they are living, which must put them to exquisite pain. And in the fens of Lincolnshire, in the moors near Bridgewater in Somersetshire, and other places, they have a most barbarous practice of pulling out the quills, and plucking off the feathers of the live geese several times in a year. None of which cruelties would be practised, if we had a due sense of the principles of mercy and humanity; nor would any government permit them, that had a proper regard to the moral conduct of the people. See this subject well treated in *two Sermons on clemency to Brutes*,[34] *printed for Dodley in 1761.* – The Turks on the contrary will not suffer any animal to be injured or tormented, but severely punish all those who behave cruelly to them. They treat their horses in particular with much lenity and indulgence, and never beat them but in cases of necessity. This makes them great lovers of mankind, especially of their masters and grooms; and they are so far from being unruly or untractable by this gentle usage, that you shall scarcely find such a horse among them. See *Busbequius's Letters*,[35] p. 163, 164 and 175. – I would further observe that the supreme court of judicature at Athens, thought cruelty to animals not below their cognizance, when they condemned a boy for putting out the eyes of Quails. See *Quintilian*,[36] *B.* v. *Ch.* 9. The Athenians also expelled a member of the Areopagus, for treating a bird inhospitably, that took shelter in his bosom from a hawk.

[34] See *Clemency to Brutes. The Substance of Two Sermons Preached on a Shrove-Sunday* (1761).

[35] Augerius Gislenius, Seigneur de Bousbecq, *The Four Epistles of A. G. Busbequius Concerning his Embassy into Turkey* (1694).

[36] M. Fabius Quinctilianus, *His Institutes of Eloquence* (2 vols., 1756), vol. I, p. 311.

We allow no one to be buried in any church or place of public worship, lest any infectious exhalations should arise from the putrid bodies, and be hurtful to the congregation:[h] but proper burial places are laid out in the form of a square round every church, planted with aromatic shrubs and flowers in a beautiful and agreeable manner, and the graves are placed in streight and regular rows. And every one must be buried so early, that the persons who attend, may have time to return home before sun set.

Whoever shall endeavour to destroy the liberties of the people, and the constitution of the state; or shall discover to our enemies, the passages which lead to our country, shall be put to death as a traytor, even though he were the governor himself. Murder and adultery also are punished with death: unless it should appear in the last case, that the guilty party was drawn into the commission of that crime by the art and contrivance of the husband or wife. And all attempts to commit any of these crimes shall be severely punished with a fine and imprisonment.

When any one is unable to pay his debts, his creditors are to make an application to the proper inspectors, who are carefully to examine into the cause of such a failure, and report it to the senate. If the senate finds it to arise from losses, illness, or unavoidable misfortunes, his debts are to be discharged out of the public stock. But if he is found to be reduced by a criminal and faulty conduct, his goods are to be publickly sold to pay his debts, and he is further to be punished for his ill behaviour.

Whoever challenges another to fight a duel, and whoever accepts of such a challenge, is not only to be fined and imprisoned for one year, but also to be turned out of their citizenship, the first for seven years, and the other for three: and during the year of their imprisonment must stand exposed to public shame four times, for the space of one hour each time at our quarterly public meetings in the chief town.[i] But if any one kills another in a duel, he is accounted guilty of wilful murder, and is punished with death.

---

[h] I am much pleased with the following epitaph at Louvain. – "Philip Verkeyen doctor and professor of physic ordered his mortal part to be buried here in the church-yard: that he might not pollute the church, and infect it with noxious effluvia." *See Keysler's Travels, Vol.* I. p. 270.

This, I suppose, is like our pillory in England, and would be a very proper and ignominious punishment for our duelists. – Du Pratz in his *History of Louisiana, Vol.* II. p. 165, tells us, that if any of the young people there happen to fight (which he adds he never saw or heard of during the whole time he resided in the neighbourhood

The head or heads of every family are in some measure answerable for the faults and ill behaviour of every person in it, especially their children. And all the families in every town or parish are answerable for the faults or crimes of every person in it, unless they bring the offender to justice: that thereby it may be the care of every one to consult the good of the whole, and to permit no idle vagabond, nor publickly wicked or immoral person to live quietly among them. And whoever instigates or excites another to the commission of any crime, or is an accomplice with him, must suffer the same punishment with the offender.

All sorts of fish in the rivers, and all fowls, birds and animals which are wild, are free for every one to take and kill. But the senate has power to limit the seasons for fishing, hunting and shooting, and also the size of the fish, under which they ought not to be killed, that the game and fishery be not destroyed.

Whoever hurts or injures another, either in his person, house, goods, &c. through folly or carelessness, is obliged to make him such a satisfaction and recompense as the jury or senate shall determine. But if it is done designedly, he must make a full satisfaction, and pay a fine also. And whoever mocks or affronts any one, meerly on account of lameness, blindness, or any other natural infirmity, must make a proper acknowlegement to the injured person for his offence.

As we live upon our own small estates with very little trade, no one can receive any usury or interest from another for any money or goods lent to him: unless for good reasons, and with the consent of the senate.

Whoever wilfully spreads any lies or false reports of another, to injure his character and reputation, must publickly ask his pardon; and pay a fine both to the person injured, and also to the public. And if any one falsely asperses another's character, only for want of prudence and better consideration, he shall be punished as the jury or senate shall direct, that it may lead all persons to a habit of caution upon so very tender a point.

The more effectually to preserve innocence and modesty untainted, whoever talks or behaves indecently, and contrary to the rules of chastity and purity of manners, is punishable for it. And all immoral

of the Natches), they threaten to put them in a hut at a great distance from their nation, as persons unworthy to live among others.

and obscene books, prints, pictures &c; are ordered to be burnt; and those that have them, to be fined, as encouragers of vice.[k]

If a senator, juryman, or inspector, or any other magistrate accepts of a bribe or present from any one, on account of a cause to be tryed by him, he shall on conviction be deprived of his office and citizenship for ever, and be further fined or imprisoned according to the heinousness of his crime. For all bad magistrates are to be more exemplarily punished than others; as it is the very design and nature of their office to extirpate vice, and to be the guardians of innocence and virtue.

No oaths are administered among us, but on extraordinary occasions: and then they are given in the most solemn manner.[l] And whoever is guilty of perjury, is not only fined and imprisoned, but is deprived of his citizenship for some years. But if it clearly appears from the concurrence of several circumstances, that he wilfully designed by his perjury to have taken away the life of another, his punishment is death.

Whoever swears or curses, or uses the name of God irreverently, pays a small fine for the first offence, which is to be doubled every time he is guilty of it.

No one can hold two civil, or two military offices, or be minister of two parishes; as he cannot faithfully discharge the duties of both places at one and the same time.

The senate has power to fix the price of corn and cattle, of bread, meat, labour and all other things, to prevent any unjust combinations.

[k] Thus the Lacedæmonians caused the books of Archilochus, one of the greatest poets, to be banished from their city, because they thought them not modest or chaste enough to be read; lest the minds and manners of their children should be corrupted by them. *See Valerius Maximus,*[37] B. VI. ch. 3.

[l] To every good man it must be a melancholy consideration, that so great a number of useless and unnecessary oaths should be required for most offices among us: especially as some of them (particularly that of the churchwardens) are almost impossible to be performed; by which many persons become perjured every year. And the loose, trifling and careless manner, in which they are too often administered, prevents and destroys the very design of them. They are also lately introduced at the elections for members of Parliament, where the electors are sometimes sworn that they have received no manner of bribe or reward for their votes, though it is well known, how much bribery and corruption prevail. But were there a sincere regard and concern for religion prevailing among us, most of these oaths would be abolished, since they are found by experience not sufficient to restrain wicked persons, and only tend to increase perjury in the nation.

[37] *Valerii Maximi Libri Novem Factorum Dictorumque Memorabilium* (1726).

Every person who is imprisoned for any offence, must be employed during that time, in such laborious works, as are of publick use and benefit. And every bad husband, wife or child, every idle and drunken person may be confined by the senate in a bettering house,*m* and obliged to work.

All the public roads are about twenty-five yards broad, run straight and regular, have a causeway or foot path raised on one side, and at the end of every mile, have a stone erected, on which is inscribed the distance from one place to another. And none are permitted to encroach upon them by any sort of buildings, nor to plant any trees close to them without first having the consent of the senate. The senate has also fixed the breadth of waggons, carts, and all other carriages, and of their wheels, that the roads may be the better preserved. And as the body of the carriage is low, and the distance between the two opposite wheels is ordered to be about seven feet, we seldom hear of any unhappy accident befalling them; for if a wheel or the axle tree breaks, the carriage only leans on one side, and seldom or never overturns.

Since we are all brethren, and God has given to all men a natural right to liberty, we allow of no slavery among us: unless a person forfeits his freedom by his crimes.*o*

---

m They have in Holland houses of correction called by this name; in which dissolute, idle, and drunken persons are confined till they are reformed and made better.

o It is surprizing that the English, who shew the greatest abhorrence of slavery, should act so contrary to so noble and generous a principle, and carry every year so many thousand negroes from their own country, their families, and every thing which is dear to them, and plunge them and their posterity into a state of perpetual and irretrievable bondage. They are chiefly transported to the West Indies, where too many of their English masters have but little religion, and less humanity. In some places, no day is exempted from labour, except Saturday afternoons and Sunday: and the negroes are obliged to work on the grounds which are allotted them for their own subsistence, which is chiefly yams. In other places where their provisions are given them, a pint of Indian corn, and a herring is all the food they are allowed during a hot and toilsome day, that their masters may be idle, rich and luxurious. – Surely sugar and tobacco &c. are not so absolutely necessary to our happiness, as to justify such inhuman and cruel proceedings! – The chief argument alledged in favour of this trade is, that these slaves are taken captive in war, and might perhaps otherwise be sacrificed to their Gods. – But in truth and reality, it is the Europeans themselves, who are often the authors of the wars among the African negroes: and it is to purchase our brandy and other goods, that they not only waste and depopulate their neighbour's territories, but sometimes even their own country, to procure slaves for us. Thus *Moore, in his travels into Africa,*[38] *p.* 65, 66, 87 *and* 91, tells us, that when the king of

---

[38] Francis Moore, *Travels into the Inland Parts of Africa* (2 pts, 1738).

Whoever steals any thing from another, or cheats or over-reaches him, must make some restitution to the person, and pay a fine to the public. If the thief or cheat cannot be found, then the town or parish must make such a satisfaction to the person for his loss, as the judges or senate shall determine.

The senate is enjoined to establish sumptuary laws, and carefully to guard against the first introduction of all sorts of luxury: and to prohibit all those arts and trades, which minister only to idleness and pride, and the unnecessary refinements and embellishments of life, which are the certain fore-runners of the ruin of every state. And though it is very commendable to be neat and cleanly in our apparel, yet nothing is more contrary to a wise and rational conduct, than to lay out too much thought and expence upon it; and a frequent change of fashions shews a vain and trifling mind. The senate have therefore regulated every one's dress according to their age and sex: it is plain, decent and becoming, but no diamonds or jewels, no gold or silver lace, or other finery are allowed of, lest pride and vanity, the love of shew and pomp should steal in among us by imperceptible degrees. Only fools and ideots are obliged to wear some gold, silver, or fine laces, to distinguish them from those of better sense. An effeminate fop or beau (being a disgrace to men) is to be fined and employed in the bettering house in some dirty and laborious public works: and

Barsally wants goods or brandy of the English, he ravages some of his neighbours towns, seizing the poor people, and selling them for such commodities as he wants. But if he is not at war with any of his neighbours; he then falls upon one of his own towns, and uses his own subjects in the same manner. – Another argument made use of to justify the slave trade is, that the white people cannot work the sugars and tobacco; and that therefore if we did not employ negroes, the French and Spaniards would engross all that trade. To which I answer, that if our colonies had no slaves at all, they would very probably soon find out some easier method of cultivating those plants. But if they could not do this, yet I cannot see, how any nation can be justified in doing what is contrary to all the laws of nature, goodness and humanity, only to get money and aggrandise themselves. If this may be done in any one article, what can prevent it from being extended to every thing else? – The number of persons carried every year from Africa into slavery is exceeding great: for the learned author of *the importance of the African expedition to the River Senegal* [39] assures us, that in the year 1725, the Portuguese alone carried away one hundred thousand slaves, and the other Europeans as many. – And though it is the interest of the planters to treat them with humanity, and to make their slavery easy to them, that they may be the better able to endure labour, and live the longer: yet *Hughes*, in his *History of Barbadoes* [40] p. 14, says that their hard labour, and often the want of necessaries destroy a number of them.

[39] Malachy Postlethwayt, *The Importance of the African Expedition Considered* (1758).
[40] Griffith Hughes, *The Natural History of Barbadoes* (1750).

the more effectually to curb the desires of the female sex, and keep them in due bounds in these particulars; it is decreed, that if they dress above their rank, or contrary to the laws, they shall not only be fined for it, but shall be obliged to appear abroad for one year afterwards, in a dress below their station, as a just punishment for their vanity and love of ostentation.[p]

We also forbid cards, dice and all games of chance, under the penalty of fines and imprisonment in a bettering house. Nor are plays, interludes or theatrical entertainments allowed of, among us, nor any public places of expence and pleasure, lest they should hurt our morals or effeminate our minds; encourage indolence, and seduce the industrious from their necessary business and employments, which would soon render labour and diligence disagreeable and irksome, and consequently prove the ruin of our state.[q]

The governor appoints a treasurer to receive the public fines and

[p] Thus at Geneva, a chamber of reform, which meets once a week, is instituted to prevent (if possible) the introduction and increase of luxury. This regulates the dress of both men and women, and forbids them to have any fine tapestry, paintings or looking glasses above a certain value. *See Keate's Account of Geneva, p. 158,* &c. – Our lives and manners are in some measure influenced by our dress, and therefore, as *Dionysius of Halicarnassus, B.* VII[41] tells us, when Aristodemus the tyrant of Cumæ wanted to corrupt and enervate the young men there, he commanded them to let their hair grow in the fashion of the young women, to wear flowers and curls, and to tie up their curls in little bags of network; to dress themselves in embroider'd coats reaching down to their ancles, to cover themselves with soft cloaks, and to live in the shade: they were also taught to dance, and to play on the flute and other kinds of musick, being attended to these schools by women servants with umbrellas and fans. – Being educated thus till they were twenty years of age, how soft and effeminate must they become, unfit for any thing that is excellent and valuable, and shamefully attached only to foppery, dress and trifles?

[q] The prohibiting public plays &c. among the Cessares, seems to be very just and right, in such a state as theirs is. For though the theatre (if well regulated) might be made a powerful instrument to inspire public virtue, and the most noble and exalted sentiments: yet experience shews us, how it degenerates into trifling and ludicrous entertainments, and too frequently excites vicious ideas. Besides which, dress, action and elocution are too apt to inflame the passions, instead of bringing them under the wise and regular government of calm and sober reason. It also greatly tends to seduce people from their business, and to make labour and industry disagreeable to them. For these reasons the people of Geneva will not suffer a theatre to be erected in their territories. And *Rollin, in his ancient history,*[42] *Vol. V. B.* 10, shews, how the passion for theatrical entertainments at Athens, was one of the principal causes of the degeneracy and corruption of that state.

[41] Dionysius Halicarnassus, *The Roman Antiquities of Dionysius Halicarnassus* (4 vols., 1758).
[42] Charles Rollin, *The Ancient History of the Egyptians, Carthaginians, Assyrians, Babylonians, Medes and Persians* (1732–8).

taxes, and to take care of the public money, stock of wheat, &c. The senate fixes the salaries allowed the governor, the ministers, public school-masters, and whoever else employs his time in the service of the public; which are paid them by the treasurer. And the governor is further empowered to order him to pay such allowances as he judges proper, to those who are sick, aged, or incapable of supporting themselves, and also to give rewards to the authors of any useful inventions. An exact account of all which is constantly kept by the treasurer, which any citizen may freely examine.

Before any town can be built, the ground is carefully examined, or bored, that if any useful mines of coal, iron &c. should be discovered, no buildings may be erected thereon, but it must be left for the public benefit. The streets of every town are laid out by the governor, or one appointed by him; are thirty yards broad, straight and regular, crossing one another at right angles. And as all the houses in the same street (public buildings excepted) have the same appearance, form and dimensions, the streets are uniform and regular, and no one outvies his neighbour: but in the back part of the houses, in the yards, gardens &c. every one may build as he pleases, provided he does not injure, overlook or darken his neighbours. Proper regulations are also made, that every town may be kept clean; and no nusances are permitted, nor any noisy, unwholesome or disagreeable trades allowed of in the streets; but for all such, proper places are assigned at a distance.

As our estates are but small, no one is permitted to plant any trees, so near as to spread any of their branches over his neighbour's grounds. The hedges on the south and east sides of every one's share, belong to the owner of that share, together with such other hedges as border on the public roads: and he is obliged to repair and constantly to keep up these bounds, and is answerable for whatever damage arises from a neglect of it.

At the trials of all civil and criminal causes, at the elections for senators, jurymen, inspectors and all other magistrates, and in all affairs transacted in the senate &c. the votes are given by ballot, that every one may vote freely, and without any restraint: and that bribery and corruption, as well as personal feuds and animosities, may be prevented. No one is allowed to vote in any cause, in which he himself is concerned. Nor can any one vote by proxy, those only having a power to vote, who are actually present.

The senate is enjoined to see, that there is always kept a public stock of wheat, sufficient to serve the whole nation for two or three years, to supply the inhabitants in any time of scarcity.'

Lastly, since history informs us, that great changes and revolutions have happened in most states, from the selfish or wicked views of one or more persons, who, to gratify their own ambitious or revengeful passions, have made no scruple to destroy the wisest government, and the best laws and regulations for the public good: so if this should ever be the case in our land; let him who shall restore our laws and constitution again to their original force and influence, be called *the father of his country.*

I am, &c.

Letter VIII.

A description of the country. The situation of Salem, their chief town, and how it is built. Of the public roads, and division of the land into shares. The estates being but small and well cultivated, the country appears very beautiful. They allow of no luxury or expensive fashions, rejecting the pride and pomp of other nations, and the unnecessary refinements and embellishments of life. What their food chiefly consists of. They drink but little beer or wine, but have grateful teas, and milk in plenty. Their employments. Their labour not great, and shewn to be moderate from the consideration of the small number of persons, who in other countries provide all the necessaries of life. Their great harmony and union, and what it is owing to. None

---

Chardin, in his travels into Persia[43], *p.* 74, informs us, that the Tartars and all the country people in the East, store up their corn and their forage in deep pits under ground; which they cover so exactly, that only they who made the pits can tell where to find them. – The Hungarians lay up their corn in caves under ground. *See Brown's travels,*[44] *p.* 7. and *Varro de Re Rustica,*[45] *B. I. ch.* 5. tells us, that corn will keep good fifty years in the ear in Italy, provided it is shut up close in subterranean pits or caverns, and inclosed on every side with straw. – But in 1707, a granary was discovered at Mentz in Germany, which had lain concealed 154 years; and the corn was found under a stratum of clay or loam, without being the least damaged. See *Keysler's travels, Vol.* IV. *p. 192.*[46]

[43] John Chardin, *Sir John Chardin's Travels into Persia* (1705).
[44] Edward Brown (i.e., John Campbell), *The Travels and Adventures of Edward Brown* (1739).
[45] Marcus Terentius Varro, *Rerum Rusticarum* (1515).
[46] See Johann Georg Keysler. *Travels through Germany, Bohemia, Hungary, Switzerland, Italy and Lorrain* (4 vols. 1756–7).

*poor or in want among them. The author concludes with a pathetic descrip-
tion of the happiness of their state.*

DEAR SIR,   Mar. 6, 1620
I come in the last place to give you some account of this country;
and of our employments, and manner of life.

As the country round about us is not inhabited, we have a very
considerable tract of land which we call our own. It is bounded on
three sides by high and craggy rocks and mountains, and on the
fourth by a large river, which for a considerable part of the year rolls
with such a torrent, as to render it difficult and hazardous to cross
it. The climate is temperate, the air healthy, the soil fertile, and the
face of the country very pleasant.

Our chief town is called Salem, to remind us of that peace and
union which ought to reign among us. It is laid out in the form of a
square, is about a mile on each side, and situated near the middle of
our country, on a large fertile plain on a moderately high ground: at
a distance from woods, marshes, lakes or stagnant waters; but has a
fine stream of clear and wholesome water, which, at it's entrance into
the town, being divided into several channels, runs through most of
the principal streets.[1]

---

[1] By this description, the town of Salem is extremely well situated. For if a town stands
too high, the air is sharp and bleak: if it stands in a low valley, it is generally damp
and unhealthy. If it is built in too confined a place, shut up and surrounded with high
hills, the free course of the wind and air is prevented, and it becomes unwholesome,
and is very hot in the summer. If it is seated on the side of a hill, or is built on several
little hills, it is very troublesome and uneasy both to the inhabitants and their horses,
to be continually going up or down hill. But a moderately high and level ground is
certainly the most convenient situation, as well as the most healthy. If a town is
surrounded with large woods, they prevent the free circulation of the air, make it
damp and unwholesome; and all low, marshy grounds, fens, lakes and stagnating
waters give bad exhalations, and produce agues and putrid fevers. – Thus Rome
becomes sickly, whenever the southern winds prevail, which come from the neighbouring fens and morasses: and the fevers which rage at Bareith in Germany every
year, are thought to be owing to a large lake near it; a great part of which is over-run
with weeds, which rot in autumn, and send out noxious effluvia: the cities also of
Ravenna and Stutgard are become more healthy, since the neighbouring marshes and
ponds have been drained. *See Keysler's travels, Vol.* II. *p.* 29. *and Vol.* III. *p.* 70 *and
Vol.* IV. *p.* 167. – Besides these things, the soil should also be considered, for a rocky
soil is very disagreeable and barren, is cold in winter, and hot in summer. A clayey
soil retains the rains, and consequently makes the air damp and unhealthy. A chalky
and a sandy soil are generally dry and wholesome, but they are not very fruitful: the
first is slippery after rain, and the water of the last is scarce and seldom good. But
the best soil in almost all respects is a good mould, a little inclining to a sand or
gravel: or else a good brick earth, which last is the most fruitful.

This town is as yet but thinly built and inhabited, but is laid out in the following manner. The streets are a mile long, and about thirty yards broad, run quite streight and regular, and cross one another at right angles. And the name of every street painted in large letters, and fixt up at every corner. The houses are neat and plain, and exactly of the same form and size, which makes an agreeable uniformity in all the streets. They are built at some little distance from one another; to enjoy a more free air, and to prevent accidental fires from spreading their flames to the neighbouring houses.*ᵐ* And we allow every house a little spot of ground for a yard, garden and other necessary uses: the whole with the house being about fifty two yards in front, and 129 in depth. The houses are low, consisting only of two floors, but have several rooms on each floor, and are covered on the top with a terrace, where in the summer we frequently enjoy the fresh air. Nor must I omit to mention, that in the middle of the streets, aromatic trees and shrubs are planted at proper distances, to perfume the air, and render it the more healthy.*ⁿ*

Several of our public roads are finished, and many more are marked out over a considerable part of the country. They are twenty-five yards broad, run in streight lines, cutting one another at right angles at every mile's distance; and thereby divide the land into squares of a mile on each side. Every such square is divided into shares, between thirty-five and fifty acres, according to the nature and fruitfulness of the soil. And the owner of every share builds a house near the middle of his estate, that he may the more easily cultivate every part of it.

Thus the inhabited part of the country, being divided into small

---

ᵐ Juan and Ulloa assure us, that there is a certain tree at Panama, with which they build their houses; which has this property, that if any fire is laid on the floor, or against the walls built with this wood, it only makes a hole without flaming, and is generally extinguished of itself by it's own ashes: *See their voyage to South America,*[47] *Vol. I. p.* 119. – In *The Laboratory, or School of Arts,*[48] it is said, that, if equal parts of brickdust, ashes, and filings of iron, be put into a pot with glew water, or size, and set on the fire till it is warm; and then be well stired together; the woodwork, which is well washed over with it, and again once more, when it is dry, will be proof against fire.

ⁿ These must make the town extremely pleasant and healthy, owing to the grateful effluvia which they emit. And it is remarkable, that the isle of Ternate in the East Indies, became sickly, as soon as the Dutch cut down their clove trees.

[47] Antonia de Ulloa, *A Voyage to South America* (1758).
[48] Godfrey Smith, *The Laboratory, or School of Arts* (1739), pp. 158–61.

shares, is well cultivated and improved: and the houses being built
at a distance from each other, surrounded with gardens and orchards,
with arable fields, and green pastures abounding with sheep and
cattle, the whole land presents a most delightful and agreeable prospect, and appears like one beautiful and fruitful garden.

I am sensible that to those who place their chief happiness in
pomp, grandeur and the refinements of luxury, we must appear in a
mean and despicable light, void of all taste and delicacy, because we
have no gold or silver to boast of, no sideboards of plate to make a
show of, no grand houses, no sumptuous furniture, no fine or gaudy
apparel, nor any foreign trade and commerce to introduce among us
those expensive fashions and needless superfluities, which come by
degrees to be considered as the real necessaries of life.* Our fields
and gardens, our flocks, herds and poultry are our only riches, supply
all our wants, and with these we are contented, being happily ignorant
of the vices of other nations, and free from the desire of those foolish
refinements, and vain embellishments of life, which cause so many
persons in Europe to destroy the peace of their own minds, and to
involve themselves and others in difficulties, want and ruin. We on
the contrary are extremely careful to prevent the introduction of
luxury, and of that pride of life, which are the bane of public virtue,
the great source of corruption of manners, and have been the ruin
of all the most flourishing states in the world.*

---

* Scopas the rich Thessalian, being asked by a friend for a piece of furniture, which
he thought was of no use to him, because it was superfluous. He replyed; alas, my
friend, the chief happiness of our lives consists in those things which are useless and
superfluous, and not in those which are necessary. *See Plutarch on covetousness, and
his life of Cato the Censor.*[49]
* So long as the Persians, Greeks and Romans were poor, and lived temperately, they
were free, virtuous and happy: but as soon as riches came among them, they immediately sunk into an effeminate and luxurious life. Then selfishness and ambition, a
general disregard to the public good, and a universal dissoluteness of manners succeeded, and they soon lost their liberty and virtue. *See Montagu's reflections on the rise
and fall of the ancient Republics.*[50] – Cyrus having asked Croesus, how he could most
effectually enslave the Lydians, who had revolted from him: he advised him to
debauch their manners, and to encourage intemperance among them: for the chains
of luxury are easily borne, and the hardest to break of any in the world. Accordingly
Cyrus commanded their arms to be taken from them, erected taverns, gaming houses

[49] *Plutarch's Morals* (5 vols., 1684–94), vol. II, pp. 112–37; *Plutarch's Lives of the Illustrious Greeks and Romans* (1713), pp. 116–24.
[50] Edward Wortley Montagu, *Reflections on the Rise and Fall of the Antient Republicks*
(1759).

You may possibly think that thirty-five or even fifty acres of land, are not enough to support a man who has a large family: but we find

and stews; enjoined them to wear vests and buskins, and to teach their sons to sing, to play on the harp, and to frequent the public houses. And thus that nation which before was remarkable for their industry and valour, now dissolved in ease and luxury, soon became a prey to their own sloth and laziness. *See Justin,*[51] *B.* I. *ch.* 7. *and Herodotus,*[52] *B.* I – And to persons, who know any thing of the extravagance which prevails in many parts of Europe, it must plainly appear, that there are several states in it, which seem to advance with a rapid progress to their ruin. *Stanyan in his Account of Switzerland,*[53] *p.* 147, 148. tells us, that even the Switzers, who have been remarkable for many ages, for great candour in their dealings, and simplicity in their dress and manners, have of late years had luxury and corruption of manners introduced among them. And that with regard to dress, if the magistrates had not wisely interposed, and put a curb upon their vanity by prohibiting all costly apparel, they would very probably have ruined themselves by it. And this account is confirmed by *Keysler, Vol.* I. *p.* 2, *and* 3. who assures us, that even in Switzerland, luxury, pomp and an infatuation for every thing that is foreign and costly have lately spread themselves, though good regulations have not been wanting nor proper endeavours to restrain them: but it is there, as it is in other places, many wholesome laws are made, but little observed. At Geneva, the very richest inhabitants are not allowed a service of plate in the city; and on that very account it is the more frequent and costly at their country houses. And in some parts of Switzerland, where the women are still under sumptuary laws, in respect of fine cloaths and new fashions; they repair, as soon as the summer permits them, to the German Spaws, there to give a full scope to their gaiety, in spite of any restraints of their own laws at home. – I wish I could say better things of the English, but what vast sums of money are now dedicated to pleasure among us, squandered away upon finery and trifles, lost in gaming, lavished away upon delicacies and profuse entertainments, and dissipated in levity and folly, in sensual gratifications and indulgencies, instead of being employed for the good and happiness of others, in generous and benevolent actions, while so many of their fellow creatures are poor and miserable about them? Our numerous taverns and ale-houses encourage idleness, drinking and unnecessary expences, and are the bane and ruin of many: and our places of public diversions administer so many temptations, that people must have a great deal of resolution and self denial, to stem the torrent of an idle and pleasurable life, and not be led into a greater expence than their income will support. And even those young persons who are still educated in a sober frugal and virtuous course; yet for want of experience and knowledge of the world, they are soon carried away by the stream of custom and fashion into the paths of gaiety and pleasure, which often end in vice and ruin. *Mr. Cole, in his discourses on Luxury,*[54] justly observes, that an ostentatious extravagance is continually displaying itself at London amongst all ranks and conditions of men. An emulous endeavour to outvie each other in all the elegant accommodations of life, seems to be not only the ruling principle of a few, but the main ambition of a vast majority, the characteristic and almost universal passion of the age. Insomuch that it is doubtful, whether the commerce of vanity and intemperance be not the principal traffick of the nation; and whether vice and folly do not support as great a trade amongst us, as all the arts and sciences, which are any wise necessary

[51] Trogus Pompeius, *Justin's History of the World* (1702).
[52] *Herodion's History of his Own Time* (1749).
[53] Abraham Stanyan, *An Account of Switzerland, Written in the Year 1714* (1756).
[54] Thomas Cole, *Discourses on Luxury, Infidelity, and Enthusiasm* (1761).

it fully sufficient.[q] We have not only corn of all sorts, beeves, sheep and hogs, but plenty of fowls, ducks, geese, turkies and pidgeons; the neighbouring mountains also afford us goats, wild fowl and game; and our rivers and brooks are full of fish. Our gardens and orchards supply us with most of the fruits, herbs, pulse and roots which grow in Europe, besides those which are the natives of this country: and in the summer we dry many of our figs, grapes, and other fruits for our winter stores. Our bees also give us abundance of honey; and we have such plenty of chesnuts, that we feed our hogs with them, which makes their flesh very good, firm and wholesome.

We drink no distilled spirits, except in cases of sickness: and but seldom wine, beer or such fermented liquors: and bring up our children to water only. It is to this abstinence that we attribute in a great measure our robust and healthy constitutions, and the calm, free, and undisturbed exercise of our rational powers[r]. Nor do we want grateful teas,

---

or, serviceable to the common-wealth. – I shall conclude this note with *Middleton's* remarkable words in his *life of Cicero*,[55] *Vol.* 1 *p.* 495. England, says he, is become the seat of liberty, plenty and letters, flourishing in all arts and refinements of civil life, yet running perhap's the same course which Rome itself had run before it: from virtuous industry to wealth; from wealth to luxury; from luxury to an impatience of discipline, and corruption of manners: till by a total degeneracy and loss of virtue, being grown ripe for destruction, it falls a prey at last to some hardy oppressor: and with the loss of liberty, losing every thing else that is valuable, it sinks gradually again into it's original barbarism.

[q] From the best enquiries I can make, I find that nine acres of good arable land are enough for any family for all sorts of corn: three of which may be sowed one year with wheat, and then lie fallow for one year, and on the third year be sowed with barley, oats or pease for their horses, hogs and poultry. One acre together with their hedges, would be sufficient for timber, and underwood for firing, if they should have no coal, peat or turf. The house, yard, barns and stable, might take up one acre more: and two acres of garden ground would be enough for all sorts of fruit, herbs and roots. And the remaining land would afford sufficient pasture for two or three cows, as many horses, and twenty sheep, which seems to be as much cattle as a Cessarean would desire. And if their garden was too small, they might plant some fruit trees for an orchard at proper distances in their fields. – The trustees of the colony of Georgia gave every man fifty acres, without any regard to the goodness of the ground: of which they were allowed a little spot of sixty feet in front, and ninety feet in depth in a town, and the rest in the country. *See Moore's Voyage to Georgia, p.* 7.

[r] My author agrees here with *Sydenham*, who observes that water is at this time, the common drink of the greatest part of mankind: who are happier in their poverty, than we are with all our luxury and abundance. This is confirmed by the many diseases, with which we are afflicted on this account: besides the injury done to the mind by volatilizing it too much, and suggesting vain and idle thoughts instead of solid reasonings: and thus rendring us drolls and buffoons instead of wise men. *See the*

---

[55] Conyers Middleton, *The History of the Life of Marcus Tullius Cicero* (2 vols., 1741).

which we make of the wholesome herbs, that grow among us or on the neighbouring mountains, which recruit our strength and revive our spirits, without intoxicating the head. We are also lovers of milk, and have plenty of it: and I dont doubt but you will readily recollect the excellent character, which Homer gives the ancient Scythians, when he calls them *Milk eaters, the most just of men*, because they had few wants, and were contented with a plain and simple diet.[s]

Our chief employment consists in gardening and husbandry, and looking after our flocks and cattle: an employment the most innocent and useful, nay even the most indispensable of all: and which alone affords an abundant supply for the life and happiness of every one.[t] And some of our leisure hours we spend in several mechanical trades, such as those of carpenters, turners, and the like, in which many of our people are great proficients: and the rest of our time we devote to the improvement of our children, and of our own minds. The

third Edition,[56] *p.* 492. – And history universally assures us, that all those nations, who use only water for their constant drink, are remarkable for their health, strength of body, and long life. And *Kolben* observes, that such of the Hottentots as drink no wine nor strong liquors live very long, and are liable to few distempers: whereas those who drink strong liquors, shorten their days, and are afflicted with diseases before unknown to them. *See his present state of the Cape of Good Hope,*[57] *Vol.* I. *p.* 48. – Such also was the happy state of the Indians on the continent of North America, till the Europeans introduced spirituous liquors among them, which have almost destroyed several of those nations: though they have often complained to our English governors, and intreated them that no such liquors should be permitted to be sent to them. But to no purpose, for the ruin and destruction of thousands is little regarded by wicked and avaritious men, if they can gain any thing by it. – *See also Douglass's state of the British settlements in North America, Vol.* II, *p.* 118.

[s] *Homer's Iliad.* B. XIII. *line* 5.[58] Bochart apprehends that the people here referred to were the ancient Scythians who inhabited the places near the Euxine sea. *See his Phaleg,*[59] *p.* 197.

[t] Rollin justly observes, that no trade can be compared to agriculture, upon which life itself depends; and which only the depravity of our manners can render contemptible. Though gold and silver should be destroyed, though diamonds and pearls should remain hid in the earth and sea, though commerce with other nations should be prohibited, though all the arts which have no other object than embellishment and splendor should be abolished; yet gardening and agriculture with a few other necessary trades would furnish us with all those things, which are needful for the subsistence, the welfare and happiness of mankind. In ancient times they were in the highest esteem; and among the Assyrians and Persians, those governors were rewarded, in whose jurisdiction the lands were well cultivated, and those were punished, who

[56] Thomas Sydenham, *Observationes Medicae* (1676).
[57] Peter Kolb, *The Present State of the Cape of Good Hope* (1731).
[58] *The Iliad of Homer* (5 vols., 1714–22), vol. III, p. 114.
[59] Samuel Bochart, *Geographiae Sacrae Pars Prior* (1646).

women take care of the household affairs, and the dairy and poultry, and spin the cotton, flax, and wool. And every child is enured to labour, suitable to it's age and strength, for none are permitted to be idle.

But don't mistake me, as if we were continually employed in a course of labour and drudgery: no, there is no necessity for this, for the necessaries and conveniences of life are easily procured.*"* This will appear at once obvious to you, if you consider how great a part of mankind in other countries live indolent lives: for not to mention the nobility, gentry, and ladies; what numbers of tradesmen and artificers are there, whose whole employments contribute to nothing but luxury and pleasure, or to promote the grandeur, splendor, and pride of life. Add to these, the military part of the nation; with the slothful and debauched, who waste their time in taverns, alehouses, in trifling diversions and amusements.*ˣ* From whence it plainly appears, that

neglected this part of their duty. And at Rome for several ages, the senators cultivated their grounds with their own hands, and their consuls and dictators were sometimes taken from following the plough. *See his Ancient History, Vol. x.* on agriculture.

" The character which Salmon gives the inhabitants of St. Helena, as he found them to be in 1701, seems to resemble in some particulars that of the Cessares.[60] But as there are three or four hundred soldiers generally residing in that island, and the East India ships frequently touch there, their virtue and innocency must be greatly corrupted. – They were, says Salmon, of a fresh ruddy complexion and robust constitutions, employing themselves in the healthy exercises of gardening and husbandry: and seemed to me to be the most honest, inoffensive, and hospitable people I had met with. I asked some of them; if they had no curiosity to see the rest of the world, of which they had heard so many fine things: and how they could be contented to confine themselves to an island scarce twenty-one miles round, and separated from the rest of mankind? – To which they answered, that they enjoyed all the necessaries of life in great plenty, that they were neither parched with excessive heat, nor pinched with cold; that they lived in perfect security, in no danger from enemies, robbers or wild beasts; had no rigorous seasons, and were happy in a continual course of good health. – That as there were no rich men among them; scarce any one being worth more than a thousand dollars (or 225 pounds sterling): so there were no poor in the island, no man hardly being worth less than 400 dollars (or 90 pounds): and that no one was obliged to more labour, than was necessary to keep him in health. – That if they should transport themselves to any other country, they understood that their small fortunes would scarce preserve them from want: besides which they would be exposed to innumerable hazards and hardships, which they knew nothing of, but from the report of their countrymen.

ˣ Had my author been an Englishman, he would have added the gypsies and beggars, who to the great scandal of our government are very numerous. Whereas no beggars are tolerated at Geneva, *see Keysler, Vol.* I. *p.* 387. And the king of Sardinia will suffer

[60] Thomas Salmon, *Modern History: or, the Present State of All Nations* (3rd edn, 3 vols., 1746), vol. III, pp. 90–1.

the number of those, by whose labour and industry all the necessaries and real conveniencies of life for the whole nation are obtained, is much less than you could at first imagine.

Before I conclude this letter, give me leave to observe that such is our happy state, that, during the whole time we have now lived together in this country, our harmony and union have not been interrupted by any broils or civil dissensions. This domestic peace is to be ascribed (under God) to the quiet and peaceable tempers of those persons, whom we made choice of to take with us: together with the wisdom of our laws, the mildness of the government, the prudent conduct of our governor and magistrates, and that concord and unanimity which have hitherto subsisted among them.*y*

Here poverty and want are unknown, as every one enjoys an equal share of land with his neighbours: and the public stock is obliged to relieve those who meet with any misfortune. Covetousness, with all those passions which arise from it, and often prove so destructive to others, is banished from a country, where no one can engross estates, and heap up riches. Vice and idleness are carefully discouraged; virtue and industry are made fashionable, and generosity and probity are the only steps to honour among us.*z*

no beggar to live in his territories by the sweat of another's brow; nay it has been made penal at Turin, to relieve a strolling beggar. *See Bishop Berkeley's Miscellanies,*[61] p. 107.

y There is in the Gentleman's Magazine for 1750 a letter from Halifax in Nova Scotia, dated December 7, 1749, which gives the following instructive account of the good effects of a wise and prudent conduct in governor Cornwallis, who landed there June 21, 1749, with 2000 persons, being the first settlers in that place.[62] – Who were at first (says this letter), tumultuous and refractory, full of discontents and murmurings, capricious in demanding favours, not long satisfied with them, and often abusing them by a restless importunity for more: yet in a few months, by his prudent management and proper generosity, by his condescension, candour, and affability, he has turned a mad tumultuous rabble into a tractable and quiet people: who now work with ten times the alacrity they did at first, and are become patient under disappointments: and when they are denied any thing, they conclude their petition to have been unreasonable, from a firm perswasion that their governor has their true interest at heart, and that they cannot ask any thing with reason, but what he grants with pleasure.

z A noble writer in his *Dialogues of the Dead,*[63] *p. 21,* justly observes, that to watch over the morals of a people, and to discourage whatever may taint or corrupt them, is one of the principal objects of a wise legislature. And certainly (says he) that is the happiest country, which has most virtue in it: and to the eye of right reason, the poorest Swiss

[61] George Berkeley, Bishop of Cloyne, *A Miscellany, Containing Several Tracts on Various Subjects* (Dublin, 1752).

[62] *Gentleman's Magazine,* 20 (1750), 72–3.

[63] Salignac de la Mothe Fénelon, Archbishop of Cambrai, *Dialogues of the Dead* (4th edn, 1760).

O happy state! founded upon and conducted by the principles of reason, goodness, and equity. Where the equal division of the land, and the moderate quantity allowed every one, without any foreign commerce, restrain pride, ambition, and luxury, and establish temperance and industry: while every one is contented and chearful, crowned with liberty and plenty, possessing all the blessings of a calm country life, and peaceably enjoying the fruits of his own labour.

O happy people! how propitiously has a kind providence crowned all your toils and difficulties. You are now a flourishing colony, in the quiet and undisturbed possession of a country spacious and fertile, which by easy labour and due cultivation yields you every thing, that is necessary to render life agreeable and comfortable: free from the disquieting fears and dread of poverty, the pride and insolence of imperious power, and the tyranny of the merciless and cruel oppressor. And if ever we should be known to the world, let us be known as a wise and a brave nation, the contemners of riches, the avowed enemies to luxury, the dread of tyrants, and the guardians and preservers of liberty. A people active, strong and healthy, enur'd to labour, plain in our dress, our houses and furniture, temperate in our diet, and of great simplicity of life and manners: a people, whose ruling principles are piety and gratitude to God, an ardent love of our country, and a sincere regard for the public good; principles, which must always influence us to every noble and worthy pursuit.

Excuse, my dear friend, the warmth of an old man, glowing with love for a people, with whom he has shared a course of difficulties, and in whose welfare he is deeply interested. Who is now fully rewarded by the pleasure and satisfaction he feels, in finding that our generous and disinterested scheme and well-designed endeavours have proved (with the blessing of God) so greatly successful, even far beyond our most sanguine hopes and flattering expectations.

I am, &c.

Canton is a much more noble state than even the kingdom of France, if it has more liberty, better morals, a more settled tranquillity, more moderation in prosperity, and more firmness in danger. – Such seems to be the happy state of the Pholeys in Africa, who are of so good and quiet a disposition, and so well instructed in what is just and right, that a man who does ill, is the abomination of the whole nation. And their chiefs rule with so much moderation, that every act of government seems rather an act of the people than of their governors. They are very industrious and frugal, of great humanity, very rarely angry, but mild; and yet brave and courageous: and drink nothing stronger than water. *See Moor's travels into Africa,*[64] *p.* 30, 32, 33 *and* 39.

[64] Francis Moore, *Travels into the Inland Parts of Africa* (1738).

Letter IX.

Early marriages encouraged among them, by giving an estate to every person on his marriage. Their friends and relations assist them to build their house, and plant and stock their farm. They are likely to double their numbers every twenty-five years. The children are instructed in several arts and sciences: in which the learned terms of art are thrown aside, and easy ones substituted in their stead. The advantage of the sumptuary laws. The sons of the governor are educated under the inspection of the senate, and why? The children are taught to sing psalms and moral songs. The people assemble four times in a year at Salem. The particular form of public worship. The conclusion.

DEAR SIR

I have already told you, that we allow of no trade or correspondence to be carried on with the Spaniards in Chili: on which account we have but lately heard, from the neighbouring Indians, of the truce which was concluded in 1609 for twelve years, between Spain and the Seven United Provinces. This truce being not yet expired, gives me great hopes, that my letters will be safely conveyed to you: I shall therefore hasten to finish them, and shall intrust them to an Indian, who is going to Baldivia, and has promised to deliver them to the captain of the first ship, that sets sail from thence for Spain, and to engage him faithfully to send them from thence by a Dutch ship to Amsterdam.

Early marriages are encouraged among us, not only because the strength and power of a state consists in the number of it's inhabitants: but also because such marriages are the best means of preserving sobriety and virtue, and preventing vice and debauchery.[a] Every

---

[a] Since God has implanted the desire of marriage in young persons of both sexes, to answer the wise ends of continuing the human race, of loving and mutually assisting one another, and of educating their children in a sober and virtuous course: whatever prevents such early marriages as nature dictates, is one great cause of that corruption of manners, and of those vicious courses, which our young people fall into. And if we examine the manners of the English nation, we shall easily see, that it is the extravagance of the present age, the destructive love and pursuit of pleasure, and the polite education which we give our children, that prevent our young people from marrying: as they are unable to live in that elegant manner in which they have been brought up, and to bear the expences which attend the married state, since every one, when single, wants to make a shew above what he can really afford. If so, what sober man would venture to marry a woman, who has been educated in a polite and genteel manner above her circumstances? as it must be a constant source of uneasiness to a husband, to find his wife discontented with that state of life, which their fortune or trade will but just support. Besides, such women being early initiated into pleasure,

one is therefore entitled on his marriage to an estate equal to his neighbours, and sufficient to maintain himself and family. But you will ask how a young couple, having no house or barns &c. ready built on their land, no cattle, or corn nor proper instruments for husbandry, will be able to undertake the cultivation of such an estate? But this objection will soon cease, when I inform you that it is a constant custom among us, for the young men to employ themselves for a year or two before they marry, and mutually to assist one another in framing houses, in making proper household goods and furniture for them, and also the necessary implements for husbandry.*b* And

and attached to the frequent change of fashions, the glitter of finery and the folly and extravagance of dress and shew; what fortune will be sufficient to gratify their enlarged desires? Having their minds uncultivated, what wretched companions must they make; and how destructive must their manner of life be to all conjugal felicity, and to every rational and domestic virtue?

b Thus the Peasants in Norway, as Bishop Pontoppidan tells us, are dextrous and ingenious, never employing any hatters, shoemakers, taylors, tanners, weavers, carpenters, smiths or joyners, nor do they buy any goods in the towns; but all these trades are exercised at every farm-house: and they think a boy can never be an useful member of society, nor a valuable man, without making himself (in some degree) a master of all these trades. And he adds, that the Swedish Peasants do the same. *See his natural history of Norway, p.* 245[65] – *Mr. Rousseau* also in his *Letter to D'Alembert against erecting a Theatre at Geneva,*[66] tells us of a people near Neufchatel in Switzerland, who dwell on a mountain which is covered with habitations, each of which is built in the middle of the lands of the owner, and affords the numerous inhabitants the tranquillity of retirement, with the sweets of society. These happy people live free from taxes, imposts and oppressions, cultivate their own lands with all possible care, and employ their leisure hours in many handicraft trades. When the deep snows in the winter prevent them from going abroad, every man shuts himself up with his numerous family in a neat wooden house of his own building, where he employs himself in useful and amusing exercises, which prevent his being tired with his solitude, and preserve his health. No carpenter, lock-smith, glazier or turner ever enters their country, for they all work at those trades themselves. They make a variety of different things in steel, wood, or paste-board, which they sell to foreigners; some of which are sent as far as Paris, and, among the rest, some wooden clocks: they also make some of metal, and they even carry their ingenuity so far as to make watches. But what seems almost incredible, is that every man understands all the different branches, into which the watch-maker's business is divided, and makes the several tools himself; so that you would take his room to be the shop of a mechanic, or the closet of some experimental Philosopher. They also make cranes, spectacles, pumps, barometers, camera-obscura's, &c: they understand something of designing, and know how to paint. Their chief amusement is to sing Psalms with their wives and children, and it is amazing to hear their strong and nervous harmony. They have also useful books, and are tolerably well instructed, and reason sensibly upon most subjects; and treated Mr. Rousseau with great hospitality.

[65] Erik Pontoppidan the Younger, *The Natural History of Norway* (1755).
[66] Jean-Jacques Rousseau, *A Letter from M. Rousseau . . . to M. D'Alembert Concerning the Effects of Theatrical Entertainments on the Manners of Mankind* (1759).

when any marriage is concluded upon, and the parties are contracted to each other; upon their application to the senate, leave is given them to chuse their estate, and then their parents, friends and relations assist them to erect their house and other necessary buildings, to plant their garden and orchard, and inclose their fields. They also present them with corn and other necessary food, with all sorts of poultry, and cattle sufficient to stock their little farm.*'* This is such an inducement to matrimony, that an old batchelor or maid is scarce known among us: and as early marriages produce a greater number of children than later ones, they make our colony increase so fast, that, by the best computation we can form, we reckon we shall double our numbers in about twenty-five years.*ᵈ* Nevertheless we are under

---

' Thus when any of the Indians at the Isthmus of Darien in America, marries his daughter, he invites all his neighbours to a feast. The men who come to the wedding, bring their axes with them; the women bring Indian corn; the boys fruits and roots, and the girls, fowls and eggs, for none come empty handed. As soon as the marriage ceremony is over, the men take up their axes, and go to the woods, where a spot is fixed upon for the residence of the young couple. There they fall to work, cutting down the woods, and clearing the ground; and as fast as they clear it, the women and children plant it with corn, or whatever else is suitable at that season. They also build a little hut for the new married couple to dwell in; and thus continue about seven days, working with the greatest vigour and alacrity imaginable. *See Wafer's voyage,*[67] p. 164, 165.

ᵈ This great increase of the Cessares is confirmed by what a learned and ingenious gentleman assures us to be the case in our English colonies on the continent of North America; where it being easy to obtain land (which with moderate labour will afford a good subsistence) people marry more early in life; from whence arises a numerous off-spring, about eight children upon an average springing from every marriage, and consequently there is a quick peopling of those countries. And their common rate of increase, where they are not molested by enemies, is doubling their numbers every twenty-five years, exclusive of the accession of foreigners. *See the Interest of Great Britain considered with regard to her Colonies, 2d Edition,*[68] p. 23, 36 and 51. – Early marriages seem also to prevail in Switzerland, for Stanyan says, that one generally finds there nine or ten children in a family, and sometimes double that number. *See his Account of Switzerland, p.* 143, 144. – The greatest number of legitimate children which I have yet heard of, begotten by one man, is expressed in the following epitaph in Heydon church yard in Yorkshire. Here lies William Sturton of Patrington who died in 1726. He had by his first wife twenty-seven children, and by his second seventeen, in all forty-four. – At Conway also in Carnarvonshire is this epitaph: Here lies the body of Nicholas Hookes, of Conway, gentleman, who was the forty first child of his father William Hookes Esq; by Alice his wife; and was himself the father of twenty-seven children: he died March 20, 1637.

[67] Lionel Wafer, *A New Voyage and Description of the Isthmus of America* (1699).
[68] [Benjamin Franklin], *The Interest of Great Britain Considered, with Regard to her Colonies* (1760).

no apprehensions of being too numerous; because the uninhabited tract of land all around us is so large, as to require some centuries before it can be fully peopled. And our children, who are generally numerous, are so far from being a burden to us, that on the contrary they are the greatest blessings, chearfully assisting us (as far as they can) in our employments, being brought up from their infancy to diligence and industry, and to such labour or business, as is suitable to their age and sex.^e

In our chief town, we have a public library, a collection of natural curiosities, and models for making every useful implement and machine. In our public schools, the children are taught some parts of the mathematics, because they tend to make a man perform mechanical works much more perfectly than he can do without them. We also give them some knowledge of history, chronology, geography, philosophy, and astronomy: sciences which enlarge the powers of the mind, enoble it's views, and bring it to acquire a justness and loftiness of sentiment, and which, from the contemplation of the beauty, order and harmony which are diffused through the universe, lead us by degrees to the one supreme, infinite, uncreated Cause of all things, the author of all excellence, and the center of all perfection. In mediating on whose wisdom, greatness and goodness, the human mind is lost in wonder, and over-whelmed in transports of gratitude, esteem and adoration. But I must observe, that in all these sciences, we have thrown aside the learned terms of art, and have introduced such new ones, as are easy and on a level with the capacities of our children.^f

Thus they are brought up to be sober and modest, enured to labour and industry, and instructed in every branch of useful knowledge, and are not educated in a state of softness and indolence, of levity

---

^e It is well known, that in some parts of Germany, the children are brought up to make toys and several other things at those ages, when the children in England are good for nothing but to break them. And Bishop Berkeley says, that in Holland a child of five year's of age is often maintained by its own labour. *See his Miscellanies, p.* 102 *and* 100.

^f This is an excellent method, which I wish was introduced among us: for if we really desire that young persons should take a delight and improve in such studies, we ought to employ the most easy and familiar terms. My author thought that even the Dutch were deficient in this particular; and yet they are remarkable for having translated many of the Greek terms of art into their own language. – And why might not a *Telescope* from τηλε *far*, and σκοπεω *to view*, be also called by us *a far viewer*: would it not convey at once a more clear idea of the use and nature of this instrument to young persons, than if we used a learned term taken from the Greeks, Romans, Egyptians or Chinese?

and folly. And as our laws enjoin a great simplicity and plainness both in furniture and apparel, our women are deprived of those vain and empty toys, and trifling ornaments, which engross the attention of the female sex in other countries, and employ the greatest part of their time, as they unhappily look upon a shewy and gaudy dress, and fine furniture, to be essential to their happiness, meerly from a bad education, and an ignorance of what is truly valuable. Whereas our young women are trained up to be loving, frugal and industrious wives, and good mothers: and our young men to be diligent in their employments, kind husbands, and prudent fathers: by which means our marriages are crowned with domestic peace, endearing comfort, and heart-felt happiness.

There is one particular I ought not to omit, which is, that as we consider all the children in general to belong to the whole community, and therefore their education is conducted under the public eye: so in a more particular manner the sons of the governor are placed under the inspection of the senate. For history and long experience shew that the multiplicity of business which engages the attention of the father, and the too great fondness and affection of the mother, have caused the education of the children of even the greatest and best princes to be very defective. A remarkable instance of this kind we have in Cambyses, the son of Cyrus king of Persia. Cyrus, whom historians have celebrated as a wise, brave, and great king, was educated in the public schools in Persia, to which he chiefly owed his most shining accomplishments. But his son Cambyses, who was educated under the direction of the queen, proved to be one of the worst of princes. For she had been brought up in Media, where vanity and voluptuousness reigned in the highest degree; and having entertained exalted ideas of grandeur, luxury and magnificence, and such extravagant notions of regal prerogative, as are utterly inconsistent with the happiness of the people; she instilled the same into her son. Hence he became tyrannical, cruel and oppressive, and devoted to all kinds of excesses. This was the case of many other princes of that empire, insomuch that Plato justly observes, that one chief cause of the ruin of the Persian state was the bad education of their princes.[g]

The senate therefore carefully examines into the education, con-

---

[g] *Plato de leg. lib. 3.*[69]

[69] Plato, *De Legibus* (1587).

duct and behaviour of the governor's sons: they are brought up at the public schools with the other children, habituated to equal diligence and industry, and instructed in the principles of religion and virtue, justice and equity, and inflexible honour and probity. They are also obliged to study our laws, to conform themselves to them, and to obey the magistrates equally with the lowest subject. And when they attain a proper age, they attend the public trials of civil and criminal causes, that they may learn to judge rightly, and may thereby be the fitter to govern, whenever any one of them shall be called to that important trust.

Before I leave this subject of the education of our children, I must not neglect to acquaint you, that we bring them up to sing psalms and such moral songs, as tend to excite to piety, and the performance of every generous and worthy action, to encourage purity of heart and manners, and a wise and regular course of life. These are infinitely more useful and instructive than the amorous, and other trifling and foolish songs, which are too often used in other countries. And whenever any person is buried, a certain number of these children walk before the corpse, and sing some suitable hymns.

We have a meeting, as was before observed, of a great number of our people at the town of Salem, on the first Monday in January, April, July and October. In the morning we assemble together at the church to return our grateful acknowledgements to the fountain of all good for his blessings to us, to intreat the continuance of his favour, and beseech him to make us a happy and an united people. When the morning service (which is but short) is over, the governor and senators go to the senate house, to hear and determine all disputes, to attend to the complaints of the injured, to redress their grievances, and to punish every criminal and oppressor. At these times also every inspector is examined with regard to the state of the people under his care; and every master and mistress of the public schools, concerning the behaviour and improvement of the children under them. The children also are brought before the assembly, and examined by the governor in those branches of knowledge, in which they have been instructed; they also produce samples of their work, the boys in several sorts of handicraft trades, and the girls in sowing, knitting and spinning: and then the governor publickly distributes rewards to those of every different age, who excell the rest. He also gives rewards to such parents, as have been remarkably diligent in instructing their children, and thereby have been worthy examples to others.

With regard to the public worship of God; though we allow a free toleration to all religious sects, yet we have hitherto been so happy, as to unite together in one society. Several forms of prayer have been drawn up by our ministers, which are short and rational, and chiefly in the words of scripture, that so no one may have any just reason to be offended. The minister makes use of one of these forms before sermon, and afterwards concludes the service with a prayer of his own composing; by which method we have united the advocates and opposers of a liturgy. But if any church chuses to alter any of the forms, or to omit them intirely, it is always left to the determination of the majority of the members of that church, to prevent all impositions.

Thus have I given you a full answer to all your enquiries: and I believe you will not easily find a better form of government, where the liberty and happiness of every individual is more carefully consulted; where every tendency to vice and licentiousness is more effectually discouraged; and where more care is taken of the right education of the children, upon which the welfare of posterity greatly depends. What alterations may hereafter be introduced among us, when the present generation is dead (who by their having lived in Europe, are thereby convinced of the great use and necessity of these regulations) I cannot say. But happy will it be for our children, if they steadily pursue the same plan, adhere to the same laws, and suffer nothing to destroy that right disposition of the heart and mind, and that amiable simplicity of life and manners, which at present flourish among us.

I am, Dear Sir,
    Your sincere Friend
        and affectionate humble Servant,
From the town of Salem, June 19, 1620.   J. VANDER NECK

Memoirs of Planetes,
Or a Sketch of the
Laws and Manners of Makar.
by Phileleutherus Devoniensis.

Φανερον τοινυν ὡς ὁσαι μεν πολιτεῖαι το κοινῇ συμφερον σκοποῦσιν, αυται μεν ορθαι τυγχανουσιν οὐσαι καλα το απλως δικαιον. Ὁσαι δε το σφετερον μονον των αρχοντων, ημαρτημεναι πᾶσαι, και παρεκθασεις των ορθῶν πολιτειων δεσποτικαι γαρ. ἡ δε πολις, κοινωνια των ελευθερων εστι. ARISTOTLE.

"It is evident then, that all those governments which have the common good in view, are rightly established, and strictly just, but those which have in view only the good of the rulers, are all founded on wrong principles, and are widely different from what a government ought to be, for they are tyranny over slaves, whereas a city is a community of free men." ELLIS[1]

Ζητουσι δ ολως ου το πατριον, αλλα ταγαθον πανιες.
ARISTOTLE[2]

1795

---

[1] Aristotle, *A Treatise of Government*, transl. William Ellis (1778), p. 132.

[2] Aristotle, *A Treatise of Government*, transl. William Ellis (1778), p. 85: 'all persons ought to endeavour to follow what is right, and not what is established'.

Phileleutherus Devoniensis to the Reader.

With whatever degree of partiality I may view the form of government here presented to you, and how fondly soever I may imagine it, in the abstract, to be calculated to ensure the happiness of mankind, I am ready to allow that in the present institutions of society, philosophy has yet much to do to prepare the minds of men to receive it. The great mass of vice and misery which pervade the lower classes of people throughout most of the countries of Europe, must without doubt be considerably diminished before any change of government can be so introduced as not to bring with it the evils of tumult and massacre; evils most fervently to be deprecated by every lover of justice and truth, but which, with sorrow does he perceive it, seem to be the inevitable result of a system of oppressive laws, and unceasing taxation. It is for this reason that every true Briton, every real friend of his country, must be anxious for such a reformation in the commons house of parliament as will restore to the people their just weight and power in the constitution: with this, we may hope for the blessings of peace, prosperity, and content; without it, we must expect the evils of anarchy, confusion, and discord. In our endeavours then to attain this desirable object, let us not be dismayed by the various obstacles every where thrown in our way by the interested and apostate. Calumnies and persecutions have ever been accumulated upon the reformers of mankind since the times of the statuary and the carpenter, but calumnies and persecutions so far from deterring the just man from a steady adherence to his purpose, very frequently tend to accelerate the success of his endeavours: nor are his enemies insensible of this truth; they have recourse therefore to other weapons, and where they are too feeble to punish or imprison, they brand with the titles of visionary and theorist. But let us allow them the use of this favourite weapon. Is theory to be despised because not immediately reducible to practice? Reason, Newton, and philosophy answer in the negative; it is corruption and desperation only that vociferate the affirmative. "It is a well-known principle of morality, says Mr Godwin, that he who proposes perfection to himself, though he will inevitably fall short of what he pursues, will make a more rapid progress than he who is contented to aim only at what is imperfect."[3] It is upon this principle that the Stoics formed their sage, and

[3] William Godwin, *Enquiry Concerning Political Justice* (2 vols., 1793), vol. II, p. 894.

the Christians have their *perfect man.*^a This then, I hope, will suffice to vindicate what may appear theoretical in the following sheets; I say *appear*, because it is unknown to how great a degree of happiness mankind may approximate, when the exactions and oppressions under which they now labour are pruned away, and when governors have no temptation to consult their own interest in preference to that of the governed.

FAREWELL.

Dated amid the vice of London,
   MARCH 16. 1795.

---

^a See an excellent note upon this subject in the xixth Remark of Melmoth's Lælius,[4] where he presents the reader with the following quotation from Quintilian. Evenit nonnumquam ut aliquid grande inveniat, qui semper quærit quod *nimium est.*[5]

[4] Marcus Tullius Cicero, *Laelius: or, An Essay on Friendship*, ed. William Melmoth (2 vols., 1777), vol. II, pp. 207–9.

[5] Said of untrained orators, who are 'so reckless in their efforts that sometimes in their passion for extravagance they light upon some really striking expression'. Quintillian adds 'But such success is rare, and does not compensate for their other defects' (*The Institutio Oratorio of Quintillian*, II.12.5; transl. H. E. Butler, 4 vols., Heinemann, 1920, vol. I, pp. 284–5).

Memoirs of Planetes, &c.

Chap. I.

Towards the close of the eighteenth century I determined to leave my native soil upon a voyage of discovery, intending among other objects to explore the south and south-west coasts of New-Holland, and having visited the Islands in the Pacific Ocean found out by Captain Cook, to trace the western coast of America. For this purpose I fitted out a brig of two hundred tons burthen, and set sail in the year 1794. The ship's company consisted of twenty men, beside the mate and surgeon. Nothing of consequence occurred till we reached the Cape of Good Hope, but in making the harbour the vessel struck, and carried away her rudder. This was an unfortunate accident, as the weather began to grow squally, and a strong current was then setting to the south-east. As the wind did not cease for many days, and by our reckoning we had been carried at least four degrees from the Cape, I conferred with the mate, whether it were more advisable to attempt again to make the Cape, or bear away at once for New-Holland. He observed that the store of provisions was ample, and therefore was inclined to the latter. About a fortnight after this one of the sailors upon the mast-head called out – Land! It proved however to be an immense Ice-island, huge pieces of which we had frequently met with. This island lay to the north-east, and in order to keep clear of it we bore away to the south, but the atmosphere growing cold and hazy, and various masses of ice thickening upon us, there was great danger of the vessel being jammed between them. In addition to these circumstances, the mate came one morning into the cabin to tell me that the men began to murmur, and did not obey orders with the alacrity that could be desired. Fortunately on the next day we discovered an opening through the ice, and in a few days arrived in somewhat a milder climate: still the murmurs of the seamen increased; they threw out broad hints that they thought me insane, and would no longer be made the tools of my romantic vagaries. It was in vain that the mate and myself harangued and expostulated with them; they had fixed their plan and only waited their opportunity. We had experienced so much bad weather during the last three weeks, that no observation could be made, but the sky now beginning to clear up, we had hopes of being soon enabled to find our situation. About sun-rise one morning, the mate being upon the look out, discovered land about four leagues a-head. This was agreeable news, and upon our approach I immediately ordered the boat out to sound the coast. At the depth of five fathoms the ship was brought to an anchor in a small bay, at the bottom of which I ordered two tents to be fixed, and the astronomical instruments, some fowling pieces, the medicine chest, and provisions, to be landed I then went ashore myself with the mate.

Chap. II.

It was here that the sailors put their diabolical plot into execution: I had proposed to the mate to ascend one of the highest cliffs in order to take a view of the country, and to do this we were compelled to make a circuit of three or four miles over very rough ground. Having with much difficulty arrived at the summit of one of the rocks, we were struck with the greatest astonishment at seeing the ship under full sail standing off to the north-west. I now blamed myself for disregarding the murmurs of the seamen. The complaints of the lower classes of people should always be listened to at their outset. If I had called a council of these men, said I, and permitted them to depute one of their number to lay their grievances before me, I should have been adored as their friend and benefactor, and not left here to perish through want and misery. The poor mate, whose name was Lawrence, and who united to a strong judgment all the openness and sincerity that characterize the British sailor, agreed with me in my observation. I dare swear, Captain, said he, these fellows have left us some provision, and the orders you gave yesterday respecting one of the boats were punctually fulfilled, for if they have not carried it off with them, it is safe moored in a small creek at the northern extremity of the bay. Besides, Sir, your faithful companion, Mungo, is close at your heels. Poor fellow, said I, he is a better friend than the generality of those who call themselves Christians. I wish, returned Lawrence, you had been more careful in your choice of the ship's company; that rascal, Jack Ratlin, is the cause of all this evil: he had just escaped from Exeter gaol, where he had been committed for a burglary, when he entered into your service. True! my friend, said I, and I will venture to say that he learnt no good there. Our gaols, instead of being seminaries of repentance for the past, and amendment for the future, generally dismiss their wretched inhabitants in a tenfold degree more depraved than they found them.[b]

Our misfortunes were not a little increased by finding the spot on which we were banished to be a small island bounded by high rocks; it appeared to be about twelve miles long, and four or five broad. We now began to descend the rock, and about midway, Lawrence, who had advanced somewhat before me, called out; If my eyes don't deceive me I see a smoke in the east part of the island. I applied my telescope, and found it true. The first thought that occurred was, that it proceeded from the fire of some Indians, and perhaps Cannibals; accordingly we quickened our pace, and soon after mid-day arrived at the spot whence we set out. Here to my great joy I found Lawrence's conjecture verified. One of the tents was left standing, with a hammock, part of the medicine chest and provisions, the boat, and a few kitchen utensils and other trifles, but the astronomical apparatus was gone. We concurred in the necessity of putting ourselves instantly upon short allowance, and barricading our tent in the best manner possible, which we did by piling large stones all around it. Until this was completed we determined to sleep in the boat within a gun-shot of the tent, and alternately to keep watch four hours.

Chap. III.

On the third day after the ship's departure we set out to explore the island, each having a gun and a brace of pistols, and the dog Mungo carrying a bag with a few biscuits. We pursued the coast, which was exceedingly rocky, but here and there interspersed with fine sand.

[b] The Reader may find some good observations upon the above subject, in the 9th Chap. Part III. of *The Complaints of the Poor*, written by that indefatigable friend of man, GEORGE DYER.[6]

[6] George Dyer, *The Complaints of the Poor People of England* (1793), pp. 68–71.

Oysters, lobsters, penguins and seals, presented themselves in abundance, there was little fear therefore of starving; and as to fresh water, if none were to be found in the middle of the island I meant to distil the sea water; this resolution was useless, as we afterwards found an excellent spring.

We had now gone somewhat more than ten miles, and judged ourselves near the spot whence the smoke had proceeded. Mungo was a considerable way before us, when on turning a sharp angle he suddenly dropt his bag, his tail stiffened, and he flew from our sight with prodigious fury. I instantly hallooed to him, and ran up with all my speed. I found him standing with his paw upon the breast of an Indian boy, who appeared senseless. Directly opposite him was a cave in the rock, that seemed partly excavated by art and partly by nature. Lawrence had now come up, and with his assistance the Indian was speedily recovered. His fears seemed to have overcome him, and indeed this was a fortunate circumstance, for in all probability had he made any resistance, Mungo would have torn him in pieces. If the boy's astonishment at seeing us was not so great as might have been expected we on our side were not a little surprised at his dress. Upon his head was a sort of turban, and round his body a shirt of the finest flannel I had ever seen to this was added a pair of trousers which reached to his ancles, and his feet were covered with shoes of caoutchouc‘ laced up beneath the trousers. He shewed signs of fear upon the approach of Mungo, but from this I soon relieved him by patting and stroking the dog, and teaching him to do the same. He spoke to us in a language that we did not understand, and pointed to the cave. Here I was going to enter with him but he gently put me back with both his hands, crying out, Yan, yan-a-roo. In about a couple of minutes after he had entered the cave, he returned bringing with him a middle-aged woman of a respectable and solemn aspect, whom I guessed to be his mother. She had on a sort of cloak of a greenish colour, thrown loosely over her shoulders and tied with a net-work bandage about her body, under this was a garment that reached to her feet, of the same substance and fineness as the boy's,

---

‘ This elastic resin, more known by the name of *India Rubber*, is the produce of South America, and among the various uses to which it is applied by the Indians, may be reckoned boots, which are impenetrable to water; bottles; flambeaux, that give a beautiful light, and are inoffensive to the smell; and a kind of cloth. – For further particulars see the *Encyclopædia Britannica.*

her shoes and turban were also similar. I now began to indulge the hope of being at no great distance from some civilized state, but my ignorance of their language was a great obstacle to every information. As we had no other provision with us than a few biscuits, I put my finger to my mouth intimating that I should be glad of some refreshment; the hint was understood, and our good hostess beckoned to us to follow her into the cave. I had forgot to mention that when she first saw us, she put some question to me in a tone and accent so different from those of the boy, that I immediately remarked to Lawrence; Certainly this is another language from what we have just heard. It appears so from the sound, returned he. The moment we spoke, the woman muttered something to the boy that ratified my opinion of having heard two distinct tongues. We had now entered the cave which was a large circular room, having a wood fire and a chimney built of stone in the centre. Over the fire was an earthen vessel with boiling water, and the furniture consisted chiefly of earthen ware, a table, and some stools, or rather chairs without backs, of an unknown wood. In short every thing bespoke a condition superior to the generality of Indians, and I was just going to make some observation to my companion, when the woman put her finger upon her lips and whispered in a soft tone Doom! Doom! If any thing could tend to increase my wonder it was this word, Doom! which I knew to be of eastern origin, and signified silence; but how it came to be used by an Indian in the middle of the southern ocean, and upon a barren island, was then beyond my comprehension. I religiously kept silence, but my curiosity was raised by her pointing to a little door in the cavern. All this time Mungo and the boy made friends of each other, much to the advantage of the former, who thereby got plenty of yams and bread-fruit. A groan as of one awaking from sleep, and which proceeded from the door above mentioned, now roused our attention. The good woman ran to the door, and after a few minutes conversation with some one within, led out a respectable old man, who immediately approached me, gently squeezed my hand and sat down by my side. In the mean time dinner was served up; it consisted of a large flat fish of the nature of turbot, a dish of yams, and some bread-fruit. The liquor was of a delicious flavour, not unlike weak mountain wine. The pleasure I took in the happiness of this small family, and the wonder how they came there, occupied so much of my thoughts that I had forgot it was time to return. Lawrence however having suggested this, I pulled out my watch and found it to be near five o'clock. Neither of our hospitable friends took much notice of the watch, though the seal which had my arms and crest upon it attracted their observation. I now rose to depart, having first thanked the old man in the best manner I was able, and then taking the youth by one hand I pointed with the other to the western part of the island, as much as to ask him to return with us; he answered by shaking his head and looking at his mother, who replied with all the sympathy of natural affection by smiling in tears. I was unwilling for that time to press my suit, and having again shaken the boy's hand, and given him one of Mungo's paws, which made him laugh heartily, we departed. The youth followed us for some time, pleased with Mungo's carrying the wallet.

Our return was considerably shortened by ruminating upon the adventures of the day. It is a matter of much wonder to me, said I, how these Indians could come here, and what was their design in so doing; an old man, a woman, and her son occupy a barren island in the midst of the great southern ocean, and what is more surprising shew no astonishment at strangers though of a different colour, dress and language; have no appendages at their nose or arms, and no baubles in their ears, dressed in the most becoming ease, and speak two languages. I am struck with equal wonder with yourself, said Lawrence, but it is my opinion that they belong to some fishermen, who perhaps are out at sea, and I am the more inclined to this belief, as I observed in a recess within the cave a large quantity of dried fish. Little Munna too (for thus the woman called the boy) though he looked at the guns for some time, yet what mostly engaged his attention were the letters upon the collar of the dog, these I am convinced he knew not what to make of, and his mother seemed equally surprised with himself. It is evident, I replied, that these people must have some communication with a civilized society, and I am determined if possible to find it out. I am heartily glad to hear it, Captain, returned Lawrence, and am willing to bear you company in such an undertaking through the whole world. We were now arrived in sight of the tent, and having agreed to sleep on shore that night, determined upon an expedition round the south part of the island the next morning.

Chap. IV.

With the fuel that the crew had left behind them Lawrence made a fire just outside the tent, in order to boil some of the lobsters that we had picked up on our return; and while he was engaged in this employment, I took a ramble towards the mouth of the bay, having my spy-glass in my hand. The moon shone bright, but the sky was full of light fleeting clouds, the wind blowing strong from the east. As soon as I had scrambled to the outer point of the bay I applied my glass through the whole horizon, and in the south-east quarter thought I perceived a sail. I continued viewing this object for near half an hour, and as it approached had no doubt of my conjecture being true; I could willingly have staid an hour longer upon this spot, but fearing that Lawrence would be alarmed at my absence, I hastened back to communicate to him the intelligence. Upon approaching the tent a sound struck my ears which I knew not to be Lawrence's; this startled me not a little, and I crept softly towards the tent to learn the result, Mungo at the same time began to growl; but my fears instantly vanished upon the appearance of little Munna, who ran up with all speed, crying out Mungo! Mungo! The dog immediately recognized his young friend by jumping upon his shoulders. Glad as I was to see him, I thought it highly imprudent in him to venture such a distance by himself; however it was my duty to treat him with all the hospitality in my power. Recollecting that I had a ring set with stone, and a bunch of red feathers, I arranged the latter in a fanciful manner and placed them in his turban, at the same time putting the ring upon his finger, but I soon perceived that I had offended him, for without saying a word he laid them both upon the table. Surely, said I, this child teaches us an useful lesson not to make baubles so dear to us; what European of his years would not have thought himself happy in such a present? Every thing I see, said Lawrence, presents a new object of admiration. Munna has not come unattended, but has brought with him a basket of fish and yams, and an earthen bottle of what he calls Ulla. We now sat down to supper, having added a dish of the ship's pease to our other fare, of which Munna ate heartily. We now began to prepare for bed, but there being only one hammock that we had spread upon some boards, I was at a loss how to accommodate my young friend. Whether or no he perceived my situation I know not, but taking Lawrence by the hand he led him out of the tent, and in about half an hour they both returned with two bundles of a species of weed, that they had gathered from the neighbouring rocks; it was dry, soft, and inoffensive, to the smell. Of this Munna made himself a bed, adding the sail of our boat by way of covering, and wrapping some of it in a cloth for a pillow. Nor was Mungo forgot, for he made him a bed of the same materials by his side.

Chap. V.

We rose with the sun, and set out with our young companion and guide to make a tour of the other side of the island. Before this took place, Munna went to look at our boat, which he surveyed attentively; he then returned to the tent, and having examined the whole of its furniture and looked often at us, I saw that he was much at a loss how to account for our conveyance hither. In order to relieve his anxiety I led him towards the mouth of the bay, and first pointing to the north-west and then to myself and Lawrence, and making as many other signs as suggested themselves at the moment, I gave him a tolerably good idea of the nature of our situation. Munna had a feeling heart, and seemed much affected with my dumb narrative. He warmly pressed my hand, and while tears stood in his eyes he gave me such a look of affection that I was at no loss to understand his meaning. Indeed it is to him and his family that I am indebted as well for my delivery from this island, as for the comforts that I received while its inhabitant. In our tour we found several more of those circular habitations, some cut out in the rock and others built of stone, but most of them at that time uninhabited. On approaching Munna's dwelling I was not a little surprised at seeing two vessels of about thirty tons burthen riding at anchor. Their structure was rather different from what I had been used to, having two short masts with each a large sail something between a lug and a shoulder-of-mutton sail. We had by this time reached our good hostess's, and perceived two middle-aged men of our own colour, though much tanned by the sun, standing near the door. Munna ran with great joy toward them, and they instantly came up and saluted us with great civility, their language however was unknown to me, except a very few words that appeared to be derived from the languages of the East. We found our hostess surrounded with several new guests, all Indians except the two above mentioned; and during our participation of her frugal table, Munna to the best of his power communicated the dumb intercourse he had had with me relative to the nature of my arrival. One of the white men, to whom I perceived some deference was paid, and whom they called Othono, appeared to me by the signs he made, and particularly by his frequently pointing to the north-west, to have seen our ship. Othono was tall and well made, and though much beaten by weather shewed a kind benevolent aspect; I thought this therefore a favourable opportunity to make him acquainted, as well as nature could dictate, with my earnest wish to leave my present abode. For this purpose, as soon as dinner was over, I took him by the hand and led him towards the place where the two vessels lay at anchor, and made all the signs I was able, that we were unhappily left upon this island far from our native country, and wished to be conveyed to some civilized spot. The voice of nature was strong, and before I thought he could perfectly have understood me, this good man ordered four of the Indians to fetch my tent and luggage, and pointed to Lawrence to accompany them. Lawrence wanted no intimation from me, he obeyed the summons with pleasure.

Chap. VI.

From my earliest years I had been exceedingly fond of learning languages, here necessity as well as inclination led me to be assiduous in my application to this subject. I took therefore the greatest pains to learn the name of every thing that presented itself to view, nor was Othono less eager to know my appellation of things. For the space of six hours did I employ myself in this manner, and from the readiness which every one shewed to assist me, acquired a decent vocabulary. My pocket-book which I never failed to carry about me was quite filled. Othono viewed the letters I made with attention, and I was also much surprized at seeing him write in a character perfectly new. Lawrence had now returned with our tent, boat, and luggage, which our friend ordered to be stowed on board one of the vessels, while our hammock was spread in a small room in the cave. We went to rest early, and I was no sooner in my room, which was illuminated by a taper of caoutchouc, than I began to meditate seriously upon my past adventures and future prospects. I must be miserably deceived indeed, said I to Lawrence, if these people have any bad intentions against us; we are now going to put ourselves under their protection, totally ignorant whither they mean to carry us. So far, said Lawrence, from thinking they mean to do us any harm, we ought to be thankful that we have met with such a humane and sociable people; and as to where they purpose carrying us, at all events we cannot do better than leave this barren spot. I verily thought that when we were first left here, we must either have been starved to death, or torn in pieces by wild beasts; instead of these we have found the most hospitable treatment, and by what I can foresee, our future prospects are better than the present: but I confess, Captain, the whole matter appears to me a perfect mystery. I am indeed myself, Lawrence, much at a loss to account for the humane treatment that we have experienced. Without any of that stiff formality that pervades every branch of European civilization, which almost withers humanity itself, by tending to render man a curse instead of a blessing to his fellow man, we meet with all that ease and freedom, which are the constant attendants upon innocence and contentment. At the same time we may be fully convinced by their dress and manners, by the order and regularity with which every thing is performed, the furniture of the dwelling, and the rigging and trim of the ships, that there is some civilized country at no great distance with which these people have communication. I verily believe it is as you say, replied Lawrence, but after all I shall be loath to part from little Munna. I heartily wish he could accompany us. I wish so too, Lawrence, but perhaps we may have some future opportunity of revisiting our young friend. We continued this sort of conversation till sleep overtook us, but the thoughts of our distance from Europe, and the uncertainty of our situation, disturbed much my repose with dreams. Methought I was placed in a garden enriched with abundance of beauteous flowers and choicest fruits. Upon examining them more attentively I found myself almost totally unacquainted both with their names and nature, but thinking it advisable to attempt to transplant some of them into my native soil, I began to collect as many roots and seeds as I was able to carry. Among the various flowers that struck my fancy was one that seemed to surpass all the rest, it was of a variegated hue, one half being of a brilliant mixt colour, and the other of a delightful white, and diffused its peculiar fragrance through the whole garden; this I was determined to add to my collection; but judge my astonishment when I found it surrounded with innumerable thistles that seemed to have been set by the hand of art. Through these I resolutely forced my way, and carefully selected two or three of its finest roots. What with the joy I felt at the idea of transporting to my own country so valuable a plant, and the pain that originated from the thistles, I awoke. Early in the morning Munna knocked at the door, calling our Captain! I was already dressed, and immediately let him in. He was very sorrowful, and shook me tenderly by the hand; I was myself low in spirits, for the goodness of the boy's heart had rivetted him in my affections. We began now to pack up our hammock and other trifles, and as Othono was waiting for us, and I thought that the shorter we were in taking leave the better, I comforted my little friend as well as I was able: I could not however think of parting from him without making him some compensation for the favours received from himself and family, having therefore brought myself to the resolution, I presented him with poor Mungo, and immediately went on board.

Chap. VII.

The wind blew fresh from the north, and our course, as I soon found, lay almost due east. A little inclined to the southward, and our rate of going was at least ten miles an hour. The crew consisted of Othono and two blacks, myself, and Lawrence. We had now sufficient time to examine the structure of the vessel. She was of great breadth upon deck, had a deep keel, and lay close in the water, which added to the shortness and consequent lightness of the masts, contributed much to her rate of going; but what pleased us most was a sort of elastic spring fastened to the main sheets, the use of which I apprehended to be this, that the increase or diminution of the wind's power might not be lost upon the action of the vessel.[d] The accommodations were

---

[d] The advantages that are likely to accrue from the use of shorter and lighter masts to shipping will, the Author hopes, sooner or later be an object worthy the attention of the British Government. The Author has been informed that one of the English men of war, when under jury-masts, sailed faster than under her proper masts. But as this work is intended to blend together the *utile dulci*, it may not be amiss here to consider the inconveniences that attend the masts now in use. First. To counterbalance their great weight and height, the resistance of the ballast must be increased. This is so apparent when the ship heels that it is sometimes with great difficulty that she is restored to her equipoise. A circumstance which not only impedes her way, but endangers her loss. Secondly. A great part of the wind's force is lost by the height of the mast; for instead of communicating direct motion to the vessel (which it would

good. In our voyage we passed in sight of several islands, which I could with great pleasure have visited, but having put myself under the direction of Othono, I deemed it improper to alter his plan. On the sixth day soon after day-break land was discovered at a great distance; as we approached I perceived it to be a large tract of country, beautifully interspersed with hill and dale, and almost covered with villages and plantations. We entered a narrow streight, between two old castles, and in a few minutes my eyes were presented with a most charming view. Figure to yourself, reader, a large expanse of water covered with shipping, and bounded on both sides with lands in the highest state of cultivation. Suppose at the extremity of this expanse a superb and spacious city, built on a gently rising ground that projected into the sea, and having in its centre a magnificent pile of building, whose lofty dome seemed towering to the clouds: you will then have a faint idea of the country and city of Makar. What then do you imagine must have been the joy of myself and Lawrence, who scarce a fortnight before thought ourselves doomed to misery and famine, and all at once as it were brought into the midst of happiness and plenty? Believe me it seemed all a dream, and I gazed with wonder and admiration.

Chap. VIII.

Othono was well known, and frequently spoken to as we passed the shipping. The quays and wharfs extended both ways as far as my eye could reach, and on landing I was surprized to see the cleanliness

do if the power were applied more centrically) it tends only to make her dip, and consequently lose her progressive motion. Thirdly, The ship's burthen is augmented, which is another reason for her way being impeded. On the contrary, by having shorter masts, the burthen of the ship is diminished, she heels less, and on that account may in proportion carry a greater quantity of sail, her progressive motion is increased, by the more centrical application of the wind's power, the expense is less, and the loss more easily supplied. Nor is it probable that the single advantage of catching the higher breezes in calmy weather will counterbalance the advantages above mentioned. At all events it would be worth while to make a trial. Respecting the elastic spring little more need be said now than that it was the invention of FRANCIS HOPKINSON, Esq. of *Philadelphia*, who received for it the Magellanic gold medal. The Author thinks the invention valuable, but it has its inconveniences. – For further particulars, see a very useful work now publishing in numbers, entitled *The Repertory of Arts and Manufactures*.[7]

[7] *The Repertory of Arts and Manufactures*, vol. I (1794), pp. 44–52.

and order with which they were kept. Othono conducted us through some spacious streets to his own house, which lay about half a mile from the landing-place. Here we were received by his worthy family with attention and respect. This family consisted of his wife, a woman of the most engaging manners, and of an excellent education, but unhappily much afflicted with disease, of two amiable daughters, and one son. For the first month of my residence my application was totally confined to their language, and at the end of this period I had made a very tolerable progress. I soon found that Othono was a man of very considerable property, and was therefore the more reconciled at taking up my abode at his house, and indeed so far from his thinking myself and Lawrence a burthen, I was fully convinced that he was happy in our company; but a fortunate occurrence tended to endear me to him for ever. His lady, whom he was doatingly fond of, continued for some time to labour under a bad state of health: this at length terminated in an intermittent fever that seemed to baffle the skill of her physician. I have already mentioned to my reader that I had carefully preserved part of the medicine chest, and having ever been partial to the study of physic, but through the perverseness and false modesty of those under whose direction I had been brought up, not permitted to practise it, I proposed one day to Othono to try my skill under the inspection of his physician. He listened to my proposal with attention, but shook his head, and observed, that he was unwilling to put his wife to any further torment, and that the physician whom he employed was of eminence in his profession. Will you then, said I, inform him of my proposal? He answered in the affirmative, and the next morning introduced to me a man of a very grave and respectable deportment, in whose face I could plainly observe the effects of study. He began with asking me several questions upon the nature of different diseases, and more particularly of the disease above mentioned. My answers gave him some degree of satisfaction. He then proceeded to examine the medicines that I had brought with me, the uses of which I clearly pointed out to him, as well as the remedies I meant to apply in the present instance. Upon this he turned to Othono, saying, I am satisfied, let this young man try his skill; possibly foreign medicines may be of service, when our native ones fail. Without troubling the reader with a recital of the various remedies I applied, suffice it to say that within the space of six days, my patient was pronounced in a fair way of recovery.

Chap. IX.

Othono's gratitude scarcely knew any bounds; I verily believe he would have given me half his property if I had chosen to accept it: but I told him that his persevering kindness and attention to me much more than counterbalanced my humble efforts; that knowledge and information were the only riches that I wished to acquire; that the happiness which I saw among all classes of people in that country; the almost total extinction of poverty, beggary, and vice; the great leniency and equality of their penal code, and particularly the utter abolition of the sanguinary and inhuman punishment of death; the facility with which every species of education, whether in arts, sciences, or manufactures, was acquired; the extreme cheapness of cloathing and provisions, with several other blessings exclusively enjoyed by the inhabitants of Makar; these I told him were topics upon which I could dwell for ever with enthusiasm, and that the knowledge of that government from which such innumerable blessings could be derived, was of more value in my estimation than all the riches in the world. They are blessings indeed, said Othono, and have not been acquired without tumult, but we have now enjoyed them for so many years that the people think not of their value. Before you mentioned this your desire of becoming better acquainted with our government, it had all along been my intention, as soon as you had obtained a proficiency in our language, to introduce you to a venerable member of our Senate; a man, Planetes, whose purity of morals and uprightness of conduct can only be equalled by his judgment, experience, and sagacity. This character I will not blush to give him thro' fear of being accounted partial. Believe me, Planetes, my venerable friend, Euthus, is almost adored by his country. He was a great actor in the Revolution, and to him we are much indebted for our present liberty and happiness, by the extirpation of a system of tyranny. The only fault that you will find in Euthus is, that you may perhaps think him too severe in his decisions. I have already mentioned you to him, and can assure you that he is very desirous of being made acquainted with you. He is eager to learn the manners and laws of your nation, the name of which neither he nor any one in this country have ever heard of. It was totally my fault that you were not introduced to each other sooner, but I determined that you should first become acquainted with our language. This amiable man,

Planetes, will be the fittest person to satisfy all your inquiries respecting our manners and customs, and therefore upon that head I shall with pleasure leave you to him. I have myself, continued Othono, been brought up almost from my infancy in the mercantile line, and it is only four years ago that I quitted my profession. At the same time habit is so strong upon me that I am perpetually making some short voyages. I was upon an expedition of this sort when I first saw you, the great preserver of my happiness, to whom – I will not permit you, said I, to proceed at this rate. Remember that if I had not met with you, in all probability I must have perished through want. But pray, Othono, can you give me any information relative to that worthy family of Indians whom we found upon the island? Here I perceived that he was rather unwilling to solve my question, the qualities of his heart were offended at the most distant revelation of their own merit. His wife whom I shall henceforth call Clarina, and who had listened in mute attention to our discourse, now broke silence. Indeed, Planetes, I must inform you the whole truth. Othono first visited that island about five years ago, and finding it to abound in a variety of fish, proposed to found an Indian colony upon it, and provide the inhabitants with all the requisite materials for fishing. This he accomplished, but the island not being inhabitable in the winter months, on account of the boisterous weather and lying at a great distance to the west from all the other inhabited islands, he sends his colony every spring, and it returns in the latter end of autumn. Othono frequently visits the island, and I sometimes accompany him. The islanders bring their fish, which they cure and dry on the spot, to our market. I thanked Clarina for her information, and admired Othono's goodness. But how comes it to pass, said I, that those poor Indians talk two languages, for both I and my friend Lawrence have persuaded ourselves that we heard two distinctly. Clarina smiled, and Othono replied, when you know us better, you will learn, that every nation, whether black or white, that traffics with us, brings up some if not all of its children to speak the Makar tongue with its own, and indeed it is now become a sort of universal language. A most excellent institution, said I, I wish our tardy Europeans would do likewise. We are always complaining of the want of an universal medium, but have not spirit enough to put it into execution.

Chap. X.

Thus ended the present conversation, and soon after breakfast the next day, Othono came to my room leading Euthus in his hand. I am come, said Othono, according to my promise, to introduce to you my worthy friend Euthus, and if I mistake not you will neither of you be displeased with the other. If from the character I had received of Euthus I had not already been prepossessed in his favour, his appearance would have inspired respect and reverence. Euthus, who was something above the middle stature, was covered with the snow of years, and in the lines of his countenance I could plainly trace the effects of deep study and penetrating discernment, at the same time there was that gravity in his demeanour that brought to my mind the inflexible Cato. I began with thanking him for his kindness in thus visiting me, and that I must place it among the many obligations that I lay under to my worthy host. Talk not, Planetes, of obligations, we are all human, we stand in need of the assistance of each other, and happy is the man to whose lot it falls to be of the greatest service to his fellow-creatures. Your observation, Euthus, is just, but surely you would not expunge gratitude from the human breast. We may be mindful, Planetes, of benefits conferred upon us, but remember that it is a duty to do good, and a virtuous man will neither expect nor desire thanks for performing his duty: the best reward that a good man can receive for his actions, is the reward of an approving mind. It is indeed true that in my younger days I have seen men receive public thanks from the State for performing very trivial services; but it was a proof of the corruption of the age; the generality of men must be bad indeed, when it is found necessary to return public thanks to the few that do their duty. Another evil attending these public thanks is, that they soon degenerate into the mere effusions of party zeal. It was in some measure from my view of things in this light that I foretold the revolution that soon followed in our government; and I think my experience will authorize me in saying, that no government can long stand that praises its own partizans, while it either totally neglects or endeavours to disparage the merits of its opponents.' There is however, continued Euthus, this misfortune

---

' Τοῑ (εφη Αντισθενης) τας πολες απολλυσθαι, ὁταν μη δυνωνται τους φαυλους απο των σπουδαιων διακρινειν.

Then, said Antisthenes, do cities perish, when they can no longer distinguish the good from the bad. DIOC. LAERT.[8]

[8] Diogenes Laertius *et al.*, *The Lives of the Ancient Philosophers* (1702), p. 252.

attending the actions of man, viz. that he no sooner escapes from one extreme than he runs into another. You will perhaps hardly give me credit when I tell you that the Makarians are so eager to reward merit, that no sooner does a man find any error, proved such before any of our committees, in their laws or government, than they enroll his name among the benefactors of his country. But I should be glad to know, Planetes, how you, who, according to Othono's account, are situated almost at our Antipodes, conduct yourselves in these matters. I assure you I expect much entertainment as well as much improvement from an account of your manners, laws, and history. By this direct accost I appeared not a little confused. I knew almost from my first arrival that the Makarians were nearly a century before us in civilization, and from what I had just heard I could have wished rather to receive a full account of the constitution and government of Makar, than enter into any particulars about my own. I was therefore at a loss how to proceed; but Euthus who perceived my confusion, very humanely relieved me by observing; Be under no fear, young man; if you have not yet made such progress in civilization as the Makarians, you should recollect that we are not arrived at perfection, but have several links in the great chain of human happiness to fill up; nor ought we to repine at this, nothing is stable that does not approach gradually to its consummation; to build an edifice that shall last for ages, it must be a work of time. Since then all governments are more or less imperfect, it is our duty to glean the virtues of each, and by applying them to our own country, endeavour thereby to remedy its defects and increase its welfare. Without further ceremony then I shall hope, Planetes, you will grant my request.

Chap. XI.

After all necessary apologies for my youth and inexperience, I began with laying before him the great valour of my countrymen, even from the descent of Cæsar. The glorious victories of Crecy, and Poictiers, and Agincourt, and Blenheim, the siege of Valenciennes and defence of Gibraltar. I stated our renown in naval tactics, describing the bravery of Admiral Benbow, the battles of La Hogue, and the twelfth of April, and the first of June. I enlarged with great fervour upon the vast extent of the British territories; that the British empire itself consisted of the three kingdoms of England, Ireland, and Scotland, beside the Principality of Wales; that his Britannick Majesty continued in the possession of the Electorate of Hanover, his hereditary dominion; that this Electorate gave him great sway in the German empire; that the Britons possessed almost a continent in the East Indies, distant from us a diameter of the world; that we had a vast empire in America and the West Indies; that the British name was known even at Oczakow and Nootka Sound. I then reverted to William the Conqueror, shewed that he was a hero of prodigious valour, but I carefully concealed the bastardy of his birth. I next went through in a cursory way the succession of our kings; magnified the vast advantages the barons had gained from John in the great charter; skimmed over the history of the civil wars among the Yorkists and Lancastrians, and rested not till I came to the glorious reign of Elizabeth; here I dwelt with enthusiasm upon the victory over the Spanish Armada, and doubted whether I admired more the virgin purity of the Queen, or the greatness of her understanding and love of justice. I then went on to the Revolution, and much admired the great condescension of William in accepting the crown. But I hope the reader will pardon my not proceeding further upon this subject. I cannot prevail upon myself so to hurt his feelings or my own modesty as to mention publicly the great and good things that I said of all the Georges, particularly of the great patriot who now fills the throne.

The next topic that I adverted to was that eminent trait of benevolence, and high sense of honour that pervade all ranks of British subjects. Here I instanced the patriotic donations to the oppressed Poles, and subsidies to our worthy ally the King of Prussia. I alledged that it was owing to these our virtues that we voluntarily paid kings for defending their own dominions, that we had thereby incurred an immense debt that we should never be enabled to discharge, and that nations borrowed of us that had no idea of refunding. Before I concluded this topic I deemed it expedient to say a few words relative to the just and necessary war in which we were then and are now most happily engaged. This then I called a war of reason against insanity, of virtue against vice, of religion against atheism. I told Euthus that all the potentates in Christendom in the least renowned either for valour, power, or wealth, for the purity of their government, or the love which they inspired into their subjects, for their high sense of justice, piety and law, had concentrated their forces against a nation consisting of the most execrable, detestable, impious, atheistical, hideous, sanguinary, obstreperous, tumultuous, vile, lawless, infernal, outcasts, cut-throats, murderers, robbers, plunderers, monsters, that ever polluted the face of the earth:[f] that the sun itself would soon forget to shine upon such complicated masses of deformity, depravity and sin; that they had either put to an ignominious death, or extirpated from their kingdom every person of probity and virtue; that though it had pleased the Disposer of events to give them hitherto the victory in the day of battle, yet that it was only to make their fall the heavier by a temporary elevation,[g] and that I entertained just hopes that a prophecy of one of my countrymen would be verified, viz. that this nation would soon be a blank in the map of Europe. Having gone through this, and a great deal more, much to my own satisfaction, I next proceeded to our laws.

Chap. XII.

And here the first thing that occurred, was what had occurred to a celebrated foreigner at a time when he resided in my country, viz. the frequency of capital punishments; but instead of looking upon it as "a melancholy truth," as a weak-nerved Judge[h] had once done, I

---

[f] The enthusiastic reader may select a few more sublime appellations from the following:

> – tatterdemalions,
> Scald-miserables, rascals and rascalions,
> Buffoons, dependants, parasites, toad-eaters,
> Knaves, sharpers, black-legs, palmers, coggers, cheaters,
> Scrubs, vagrants, beggars, mumpers, ragamuffins,
> Rogues, villains, bravos, desperados, ruffians,
> Thieves, robbers, cut-throats, &c.
>
> ROLLIAD[9]

[g] Consuesse enim Deos immortales, quo gravius homines ex commutatione rerum doleant, quos pro feelere eorum ulcisci velint, his secundiores interdum res, et diuturniorem inpunitatem concedere. CÆSAR. B. G. Lib. I. Cap. XIV.[10]

The immortal Gods are accustomed to grant a considerable degree of prosperity and a long impunity to wicked men, that they may feel their punishment the heavier by a change of circumstances.

[h] It is *a melancholy truth*, that among the variety of actions which men are daily liable to commit, no less than an hundred and sixty have been declared by act of parliament to be felonies without benefit of clergy; or in other words, to be worthy of instant death. So dreadful a list, instead of diminishing, *increases* the number of offenders. BLACKSTONE[11], Vol. IV. Chap. I.

[9] *The Rolliad, in Two Parts; Probationary Odes for the Laureateship; and Political Miscellanies* (1795), p. 104.

[10] *Civilli Caesaris Commentariorum, De Bello Gallico* (1654), p. 10.

[11] William Blackstone, *Commentaries on the Laws of England* (11th edn, 4 vols., 1791), vol. IV, p. 18.

magnified the great advantages that accrued therefrom to the more peaceable part of our society. Euthus, who till now had preserved the most becoming silence, here interrupted me by asking how many crimes were liable to be punished with death? I answered about two hundred. My answer I perceived evidently astonished him. And are you certain, Planetes, of what you say? O yes! returned I, it is as true as that you are a Makarian, and I a Briton; I have seen ten or twelve hanged on one day with my own eyes. Nor ought he to wonder at the equality of punishment, for that there had existed upwards of two thousand years ago, a certain sect of philosophers who maintained that all crimes were equal, and therefore it followed of course that punishments should be so likewise. I now entered into an account of the names and nature of our different laws, but as it would be impertinent and useless to trouble my countrymen, of whose education this study makes a necessary part, I shall not repeat a tedious detail of burglaries, felonies, recognizances, certioraries, excise, bastardies, petit-larcenies, and black-acts. Neither shall I lay before them the manner how I enlarged upon the great benefits attending the amazing length of some of our law causes, the infinite number of our lawyers, or the refinements, forms, ceremonies, and fictions, with which those bulwarks of our constitution have strengthened the pillars of the state. No! I will leave entirely to their own candour to suppose that I forgot neither writs, pleadings, or misnomers; detinues, trespasses, actions upon case; replications, surjoinders, rebutters, counts and bars; pones, sub-poenas, or qui-tams. Suffice it to say that after a nine hours speech of the historical and natural epitome of the laws; I concluded with observing that the laws themselves would occupy a space of five or six hundred folios, and that three lives of man were insufficient to procure a competent knowledge of their value, but that the study of the laws was so intoxicating that no man ever sat down to them without receiving pleasure and improvement. Lastly I proved that the quantity of law was calculated only to increase the liberty and security of the people.

I now told him that I was willing to proceed with the history of our constitution, but as it consisted of three parts, each in itself a whole, I thought it right to arrange my ideas into some method, and therefore if he pleased would delay it till to-morrow morning. To this proposal Euthus spontaneously assented.

Chap. XIII.

We were now called down to dinner, and tho' I was not at all fatigued with my labours, for who can possibly be fatigued with recounting the virtues of his country? yet I deemed it proper to comply with the rules of the house, and therefore obeyed the call. Euthus was remarkably reserved all dinner-time, which I attributed to the conviction I had produced upon his mind of the excellence of our laws, so that the same cause that effected his silence contributed to the exhilaration of my spirits. As soon as dinner was over, I returned to my apartment, and began to ponder upon the powers of my own eloquence that could produce conviction upon the mind of a total stranger of such acuteness and soundness of judgement; for I then concluded very naturally that as Euthus had not dissented from any thing I had asserted, nay! had scarcely once opened his lips, so he must have been fully convinced of the rectitude of what I had advanced, and hence I judged that my former opinion concerning our laws, viz. that some trivial errors during the last ten centuries had crept into them, was erroneous. Emboldened by these considerations, I sat down with pleasure to draw up an epitome of our excellent constitution. But here a serious obstacle presented itself; I knew that almost all our great men had allowed, particularly when they were out of place, that it stood in need of reformation, and consequently in all probability was somewhat defective, but as I was unwilling to point out any of its defects, I thought it best to omit them altogether, and leave it to the sagacity of Euthus to find them out. With this resolution I drew up, and presented to Euthus the next morning the following sketch of the English constitution.

Chap. XIV.

The English constitution then consists of king, lords, and commons. In the king who is an hereditary monarch is vested the executive power, and it is from the stability of this power that many important advantages flow to the people. Among others the liberty they enjoy in assembling freely to deliver their sentiments on the abuses that may have crept into the constitution, and their right to petition for a remedy of those abuses; that although it is a maxim of the English law that the king can do no wrong, that is, that his person is inviolable, yet as he cannot act without ministers, ministers are made responsible for his actions; that the king has the prerogative of making war or peace, but that taxes the sinews of war, are lodged in the hands of the representatives of the people; that the king is the head of the courts of laws, and has the power of remitting punishment to criminals; he is also head of the church; that though he has a share in making laws he is obliged to abide by them when made, that he is guided in all his actions by the advice of his privy council, that is, by some of the greatest men in the nation; and that he cannot keep a standing army without consent of parliament.

The House of Lords is a sort of mean between the king and commons, curbing by its rectitude and impartiality as well the violence of the latter as despotism of the former. I set forth that it is the great bulwark of the landed interest; that it is composed of the ablest, the most virtuous, and richest men in the kingdom; that it is the great point of honor to which the members of the lower house aspire as a reward to their merit; that part of their body is composed of the dignitaries of the church, men of the strictest morals, and chosen only on account of the eminent qualifications they possess to further the progress of religion and virtue, that these holy men being totally unbiased in their opinions and generally acting together, tend wonderfully to maintain the balance of the constitution[i], and that on these accounts it has been thought proper to enrich them with large benefices: that another portion of this assembly consists of the judges of the law, chosen like the bishops on account of their superior knowledge and virtues; that all impeachments of state criminals are brought before this august house, and that from its decisions there lies no appeal; that lastly, by reason of the eminent services it has done the state, its honors are hereditary, which honors are in the gift of the king, who is unlimited in his use of them.

The House of Commons is the representative of the nation, chosen by the different counties into which the kingdom is divided, by certain towns, and by certain boroughs, has the immense prerogative of

---

[i] How ridiculous then does the following affirmation of the Duke of Argyle appear, 'That the clergy in all ages have delivered up the rights and privileges of the people?' – SMOLLETT.[12] Vol. 2. B. I. Ch. x.

[12] Tobias Smollett, *A Complete History of England* (4 vols., 1758), vol. IV, p. 367 (Bk 8, ch. 10)

laying on taxes, and assists in making laws; that it is prorogued or dissolved at the will of the king; that the regular period of its power is seven years, but that it was formerly triennial, and before that annual; that each of its members must have certain qualifications in landed property; and in order to prevent undue influence, there are heavy penalties against bribery, and no peer or officer of the crown is allowed upon any account to interfere in elections; that this house is generally divided into parties variously denominated, such as ministry and opposition, court and country, tory and whig, aristocrats and republicans, &c. &c. but that each of these parties has no other view in its debates and disputations than the good of its country.

Such, Euthus, are the constituent parts of the English parliament, whose power is in all cases supreme, except that it can neither alter a fundamental principle of the constitution, nor 'make a man a woman, or a woman a man.'[j]

Chap. XV.

In addition to the above blessings, which the candid reader will undoubtedly conclude, from the nature of conversation, that I expatiated upon with much greater fulness than I have here represented, I observed that both houses of parliament were allowed the utmost freedom of debate, and that with respect to the nation at large, the liberty of the press was almost unbounded, but that the chief prop of the constitution was founded on the TRIAL by JURY. Here the genuine Briton will necessarily suppose that I left no argument untried that tended to enhance the value of this mode of judicial proceeding. I told Euthus that it was the greatest check we had upon the arbitrary proceedings of tyrannical kings, corrupt ministers, and profligate judges; that these men were so well aware of this circumstance, that several daring attempts had been made to undermine this corner stone of our liberties. Juries had been packed; sheriffs' books corrupted; judges had summed up causes with partiality, and put their own arbitrary construction upon the written laws of the land; and that the time was when juries had been punished with

---

[j] 'It is a fundamental principle with the English lawyers that parliament can do every thing, except making a woman a man, or a man a woman.'
DE LOLME on the Constitution.[13] Chap. x. in a note.

[13] J. L. De Lolme, *The Constitution of England* (1789), p. 134.

fine and imprisonment for delivering a verdict according to their consciences; but that at present the rights of juries were so well know, that even supposing attornies could be found to commence, or judges to superintend prosecutions professedly against the rights of the people, juries were also to be found whose hearts would vibrate in unison with an approving audience, and whose tongues would utter, amidst a shower of applause, the verdict of their rights.

To conclude, I observed that a government composed of a well tempered mixture of monarchy, aristocracy, and democracy had been for ages the admiration of the world, that two ancient philosophers of great eminence had written in its praise, and that a celebrated historian had treated it as a subject more worthy of admiration than likely to come to pass, adding at the same time that if ever it did come to pass, its existence would be of short duration.*ᵏ* And indeed, said Euthus, fetching a deep sigh, I think the historian is in the right. Reader! have you ever seen a sportive schoolboy whipping off the tops of the stately nettle? or have you ever been in a London mob, and spied a roguish hand pop from a baker's basket, pulling therein the periwig of some enraged wight? or lastly, have you ever seen a handsome beau tipped on the shoulder by the ugly bailiff? If you have,

---

ᵏ Πολιτειαν δε αριστην, την μικτην εκ τε δημοκρατιας και βασιλεια και αριστοκρατιας. – DIOG LAERT. in ZENONE.[14]

Statuo esse optime constitutam Rempublicam quæ ex tribus generibus illis, Regali, Optimo, et Populari, modice confusa. – CIC. FRAGM. ut fertur.[15]

Cunctas Nationes et Urbes, Populus aut Priores aut Singuli regunt. Delecta ex his et constituta Reipublicæ forma laudari facilius quam evenire; vel si evenit, haud diuturna esse potest. – TACIT. An. lib. IV.[16]

The two last quotations are taken from De Lolme[17]; and to these may be added the following from Aristotle.

Ενιοι μεν ουν λεγουσιν ως δει την αριστην πολιτειαν εξ απασων ειναι των πολιτειων μεμγμενην. And again; Βελτιον ουν λεγουσιν δι πλειους μγνυντες ή γαρ εν πλειωνων συγκειμενη πολιτεια, βελτιων.

Politic. Lib. II

[14] Diogenes Laertius: *Vit.*, n7.131.5–6: 'The best constitution is that which is a mixture of democracy, monarchy and aristocracy.'

[15] Cicero: 'I think that the best state is that which is a mixture of the three types, monarchic, aristocratic and democratic.'

[16] Tacitus: 'All nations and cities are ruled by the people, the nobility, or by one man. A constitution, formed by a selection out of these elements, it is easy to commend but not to produce; or if it is produced, it cannot be lasting' (*Annals*, IV.31)

[17] Aristotle: 'Some, indeed, say that the best constitution is a mixture of all the types of constitutions' (*Politics*, 1265b.33–4); and: 'But better are those which combine many forms. For the constitution which consists of many elements is better' (*Politics*, 1266a.4–5); cf. Aristotle. *A Treatise of Government*, transl. William Ellis (1778), p. 70.

reader! you may form some inadequate judgement of the abasement, surprize, and rage that pervaded my whole frame at this solitary remark of Euthus. Although I was satisfied that my abilities were insufficient to set forth our glorious constitution in its genuine colours, yet by the silent attention that Euthus had paid to every thing that I had advanced, I had buoyed myself up with the hopes of receiving his warmest applause; but alas! these hopes were all blasted.

Chap. XVI.

I perceive, young man, said Euthus, that my answer has somewhat disconcerted you; perhaps you do not sufficiently understand my meaning. Let me explain myself. I believe it then morally impossible that a government consisting of three equal and distinct parts ever did, or ever can exist. For first with respect to your own, whenever any motion *of importance* is brought forward by the ministry, the two houses must either agree to it or disagree, if they agree, it appears to my mind to be a play upon words to call such a government mixt; and if they disagree, the wheels of government will be clogged. True! Euthus, but it is presumed that each house has the good of its country so much at heart, that it would of itself agree to the more material points, and yet be a powerful check upon all rash, improper or unlawful measures. I willingly concede to you, Planetes, this inhibitory power, but in that case your government becomes a monarchy under certain restraints. Now provided that these restraints are pure and effective, a circumstance which I may hereafter have occasion to discuss, I am ready to allow that such a government is best adapted of any to the present state of your nation: but this has little to do with the subject before us. Another reason then for my disbelief in the existence of a triple government is the following. From the whole tenor of history we may safely conclude that whenever two or three distinct powers arise in any state, each will be in perpetual struggle for mastery, and this mastery will inevitably be obtained either in secret or openly, by force of arms, or dint of bribery and corruption. In addition to the above I may observe, that neither the philosophers or historian whom you have cited meant by democracy any other than the viva voce government of the people, nor did they dream of the representative system, such as yours is or ought to be, and which I esteem a vast improvement upon the other. But let us examine this matter a little more closely. You have said, Planetes, that your house of lords is a sort of check upon the other parts of the constitution. Now without entering an inquiry into the nature and process of electing bishops, how can you reconcile such a declaration with the prerogative that the king possesses of creating peers at will? This single reflection, even allowing that the king uses his power in the most cautious and prudent manner possible, necessarily overthrows your argument. With regard to the lower house, I see so many proofs of its not always being the voice of the people, that I hesitate where to begin. The existence of such innumerable laws,[*] the immense burthen of your taxes, and the greatness of your national debt, to which I might add the dreadful consequences of these evils, viz. beggary, vice, and poverty, are sufficient proofs of themselves that all is not right; but pray, Planetes, let me ask you two questions: What is the cause of the constant opposition in the lower house, for constant it must be by the appellations that both parties give each other? and in what manner are the members for the boroughs returned? Here I hesitated, and was covered with confusion. Euthus, with a severity upon his countenance that I had been totally unaccustomed to, immediately remarked; I tell you what, young man, though I rejoice at seeing the colour of virtue upon your cheeks, yet it is necessary that you should know, that the inhabitants of Makar are a plain honest people, and detest all shuffling and deceit; if you mean therefore to continue in my good opinion, you must act with candour and sincerity. Believe me, continued Euthus softening a little, a true lover of his country will rather endeavour to lay open the defects of its government in order to procure their abolition, than strive to conceal them; the confined flames, Planetes, burst forth with the greatest fury. Euthus! said I, let me intreat your forgiveness. I confess that many and great defects allowed such by our best statesmen and philosophers, have crept into our constitution. I moreover confess that, from the violent opposition which every proposal of reform has hitherto met with even from those who had been previously esteemed its greatest advocates, I am inclined to believe that there is little hope of its ever taking place; I fear, Euthus, that the evil has now increased

---

[*] Corruptissima Republica plurimæ leges.

TACIT. An. Lib. III.[18]

[18] Tacitus: 'laws were most numerous when the commonwealth was most corrupt' (*Annals*, III.27)

beyond remedy; and this circumstance gives me the more uneasiness, because I am persuaded of the truth of your observation, that all things considered, the mixt government is the best adapted to the present state of my nation. Do not despair, Planetes, the voice of the people is no feeble voice, it must be attended to sooner or later. And now since you have confessed your error, I will no longer hurt your feelings by prying into the defects of your government, the nature of which I am but too sensible of, as well from the description that you have just given, as from the similarity between your ministry and our Schumalahs (that is, counsellors to the king) previous to the revolution; a concise account of which I will with pleasure now lay before you.

Chap. XVII.

The Makarians were originally under the dominion of Schums,[m] and during that period which lasted for many centuries, their history like almost all the histories of the world presents little more than a mere recital of various acts of oppression, corruption, and slaughter. The advice which one of our Schums had given his son, never to suffer the Makarians to remain long in peace, was religiously put in execution by his successors.[n] Pretexts for war were never wanting. Friends, brothers and relatives were equally our enemies. To-day we should embrace as allies those whom to-morrow we should endeavour to destroy, and the soldier was led out a mere automaton to butcher his fellow creatures in cold blood. All this time philosophy the parent of freedom lay buried in obscurity, while ignorance the guardian of slavery and superstition made rapid strides throughout the nation. It was not however in the nature of things that her dominion could last for ever, and our learned men assert that there is a regular chain of

[m] The original meaning of the word *Schum* is *great* or *vast*, and in the sense here taken answers to our *King* or *Emperor*. Here it is proper to inform the reader, that in order not to alarm him by outlandish terms, I have for the most part, a few instances only excepted, presented him with these memoirs of Planetes in an English dress.

[n] Some of my readers may be surprized to hear that this 'was the dying injunction of Henry IV. He advised his son, *never to let the English remain long in peace*, which was *apt to breed intestine commotions*; but to employ them in *foreign expeditions*, by which the prince might *acquire honour*, the *nobility* in *sharing his dangers* might attach themselves to his person, and all the *restless spirits* find occupation for their *inquietude.*'

V. Encyc. Britan.[19]

[19] *Encylopaedia Britannica* (2nd edn, 1779), vol. IV, p. 2780.

causes by which civilized man arrives at perfection in government. From one and nearly the last link of this chain depends the state of Schums. The truth seems to be that man will not exert his powers without opposition; while the means of living are easy of attainment, he does not much concern himself about his governors, but when these means are rendered difficult, owing perhaps to the nature of government by Schums, it is then that he opens his eyes, and inquires into the cause of the evils that surround him: in this inquiry he is aided by the first beams of philosophy, which soon brighten into mid-day and illumine him for ever. Thus it was with the inhabitants of Makar. Within the two last centuries had arisen several patriotic writers of abilities and virtues, and among others two of great eminence, who dared not only to expose to the people the defects of their own government, but freely to discuss the subject of government in general. These men became objects of detestation to our rulers, and in spite of their integrity and popularity were persecuted, condemned and executed. The severity of these measures destroyed their efficacy; it is true indeed that for a short period the spirit of the people seemed broken, but the seed of liberty was sown and the harvest was soon to be abundant.

But to proceed; the system of wars continued, and, upon every trifling advantage gained, prayers and thanksgivings were offered up to Vishnou,[*] for having given us the victory in the day of battle, adding at the same time entreaties for a continuance of his all-powerful aid and protection: upon defeat, nothing was to be heard of but fasts and supplications. But supplications, fasts, thanksgivings, and prayers, had lost their effect upon the people. Those clouds of ignorance, superstition, and credulity, which had for so many ages hung over mankind, now began to be dissipated, and the nation was determined no longer to submit, without murmur, to that accumulation of misery and wretchedness which oppressed them, as well from iniquitous and sanguinary laws, as from overburthened taxation. They resolved, therefore, to enter a strict inquiry into the cause of that system of warfare in which they were constantly immerged; and to this inquiry they were urged by innumerable writers, who, fearless of prisons or punishment, which nevertheless were profusely bestowed upon them,

---

[*] Vishnou was the *name* then given by the Makarians to the Author of the Universe. He is now generally styled *the Supreme, the Unknown*. N. B. Vishnou was one of the names of Foe the Indian Divinity.

dared to publish to the world the wholesome dictates of truth and justice.

There is a proverb, Planetes, among the Makarians, that evils generally bring with them their remedies; this was soon to be verified. Our last Schum was a plain, simple, well-meaning, harmless man, but extremely unfortunate in the choice of his counsellors. These were for the most part men of boundless ambition; rash and intemperate in their undertakings; proud and insolent to those who thought differently from themselves; scorning openly to take advice, but secretly adopting the measures that they had pretended to despise; mock-patriots who at a time when their tongues were employed in speaking words of comfort to the nation, were engaging in measures that tended inevitably to augment its misery; men who bestowed without limit every place of profit, honor, or importance upon themselves, relatives, or friends, but persecuted without mercy those who had the resolution to oppose their proceedings. Such men were our last Schumalahs, and the chief of these, whose name was Baltrolph, excited more odium than the rest from his having first brought himself into notice by a determined opposition to their measures, and steady support of the rights of the people. These men retained their power principally by means of a system of spies and informers, that would have disgraced a nation of Ourans.*

I was at this time a great favourite with the people, and consequently the chief object of resentment and hatred with the Schumalahs. Every term of reproach, every species of misrepresentation, were profusely heaped upon me, but misrepresentation and reproach frequently attack merit.* They had not yet dared to touch my person: in this their courage failed them. The truth is, that independently of the support and protection that I drew from the people, I had several powerful friends in higher life who seconded my endeavours to alleviate our sufferings. But here was the vulnerable part. The Schumalahs finding their efforts against me ineffectual, determined to lay siege

---

* The particulars relating to the Ourans have really escaped my memory, but I perfectly recollect it was a nation where spies and informers abounded, and where power was upheld by every species of corrupt influence; by bribes, contracts, jobs, salaries, pensions, places, perquisites, expectations, promises, alarms, threats, frowns, nods, winks, smiles, &c. &c. – PLANETES.

* Απτεται δ'εσθλων αει. – PINDAR.[20]

[20] Pindar: 'Envy always fastens upon the brilliant.'

to my friends; every weapon in their power was employed in the attack, and sorry am I to say that partly by bribery and promises, partly by alarms and fears, they carried their point, and several of those men in whom I had hitherto been accustomed to place the greatest confidence all at once deserted me and my cause. This event gave me at first considerable uneasiness, but I found consolation in reflecting on the justice of the cause in which I had engaged, and in considering that those few friends who still remained true to me, would on this account be the more stedfast and persevering. The sun's rays never burn more intensely than when converged to a focus.

Not to trouble you, Planetes, with a tedious narrative; a new war brought on a new and incredible load of taxes; provisions and cloathing were advanced in price; commerce was rapidly on the decline: misery and poverty increased among the lower classes of men, and luxury and gluttony were not diminished among the higher. In short the passions of the people were inflamed to the highest pitch, and after every other method had failed of redressing their wrongs, they framed a remonstrance, drawn up with moderation and firmness, against the destructive measures of the Schumalahs, and deputed me to present it to the Schum himself. This being a step that was never taken but in times of the greatest difficulty and distress, the whole nation stood in anxious expectation of the event.

Chap. XVIII.

I know not how it is, continued Euthus, but when wicked men have arrived at a certain degree of depravity, they continue to plunge themselves deeper and deeper into error, until they are entirely overwhelmed. Instead of taking warning from these spirited proceedings of the people, and relaxing in the violence of their measures, the Schumalahs had the audacity or rather insanity to surround my house with a considerable body of the military, who hurried me instantly to prison. I asked the commanding officer upon what authority he warranted his conduct, but the only answer that I could obtain was, that he obeyed orders. The fury of the people was by these means kept under, and indeed had it not been so, I should have been the first to dissuade them from all tumult and violence. Reason and truth are the only weapons with which I would encounter my adversaries, and fully am I assured that reason and truth are more powerful than the sword, the bayonet, or the gallows: indeed it has always been a favourite maxim with me, that we have no right in any case whatever, except self-defence, to put a fellow-creature to death. But more of this hereafter. Much time was not allowed me for deliberation upon which law of the land I was thus imprisoned, for very soon after commitment I was given to understand that an indictment for high treason was preparing to be brought against me by the chief Schumalah, Baltrolph, setting forth that I, not having the fear of Vishnou before my eyes, but being moved and seduced by the instigation of Oonnanoo, did compass and imagine the death of my sovereign the Schum; and secondly, that I had levyed war against my sovereign the Schum in his realm, by an attempt by intimidation and violence to force the repeal of law.[r] Though I was well aware of the frivolousness and wickedness of these accusations, and made no doubt that any upright judge would instantly and honourably acquit me; though I could prove by innumerable witnesses the domestic tranquillity of my whole life, and my professed enmity to every species of violence and bloodshed; yet I was ignorant to what degree of desperation my enemies might be driven: they knew equally with myself how much philosophy had illumined the understanding of the nation, and that the impaired edifice of the constitution without further investigation was in danger of falling and crushing them to atoms. Of this investigation I had myself been ever the strenuous advocate and promoter. It was an argument therefore with my opponents that if the leader were punished the followers would be intimidated. How futile are the expectations of man! How little is he prepared to avert those evils from himself, which he is planning for others! The rage of the people had increased almost to madness, and they called aloud upon the soldiery to join their cause; several of them immediately obeyed, and the nation was upon the verge of a civil war.

As soon as the Schumalahs found how matters went, they not only released me from prison, but deprecated my wrath with the most cringing servility. Arrogance indeed in prosperity, and meanness in adversity are the characteristics of base minds, and never was that

---

[r] I hope the candid reader will not accuse me of any discordance on account of my having rendered the above passage in words more familiarized to my ear. He may rest assured that the substance of the narrative of Euthus is faithfully recorded, and trivial defects it is hoped will be overlooked. N. B. Oonnanoo was the devil of the Makarians before the revolution.

truth better exemplified than in the present instance; but it was too late, and no longer in my power to stem the torrent. The convulsion increased; the greatest part of our rulers fell a sacrifice, and it was with the utmost difficulty that myself and friends upon our knees could preserve the life of the Schum himself. An annual allowance was afterwards granted him, and he retired to a private station, where he died of old age about fifteen years ago.

Like a phœnix just risen from its ashes, the people began to feel their mighty strength. The corruption of the state had been known hitherto only by its effects, it was now exposed to view in its most secret operations, the extent of which was inconceivable. But this is a topic, Planetes, that it gives me pain to dwell upon; I shall therefore hasten to subjects of more material consideration.

The revolution commenced; the people with arms in their hands demanded a restitution of their rights, and that a new constitution should be founded upon those rights; that hereditary distinctions and primogeniture systems should cease, and that a new code of laws should immediately be framed upon the rights of man; they boldly asserted that it was unjust that they should pay for the extravagance of their ancestors, or servile compliance of their governors, and therefore insisted upon the abolition of taxes and national debt. They moreover declared their resolution not to lay down their arms until their demands were complied with.

This event I had long foreseen, and as it had ever been a favourite maxim with me, 'never entirely nor at once to depart from antiquity,' I had given those in power, every possible warning of its approach, that by timely reformation they might have prevented it. I had proceeded too upon another principle. The immediate effects of a revolution in government are generally disastrous, and even allowing the ultimate consequences to be general happiness, it is the part of a just man not to do evil that good may come. My admonition, as I have already mentioned, had been received with contempt; and the event which I had predicted having come to pass, it became my duty to render the evils attending that event as little felt as possible. Happy am I in being able to say that, the Schumalahs excepted, not a single life was lost.

Chap. XIX.

The people now proceeded to the choice of delegates of the several districts to form their new constitution. The first question that came before us was, whether the Makarian government should be a limited monarchy, or a representative republic?[s]

The advocate for the former began with observing, that he saw with concern the bias of the people to a republic, but was nevertheless convinced that they were as yet unprepared for such a change in their government: that a proper degree of veneration should be held for the sentiments and institutions of our ancestors, and that, when the abuses that had crept into our monarchy should be pruned away, and the responsibility of its agents fully established, taxes would be speedily diminished, commerce recovered, and the people be rendered free, prosperous, and contented. He advised the house by no means to listen to the specious arguments of artful and designing men, who had no other object in view than to work upon the passions of the people, and thereby make them a step-ladder to their own exaltation. He observed that monarchy was best adapted to large states, which require vigour, union, and celerity in action; that it prevented the evils attendant upon ambition, and rewarded talents by affording them protection; that it nourished the polite arts; secured property, and encouraged obedience to law. That in a republic every thing was anarchy, confusion and inconstancy; where every one was master no one would obey; that the mass of the people being doomed by their situation to ignorance, would always be liable to the impositions of factious leaders, and even allowing that men of virtue would sometimes get the ascendancy, their virtue would be represented only as a mask, and they themselves fall under the suspicion of an endeavour to usurp the rights of the people; that property would be rendered insecure; that laws would be broken with impunity; that the house of representatives would be divided, and that this division would inevitably engender civil wars; hence all the peace and prosperity of the country would be destroyed, and barbarism would ultimately ensue.

Here again I beg leave to inform the reader, that for the sake of perspicuity, and to avoid a greater number of notes, I have used those words that best accord with his ideas and mine.

Chap. XX.

To this mode of reasoning it was objected on the other side, that monarchy was adapted only to the rude uncultivated state of mankind, when being but a little removed from the brute creation, they required a hero to lead them out to battle, and keep them from cutting their own throats at home; that man was now arrived at such a state of civilization, as to admire the blessings of peace, and hold all wars,' except those of self-defence, in just abhorrence, and therefore stood in need of no such hero or governor; that on this account monarchy was an evident usurpation upon the rights of the people; it was also an injustice to the individual himself;" it was a school of pride, ignorance and falsehood; the monarch being required to do more than human powers enabled him, was obliged to use the eyes, ears, and understanding of others, whose services it was impossible to obtain without some recompense; that hence arose a cloud of evils too long and too well known to enumerate; that one of the greatest evils is, that the governors have a separate and distinct interest from the governed, and therefore in such an institution freedom has always a powerful foe to her advancement; virtue too and talents are obliged to give way to interest. As to the responsibility so much boasted of, it is and always has been a creature of the imagination. What successor to a minister will be eager to punish his predecessor, when he may hereafter tremble for the same fate himself? It has been argued that the nation is not in a fit state at present to change their form of government; monarchy surely is not the proper school to give them the education required; in monarchy man is brought up even from his infancy a *subject*, that is, a slave, and can any thing be so absurd as to suppose that a monarch will either teach his subject himself, or suffer him to be taught by others, the true nature of subjection? Besides what an insult is it upon the understanding of mankind to tell them that they are born and must continue all their lives in a

---

' Wars indeed are almost incompatible with the nature of republics. – See Godwin on Political Justice, B. v. Chap. xvi.[21]

" This is true without insisting upon the observation of Aristotle, Τον μεν αρχοντα τελειαν εχειν δει την ηθικην αρειην Polit. Lib. i.[22] That the governors should be perfect in moral virtue.

[21] William Godwin, *Enquiry Concerning Political Justice* (1793), vol. ii, p. 513.

[22] Aristotle, *A Treatise of Government*, transl. William Ellis (1778), p. 41.

state of subjection, and that such a state is instituted for their happiness. Such argument is little more than a revival of the old exploded doctrine, 'that some men even from their birth have a certain portion of gold and silver blended in their natures, while others who are destined to travel in the more humble walks of life, have only brass and iron.'[r] But to leave the present topic, to tell men that they are unfitted to change their government, is nothing more than to tell them that they live in ignorance and deception, and unfit to receive the impressions of truth. Away with such stupidity. When the advocates for monarchical power asserted that monarchy was best adapted to large states, they should have supported their assertion by strong arguments; the reverse appeared to be the fact; when unbiassed representatives were returned from all quarters of the nation, they certainly must have better information to proceed upon than a prejudiced and interested ministry.[s] It was said that monarchy prevented the evils of ambition; what ambition did it prevent? It prevented that just ambition which virtue and talents had to distinguish themselves, by raising themselves to their proper level in society; but it may be asked, did not monarchy give encouragement to the worst of ambitions, the ambition of being distinguished by the smiles of those in power? But monarchy fostered the polite arts. It fostered the arts of intrigue,

---

[r] Φησι δε, τοις μεν ευθυ γινομενοις μιξαι (θεον) χρυσον, τοις δε, αργυρον χαλκον δε και σιδηρον τοις τεχνιταις μελλουσιν εσεσθαι και γεωργοις – ARISTOT. Politic. Lib. II.[23]

[s] See some accurate reasoning upon these subjects towards the beginning of the second volume of Mr. Godwin's Inquiry concerning Political Justice;[24] a work which for solidity and justness of argument is equalled by few, and surpassed by none; that it has defects cannot be denied, but it may safely be asserted that no unprejudiced person can sit down to an attentive perusal of it, and not rise up from that perusal wiser and better.

Ωσθ' ο'πον μπ μικρα πολις, πολιτικωτερον πλειονας μετεχειν των αρχων, και δημοτικωτερον κοινοτεροντε γαρ, καθαπερ ειπομεν, και καλλιον εκαστον αποτελεται υπο των αυτων, και θαττον. – ARISTOT. Polit. Lib. II.[25]

So that where a state is large it is more politic and more popular that a greater number of persons should be admitted to share in the government; for this is more for the common benefit, and thus every thing is done better and with greater speed.

[23] Aristotle: 'But he [Socrates] says, in some [God] mixes gold at the very moment of their birth, in others silver; but bronze and iron in those who are meant to be craftsmen and farmers.' See Aristotle. *A Treatise of Government*, transl. William Ellis (1778), p. 64.

[24] William Godwin, *Enquiry Concerning Political Justice* (1793), vol. II, p. 413.

[25] Aristotle, *A Treatise of Government*, transl. William Ellis (1778), p. 105.

cunning, and dissimulation, and annihilated the manly virtue of sincerity: in monarchy a man was every body's, even his enemy's, obedient humble servant, in a republic, his friend or fellow citizen. But a well regulated republic had not only the negative qualification of being exempt from the above evils, to which indeed might be added others of equal or greater importance, those of oppressive laws, and overburthened taxes, but it was the nurse of freedom, justice, courage, science and truth; it called forth the latent energy of mind in the obscurest individual; it gave encouragement to virtue and talents; it suffered not corruption to creep into it, and consequently was always in its youth and prime. It could scarcely be denied that all the errors attributed to a republic originated from the ignorance of the people, that it was the interest of monarchy, and its attendant aristocracy to cherish this ignorance, and that the moment this darkness was removed by the light of philosophy, the perfectibility of man in moral and intellectual endowments would become apparent; having no longer the false glare of riches and titles to mislead him, he would learn to love truth, and submit his actions to her dictates.^{x} A republic tended to remove all these obstacles to the happiness of its citizens, and in short by teaching them to know and value themselves, it taught them also to know and value their country.^{y}

Chap. XXI.

These, Planetes, were the chief arguments that I at present recollect to have been used in that important debate, and the question of a republic being put was carried by a considerable majority. A committee was instantly appointed to draw up a plan best adapted to the circumstances of the country, and the following, after a proper interval, being reported, passed unanimously.

Here I deem it necessary to inform the reader, that the above narrative of Euthus did not pass without frequent interruptions, but I have thought it best to deliver it rather as one continued discourse, than in a broken and disjointed manner. The same method I mean

---

^{x} The road to the improvement of mankind is in the utmost degree simple, to speak and act the truth. – Godwin. Vol. II. B. v. Chap. XIV.[26]

^{y} 'To make us love our country, our country ought to be lovely.' – Burke's Reflections.[27]

[26] William Godwin, *Enquiry Concerning Political Justice* (1793), vol. II, pp. 494–5.

[27] Edmund Burke, *Reflections on the Revolution in France* (1790), p. 116.

to adopt in the following sketch of the constitution and government of Makar.

The preamble began with setting forth that all governments were more or less usurpations upon the rights and liberties of mankind, inasmuch as an education which instilled into the minds of men the perpetual practice of justice and truth would speedily annihilate the necessity of such regulations. Government therefore was manifestly an evil; but as in the existing circumstances of the country, owing to the corruption every where dispersed from ancient institutions, this evil is become absolutely necessary, the committee have with pleasure sat down to accomplish according to the best of their abilities the task imposed upon them: at the same time they declare that it is their earnest hope, founded upon the perfectibility[z] of man, that such necessity will gradually diminish: and in order to accelerate so desirable an object, they have inserted a clause in the constitution relative to periodical reformation. This they flatter themselves will the more readily meet the approbation of the house, when it takes into its consideration that the want of such a species of censorship has been the chief cause of the abuses of government in general.

The preamble next proceeded to state the various evils attendant as well upon monarchical and aristocratical institutions as upon those of pure democracy, and it was therefore to keep clear of those evils that it had been decreed that the Makarian government was a representative republic founded on the indefeisible and inalienable rights of man.

Chap. XXII.

The first article was, that the kingdom should be divided into districts, and that every male who had attained the age of twenty-four years should be entitled to vote at elections.

2. That every two thousand of such males should return one member to the house of representatives.

3. That every person be eligible to such office who had resided six months in the district for which he might be chosen, previous to the day of election.

---

[z] 'There is no characteristic of man which seems, at present at least, so eminently to distinguish him, or to be of so much importance in every branch of moral science, as his perfectibility.' – Godwin. Political Justice. Book I. Chap. VI.[28]

[28] William Godwin, *Enquiry Concerning Political Justice* (1793), vol. I, p. 43.

4. That every person who is elected be compelled to serve; no regard being had to such person's inclination.*^{aa}*

5. That the house of representatives never cease to exist.

6. That one third part of the house be renewed annually.

7. That the resigning members be debarred sitting again in the house for the space of three years.*^{bb}*

8. That after the lapse of every ten years the people do elect delegates from the several districts, for the sole purpose of inquiring into the abuses that may have crept into the laws or constitution, and pointing out their remedy.*^{cc}*

9. That such delegates be chosen in the same manner as the representatives.

---

^{aa} το αντον αιτεῖσθαι τον αξιωθησομενον της αρχης, ουκ ορθως εχει. δεῖ γὰρ καὶ βουλομενον καὶ μη βουλομεον αρχειν τον αξιον της αρχῆς. – ARISTOT. Polit. Lib. II.[29]

It is not right that any man who shall be deemed worthy of being a magistrate should canvass for the office; for such a one ought to serve whether willing or not.

^{bb} Εν μεν ουν τᾶις πολιτιηᾶις αρχᾶις τᾶις πλεσταις μεταραλλε το αρχον καὶ το αρχομενον εξ ισον γαρ ειναι βουλεται την φυσιν καὶ διαφερειν μηθεν. – ARISTOT Polit. Lib. I.

In most civil governments the rulers and ruled change places, for men are by nature equal.

The reader perhaps will not be displeased with the following translation of another passage from Aristotle.

Wherefore in civil governments, which are founded upon the equality of the citizens, it is deemed right that every man should take his turn to govern. Formerly indeed, as was natural, it was thought just to serve the public by turns, that each man, by having himself first contributed to the welfare of others, might expect to reap a reciprocal benefit from them. *But now, on account of the emoluments deriving from the administration of public affairs, men are desirous of continuing in power,* as if it happened that those who are diseased become sound by being in office, in which case indeed there might be some reason for their so eagerly canvassing for magistracy. – Polit. Lib. III. Cap. VI.[30]

^{cc} The necessity of a periodical reformation of the various evils that prevail more or less in all human institutions is evident to every well informed mind; but different men have proposed different remedies. I beg leave to instance the following one of Mr. Locke, in his Laws of Carolina.[31]

LXXIX. 'To avoid multiplicity of laws, *which by degrees always change the right foundations of the original government,* all acts of parliament whatsoever, in whatsoever form passed or enacted, shall *at the end of an hundred years after their enacting,* respectively *cease and determine of themselves,* and *without any repeal become null and void,* as if no such acts or laws had ever been made.'

[29] Aristotle, *A Treatise of Government*, transl. William Ellis (1778), p. 93.
[30] Aristotle, *A Treatise of Government*, transl. William Ellis (1778), pp. 38, 131–2.
[31] *The Works of John Locke* (9th edn, 9 vols., 1794), vol. IX, pp. 191–2.

10. That the ministers of the executive, be chosen by the legislative authority, to which they are to be responsible.

11. That the government has no right to interfere in matters of religion.

12. That every religion be admitted.

13. That oaths be abolished.

If reason had been allowed her due share in the formation of political constitutions, there would no doubt have existed some such regulation as the above in all the governments of the world. What can be more unwise in itself, or injurious to the happiness of nations, than the acting upon laws that passed centuries before? Is man to prescribe to his fellow-man the bounds of his intellectual improvement? Is one man to make another's ignorance the stepping-block to his own elevation? Or are we to cut the misletoe and worship the Pope for ever? Reason, truth, and philosophy say no; and shall we sacrifice the dictates of reason, truth, and philosophy at the shrine of hobgoblins and chimeras? Let us for once be wise; let us apply the knife to our own wounds before they become gangrenes and mortifications. Time was; time is but time will soon be passed. 'Mere words! cries the objector, we are actually in a state of improvement; we do not worship the Pope; we do not cut the misletoe.' Look at the misery and wretchedness that crowd the streets of our metropolis, and ask your conscience whether such a state deserves the appellation of improvement? Search for the laws that tend to pluck up this growing evil by the roots. Do you not venerate Old Sarum? Do you not religiously adhere to the remnants of feudal rights? And is not the nation disgraced by test laws and corporation acts? Above all, an honest man's heart must bleed when he peruses the penal code of what once was Britain. But not to wander too far, let us hear what Mr. Locke says upon the present subject.

'Things of this world are in so constant a flux, that nothing remains long in the same state. Thus people, riches, trade, power, change their stations, flourishing mighty cities come to ruin, and prove in time neglected desolate corners, whilst other unfrequented places grow into populous countries, filled with wealth and inhabitants. But things not always changing equally, and private interest often keeping up customs and privileges, when the reasons of them are ceased; it often comes to pass, that in governments, where part of the legislative consists of representatives chosen by the people, that in tract of time this representation becomes very unequal and dispropor-tionate to the reasons it was at first established upon. To what gross absurdities the following of custom, when reason has left it, may lead, we may be satisfied when we see the bare name of a town, of which there remains not so much as the ruins, where scarce so much housing as a sheepcote, or more inhabitants than a shepherd is to be found, sends as many representatives to the grand assembly of law-makers, as a whole country numerous in people, and powerful in riches. This strangers stand amazed at, and every one must confess needs a remedy; though most think it hard to find one; because the constitution of the legislative being the original and supreme act of the society, antecedent to all positive laws in it, and depending wholly on the people, no inferior power can alter it. And therefore the people, when the legislative is once constituted, having in such a government as we have been speaking of, no power to act as long as the government stands; this inconvenience is thought incapable of a remedy.'

LOCKE on Civil Government.[32] Chap. XIII.

[32] *The Works of John Locke* (9th edn, 9 vols., 1794), vol. IV, p. 432.

14. It appearing to the committee that all laws were more or less infringements upon the rights of man, they recommended a reduction of the existing code to such a number of laws only as may be deemed after a strict investigation absolutely necessary to the well-being of the country in its present circumstances: they further recommended that these laws should be simplified, or rather reduced to such a form as to be perspicuous to the meanest capacity.

15. That previous to the enacting of any law it should undergo three distinct discussions in the house, with at least six days interval between each discussion.

16. That a majority of at least two thirds of the house be necessary to the enacting of any law.

17. That the mode of Trial by Jury be adopted, that is, every jury is to consist of fifteen members, three of whom may in all cases acquit the prisoner.

18. That the present penal code be abolished, and the greatest punishment in future be imprisonment.[dd]

19. That every accused person be supposed innocent until he be convicted of guilt.

20. That the accused be brought to trial as soon after the supposed commission of a crime as possible.

21. That for this purpose there be resident judges in every large town in the kingdom.

22. That primogeniture laws and laws of entail from henceforth cease; for it appears to the committee that, exclusive of the injustice of these systems to the younger branches of the same family, they

---

[dd] The inutility of capital punishment is fully proved, especially in our own country, by the frequency of its occurrence. This circumstance alone ought to have induced legislators, and have indeed induced some to discontinue it. In addition to the inutility, what can be more unwise? There can be no doubt that many an individual is sent out of the world, for the commission perhaps of a *single crime*, to which he may have been urged by the pressing calls of a starving family, who might by proper instruction have been restored to society an useful and valuable member. But what shall we say to the wickedness and impiety of such a practice? Legislators endeavour to inculcate into nations a belief of the *benevolence* of the Deity; let us see how far their own benevolence extends. When a fellow creature has committed a crime, do they endeavour to make him sensible of the injustice of his conduct? Are they eager after his amendment? No! their benevolent hearts teach them only to get rid of him. In short, there can be no doubt in the mind of an upright man, that we have no right to take away the life of another except in self-defence.

engender poverty in the lower classes of the people, and poverty is frequently the cause of sedition and crimes.*

23. That the property of every man who dies intestate be divided equally among his children.

24. Great evils arising from the ignorance of the people, it is earnestly recommended to the house, to give all due encouragement to literature and science; and that all sciences be freed from abstruse terms which are now the clog to education.*

25. That every valuable foreign work be translated into the Makar tongue.

26. In order still more to further the progress of philosophy, the committee most seriously recommend the establishment of an universal language; and it appears to the committee that the easiest way of bringing about so desirable an object is, to appoint or cause to be appointed schools in every town or village where the Makarian gov-

---

* I cannot forbear remarking that these laws of primogeniture and entail are to be ranked among the causes of the decrease of population in the countries in which they are established. Aristotle has observed that a state will considerably increase in population where the property is more equally distributed; and the observation is just.[33] The lesser the portions into which land is divided, the better will that land be cultivated, and consequently the greater number of inhabitants will it maintain. Upon this ground it is much to be wished that those men who inherit a vast landed property would divide that property into as small farms as possible. In the following observation of Dr. Franklin there appears to me to be truth blended with falsehood. He observes that 'people increase in proportion to the number of marriages, and that is greater in proportion to the ease and convenience of supporting a family. When families can be easily supported more persons marry, and earlier in life.' I say that there is truth blended with falsehood in this observation; for in my opinion the population of a country does not increase in proportion to the number of marriages; its increase depends solely upon the facility of procuring the necessaries of life: where these are difficult of attainment let marriages be never so frequent the offspring of such marriages will be cut off in the bud for want of proper nutriment. This evidently is one of the causes of the decrease of population in large cities. But I willingly refer the reader to Dr. Franklin's observations upon the peopling of countries.[34]

* What is the reason that sciences are so difficult of attainment? One of the reasons is because they are inveloped in a mass of unintelligible names. If in lieu of the Greek, Latin, and fanciful appellations with which Astronomy, Anatomy, Botany, Chemistry, &c. are at present surrounded (and which constitute as it were a monopoly of those sciences to the Grecian and Roman) they were illustrated by plain English terms that *convey meaning*, to how much greater perfection would these sciences speedily arrive?

[33] Aristotle, *A Treatise of Government*, transl. William Ellis (1778), p. 90.

[34] Benjamin Franklin, 'Observations Concerning the Increase of Mankind', in William Clarke, *Observations on the Late and Present Conduct of the French* (1755), pp. 48–54.

ernment has influence, for the sole purpose of teaching the children of such town or village the Makar language with their own.*

27. That marriage be considered as a civil right, and that the mere consent of a man and woman before three witnesses do constitute marriage.

28. That the parties be disunited by mutual consent of half a year's continuance.

29. That the liberty of the press be unbounded.

30. That with respect to other nations the Makar government will neither interfere with them, nor suffer them to interfere with it.

31. The committee, fully convinced that it is the duty of legislators to consult the interest of the people, and that where that interest is not consulted no government can long stand, have endeavoured to the best of their power to perform that duty in the above plan: at the same time they earnestly request the house carefully and thoroughly to investigate every clause of it, as by so doing they can only secure what ought to be the end of all governments, the happiness and prosperity of the people.

Thus, Planetes, have I given you a rough sketch of our constitution, nor have I thought it necessary to enter into a more minute detail, which you may learn with more advantage by observing its effects upon the manners of the people.

Chap. XXIII.

Euthus having concluded, I returned him my sincerest thanks for the knowledge with which he had enriched my mind. But there remain two things, Euthus, which you have not yet explained. The first is, how the war ended? and the second, what became of that enormous load of debt and taxes with which the nation was oppressed? The war, replied Euthus, ended without difficulty; our enemies were as desirous of peace as ourselves, and every thing was restored to the footing on which it stood previous to the war. With regard to the national debt; the people were with great difficulty restrained from

---

* Upon this subject it is needless to enlarge. The proof of its practicability is in our own possession. Both in Wales and Scotland the children are brought up to speak the English language with their native tongue; and if all the nations of Europe were in the same manner to be instructed in the French language, the work is done; an universal language, as far as regards Europe, is at once established.

cutting it off at one blow; but the immensity of the evil that was likely to ensue from such a rash proceeding, determined me strenuously to oppose it. I at length succeeded, and it was agreed that the interest of the debt should diminish a fortieth part every year; this was easily effected, and we have now few, very few taxes remaining. These are chiefly employed in improving the roads, canals, bridges, wharfs, public buildings, &c.; in bringing to perfection any expensive invention of individuals; and in succouring oppressed neighbouring states, &c. &c. I could heartily wish, said I, to fix my residence among so contented and prosperous a people, but there is a something, Euthus, that calls me back to my country with all its imperfections. Imperfections! replied Euthus, it would be cowardice indeed to forsake your country because of its imperfections. An honest man would rather hasten his return in order to exert his utmost endeavours to amend them before they bring on a revolution. Believe me, Planetes, the tree of your constitution is well adapted to your soil; it is sound at heart; and though two or three of its best branches have been lopt off by some desperate and wicked hands, yet I perceive that vital principle in the root, which will cause them to spring out afresh, and blossom for ever. Yes, Planetes, in all probability you have some statesman among you, who knows what is right, and dares to practise it; make haste to enlist under his banners; calamity will teach the people to know his worth, and peace will shower down upon you the blessings of content. Alas! Euthus, my efforts are but feeble and the corruptions are strong. No efforts, Planetes, are feeble that have truth to support them. Shew the people the advantage and necessity of a well-timed reformation, and when they have once raised their voice, no minister can long withstand it: if, on the contrary, they suffer themselves to be duped, and the corruptions perpetually to increase, there can be no doubt that a revolution will, sooner or later, be the inevitable consequence. And if ever such a calamitous event should take place, may it be attended with no worse consequences than those which attended the revolution of Makar.

Here Euthus took his leave, and his last words made so deep an impression upon my mind, that I thought I should be deficient in duty to my country if I did not immediately accelerate my departure to communicate what I had seen and heard. Fired with this idea I instantly went to Othono to beg his assistance in procuring a vessel to carry me to some settlement of Europeans, whence I might procure a passage to my native soil. He expressed his deep regret at my resolution of leaving him, and intreated me to return to Makar at some future period, observing that I had yet much to learn respecting their manners and customs. I replied that if I found that my country-men profitted by the knowledge which I had already obtained I would with pleasure repeat my visit. At the same time I told him that his great kindness and attention to me would ever be had in remem-brance to the last day of my existence. He engaged to procure me a vessel as soon as possible, and insisted upon accompanying me to whatever settlement I chose to fix upon. Finding it in vain to resist his determination, I complied. And now, Planetes, while things are getting ready for your departure, let me intreat you to bear me com-pany to my house in the country; it is but thirty miles distant, and I will not detain you above a week. I replied that I should accompany him with much pleasure; and this I did the more readily as his family had been gone some days before, and taken Lawrence with them. Accordingly next morning we mounted on horseback, and proceeded on our journey.

Chap. XXIV.

Never was a country more populous, or so richly cloathed; not a spot of ground was to be seen uncultivated. The first fifteen miles were almost one continued garden of olives, vines, and corn, interspersed with innumerable farms and villages. Contentment smiled upon every face we met, and beggary and poverty were unseen. Good God! exclaimed I, how is all this possible? I surely am dreaming, and this is Paradise. You may well be surprised, returned Othono, this was not so formerly. My father, who died about ten years ago, used fre-quently to tell me, that all this country which we have now passed was, when he was a young man, in the possession of five or six petty Schums[hh], and its chief inhabitants were, the poor half-starved families of hard-working labourers, and about a dozen rich over-grown farmers. A great part of the land lay either desolate or only half tilled, or was laid out into extensive parks, beautiful indeed to the eye, but useful only to the few; it is now, as you see, divided into thousands of small freeholds and supports millions. As we proceeded,

---

[hh] These answer to our great lords.

my attention was arrested by some inclosures that I perceived at a little distance from the road, which from several spots of earth newly turned up, and a few upright stones scattered here and there, I imagined to be burying-grounds. True, said Othono, they are the burying-grounds belonging to Euthus-town, so called from my worthy friend, where we shall soon arrive, and the few upright stones that you see, are the remains of the old superstitious practice of monuments, which some people cannot yet forsake. The Makarians think it unwholesome to bury their dead in towns amongst the living, and therefore carry the bodies to a distance. Your having mentioned superstition, Othono, brings to my remembrance a question that I have for a long time been desirous of asking you. Pray, what is the religion that chiefly prevails among the Makarians? Every kind of religion, Planetes, being admissible, you may readily suppose that various opinions are held among us. Some men for instance believe in the existence of two Gods, others in that of three Gods and a Goddess, and there are some who believe in two Gods and a half; but all these opinions are in their wane, and the prevalent belief is that there exists only one Supreme, whose nature is totally unknown to men, and from whom are supposed to be derived the primary laws which direct and regulate the universe. It is believed that prayers, sacrifices, offerings, and supplications are of no avail, and that the only road to happiness is, to practise justice and benevolence to our fellow-creatures. And have you, said I, no priests nor bishops? No! thank truth! replied Othono, nor creeds, nor collects. The Makarians are too wise to hamper their intellectual faculties by such clogs. Why surely you must perceive, Planetes, that religion, like all other things, has hitherto been perpetually varying; and to what cause can you attribute such variation, but to synods, and state politics? where the interference of these is annihilated, religion will soon find its proper station. But priests and bishops are not the only beings whose political existence is destroyed. That arch-enemy of freedom, and friend of usurpation and aristocracy, the political Schum of evil, Oonnanoo, finding no support in a government founded on the rights of man, has abdicated his throne for ever.

As the discourse now began to grow unpleasant I was not a little rejoiced that Euthus-town appeared in view. It was market-day when we entered; and if I was pleased with the cleanliness and regularity with which every thing was conducted, I was quite charmed with the honesty and integrity of the people. No one demanded either more or less for his goods than their just value, nor was a man to be found that would receive two-pence for a dozen of yams when they were worth only one penny. Surely, said I, things are not always thus; you must undoubtedly, Othono, have some examples among you of dishonesty and injustice. Dishonesty and injustice, Planetes, are looked upon as wonders, and I do not suppose that there are ten instances to be found in the whole nation of vicious or depraved persons. We have prisons, it is true, but they are empty. Among a people that are taught from their infancy to love and practise truth, where do you think dishonesty can rest herself? If any man were so unprincipled as to commit an act of injustice, he would meet with a monitor in every person he saw; and if he were not altogether dead to a sense of shame, he must either instantly reform or quit the country.*"* Just heaven! said I, and is human nature capable of such perfection? Capable! Planetes, abolish unjust and oppressive laws, leave mankind to themselves and virtue, and the work is half done.*"*

Chap. XXV.

Having refreshed ourselves and cattle at Euthus-town, we proceeded on our journey, and in the evening arrived at Aschol farm. Nothing could exceed the delightfulness of the situation, or the proofs of industry that prevailed around it. The house stood upon a gently rising ground embosomed in woods and olive-grounds, having in front a small meandering stream, which emptied itself into a navigable river about a mile below. The surrounding country was picturesque, being on every side diversified with hill and dale in high cultivation;

" 'In the mean time all necessity for causing the punishment of the crime to pursue the criminal, would soon at least cease, if it ever existed. The motives to offence would become rare; its aggravations few: and rigour superfluous. The principal object of punishment is, restraint upon a dangerous member of the community; and the end of this restraint would be answered, by the *general inspection* that is exercised by the members of a limited circle over the conduct of each other.' &c. – GODWIN. Book V. Chap. XXII.[35]

" 'Men are weak at present, because they have always been told that they are weak, and must not be trusted with themselves. Take them out of their shackles; bid them inquire, reason, and judge; and you will soon find them very different beings.'
GODWIN. Book VII. Chap. VIII.[36]

[35] William Godwin, *Enquiry Concerning Political Justice* (1793), vol. II, p. 565.
[36] William Godwin, *Enquiry Concerning Political Justice* (1793), vol. II, p. 776.

there was indeed no regular town or village to be seen, but innumerable cottages were scattered up and down, in one view appearing upon the brow of a hill, in another just peeping from the woods. We were received with welcome by our amiable friends, and as soon as the first salutations were over, Othono addressed Clarina by saying; I have great need of your assistance, our friend Planetes purposes to leave us in about ten days, try whether your oratory will prevail upon him to prolong his visit. I hope, replied Clarina, that Planetes is convinced that his company increases our happiness. I return you thanks, Clarina, and could with pleasure live and die among you; virtue indeed seems banished from the rest of the world, and has taken up her abode among the inhabitants of Makar; but Othono knows my reasons for returning to my native country. Well, well; said Othono, as you have promised upon certain conditions to return I will not press my suit. Lawrence all this while was remarkably dejected; nor could I then conjecture the reason, but the next morning upon his entering my room with a sorrowful aspect, Well, said I, Lawrence, what is the matter? you do not seem much pleased with the thoughts of returning to your country. No indeed, Captain; a man's country in my mind is where he can live most happily, and to say truth, I could wish to remain here among the Makarians; they are the most frank and honest people I have ever met with; during the whole time of my residence among them, I have not seen a single instance of dishonesty, nor heard an untruth. Besides, Sir, they have no taxes nor press-gangs, and provisions of all sorts are not above one third the price that they are in England. At the same time, Captain, I am under so many obligations to you, that rather than incur your displeasure, I am ready to follow you to the world's end. Thank you, Lawrence, but if I can contribute in the least to your happiness, I will do it with pleasure, and therefore you have my free consent to remain at Makar. But there are two things which you ought to consider before you determine. One is, whether your friends and relations in England will not be made unhappy by your separation? and the other is, whether such a proposal will be acceptable to Othono, as I conceive that you must in some measure live upon his bounty? As to my friends, Captain, except yourself, I have but one friend in the world who has shewn any great attention to me, and he was pressed on board of a man of war just as he returned from the East Indies; and I understand that it almost broke the poor fellows heart, more, I believe, on account of his wife and family than himself; so that where he is now I know not. As to relations, I have none living. Respecting the second question, I am not at all uneasy, for upon mentioning my determination to Othono's son, and telling him that I could be useful in the seafaring line, he seemed much pleased, and promised to make me captain of one of his own vessels. And now, continued Lawrence, I have one request to make to you. You have hitherto, Captain, been my friend, and I hope will continue so. Here the poor fellow's courage failed him, and he appeared confused. I am, and will be your friend, Lawrence; pray take courage and speak your mind freely. Why then, Captain, I have taken a great fancy to Miss Othono, and as I have reason to believe she is not displeased with me, I wish to have your consent to the match. Truly, Lawrence, this is a matter quite unexpected, and requires serious consideration. I do not know how such a proposal may be relished by my hospitable friend. He knows very little of you, and is a man of considerable property and connections, whereas you are here a total stranger without house or home. This is all very true, Captain, but Clarina tells me, that if I can obtain your consent, there is no doubt of getting Othono's, for the Makarians in marrying their children think neither of connections, nor property, they study only to make them happy. This conversation made me very reserved during breakfast, and Othono, I thought, was not in such spirits as usual. Breakfast being finished, Othono asked me if I were inclined to take a walk? to this I readily assented.

Chap. XXVI.

Othono began the conversation by informing me of Lawrence's proposal, and desire of remaining in this country; that with regard to himself, he could not have the smallest objection to any match in which his daughter's happiness was concerned, but had refrained from giving his consent, lest he should deprive his guest of a companion and friend. If that be all, said I, objections may cease; my only fear was on account of the wide difference between you in respect to fortune and connections: Lawrence, though he has a good heart and a sound intellect, yet is without friends or property, whereas you – I wish, replied Othono, with a smile, that Euthus was here; he would instantly exclaim; This young man cannot unlearn his errors, he thinks himself still in a country where the happiness of man is second to wealth. Indeed, Planetes, you must judge more favourably of the Makarians; they consider two things only of importance, namely, the happiness of others, and the improvement of their intellect. As to property, there are few, very few individuals in the kingdom that have any considerable share of it; nor is it possible to be otherwise, for every man's fortune is, generally speaking, divided equally among his children. I say generally speaking, because where a father has several children, and one may be married and have a large family, another may be engaged in an expensive business, &c. he will perhaps enlarge this or that one's portion accordingly; and if a father were so unjust as to bequeath all his property to one child in prejudice to the rest, a jury would immediately set aside the will. Thus two or three generations must disperse the largest property in the kingdom. Perhaps, Planetes, you may have observed that I am myself one of the exceptions to this rule. True! the merchants in general are the men who possess the greatest wealth; and the expence of ship-building, and risk of trade will in some measure justify the accumulation of property, though even this for several reasons is on the decline. In short, my friend, I consider myself as holding my property only upon trust, and therefore the more useful I am to others, the happier shall I be. And is this, Othono, a principle that pervades the chief part of your nation? Undoubtedly it is. The generality of men divide their time between labour and study,[kk] and therefore having no occasion for the superfluities of life, seek only where to bestow them with the greatest utility. Happy people! said I, Lawrence has chosen an enviable lot. But from your mentioning the riches of your merchants, Othono, I presume that your commerce is widely diffused. Certainly, said he, like the pebble in the lake, we endeavour to spread the circles of our own happiness to as great an extent as possible. Nor is it unjust to seek a return. If we abound in any commodity useful to mankind, iron for instance, and another nation has a like surplus of

---

[kk] The situation which the wise man would desire for himself, and for those in whose welfare he was interested, would be a situation of alternate labour and relaxation, labour that should not exhaust the frame, and relaxation that was in no danger of degenerating into indolence. Thus industry and activity would be cherished, the frame preserved in a healthful tone, and the mind accustomed to meditation and reflection.

GODWIN. Book V. Chap. xiii.[37]

[37] William Godwin, *Enquiry Concerning Political Justice* (1793), vol. II, p. 485.

some other such commodity, suppose wool; is it not natural and just that we should exchange our iron for their wool? nor is this all; commerce is of greater advantage to mankind than the opposers of commerce are aware of. The sciences of navigation and astronomy are advanced by commerce. The happiness of man in a moral view is likewise increased thereby, inasmuch as the laws, manners, customs, and improvements of nations, are thus made known to each other: the less civilized therefore may reap advantage from the more advanced in civilization. I am fully sensible, replied I, of the benefits deriving from commerce; but do you meet with no interruption, no obstacle in the pursuit of it? Explain yourself, Planetes, I really do not comprehend you. Why, have you no foes, no turbulent nation near you, who occasionally injure your trade by the calamities of war? Here I plainly perceived that Othono could scarce refrain from laughing. Surely, my friend, said he, you are not serious; or if you are, you talk so much after the fashion of the old school that I really am at some loss how to answer you. Can you for a single moment suppose it possible that any people can be so completely insane, as to make war upon a nation, the most populous in the world, united to a man among themselves, and enthusiastically partial to their laws, their liberties, and their rights? but granting for the sake of argument the possibility, I am ignorant how we should treat them. Some of us probably might commiserate them, and endeavour to give them instruction. Others would advise correction, after the old manner of correcting school-boys, and that being completed, would send them home to their masters with a lecture in the horn-book of truth and liberty; this in all probability would be of more powerful operation than the sword. On the side of offensive war, it is almost needless for me to say a word. The great principle among the Makarians is to do all the good they can; to stop the progress of wars and slaughter, and root them from the face of the earth; to disseminate the principles of universal philanthropy, to shew men that they are brethren, that they are all citizens of the world; improbable then in the highest degree is it that such a nation should be the first to commit injustice. Wars originate in the sway which the few have over the many by the influence of accumulated property over accumulated misery.[u] Wars

---

[u] It is only by means of accumulation that one man obtains an unresisted sway over multitudes of others. If Europe were at present covered with inhabitants, all of them possessing competence, and none of them superfluity, what could induce its different

then can have no place among a nation where misery is unknown, and where accumulated property is perpetually diminishing, is perpetually breaking out into diverse channels. Believe me, Planetes, there is no man among the Makarians rich or powerful enough to force others to join him in such measures, and rest assured that no man is fool enough, or base enough, to follow him of his own accord. We are happy, we are contented, we are free; what have we more to desire? And are these sentiments, Othono, disseminated among the whole people? Unquestionably they are, Planetes, not a child of twelve years old is ignorant of them. Good God! said I, how various are the manners and customs of nations! As soon as I publish what I have now learnt in my native country, I shall be branded with the titles of visionary, and theorist, a disturber of the public peace, a jacobin, a democrat, and I know not what; perhaps I may be sent to a lunatic hospital, and ranked among the incurables. How much, Othono, do I wish to remain among you! How enviable is the lot of Lawrence!

Chap. XXVII.

We were now arrived within sight of the house, and Lawrence came out to inform us that dinner had been waiting for a considerable time. His countenance shewed strong marks of hope, fear, and anxiety, but, upon my communicating to him the joyful intelligence that he had both mine and Othono's free consent to the match, and entire approbation of his continuance at Makar, they were succeeded by a flood of tears that choked his utterance. We gave him no time to recover, but hastened into the house where we found the family just sitting down to their frugal table. Indeed the Makarians are almost total strangers to luxury; they are plain and simple in their diet, living chiefly upon the various fruits of the earth, and eating very little animal food, and even this little is for the most part consumed in soups. Dinner being finished, Othono informed Clarina and his daughter of the subject and event of our morning's conversation, and for my part, I never received so much real pleasure as from the happiness which I had been instrumental in communicating to this

countries to engage in hostility? It is property that forms men into one common mass, and makes them fit to be played upon like a brute machine.

GODWIN. Book VIII. Chap. ii.[38]

[38] William Godwin, *Enquiry Concerning Political Justice* (1793), vol. II, pp. 811–12.

amiable family. It was settled that I should be present at the nuptial ceremony, and that it should take place on the morning of my departure.

During this interval I employed my time chiefly in augmenting my stock of knowledge by a strict attention to the manners of the people. What principally struck and delighted me was, that love of truth and sincerity so conspicuous among them. The English proverb, that truth is not to be spoken at all times, found no receptacle there. If a man did wrong, he was sure to be told of it. Riches afforded no shelter to error. The Makarian, being grounded in the principles of true equality; knows and feels that he is a man speaking to a man; he therefore banishes all superstitious awe and reverence towards a fellow-creature.^{mm}

In conversation they accost each other either by their simple name, or by the distinction of friend. In their epistolary correspondence, Grecian simplicity prevails, nothing more is superscribed than, 'Othono to Euthus,' or 'Euthus to Othono.' There is no hypocrisy, no 'most obedient, most respectful, most devoted humble servant.' In their literary works you will find no superfluous argument, and much less of the flowers of rhetorick, as they are called, than might have been expected. Plain simple facts, and energetic reasoning are their predominant features. I am sure my countrymen will be overjoyed to hear that some of their best works are comprized in one or two octavo volumes. Nay, I have frequently seen a small duodecimo that would have put Hoadly to the blush.

From their manner of life the people are cheerful and healthy, and very eager to improve their intellectual faculties. I have already mentioned the extreme facility with which the various arts and sci-

---

^{mm} He that cannot speak to the proudest despot with a consciousness that he is a man speaking to a man, and a determination to yield him no superiority to which his inherent qualifications do not entitle him, is wholly incapable of sublime virtue. – GODWIN. B. V. Chap. vi.

Every man ought to feel his independence, that he can assert the principles of justice and truth, without being obliged treacherously to adapt them to the peculiarities of his situation, and the errors of others.

Ib. B. VIII. Chap. vi.[39]

It is a ridiculous education that does not qualify a man to make his best appearance before the greatest man and the finest woman to whom he can address himself.

SPECTATOR. 484.[40]

[39] William Godwin, *Enquiry Concerning Political Justice* (1793), vol. II, pp. 430, 854.
[40] *The Spectator* (8 vols., 1794), vol. VII, p. 113.

ences are there acquired by being stripped of the abstruse terms in which they were formerly enveloped. Every bone for instance in anatomy is called by some name that conveys to the student a correspondent idea. It is almost incredible to those who are unacquainted with the immense injury done to science by preserving the unmeaning names given to it by its original cultivators, who lived perhaps in foreign countries, centuries ago, and whose language is now lost; I say it will appear almost incredible to them to be told, that a science which now seems extremely difficult of attainment, may in that case be acquired with great facility, in a very short time, and by the most trivial capacity.'''

Their women are chaste, handsome, and well educated. It is rare to see a woman of twenty years of age married, or one of thirty unmarried. They think that the fruit of too early marriages is debilitated. The mother, unless incapacitated by disease, never fails to suckle her child; to do otherways would be deemed criminal, and she would be severely reprimanded for it by those around her. Adultery is unknown. If a man and wife are unhappy in each other's company, and are resolved to separate, they have no more to do than to signify in writing such resolution to the witnesses of their marriage, which, if such resolution remain in the mean time unaltered, is dissolved accordingly after a lapse of half a year. I mention this only as the law of the land, for it seldom takes place. A large family of children is supposed in England to be a misfortune; a large family of children is supposed in Makar to be one of the greatest blessings: this, as I

''' The Greeks and Romans from whom most of our knowledge is derived, very naturally and wisely gave appellations in their own tongue to their various improvements and discoveries. The greatest part of these appellations European nations religiously adhere to, so that the modern student is under the necessity of cultivating the Greek and Roman languages previous to his acquisition of this or that science. Nor is this all. Several of the original appellations being proved by subsequent discoveries to be absurd and fanciful, the student has to wade through additional difficulties to understand whence they originated. But the truth is, that arts and sciences are for the most part monopolized by a few, and innovation and reformation are Democratic Fiends who would bring 'this our craft into danger.' I am the more desirous of propagating this improvement of science, as the English language is peculiarly adapted to compound expressions, and I shall be much mistaken if words that convey appropriate meaning cannot be discovered for nineteen twentieths of every art or science. The inventors of the new chemical nomenclature seem to have done the reverse of what is here represented; they have given new appellations, but have increased the difficulty. A specimen of what is now alluded to will in all probability be soon presented to the public by a friend of the author.

have already mentioned, is chiefly to be attributed to the facility of procuring the necessaries of life. I should here observe that it was once proposed in the house of representatives, that the institution of marriage should be abolished, and the intercourse of the sexes freely allowed: but the proposal was received with contempt. Among other reasons assigned for rejecting it, were the following. That in such case a man being ignorant of his own offspring, it was probable that such offspring would be little attended to, and certainly, comparatively speaking, would be badly educated. That it would deprave the morals of men, by giving encouragement to debauchery; and that by so doing it would diminish population, in which the aggregate happiness of nations consists. That promiscuous connections would annihilate that domestic happiness now deriving from the matrimonial state. That such a proposal is useless, because the evil so much complained of, viz. being tied down for life to a partner of different habits and sentiments, is already obviated. Lastly, that if it be true that not only the fruit of too early connections is comparatively feeble, but that they tend to debilitate the parents themselves, and consequently to the degeneracy of the human race; these are strong objections to the proposal being carried into execution.[oo]

The Makarians divide their year into seventy-three weeks, each containing five days, and their hours of the day commence at six o'clock in the morning, and the hours of the night at six in the evening: the old ridiculous custom of calling the depth of midnight one o'clock in the morning was abolished at the revolution.

I can assure the reader that this happy people know how to employ their time well. An idler or lounger would be esteemed a prodigy; every man is engaged either in the improvement of his intellect, in the cultivation of the earth, in manufactures, or commerce. Gaming

[oo] Among the various customs of the Germans Caesar relates, Qui diutissime impuberes remanserunt maximam inter suos ferunt laudem: hoc ali staturam, ali hoc vires, nervosque confirmari putant. Intra annum vero vicessimum feminæ notitiam habuisse, in turpissimis habent rebus. – Bel. Gal. Lib. vi. Cap. 21.[41]

Those who are inclined to see the arguments that are brought against the institution of marriage may read GODWIN. Book VIII. Chap. vi.[42]

[41] Caesar: 'Those who, for the longest period, have remained chaste, receive the greatest praise from them. By this they think that the stature is increased, the strength maintained, and the nerves braced. They consider it one of the most disgraceful things to have had knowledge of a woman before twenty years of age.'

[42] William Godwin, *Enquiry Concerning Political Justice* (1793), vol. II, pp. 848–52.

is unknown. I had once the curiosity to ask Othono's son, for I was afraid to put such a question to his father, whether his countrymen ever played at cards? Cards! said he, what are cards? Here, though I already began to repent of my foolish curiosity, I explained to him to the best of my power, what cards were. I told him that they were papers cut into an oblong form, and painted with certain figures; that they were much used in all the civilized parts of Europe, particularly by the fair sex, who usually meet together every evening during the winter, and not unfrequently during the summer months, to sit down for hours at play with them: to this I added that their chief use and design were to employ time agreeably and profitably. Believe me, said he, the Makarians have no such agreeable and profitable employment, and, whatever might be the opinion of other nations, they would esteem such things as the inventions of knaves for the use of fools.

Chap. XXVIII.

The day fixed for my departure being arrived, and the nuptial ceremony being completed by the parties giving their consent before three witnesses, I took a short leave of my happy friends, and immediately set out with Othono for Makar. We returned by way of the canal, on which we embarked about a mile below Aschol. The barges here are of small dimensions, the reason of which I found afterwards to be this: On account of a deficiency of water in the summer months, there are no locks upon this canal, but the barges are moved from one degree of elevation to another by means of inclined planes. Here however there is a considerable improvement upon the Chinese method. As soon as the barge arrives at the bottom of one of the planes, it is haled into a recess just large enough to receive it, in which recess is placed a very simple machine upon four wheels that exactly fits the bottom of the barge; the machine being well fixed, the barge becomes a sort of waggon, and is drawn up the plane by means of a capstan, a drag-chain is then applied to one of the wheels, and it descends gently into the lower canal.

Upon my arrival at Makar, Euthus immediately waited upon me. He observed that he came not to interrupt the preparations for my departure, for however he might regret my loss, he could not but applaud the motives that induced me to return; he came only to take his leave, and to inquire whether there were any thing that he could do to serve me? You have already, Euthus, done me the greatest of services, you have proved to me that the human race are capable of being made virtuous, peaceable, and happy, and the only addition that I can desire is, that you would inform me how to make my countrymen so. Every thing in season, said Euthus with a smile. Vice, wretchedness, and an inhuman thirst of warfare, seem to prevail among you at present. These evils are, I am afraid, of considerable extent, and for the last century appear to have been increasing with giant strides, you must not therefore be so rash and imprudent as to attempt to extirpate them at once, for by so doing you will perhaps augment your misery. How then, Euthus, am I to act? am I to sit down in hopeless despair? By no means, Planetes; despair does not become a philosopher. Sow the seeds of justice and truth among your countrymen. Sow them deep. And the noisome weeds that now overspread the land, and seem to choke their growth, will be totally lost in that strength and energy with which they will in their due time vegetate into maturity. Farewell.

Farewell, returned, I thou friend of man. I will obey thy instructions, nor will I think that feeble, which is done with the best intention.

Chap. XXIX.

Every thing being now in readiness, I embarked on board the ship that Othono had prepared for me. He insisted upon being my conductor to the Cape of Good Hope, to which I assented upon condition that if we met with any European vessel he would put me on board. About the distance of three weeks sail from the Cape, a Portuguese East Indiaman hove in sight. We very soon came up with her, as she was little better than a log upon the water. I instantly hailed her in the French tongue. This most unexpectedly threw her crew into great confusion, for we were so close as plainly to perceive the sailors crowding upon each other's shoulders down the hatches and gangways, while the few who remained upon deck were falling upon their knees. Poor Othono was quite alarmed, having never seen the power of a few words so instantaneous in their operation. He began seriously to question me upon the cause of the tremour that prevailed among them. I told him that the Portuguese nation were much under the influence of superstition, and that the French nation, in whose language I had hailed them, had been represented to them by their priests as cannibals; which I apprehended to be the cause of their alarm. As soon as I came on board, and had dissipated their fears, they began to grow prodigiously courageous, singing pater-nosters, and chaunting hallelujahs. We found them much in want of water and biscuits, and indeed of most other necessaries, for they had been out two months longer than they expected, and were one hundred leagues out of their reckoning. Having agreed with the commander for my passage, I bid my valued friend Othono adieu.

I did not remain long with the Portuguese, for within a fortnight's time they were again thrown into hysterics by the appearance of two large frigates, these however proving to be English, I was taken on board, and landed without further adventure on British soil.

The Commonwealth of Reason
by William Hodgson,
NOW CONFINED IN THE PRISON OF NEWGATE, LONDON, FOR SEDITION.

'The Privileged Orders may pass away,
but the people will be eternal.'

Mirabeau[1]

1795

[1] *Speeches of M. de Mirabeau, the Elder* (Dublin, 1792), p. 120: 'Privileges shall have an end, but the people is eternal'.

The Commonwealth of Reason.

Plan, &c.

Argument.

Experience having proved CORRUPTION to be the most dreadful evil that can possibly affect either public or private life, it is of course that which men should be most studious and zealous to avoid; any endeavour, therefore, to raise up barriers against this all-destructive vice, may be considered as one of the noblest efforts of the human understanding; as from thence has proceeded all those arbitrary and diabolical actions we have at different periods witnessed; and of which such innumerable examples, that have justly called down the execration of mankind, are furnished in the history of the world.

As corruption is generally the result of power long continued in the same individual, and prevention more humane and far better than detection, it is my intention, in this Plan, to make every situation in the Commonwealth, to which is attached either trust or power, REVOLUTIONARY or ROTATIVE; thereby taking what I conceive to be the best remedy for, and precaution against, this most inveterate enemy to public happiness; this epidemic, that has hitherto baffled the most strenuous efforts of the most able physicians; this political Upas,ᵃ under whose baneful and malignant branches every virtue finds immediate death.

Philosophers must have long since been convinced that the abuse of power is much more the consequence of long and uninterrupted possession in the hands of individuals, than of any other cause whatever: and as it is an axiom in politics, *that wherever there is power there*

ᵃ The name of the Poison Tree, that grows in Japan.

will be abuse, I imagine, that by making the power necessarily vested in a part, to be exercised for the benefit of the whole, as fleeting, and of as little duration as possible, in the same individual, I obviate the great error in political institutions, which seems to have been the delegation of those powers, to be exercised without a just controul, and for a long and sometimes an indefinite space of time, that require the eyes of an Argus, and a frequent change of persons, to prevent them from degenerating, by corruption, into tyranny and oppression.

As pretended distinctions amongst men, who are all equal by nature, and are all unquestionably equally helpless in infancy, and equally cold in the embraces of death, have a tendency to create a difference of interests in the same community, in which the weaker is invariably swallowed up, and destroyed, by the stronger; and human beings, otherwise naturally friends and brothers, are thereby set at enmity with each other, for the enjoyment of paltry titles, that do not *really* distinguish the possessors from the mass of mankind, except in particular and local situations: I propose, that in my Plan, no grade, or title of distinction whatever, shall exist among the citizens of the Commonwealth, except what the exercise of superior benevolence and virtue shall obtain from the general respect of society, or what the temporary possession of the public functions shall necessarily demand for the moment. Thus all being citizens, equal in rights, none will have an interest separate from that of his neighbour, since no one will be capable of infringing or invading the right of another, without involving not only his own, but that of the whole Commonwealth of which he himself makes an integral part; of course, every such attempt will, in this state of perfect equality, be resisted not only by the citizen attacked, but by the collective force of the whole community, whose direct interest will effectually point out the absolute necessity of the opposition: whilst daily experience teaches us to know, that in those states where an inequality of rights does exist, it frequently becomes the interest and desire of one grade or class to subvert and destroy the rights of another grade or class, thereby, as they falsely conceive, the more effectually to establish and support what the errors of their constitution have led them to consider as their own. Thus, in such states, it very rarely or never happens that the collective body of the citizens find an occasion, where their common interest is united. On this principle we may account for the fall of those vast and mighty empires which History informs us once had existence, and of which we have not now left a single vestige, whereby to descry their ancient power and grandeur, except the traditionary detail, handed down to us by our ancestors; for it is an old proverb in England, the truth of which has been universally admitted – '*That an House divided against itself cannot stand.*'

As the accumulation of immense wealth in the hands of individuals, by any other means than personal industry, or equitable inheritance, may with great truth be considered as the primary and most effectual means by which the fiend, CORRUPTION, secretly undermines, and finally overturns the best and wisest institutions: the endeavour to destroy this channel of abuse, *this panacea, that infallibly turns all virtue into vice*, without rendering injustice to any one, is surely highly deserving the consideration and attention of mankind; and as such, will form a part of my Plan. Seeing, therefore, that ENTAILED ESTATES, the laws of PRIMOGENITURESHIP, and other unequal and unjust decrees, respecting the distribution of property, are the causes of these mischievous masses of wealth, so highly dangerous to, and incompatible with, the existence of LIBERTY, and which have been always found to furnish the ready means of CORRUPTION, OPPRESSION and TYRANNY, I propose, that in no possible case shall the different children, whether male or female, of the same father, divide in other than equal portions, the property of which the sire may die possessed. Thus we shall prevent that disgraceful inequality of patrimony in children of the same parent, that at present furnish not unfrequent instances, where the head of the family, as he is called, has a revenue of, perhaps, *forty thousand pounds a year*, whilst the younger branches have scarcely a sufficient income to support the appearance that custom has rendered absolutely necessary to enable them to dine at their elder brother's table; to provide for whom, without injuring the possessions of the elder son, an almost incredible number of SINE-CURE places, and of trifling and useless offices, have been created under the different governments the world has hitherto witnessed; the burthen of which has, without exception, ultimately fallen on those, who, it must ever be acknowledged, form the great bulwark of every state, the INDUSTRIOUS ARTISAN and LABORIOUS CULTIVATOR, as the payment of these places is usually provided for, by taxes levied on articles of the most general consumption, and of the first necessity: Independent of which, these rich men, to preserve whole and inviolate whose property so much shameful injustice is done to the body of the citizens, become themselves the *servile* TOOLS and *abject* SLAVES of the executive power; as upon no other condition can they reasonably hope to make provision for their poorer relatives. Thus the only return the citizens receive for encouraging this immoral and partial distribution of the father's estate, is the deprivation of the independent assistance of those whom, by the most flagrant injustice, they have loaded with riches. For these reasons, I also propose, not to admit in the Commonwealth of any sinecure place, than the existence of which nothing can be more absurd; for no one can, consistently with honesty, accept of payment for services he has never performed, nor has the remotest intention of performing: indeed, sinecure places may be literally denominated, A ROBBERY COMMITTED ON THE NATION, UNDER THE FALSE COLOUR AND SPECIOUS PRETEXT OF HAVING A PUBLIC EMPLOYMENT; and the existence and duration of such emoluments can only be built on the disgraceful ignorance and culpable inattention of the greater part of the citizens composing the Commonwealth; since no man in his senses would, knowingly, pay his baker for a loaf he never had or was to have. Neither do I propose to suffer the establishment of any useless office or employment in the Commonwealth which can only be harassing to the citizens, and destructive of their common interest: Or to admit any enormous or disproportionate salary to be annexed to the execution of the necessary public functions: for as no citizen ought to refuse to take upon him, in his turn, that public employment, which a majority of his fellow-citizens shall call him to the exercise of; and as the due, faithful and impartial discharge of it is as much for his own security, happiness and advantage, as for that of the Commonwealth, so no citizen, who really wishes to promote the general prosperity of the Commonwealth, can or ought to have a desire of wickedly enriching himself at the expence of the community; which he certainly does whenever he accepts, as a remuneration for his public services, of a sum greater than will defray the necessary expences and consumption of time that has attended them, or of a sinecure place, or of a pension, or of a place of profit, the functions of which produce no general good to the citizens. The not suffering, therefore, any of these places or profits, *the existence of which, in the governments we have hitherto witnessed, may be justly stiled a radical error*, is the best and most certain way to prevent the dreadful necessity of reforming abuses, that we ourselves are the authors of, by permitting such temptations to be thrown in the way of evil-disposed, avaricious and designing men: for as it is an axiom in metaphysics, *that no effect can possibly exist without a cause*, it is also an axiom in medicine, *that if you can remove the cause, the effect will cease.*

As the existence of EXCLUSIVE PRIVILEGES is the grand means by which those unhappy jealousies, shameful dissentions, and destructive animosities, that have ever been found to be absolutely necessary to the support and existence of ARBITRARY OPPRESSION, DESPOTIC POWER, and LAWLESS CORRUPTION, are fomented and kept alive, and which effectually prevent that harmony that ought ever to subsist among the members of the Commonwealth; it must appear evident to every thinking and reasonable being, that those customs, *such as a rich man being* ALONE *permitted to destroy a bird or animal, that has perhaps been nourished at the expence of his poorer neighbour; or A being suffered to arrest B, for a sum of money, that B may stand indebted to A, whilst B shall have no such remedy against A, when it happens that A stands indebted to B*; which have no other tendency than to destroy the happy union of interests, so requisite to the furtherance of the happiness and prosperity of the citizens, can only have originated with those monsters, for I will not disgrace the name of man, by giving them that appellation, who, lost to every social virtue, and wishing to trample with impunity on the SACRED and INDEFEASIBLE RIGHTS OF MAN, have cunningly introduced a system OF OPPRESSING ONE MAN FOR THE PROFIT OF ANOTHER; which, from the extreme ignorance of mankind, and their but too general inattention to their true and genuine interests, they have been able to pass on their blindness and credulity, as favours and advantages; and who, by these nefarious means, having acquired the direction of the public force, have, whenever the CHEAT has been discovered, *and men have attempted to regain their original state of happy equality*, made use of that command; thus surreptitiously obtained, to perpetuate a system, by which alone such MISCREANTS and VIOLATERS OF JUSTICE, knew they could be enabled to commence with safety, and continue with impunity, their diabolical measures, enormous peculations, and sanguinary administration. For these reasons, I propose, that in my Plan no such heterogenous and corrupt monsters of injustice, as PRIVILEGED ORDERS, GAME LAWS, MANORIAL RIGHTS, EXCLUSIVE CHARTERS, CORPORATIONS, and OTHER SUCH PARTIAL, WICKED, AND OPPRESSIVE PRIVILEGES shall have existence: for nothing seems more irrational, than that the birds of the air, wild animals, or the fish of a river, which nature certainly has not stamped or marked with any particular man's name, and to which no one man can justly and honestly shew a superior claim over his neighbour, should be made the exclusive property of the rich man, and the poor man be punished for the killing and appropriation of that which nature seems to have sent for the express purpose of appeasing those appetites she has given him in common with the most wealthy and affluent. And it can never, surely, be argued, that the destroying of these creatures is in itself an immoral act; as, supposing such argument to be just, it could not but be admitted at the same time, that if it is immoral in the man of poverty, it is equally so in the man of riches: unless, indeed, men can be so weak and stupid, as to imagine that a rich man, lord of the manor, or other privileged person, has a licence and authority from Heaven, which purges the guilt from him, that attaches on the poor man's shoulders; and yet, ridiculous as this supposition must appear to every man of common sense, we nevertheless hear of some men whose infallibility is accredited, and even held sacred, with a great part of the world; which acknowledgment, on their parts, is absolutely supposing the existence of this monstrous and incomprehensible absurdity. Neither can any thing be more ridiculous, cruel, and unjust, than that A should have a remedy against his neighbour B, that B has not in like cases against his brother citizen A, since what is punishable when done by B, can or ought to be no less so when committed by A, however ignorant men, by absurd and nonsensical privileges, accorded to A, may have sheltered him from common justice, and enabled, and indeed encouraged him to commit, without fear of inquiry, or punishment, those acts of dishonesty and oppression to B, for which, but strip him of his talismanic garments, he would be held in utter and general detestation.

As what are called, NATIONAL RELIGIOUS ESTABLISHMENTS, have been found to be the greatest scourge that ever afflicted mankind; and have, at different periods, been perverted from what even the original institutors themselves meant should be their object; and have been called into the aid of, incorporated with, and made part of almost every national government, by which means CORRUPTION has engendered, at the moderate expence of a few mitres and other such baubles, an additional and most implacable enemy to the natural independance of man: and have by instilling the monstrous and incongruous doctrine of eternal damnation to such as differ in opinion from the national theology, robbed a great part of the citizens of their JUST, NECESSARY, and INDEFEASIBLE RIGHTS, under the specious, and diabolical pretence of heterodoxy; and compelled the inhabitants of one country, to murder the citizens of another, for the propagation of what, EACH HAS CALLED THE TRUE RELIGION, to their mutual disadvantage, and in direct defiance of the morality inculcated by all; – one of the great and principle tenets of these religion-mongers, being, according to their language, though not according to their practice, *to promote brotherhood and good-will amongst men*; yet, how far this principle actuates those who call themselves orthodox, *which each does in his turn*, may be best collected from the reciprocal benevolence they exercise towards each other; from a Jew being condemned to the Auto-de-Fe in Spain and Portugal, because he will not believe that Jesus Christ was the son of God; from a Christian being held in general abhorence by the Turks, because he doubts the truth of Mahomet's having ascended seven Heavens, and held converse with the Almighty; from a Roman Catholic being prevented in Protestant countries holding any public office or place of trust and profit merely because he believes the wine and the wafer he receives when taking the sacrament, is the body and blood of his friend Jesus Christ, whilst the true believer, as he is stiled, under what the persecuted catholic calls an heretical government, says, they are only taken in remembrance of their Lord and Master; betwixt whom and his present followers, there is no more resemblance, 'than I to Hercules;' – and a thousand other wicked and diabolical pains and penalties attached to the great, enormous, and never to be forgiven crime of a man's thinking and judging for himself, in what is called the most material concern of his life, the salvation of his soul; not to mention the cruel and murderous wars that have been carried on by Jews against Gentiles; Christians against Turks; Turks against Infidels; and one sect of Christians against another sect of Christians; in which barbarous, bloody, and blasphemous contests, millions of infatuated men have lost their lives, without the point in dispute being yet determined; the combatants having been always reduced to the situation of the hare and the hound: – WHERE ONE WAS TOO FATIGUED TO FOLLOW, AND THE OTHER TOO TIRED TO RUN AWAY; therefore, as every establishment in a Commonwealth should be really and truly to promote FRATERNITY among the citizens, and to draw closely the bonds of union in society; it follows of course, that these institutions, experience having proved them to be productive of contrary effects, should by every well wisher and friend to the repose and happiness of mankind be avoided. And as religion seems to be a subject on which men may perhaps never be perfectly agreed; since no one can, by any thing like demonstrative evidence, prove that the tenets of the particular sect to which he belongs, is more acceptable to the Supreme Being, than those of another sect, whether he be BAPTIST, JEW, GENTILE, MAHOMETAN, ARMENIAN, CHRISTIAN, ANTICHRISTIAN, ADAMITE, DUNKER, SWEDENBURGIAN, WORSHIPER OF THE SUN, WORSHIPER OF THE MOON, UNIVERSALIST, EUTYCHIAN, ADRAMMELECHIAN, PHILADELPHIAN, QUARTODECIMANIAN, PRE-DESTINARIAN, AGONYCLITE, BONASIAN, BASILIDIAN, HOTTENTOT, NESTORIAN, CARPOCRATIAN, ANTINOMIAN, MARONIST, CARTESIAN, SCOTIST, THOMIST, SCRIPTURIST, SACRAMENTARIAN, WORSHIPPER OF FO, GNOSTIC, IDOLATOR, QUIETIST, SABATTARIAN, MANICHEAN, ROMAN CATHOLIC, TRINITARIAN, ANTITRINITARIAN, RHETORIAN, MENGRELIAN, ANNOMÆAN, BROWNIST, WHITFIELLITE, CATAPHRYGIAN, MESSALIAN, PELAGIAN, SEMIPELAGIAN, ELCESACITIAN, ANTHROPOMORPHITE, MILLENARIAN, ANTIDICOMARIONITE, CERDONIST, ELATERIST, STERCORANIST, JACOBITE, GEORGIAN, ANTITATITE, CONGREGATIONALIST, COLLUTHEAR, BERULIAN, EUDOXIAN, SOLIFIDIAN, PRISCILLIANIST, MELCHITE, HERODIAN, CERINTHIAN, APPOLLINARIAN, AGYNITE, PAPIST, QUINTILLIAN, SCEPTIC, CIRCUMCELLIAN, DISCIPLINARIAN, EUNOMIAN, ALBANGIST, METEMSYCHITE, LOLLARD, HEMEROBAPTIST, FRATRICELLIAN, ARCHONTICK, ETERNALIST, DISSENTER, SAMARITAN, REMONSTRANT, OPINIONIST, PATRIPASSIANIST, ARTOLYRIST, AQUARIAN, UBIQUITARIAN, PHOTINIAN, MARIANALATRIST, SUBLAPSARIAN, SUPRALAPSARIAN, METAMORPHIST, EBIONITE, JANSENIST, ROGATIST, MENNONITE, SABEAN, APELLITIAN, MARCIONIST, DULCINIST, CATHARIAN, ASCORDRIGILIAN, MACEDONIAN, AUGUSTINIAN, MONTANIST, CHILIAST, MUNCERIAN, LIBERTINE, BONGOMILIAN, REBAPTIZER, BARDESANIST, SEVERIAN, GENTOO, BARULITE, APOSTOLIAN, BACCHANALIAN, ARIAN, SABELLIAN, QUAKER, BAGNOLENSIAN, PHARISEE, VAUDOIS, ERASTIAN, PETROBRUSIAN, TIMOTHEAN, LUCIFERIAN, BAANITE, EUSTATHIAN, FLAGELLANT, MONOTHEIST, SOCINIAN, TRITHEITE, STOICK, GORTINIAN, SOFFEE, BRAMAN, SETHIAN, FASTER, PROTESTANT, SANDEMONIAN, LUTHERAN, CALVINIST, FIFTHMONARCHIST, SELEUCIAN, NEW JERUSALEMITE, POLYGAMIST, FATALIST, POLYTHEIST, NAZARITE, GAU-

LONITE, FLORINUSITE, SABATHIAN, VALENTINIAN, JOVINIANIST, SADDUSEE, PYRRHONIST, PYTHAGOREAN, PRESBYTERIAN, METHODIST, OPTIMIST, DONATIST, MORAVIAN, MUGGLETONIAN, DEIST, NOVATIAN, TAO-SSE, UNITARIAN; it follows of course, that setting up one species of religion, in preference to others, or nationalizing it, by countenancing, protecting, and supporting in idleness and luxury such drones as MUFTIS, POPES, TA-HO-CHANGS, GREAT LAMAS, PARSONS, ARCHBISHOPS, DEACONESSES, RECTORS, HIGH-PRIESTS, ELDERS, FAKIRS, BISHOPS, DEACONS, MUSTAPHIS, ARCHDEACONS, DRUIDS, PRIESTESES, LEVITES, PRIORS, CANNONS, DEANS, PRIESTS, DOCTORS OF DIVINITY, HO-CHANGS, NUNS, RABBIS, MONKS, ABBES, CARMELITES, JESUITS, CARTHUSIANS, DOMINICANS, FRANCISCANS, LADY ABBESSES, MASORITES, LAMAS, CARDINALS, EMIRS, VICARS, PROPHETS, PREBENDS, TALAPOINS, BONZES, BRAMINS, APOSTLES, SEERS, PRIMONTRES, BENEDICTINES, JACOBINES, FEUILLANS, BERNARDINES, FRERES DE L'ORDRE DE LA MERCY, CORDELIERS, CAPUCHINS, RECOLLECTS, FRERES DE LA CHARITE, MINIMES, ORATORIANS, CHARTREUX, PREDICATEURS, PICPUCES, CARMES, AUGUSTINS, URSULINES, CALVERIANS, CLERINES, SOEURS DE LA CROIX, BARNABITES, SOEURS DE LA CHARITE, ANNONCIATS, SOEURS DE ST. THOMAS, CARMES DE CHAUSSEE, PETIT PERES, DAMES DE ST. CLAIRE, LAZARISTS, ORDRE DE ST. BENOIT, DAMES DE LA VISITATION, CELESTINES, CHAPITRE NOBLE DES FEMMES, CHANOINS, TRAPISTES, INCAS, FRIARS, CURATES, CLERGYMEN, CHAPLAINS, and other such useless beings, or *as they emphatically style each other* IMPUDENT IMPOSTORS, who being too proud and lazy to work, have availed themselves of man's credulity, and the corruption of the executive power, to get laws enacted, enabling them to steal with impunity from the laborious and industrious citizens; and who not content with thus cheating mankind, have contrived to defraud each other in the division of the spoil, by giving to one, because he wears a cap of a particular form, and of his own invention, TEN OR TWELVE THOUSAND POUNDS A YEAR, whilst the poor devils who read all their tenets to the infatuated multitude are allowed by these *meek, moderate, temperate, sober, honest, chaste, virtuous, modest, dignified,* and *superior* interpreters of what, *as they say of each other,* each impiously chooses to call God's holy word, perhaps FIFTEEN OR TWENTY POUNDS A YEAR; but then their motto is *patience, and perhaps I may be a cardinal, bishop, pope, mufti, Ta-ho-chang, Great Lama, or high-priest*; it follows, I say, that these establishments, which produce such caterpillars, who pretend that an all just God has sent them to devour the good things of this world, without contributing to the labour of producing them, can be attended with no other consequence than that unhappy one of exciting the most rancorous animosities and implacable resentments betwixt those whose immediate interest consists in preserving the utmost cordiality, harmony, and fraternity, with each other, because they are at every instant endeavouring to gain superiority the one over the other, by engendering the most vicious hatred in their followers against all who happen to dissent from their particular doctrine; I therefore propose, as religion is a subject merely of opinion, and consequently ought to be free as the circumambient air, not to suffer the building, at other than private expence, any CATHEDRAL, MOSQUE, SYNAGOGUE, CONVENT, PAGOD, CHURCH, MONASTERY, TABERNACLE, CONVENTICLE, ABBEY, MEETING-HOUSE, NUNNERY, PANTHEON, CHAPEL, TEMPLE, ALTAR, or other edifice, to be appropriated to the purpose of what is called NATIONAL RELIGIOUS WORSHIP; or the endowment of any MONASTRY or NUNNERY; or the existence of any tythes, or other provision for what are called the REGULAR and NATIONAL CLERGY; taking it for granted, that the citizens can never be more happy, or the Commonwealth more flourishing, than when they follow that precept in ethics, of DO UNTO ALL MEN AS YOU WOULD THEY SHOULD DO UNTO YOU; which great and immutable principle of morality is invaded whenever one man attempts to deprive another of any of his rights, merely because he happens to differ from him in religious opinions; for who will say, that the Swede, when he castrates the deluded Roman Catholic priest, who has the misfortune to be found in his country, would not think himself ill used by being served in the same manner, whenever he chanced to go to Rome; and nevertheless this is one of those savage customs, amongst a prodigious number of others, equally barbarous, that have been introduced by these religionists, who, with unblushing effrontery and unparalleled impudence, tell you, that in so doing they zealously serve the Supreme Being, promote the happiness of man, and propagate the doctrines of that great and good man, Jesus Christ, of whom it is recorded, in the New Testament, a book which these hypocrites themselves pretend to believe the truth of, that he was of so meek a disposition, that, in his advice to his disciples and followers, he said, '*If any man smite thee on the right cheek, turn to him the left also.*'

And as the establishment of laws, however good and wholesome they may be, can be of no real use or service to the citizens, whilst the most effectual care is not taken to obtain a fair, impartial, and speedy execution of them; and as all experience must have long since convinced men that suffering of the law to be practised by individuals, for their own peculiar benefit and advantage, thereby making a trade of that which should form a principal and prominent feature in the executive power of the Commonwealth, is a principle that is radically founded in error, militates directly against a due and equitable administration of justice, is attended with the most injurious consequences to society; with the most melancholy examples of ruin and poverty to the parties seeking redress, and above all, has become in the hands of CORRUPTION a very principal means of enslaving nations, of destroying the great and sacred rights of man, and of rending asunder those fraternal bonds, which should ever unite the citizens in the most brotherly affection to each other; and the laws having, in most countries, under the flimsy pretext and specious assertion of maintaining peace, order, and good government, of every one of which they are at present entirely subversive, no doubt, expressly with a view to the particular interests of those legal wolves, who are continually prowling in society, seeking whom they may devour, become so complicated and entangled, that a whole life spent in the most unremitting study of them, is not sufficient to ascertain, with precision, what is or is not law, whereby the great bulk of the citizens of most countries are left in ignorance, and the most shameful state of blindness, of what ought to constitute their principal instruction, namely, a clear and accurate knowledge of those laws under which they live, are governed, and by which their lives, fortunes, and honour, are liable every day to be judged; and as the present method of administering public justice in most countries is such, that the greater part of the citizens are imbued with a belief that they have no occasion to obtain a knowledge of the laws of their nation, since they can always be able to find men who have studied them in a manner that is termed *professional*, and these to keep up the delusion and error, purposely contrive to render them so intricate and perplexing that the generality of men are deterred from entering upon an examination of their principles, and, by this trick, the public justice of a country is held up to sale like goods at an auction, where the best bidder generally is the purchaser, with this difference, that whereas in the auction, the buyer may perhaps be benefited by his bargain, the gainer of a law suit is but too generally ruined, and in a worse condition than if he had quietly put up with the first injury, – indeed, the lawyers are, in fact, in almost all countries the most zealous, and strongest inculcators of Christianity; for experience soon teaches all their clients, to their cost, that it is much more for their advantage to follow that precept of Jesus Christ, where he says, . . . *'And him that taketh away thy cloak forbid him not to take thy coat also, and of him that taketh away thy goods, ask them not again,'* than employ an attorney to recover them, for frequently in attempting to recover his hat, the citizen has the misfortune to lose his coat, waistcoat, shirt, stockings, and breeches; it should seem, therefore, that those societies, who are established for the purpose of propagating the Christian Faith, would do well to recommend to the Pope the supplying all vacant church establishments with these strenuous supporters of the Doctrines of Jesus Christ, instead of those clergymen, who, by their conduct, seem determined rather to bring Christianity into disesteem than promote its interests; and as distributive justice demands that every where the laws ought really to be what the English judges say the law of their country is, equally open to the poor and the rich; although how far this is the case in most countries may be best judged of by the daily occurrences, where, if a man have not wherewith to see an avaricious attorney, his complaints, however just, against his neighbour must remain unheard and unredressed, whilst there are not wanting abundance of instances, where the man of wealth, by the mere dint of money, *properly applied, as the men of law professionally term it,* has been able to harrass, oppress, and ruin his fellow-citizen, without any just cause whatever; and to what is all this to be attributed but that which is considered by the profession as their sheet anchor, and emphatically termed the GLORIOUS UNCERTAINTY OF THE LAW, which rendered into plain English, is, *whose attorney is the greatest rogue, who has the longest purse, and the most convenient witnesses*; and as this glorious uncertainty of the law, so much valued and boasted of by its professors, is, or ought to be, its greatest reproach, because the law should equally apply to all the citizens, and none be suffered to be ignorant of it; should be definite, and never be so made as to admit of two or more constructions; and as delay in the determination of causes, is of all things the most destructive of justice, by opening a wide and extensive field for CORRUPTION, PERJURY, and OPPRESSION, and is highly harrassing, and cruel to the parties accused; there being a variety of examples where citizens who were extremely innocent of the crime alledged, have been detained in prison for SIX, NINE, TWELVE MONTHS, and more, without being ever brought to trial, and at last discharged without any thing like evidence being offered of their guilt; therefore, to remedy these evils, I propose, in my plan, not to suffer any attorney or advocate to be paid at the private expence of the individual seeking justice, but propose, that the law, the just and equitable administration of which is a circumstance mutually interesting to the whole body of the citizens, should really be what the administrators of English jurisprudence say of their laws equally attainable by the affluent and the needy, and for this purpose, I propose, that it should at all times be administered at public expence, and without any unnecessary delay; thus preventing any useless and inconvenient disbursement of money on the part of either plaintiff or defendant, and giving every citizen his remedy against oppression; thus restoring JUSTICE to her original purity, by taking out of her beam that bias which at present but too often causes one of her scales to preponderate, and never permitting her sword to strike but when truth directs the blow.

Plan, &c.

I shall now proceed to lay down the outlines of my plan for a COM-MONWEALTH, and here I must entreat the candid reader to bear in mind, that if any part or the whole of it, may appear incongruous, I shall feel the greatest pleasure in seeing my feeble attempts taken up by a more masterly hand, and that happiness, which is the undoubted right of and which I most fervently wish my fellow creatures to possess, placed by superior abilities, within the reach of oppressed mortals, by the proposition for a rational Government, to be founded on the indefeasible rights of man; the non-existence of which in most countries has hitherto so cruelly scourged the human species, sinking them in slavery, sloth and baseness; making them hug those chains they ought to rend asunder; corrupting their morals, degenerating their habits, and submitting them to the cruel and rapacious tyranny of a few crafty knaves and designing villains, that punish the imbecility of those, who imitate their example with the most bloody and dreadful tortures; thus filling their prisons with the wretched victims of their savage policy, or else strewing the earth with the dead and mangled carcases of those who left destitute by the negligence of society have been forced into criminal pursuits to obtain that provision which their physical wants have rendered absolutely necessary; but which the injustice and rapacity of these unfeeling gaolers of the human mind, has prevented them from being capacitated to obtain by other means, than depredating in their turn upon those who never cease, for an instant, to pillage and ravage their fellow-citizens to support themselves in the most shameful debauchery, and extravagant dissipation: – Regardless of the misery and wretchedness which they everywhere diffuse, by the gratification of those inordinate and desolating passions, that reduce them in the eyes of the honest and virtuous man, far below the level of the beasts of the field. Indeed, government, in the most part of the present societies, may be compared to caterpillars and locusts, who destroy, without remorse, the produce of the industry and labour of others, without ever dreaming of giving in any manner, their assistance in return.

I can truly say, that the endeavour to point out the means of establishing such a government has been the most prominent motive for the present publication; conscious of the deficiency of my own acquirements, in the prosecution of this design, I can flatter myself with nothing more than the hope, that I may by it excite in the bosom of the PHILOSOPHER, and man of reflection, the desire of ameliorating the miseries of his species; which, whatever may be the difference of opinion between men, on the best means of remedying them, must at all events be universally acknowledged but too fatally to have existence, and to cry aloud for redress: no man of humanity can look at the cottager, and see him meagre, half famished, and worn down with excessive toil; his children naked and uneducated, and at the same time, view the plumpness and healthy appearance of the coach-horse, that drags his Lord in enervating idleness past the humble thatch, and not be ready to allow, that wherever such a wicked disparity between the condition of the human and brutal species exists, the government must be radically wrong, infamous, and little calculated to produce the desirable end for which government was originally instituted.

To the critics, I can only say, I shall chearfully submit to their lashes, while they inflict them only in conformity to justice and reason; and that far from feeling myself angered by their animadversions, however severe they may be, I shall be happy in having my mistakes rectified, and to be drawn from my wanderings into the path of TRUTH; to be imbued, with whose sublime doctrines forms the most zealous wish of my heart, and to inculcate the fascinating, beautiful and delicious tenets of this long neglected, though radiant sun of human felicity, bounds the utmost ambition of my soul; and should I ever again appear before the public tribunal, I shall feel it the most honourable part of my life, candidly to acknowledge my errors, and thankfully to recognize the benefits that I may have received from the impartial observations of the LEARNED, and the honest criticisms of the friends of HUMANITY and TRUTH.

This premised, I think it proper and suitable to my subject, to set out with a declaration of rights, founded on the broad and permanent basis of LIBERTY, FRATERNITY and EQUALITY, as I conceive it is on the imperishable foundation of these rights alone, that those laws and regulations can be built, which shall truly and faithfully have for object, what ought to be considered the most important of all human pursuits – THE HAPPINESS OF THE HUMAN RACE LIVING TOGETHER IN SOCIETY.

Declaration of Rights.

Article First.

All men, when they come out of the hands of nature, are equal and free. This freedom and equality they can never infringe without committing injustice to themselves; they ought always to remain equal and free: no distinction ought to exist amongst the citizens but what is conducive to the general utility and happiness of society; any privilege, therefore, granted to a member of society for his own particular advantage becomes an injustice to the rest of the citizens.

Article Second.

The legitimate end of all association whatever, is the conservation of society, and the preservation of the natural and imprescriptible rights of each of its members: these rights are Liberty, Security, and Resistence against oppression of every kind, and are founded on the nature of man.

Article Third.

The SOVEREIGNTY ought to reside in the majority of the citizens who compose a nation. No *body of men* of less amount than the absolute majority; no *individual*, unless authorised by a complete majority, can legitimately exercise any authority over the citizens, because nature has willed that its part shall always remain subordinate to the whole.

Article Fourth.

LIBERTY consists in the power of doing every thing for the advantage of the individual which does not trench upon the rights of another: thus no restriction ought to be laid on the rights of any man, because, whenever the exercise of a function becomes injurious to society, it ceases to be Liberty, and becomes LICENTIOUSNESS; but as every man may not be able to form to himself an accurate and precise idea of what constitutes Licentiousness, the law, which, to be just, must be the expression of the will of the absolute majority of the citizens, fixes boundaries to the actions of men. The true and sole limitation of Liberty is, the not doing that to another which you would not wish he should do unto you.

Article Fifth.

The law can acquire no right to forbid those actions which are not injurious to society. Everything that is not forbidden by the law, each citizen ought to be allowed to do with safety, and ought to be by the law guaranteed in doing; but no citizen ought to be obliged to do that which is not prescribed by the law made antecedent to the compulsion.

Article the Sixth.

The law ought to be the expression of the will of the majority of the citizens comprising a state; a majority of the citizens, by themselves or their representatives, ought to consent to the law before it can have effect: it ought to be the same for every citizen, otherwise it would degenerate into injustice.

Article the Seventh.

Every citizen being equal in rights, ought to be equally admissible to the occupation of that post which a majority of his fellow citizens shall call upon him to hold; each citizen ought to be compelled to accept the public offices in his turn, if a majority of his fellow-citizens think fit; but no citizen ought to be obligated to hold a public situation twice until every other citizen shall have filled the same post.

Article the Eighth.

Religion being a matter of opinion, ought to be free as the circumambient air. No citizen ought to be compelled to adopt any particular religious tenets, or be excluded from his rights as a citizen on account of his faith, while the manifestation of it does not tend to injure the society of which he forms a part.

Article the Ninth.

No citizen ought to be accused, arrested, or detained, except in cases determined by the law, and according to the forms which shall be prescribed by the law. As punishment ought to attach to illegal arrest or detention of any citizen, so no citizen ought to withhold an obedience to the law, and resistance to it becomes a crime.

Article the Tenth.

The law ought not to establish any punishment that is disproportioned to the crime committed; and punishment to be legitimate, ought to have been decreed and promulgated antecedent to the offence, and be applied according to the forms prescribed.

Article the Eleventh.

Every citizen being presumed innocent until such time as a jury of his fellow-citizens shall have declared him guilty; whenever it shall be deemed necessary to the public safety to seclude a citizen, all co-ercive force, not absolutely necessary to the detention of his person, ought to be criminal.

Article the Twelfth.

The free communication of thought and of opinion is one of the most irrefragable and precious rights of a citizen. Every citizen therefore ought to be allowed freely to speak, write, and publish his sentiments, and opinion, upon any and every subject, when such writing, speaking, or publishing is not injurious to the interests of individuals: the law ought, therefore, to apply remedies to the abuses of the press and of speech, only in the cases of individuals.

Article the Thirteenth.

The keeping of any armed force on foot, other than the citizens of the state, being inconsistent with the liberties of the citizens, ought to become criminal in the parties concerned: the armed force being for the benefit of all ought not to be applied to the sole use or advantage of any individual, except in protecting his natural rights.

Article the Fourteenth

Society has a right to reimburse those expences which it incurs, by a levy on each of its citizens; this impost ought to be equally sustained by all the citizens, according to the abilities of each.

Article the Fifteenth.

Every public functionary ought to be responsible to the society for his administration; from this responsibility he ought not to be absolved.

Article the Sixteenth.

Every citizen has the imprescriptible right by himself, or by his representative, to give his voice concerning the necessity of the contribution to be levied; it ought not to be levied without the consent of a majority of the citizens previously obtained; every individual has a right to investigate the public accounts, and any attempt to prevent the exercise of this right, is an infraction of the rights of man, and ought to attach criminality.

Article the Seventeenth.

Society ought to guarantee to every citizen the exercise of his natural and unalienable rights; whenever these are attacked, each citizen has an indefeasible right to call upon society for protection against the invader – Society ceases to be just when it refuses this assistance.

Article the Eighteenth

Every citizen has a right to the protection of society in the enjoyment of his property honestly acquired; no power can deprive him of any part of it, except when a majority of his fellow-citizens shall have declared it necessary to the safety of the state, and in that case, society is bound to make him an indemnity.

Representation and Executive Government.

Men, in forming themselves into societies, have tacitly made a COV-ENANT, by which they engage to be mutually serviceable to each other, and to do nothing that can be injurious either to their individual or collective capacity; yet the nature of man rendering it indispensably necessary that he should at every instant search after happiness, which he always makes consist in the gratification of some passion, it becomes necessary to direct these passions in such a manner that they may concur to the general prosperity, by which alone individual happiness can be truly said to exist; for this purpose LAWS are established, by which it is or ought to be ascertained, from the united wisdom of society, what actions are or are not conducive to the maintenance of association, and the felicity of its members. But that these laws may be equitable and receive a general obedience, it is also necessary, that they should, at all times, be the expression of the public will, indeed, whenever they are not the result of the FREE CONSENT of a majority of the citizens who compose a state, they are an infraction of the rights of man, an unjust USURPATION, and a direct ROBBERY. And, as in numerous associations, an assembly of the whole citizens to discuss public measures is altogether impracticable, and could not be held without engendering tumults and disorder; it has been found necessary to choose from amongst the citizens, individuals in whom society places a confidence, to be the organs by which the general will, that is to say, the will of the majority of the citizens is expressed; these are intrusted with a certain degree of power, to make such regulations and laws, as they may judge expedient and necessary to the happiness and well-being of the community, of which they themselves form a part.

CORRUPTION, that dreadful weapon in the hands of wicked and designing men, found means to spread its baneful influence into this wholesome and salutary institution, and by degrees to enlarge the powers of the deputy by restricting those of the elector; till at length the most profligate of the representatives, in many instances, separated themselves from their companions; assumed the sovereign authority, and having surreptitiously obtained the command of the public force, they turned that which was originally meant for the protection of society, against society itself; and through the ignorance and stupidity of man, thus made the abject slave of those who first received their appointments from him, the servant became the master: use familiarised them to the assumption; ignorance and credulity concurred to rivet their shackles; until, at last, man entirely lost sight of the first intention of his association, and in his delirium and blindness, he committed for these very men, who had usurped over him an absolute authority, the most cruel and oppressive acts against his fellow-citizens; the interests of society were divided, and man became an easy prey to the ambitious and designing knave.

Elevated souls at different periods, feeling the natural dignity of man debased, his rights torn from him, and commiserating the wretchedness which every where pervades human association, have endeavoured to draw society out of this state of degradation, and place its members once more in the possession of their legislative rights; but an unfortunate principle that has hitherto infused itself into almost all their schemes, I mean that of dividing the representative and executive power, and making certain situations hereditary, has rendered, for the greater part, their most strenuous efforts nugatory and abortive.

And as the sending men to legislate without giving them the necessary power to carry their laws into execution would be an absurdity; so the separation of the executive and representative body, seems to have had its origin in an intention to deceive and defraud the people of their just rights; under a pretext as flimsy as it is fallacious; and not from any evident demonstration of its being productive of superior benefits to society: therefore, I propose that the representative and executive government shall be the same. The great desideratum then seems to be, to obtain a perfect and practicable equality of representation; and to give to every citizen a due participation in the choice of those persons, to whom is delegated the power of disposing of a part of that property, which can only legitimately be the offspring of industry, and of making those laws which may abridge a part of man's original liberty, in order to secure the safety and felicity of every component member of the Commonwealth; and here I must dissent from that distinction, which has hitherto been held as an axiom not to be departed from, that of causing property, and not persons, to be represented; and my reason for thus dissenting is this, that in all cases it is persons, and not property, that must protect both the laws and society; for all the gold, silver, and other valuables that ever came out of the bowels of the earth, could never have been able, without the assistance of men's bodies, to have protected a single individual against the depredations of rapacious villains and titled robbers. Property, therefore, in my opinion, should never be considered in any other light than as an adventitious circumstance, enabling the citizen who possesses it to gratify more sensual appetites, than the citizen who has no such appendage; but as by no means giving the possessor any advantage in point of right or privilege over his poorer fellow-citizen; whose body, without this casualty will form as strong a rampart against the enemies of society, as that of the richest NABOB that ever left the insulted and enslaved shores of HIN-DOSTAN, glutted with BLOOD, DIAMONDS, and WRETCHEDNESS!!!

I therefore propose that the COMMONWEALTH, shall be divided into districts, containing, as nearly as possible, each TWENTY-FIVE THOUSAND inhabitants intitled to vote; that is to say, male citizens, who shall have attained the age of eighteen years, and who shall not be incapacitated by crime or insanity, and that this may be obtained as precisely as possible, I propose that a general census of the people should be taken, and when the districts are formed, the inhabitants of each shall choose, from amongst themselves, by an absolute major-ity, that is to say, by not less than TWELVE THOUSAND FIVE HUNDRED AND ONE suffrages, a fit and proper person to be their REGISTER, or keeper of the archives; whose functions shall consist in enrolling the names of all the inhabitants of the district qualified to vote; which qualification, as I have before stated, shall only be, *having attained eighteen years, being a male unattainted by crime, of sane intellect, and a native of the country, or if not native, one who shall have had passed in his favour, by an absolute majority of the whole representative body, a vote of* DENIZATION.

This REGISTRY ought to be at all times open to the inspection of the citizens of the district to which it shall belong, and no one ought to have the right of citizenship who shall have neglected to enter his name, situation and place of abode in the Register; and he shall, at the time of enrollment, be obliged to bring TWO CITIZENS, whose names shall already be on the register, as vouchers to prove his qualification and right to be so enregistered, and any citizen who shall give a false voucher for another in order to obtain his enrollment shall, upon such falsity being proved to the satisfaction of a jury, be disenfranchised for seven years; and if convicted of a second offence, for ever; but this in no case to affect his children; and in order that the citizen who may happen to have residences in different districts, shall not be, from that circumstance, enabled to obtain an undue influence over his fellow-citizens, by having in consequence a plurality of votes, I propose that the citizen being possessed of such different abodes, shall, at the time of his being enregistered, give in the titles and designations of such habitations, in each district where such possessions may be, signifying in each the district in which he means to exercise his right of suffrage, and this, under penalty of forfeiture for seven years of his elective franchise for the first offence, and perpetually for the second, upon conviction before a jury of having given in a false account to the register: the same regulations to be observed upon any citizen becoming possessed of any other residence subsequent to his enrollment; the account to be given in ten days next after such acquisition, provided no election shall intervene during the ten days, should that happen he shall then be bound to do it immediately; and in case of removal from one district to another, he shall observe the same mode of procedure, giving notice to the register to strike off his name from the roll of the district from which he shall depart: and I propose that every fourth day a list of all cases of death, crimination, and lunacy, shall be published by the municipal officers, and be by them transmitted to the register of the district, that he may accordingly rectify his registry. And that no district may encrease or diminish in too a great a degree, and thereby render the representation unequal; I propose that every THIRD year the representative body shall have laid before them the different registers, that they may compare the numbers of each, and join together, or separate, or otherwise modify such as shall have encreased or decreased in such manner, that each body of electors may be composed as nearly as possible of TWENTY-FIVE THOUSAND citizens possessing the elective franchise, who shall be entitled to send FOUR representatives. And, as I propose, that in the Commonwealth, no place or office of any kind shall be held for a longer time than ONE YEAR, so I propose, that one month previous to the expiration of each year, the citizens shall by a number of twelve thousand five hundred and one electors, being an absolute majority of each district, choose a register for the year ensuing: the SALARY of the REGISTER to be fixed at THREE BUSHELS OF WHEAT PER DIEM, or a consideration in money equal to the value of such wheat, to be ascertained by the respective returns of the average price of grain in the district where he is chosen. His QUALIFICATION to be, being *a resident in the district, and having elective franchise, having attained the age of twenty-five years, uncontaminated by crime, and of a sane mind.* The mode of ELECTION to be by BALLOT.

The manner of electing the FOUR REPRESENTATIVES, for each district of twenty-five thousand electors, I propose to be by ballot, to take place one month previous to the expiration of each year; the only period for which I propose they should enjoy their representative capacity; no citizen to be declared to have been chosen unless he has an absolute majority of the citizens having elective franchise in his favour; that is to say, not having a less number of votes than TWELVE THOUSAND FIVE HUNDRED AND ONE.

The qualification for a representative to be, having attained the age of twenty-five years, having been an inhabitant of the district which he is to represent for the year antecedent to his election, having elective franchise, that is to say, being uncontaminated by crime, and of a sane mind.

The representative to be incapable of holding any other public situation or office during the year of his deputation; and to be paid FOUR BUSHELS of wheat per diem, or an equivalent in money equal to the wheat, taking the average price of the grain in the district where the representative body meet for the standard; and to be allowed such travelling expences as a jury of TWENTY-FIVE of his constituents shall deem reasonable; the jury for this purpose to be chosen by lot.

At the same time, when the election for the four representatives takes place, I also propose that there shall be chosen four *supernumeraries*, who shall succeed to the representation in case of the death of the member, or of his impeachment, or removal, &c. and to perform the duty of the representative in case of sickness; the supernumerary to receive the same salary as the representative when on actual service; and to be allowed travelling expences, to be settled by jury as already stated; and in case of his succeeding to the representation by the death, or dismissal of the former member, then the citizens of the district to proceed immediately to choose another supernumerary.

I also propose, that the electors shall at any time when they shall to the number of TWELVE THOUSAND FIVE HUNDRED AND ONE, agree that the representative or his supernumerary has forfeited their confidence be possessed of the power of removing such deputy or his supernumerary, and proceed to the election of another.

Committee of Government.

The representative body, when met, shall proceed to choose from amongst their own body, a COMMITTEE OF GOVERNMENT, to be elected by ballot, and each member to be considered only as having his election by having in his favour an actual majority of the representative body: for example, if the deputies consist of four hundred citizen, then it shall be absolutely necessary for each member chosen into the committee of government, to have the suffrages of TWO HUNDRED AND ONE representatives. I also propose, that four of the members of the committee shall go out monthly by rotation, and be replaced by four others chosen, in the same manner as the first. This committee to have no other power than that of executing the decrees of the representation, and laying before them, for consideration, such measures as they may deem necessary to the public advantage; but not to put any measure into execution until after it shall have received the sanction of an absolute majority of the representatives of the people. This committee to have under them SIX CLERKS, to be chosen annually from among the people, by an absolute majority of the representative body, one month previous to the expiration of each year; each to be paid TWO BUSHELS of wheat per diem, or an equivalent in money at the average price of grain in the district where the representatives shall hold their sittings.

Committee of Finance.

I also propose, that the representative body shall choose from amongst themselves, observing the same forms as in the choice of the members composing the Committee of Government, a COMMITTEE OF FINANCE, to consist of twelve members, FOUR of which shall go out monthly by rotation, and be replaced in the same manner as the citizens of the committee of government. This committee to have under them SIX CLERKS, to be chosen from amongst the people, in the same manner as the clerks of the committee of government; and each to be paid TWO BUSHELS of wheat per diem, or an equivalent in money according to the value of the wheat at the average market price of such district, where the representative body are assembled.

The functions of this committee, I propose, to be the receipt of the taxes; the care of the national treasure; and the payment of all salaries; the inspection of public roads, buildings, canals, and rivers, and to report to the representative body, when, and where it is necessary to amend old ones, or make new ones; but not to put them into execution, until they shall have been decreed by an absolute majority of the national representation. It shall be their duty to inspect the public works of every sort, and make the necessary payments; but, previous to any such payment taking place, they shall report upon it to the representative body, and receive their sanction. Their accounts to be always subject to the inspection of the citizens composing the representation: and every month they shall publish an account of their receipts, and expenditures, and of the money in their hands, signed by the names of the whole committee, with the names of the districts they represent: these accounts shall be deposited with the registers of each district for the inspection of the citizens.

Committee of Agriculture, Trade and Provisions.

I also propose, that the representative body shall choose, from among themselves, a COMMITTEE OF AGRICULTURE, TRADE AND PROVISIONS, observing the same forms as in the two other committees, FOUR of which shall vacate their stations monthly, by rotation, and be replaced in the same manner as in the other committees. This committee to have under them SIX CLERKS, chosen from among the citizens in the same manner as the clerks to the other committees, and each to be paid TWO BUSHELS of wheat per diem, or an equivalent in money, at the average price of the district where the representation are communed.

The functions of this committee, I propose, to be the inspection of the agriculture of the country; the state of the trade; and the taking measures for providing provisions and fuel for the different districts; they shall every month make a report to the national representation, signed by all the members composing the committee, stating the districts which they represent; these reports, I propose, shall be sent to the registers of each district for public information.

The qualification for a CLERK to the COMMITTEES to be, having attained the age of twenty-one years, and having elective franchise, that is to say, uncontaminated with crime, of sane intellect, a native of the country, or naturalized.

I also propose, to prevent any stagnation taking place in the prosecution of the public business, that at the dissolution of one representative body, the COMMITTEES, who shall be in office, shall remain until they are replaced by the regular monthly succession of four members of the new representation.

And as laws to be equitable, should always be the expression of the will of the majority of the citizens, I propose, that no act, regulation, or decree, shall take place and have effect, or be binding on the citizens, unless it has received the sanction of an absolute majority of the whole representation; that is to say, if the deputies are five hundred in number, then to every act that shall have force, two hundred and fifty-one members shall have given their assent, and their names, and those of the districts which they represent, shall be annexed to every such decree on its promulgation, or else it shall be considered as void, and of none effect. Thus every act of the LEGISLATURE being sanctioned by an absolute majority of the DEPUTIES, and these representatives being themselves deputed by an actual majority of the citizens, it would be a fair inference to suppose all such acts to be the expression of the public will, and to convey, as nearly as human possibility admits, the genuine sense of the community. The same inference will hold good with respect to the committee of executive government, which, being chosen by an absolute majority of the representative body to which every citizen is eligible, whatever they do may be justly considered as springing from the free consent of a majority of the whole citizens. I propose also, that a copy of every act of the LEGISLATURE be sent, properly signed, to the registers of each district, for public inspection, and also to the offices of the JUDICIAL ADMINISTRATORS.

But as the long possession of power has been found, by experience, to corrupt the human mind, and make men take illegal and surreptitious means to continue the enjoyment of it, I propose, to remedy this evil, hitherto found to be fraught with such destructive consequences to the LIBERTY of the human species, that after having served the office of representative for one year, the citizen shall be incapable of being again chosen for two years after: this will have two good effects – the one will be, that the representative being necessitated to return into the mass of the citizens, will be careful not to give his sanction to any arbitrary measure, because he will, in that case, be subjected himself, for two years, to all the evils of his own decrees; – the other is, that, by this means, the business of legislating and governing will be more generally diffused amongst the people; and thus the principle of public happiness will become more universally understood, and the opportunities of CORRUPTION be considerably if not entirely removed.

Administration of the Laws.

As I conceive, that the administration of the laws, which ought to be made only with a view to the public good, requires nothing more than integrity and industry; and, as nothing can be more unjust, or implicate a greater absurdity, than that those institutions, which are meant for the benefit of all, should be exercised for the particular profit and advantage of a few; so the establishment of attorneys, council, judges, &c. to be paid by the individual who feels it necessary to recur to the justice of his country, seems to be a practice that has originated in corruption, the continuation of which must ultimately be destructive of all morality, and subversive of that equality of judicial administration, that alone can render it beneficial and estimable in the eyes of men. It is the boast, indeed, of some countries, that the law is equally open to the rich and the poor, the same may be said of a banker's shop; but as it needs no argument to prove, that in the latter instance, the man who is unprovided with a good draft will not be allowed to receive money: so it is equally demonstrable, that, in those countries, where the law is administered at private expence, the man, who is destitute of a long purse, will be equally unable to obtain either law or justice. Thus, in such countries, the rich man is enabled to Lord it over his poorer neighbour with impunity. This generates strife amongst the citizens, and divides their interests, which, that they may retain their liberty, and live in perfect security, they should always endeavour to concentrate and unite.

I propose, therefore, that in each district the citizens shall choose, annually, from amongst their own body, by an absolute majority, a citizen, whose duty it shall be to preside over all complaints, both criminal and civil, that may arise in the district, and adjudge them, with the assistance of a jury, to be chosen by lot from the registry of the district, according to the laws of the commonwealth. This JUDICIAL ADMINISTRATOR, I propose, to be assisted by THREE CLERKS who shall also be chosen by an absolute majority of the electors of the district yearly: The election to take place one month previously to the expiration of each year. This tribunal, I propose, shall be open every day for the distribution of justice. To all parties accused, I propose giving the right of a peremptory challenge to as many jurymen as the number of which the jury by which they are to be tried, shall be composed. Thus suppose FIFTEEN citizens to be a jury, and this is the number I would propose; THIRTY shall be summoned by lot, out of which he shall have a right to reject fifteen: the other FIFTEEN to try the cause, with the assistance of the administrator of justice, who shall read the law upon the case, and in the event of the party accused being found guilty, pass the sentence affixed by the law immediately, and in all those cases, where the punishment is not precisely expressed by the legislature of the Commonwealth, then the jury, to award such punishment as they shall deem consistent with equity; and if the party sentenced under this last circumstance be dissatisfied, then an appeal to lie to the committee of executive government, who shall report the affair to the representation, an absolute majority of which shall finally decide the cause.

I also propose, that the same jury shall never try two successive causes, either criminal or civil; but that for as many causes as there are to be tried, so many times thirty jurymen shall be chosen by lot, and summoned to attend; the names to be enrolled, and called over in rotation, and each FIFTEEN, as they are left after the challenges, to be the jury to try the cause. This will prevent the possibility of bribing a jury, because it will be utterly impossible to know what jury will try any given cause.

The qualification for a judicial administrator to be, having attained his thirtieth year, having been a resident in the district for three years previous to his election, having the elective franchise, that is to say, uncontaminated with crime, and of sane mind. – His remuneration to be fixed at THREE BUSHELS of wheat per diem, or an equivalent in money, at the average market price of the district.

The qualification of a clerk to be, having attained twenty-five years, having resided in the district for two years antecedent to his election, and having elective franchise: the salary to be TWO BUSHELS of wheat per diem, or an equivalent in money.

I also propose, that the laws should be administered immediately, and without intermission, allowing only to the parties the time necessary to prepare their documents; and in no case do I propose that the administration of justice shall be attended with one farthing expence to either party, except what a jury shall adjudge against those parties whose suits they may pronounce litigious and vexatious, for as justice ought to be distributive and impartially administered, nothing can be more absurd than to make the obtaining of it a matter of expence to the citizen who applies for it; this being, in fact, nothing more than establishing a dangerous pre-eminence in the man of property over his more needy neighbour, and deciding the point in dispute by the strength of the purse, and completely and effectually secluding POVERTY, from obtaining that redress which is equally its right with the greatest WEALTH and AFFLUENCE.

Liberty of the Press.

This being one of the most sacred rights of a citizen, and perhaps the only means of ascertaining, what most certainly ought to be the principal object of every citizen's pursuit, TRUTH, I propose, that, in the Commonwealth, in no possible case shall any restriction be laid on the writing, publishing, or delivering any discourse or opinion, on any subject whatever. Indeed, TRUTH being the end most desirable in all well regulated states, the investigation of principles ought to be free to every one, and rather meet with encouragement than restraint; therefore no licence or authority ought to be necessary for the printing, publishing, or delivery of any doctrine, or of any animadversion on the public administration; and these are my reasons; the doctrine, if good, and capable of producing a majority of the people to declare in its favour, ought, most assuredly, to be received; if otherwise, its own want of importance will be its surest and best destruction with free-men; and all experience has shewn, that the attempt to suppress opinions is the most infallible means of bringing them into esteem: indeed, that which in itself is stupid and irrational, does not want the *keen* and *critical* eye of a public accuser to point out its absurdity; and if it is reasonable and just, it only marks the ignorance, folly, and wickedness, of those who are willing to smother it; for in a Commonwealth, where every one has an equal interest in supporting the happiness and tranquillity of the nation, no one will be able, by any argument, however plausible, to injure a society whose members will, at all times, be ready to resist every attempt at subverting that felicity of which they feel the beneficent effect. Thus, when the government shall be RATIONAL, JUST, and EQUITABLE, all the citizens will find their greatest advantage in defending it from insidious attacks, and they will be a much better security for its stability than PROSECUTIONS FOR HIGH TREASON, or IMPRISONMENT FOR SEDITION. The wings of LIBERTY are deprived of their feathers whenever the press is laid under restraint.

In cases of LIBEL on private characters, I propose, that the person who makes the attack, if called upon, shall either be bound to substantiate the charge, or be liable to such penalty as a JURY of FIFTEEN MEN, chosen by lot, shall inflict, and also the citizen convicted, shall be deprived, *for seven years*, of his elective franchise.

Inheritance and Bastardy.

I propose, that, in all cases, the children shall divide, in equal portions, the property of which the father may die possessed; if the wife be also alive, she shall be entitled to participate, and receive her dividend accordingly: when she dies, I propose, the children shall again divide equally.

And as nothing can possibly exceed the cruelty and injustice of the laws of bastardy, which are, in fact, *inflicting punishment on those who never yet had it in their power to offend*, I propose, that in the division of the father's effects, all the children, without exception, shall be included, whether born in wedlock or otherwise, for if any crime can attach, it must be to the father and mother, and not to the child, who is brought into this world without his consent; and surely no one will attempt to deny that the bastard, as he is called by the crooked policy of some governments, is as much the child of the father, and a citizen of the state, as the present legitimate inheritors of the parents' wealth. These laws, which seem to have originated in an intention to restrain men from forming promiscuous connexions, like most others, have been found, by experience, to be sadly deficient in means to the end proposed. Indeed, what absurdity can be more apparent than making those the only sufferers by any particular act, who had no knowledge or share in the commission of it. Would it not be considered as iniquitous, to hang the son because the father had committed a robbery? – And yet the laws of bastardy form a parallel case in all those countries where they have existence. In my apprehension, the only result of the laws of bastardy is the rendering a certain portion of the citizens vicious and the enemies of those societies who deprive them in the most cruel and unjust manner of the immunities of a citizen, for that in which they participated not, and could not avoid.

In cases where there are no children to inherit, I propose, the possessor of property to be at liberty to leave it as he pleases; and if he dies intestate, the property to go to his nearest relation.

Price of Labour.

And that the INDUSTRIOUS MANUFACTURER, LABOURER, or CULTIVATOR, may at all times be enabled to live comfortably, and bring up his family in a manner suitable to become good and useful citizens, and that they may never be oppressed by their richer associates, I propose, that no labourer or workman shall be paid at a less rate for his day's labour than ONE BUSHEL of wheat, or the value of it in money, at the average market price of the district where he is employed – This will always enable him to satisfy all the real wants of his nature, and make provision for his old age; and surely no one can be more justly entitled to be rendered comfortable than he who by his labour contributes to the comfort and happiness of others. I also propose that every citizen shall be at liberty to follow that occupation which most pleases him, and in any part of the Commonwealth without restriction.

Register of Births and Burials.

I propose, that all citizens shall, on pain of losing their rights of citizenship, be obliged to give in regularly an account of all BIRTHS and DEATHS that take place in their families, to the municipal officers, who shall transmit them, every fourth day, to the register of the district. I also propose, that no dead body shall be suffered to be interred at a less distance than ONE FURLONG from the city, village, or town, because experience has proved, that suffering burial grounds in populous places is destructive of health.

Public Taxes.

When taxes are levied on the people, they ought to be of such description that they may fall as equally as possible on all the citizens, according to their respective abilities; and not to be of such a nature as to be easily avoided, because, this again has a tendency to separate the interests of the citizens, which all institutions ought to endeavour to unite; for this purpose, the only tax I would propose in the Commonwealth, is so much per acre on land, to be paid yearly, by the citizens, when they go to ballot for representatives, into the hands of the REGISTER, any citizen who shall neglect to pay his quota, or use any kind of subterfuge to avoid paying for his full number of acres, to forfeit four times the tax. The COMMITTEE OF AGRICULTURE, TRADE AND PROVISIONS shall cause surveys to be made in the different districts; and each citizen, when he enrolls his name with the register, to declare the number of acres he holds absolutely in his own possession; but as the tax thus levied would be extremely small it would scarcely be a temptation for any one to evade it; and in this mode it would be collected without expence. I calculate that FOUR-PENCE per acre would overpay all the expences of a good government. These taxes to be paid into the hands of the COMMITTEE OF FINANCE, and to be deposited in the national treasury, within one month after the receipt, this would preclude those hordes of TAX GATHERERS, EXCISEMEN and CUSTOMHOUSE OFFICERS, that swarm in every country, and are almost always the *enemies* of the people.

Religion.

I propose, that this being entirely a matter of opinion, in which no one can prove his infallibility, the Commonwealth should not adopt any particular religious tenet, nor pay any priest; of any persuasion, nor build any house of religious worship; but that each citizen should be left entirely at his liberty to follow that form of religion which is most accordant to his ideas. On no account would I propose that it should interfere in any manner with the political government of the COMMONWEALTH, nor ever allow it to become a subject of discussion in the LEGISLATURE.

Bread and Fuel.

These being articles of the first necessity, without which human nature cannot long subsist, the supply of them to the citizens at an easy rate should of consequence form a prominent feature in the administration of every good government, for nothing can be more scandalous, or a greater reproach to any government in any country, than either to see a scarcity of these necessary articles, or that they should be at an exorbitant price, I therefore propose, that the COMMITTEE OF AGRICULTURE, TRADE AND PROVISIONS, shall make it an indispensable part of their duty to see that every district has a proper supply of these commodities at the most reasonable rates; and in those places that depend for a supply from other parts of the Commonwealth by water carriage, I propose, that they shall establish large national magazines, in which six months provision of these necessaries shall always be kept ready for the public use: this will prevent the prices being affected by frost, or other casualties, and enable the inhabitants to be continually in the enjoyment of a plentiful supply at a moderate price. And that this object may be continually kept in view, I propose, that the REGISTERS shall make a monthly report of their districts; on this subject, to the COMMITTEE OF AGRICULTURE, TRADE AND PROVISIONS, who shall lay them regularly before the national representation, with their own remarks. The registers and the committees to be answerable for the truth of their statements. This mode would destroy those disgraceful monopolies that frequently render these articles so dear as scarcely to be within the reach of the poor. In ENGLAND, if this mode was pursued, COALS would never exceed SIX-PENCE OR SEVEN-PENCE the bushel; or BREAD THREE-PENCE OR FOUR-PENCE the quartern loaf, even under the present system.

Marriage.

It is, I believe, an incontrovertible principle, that the strength of a state depends upon the number of its citizens; to encourage population, therefore, should be the maxim of all wise governments; for this purpose they tell us, the marriage ceremony in most countries was instituted, but I apprehend it will not be denied, that to render this means adequate to its end it should necessarily be productive of the felicity of the parties contracting: this can never be the case while two persons, who, after living together for a certain time, find their tempers unaccordant, and whose manners are but little calculated to promote each other's happiness, have no power of dissolving the bond of their union, from thenceforth, contrary to nature, and useless to the purpose for which it was designed, that of procreating their species, and augmenting human happiness. The hymenial lamp expires when love ceases to furnish oil. To remedy this evil, and render the connubial state really conducive to the happiness and increase of the human species, I propose, that MARRIAGE shall be merely a civil contract, and be entered into before the magistrate of the place, unattended with expence, a copy of it being transmitted to the register of the district; and that it shall at all times be liable to dissolution, upon sufficient cause being shewn to a jury, who shall be immediately summoned upon the complaint of either the husband or wife, to the administrator of the district – This would prevent those shameful bickerings that but too frequently send the husband one way and the wife another, to their mutual destruction; because any thing is preferable to the company of those who have ceased to merit our affections. I also propose, that the male, at the age of eighteen, and the female, at the age of sixteen, shall be deemed marriageable – This will have a tendency to lessen those dreadful scenes of wretched pollution that every where disgrace the moral institutions of civilized nations, and, which are principally kept in existence by the impolitic restraints which has been laid on the youth of both sexes entering into the hymenial bonds at a period when nature has given vigour to their passions, and that greediness of wealth that frequently induces parents to oblige their children to render themselves unhappy for life, by an intermarriage with decripitude, age, or a person that is their utter aversion, merely because it is what the world very unjustly calls *a prudent match*. Thus the youth disgusted at home, seeks amongst those unfortunate females whom a similar policy has driven into a state of prostitution, to satisfy those passions that nature has implanted strongly in his breast. I therefore propose, that no consent whatever shall be necessary to the junction of a male and female, except their own; for as this is a matter in which their future happiness or misery is concerned, it seems but rational and just that they alone should be consulted on an affair of such importance to their welfare – These regulations would also remedy another evil, which is the immense expence that attends the obtaining of a divorce in most countries, and which frequently obliges a man and woman, for want of the money necessary, to live together, although they are conscious of each other's infidelity.

Canals, Public Roads, and Rivers.

I also propose, that no canal shall be dug, public road made, or river cleansed at other than public expence, and this is my reason, these things being a benefit to the whole community, either immediately or consequently, ought to be defrayed by the generality of the citizens; they will also, by this means, be done much better and more effectually. I propose, therefore, that when the inhabitants of any place shall deem it necessary to widen a river, make a road, or cut a canal, they shall lay their observations before the COMMITTEE OF FINANCE, who shall cause inspection to be made, and report thereon to the representative body immediately, on pain of impeachment for neglect. In every well regulated state, CANALS should intersect the whole country, in order to facilitate the transport of the superfluity of one part to another, at easy rates, and diminish the breed of HORSES, who consume that produce which ought to nourish man, and by this means increase the price of provisions.

Waste Lands.

The existence of these are a reproach to any government, because they have a tendency to check population, and augment the price of provisions, both of which are in their consequences injurious to the Commonwealth, however beneficial they may be to some few of its members. I therefore propose, that no land whatever shall be suffered to remain uncultivated, either for parks, pleasure grounds, common, or otherwise, but that the COMMITTEE OF AGRICULTURE, TRADE AND PROVISIONS shall make it their duty continually to see that all the soil of the Commonwealth is in a state of culture, either for pasturage or produce; and in case of any citizen's refusing to cultivate any part of his lands, the committee shall take such lands into their own hands, and cause them to be cultivated for the benefit of the state, reserving half the profits towards defraying the public expenditure, and paying the other half into the hands of the owner of the land, who shall be permitted to reclaim them, on giving SIX citizens, having elective franchise, as security for their future cultivation. To see an acre of land uncultivated, and a citizen without employ in the same state, denotes a culpable inattention in the legislature, and demands the strictest enquiry of the citizens into the causes of this shameful neglect.

Magistracy.

Every TOWN, CITY, and LARGE VILLAGE, I propose, should have a MUNICIPAL OFFICER, with clerks to assist him, for the regulation of the police; these officers and clerks, I propose, to be chosen yearly, by ballot, by an actual majority of the whole inhabitants of the municipality, having elective franchise; the number of these municipalities to be settled by the national representation, marking the dependencies of each. The salaries of these municipal officers to be THREE BUSHELS of wheat per diem; their clerks TWO BUSHELS of wheat per diem; to be paid by the inhabitants of the municipality, and to be assessed yearly by a jury of TWENTY-FIVE of the citizens of the municipality, to be chosen by lot.

Lame, Blind, Lunatics, Deaf and Dumb.

These description of citizens being in most instances incapacitated by nature from contributing by their exertions to the common stock, most justly claim the support of their more favoured fellow-citizens, I therefore propose, that all such, after declaration of the fact, by a jury of TWENTY-FIVE men of the district, chosen by lot shall be pensioners of the Commonwealth, and receive ONE BUSHEL of wheat per diem, or its equivalent in money, unless the jury are of opinion that their circumstances do not require it. For such LUNATICS, whose being at liberty may be deemed prejudicial to society, by a jury of TWENTY-FIVE, chosen by lot, public edifices should be erected; these to be under inspection of the COMMITTEE of FORTY; the KEEPER to be chosen yearly by an absolute majority of the representative body.

Public Prisons.

If such disgraceful buildings, which are always a reproach to the legislative body, and can scarcely ever obtain in a well regulated state of society, are rendered necessary by the degeneracy and corruption of man, at least they ought to be rendered the instruments of public utility, and the means of reconducting the citizens into the paths of TRUTH, VIRTUE, and REASON; and not as they are in most countries, the nurseries of vice and infamy, where the novice is hardened in crime, and the profligate lose all sense of shame and of their duty to their country.

I therefore propose that in those districts where the national representation shall deem it expedient to have prisons, they shall always be situated at least two miles from any city or town, in an open airy situation; that the KEEPER and his servants shall be chosen yearly, by an absolute majority of the citizens of the district, having elective franchise, that is to say, by the suffrage of TWELVE THOUSAND FIVE HUNDRED AND ONE votes; that they shall be paid by the nation, and not suffered on any account to take any fee or other emolument whatever from the unhappy citizens committed to their care, on pain of attaching criminality; their salaries to be THREE BUSHELS of wheat per diem to the keeper, and TWO BUSHELS to each of his servants, or an equivalent in money. And that no extortion or other ill treatment of prisoners may obtain, I propose, that THREE members of the legislative body shall be chosen by an absolute majority of the representation every month, who shall visit all the prisons, and make a report, signed with their names, and the districts they represent, to the representation; this report shall be printed and sent regularly to the register of the districts, for public inspection. I also propose, that all the prisoners shall be made to work at some useful occupation; the profits of their labour to be their own property, after deducting a certain portion towards defraying the expence of the prison establishment, unless otherwise decreed by their jury, and during their seclusion to be fed at the charge of the COMMONWEALTH, in a mode to be settled by the REPRESENTATION.

Abolition of Capital Punishments.

As nothing can be more unnatural than that man should destroy his fellow man, so society, in my opinion, can never acquire the right of inflicting the punishment of death on any of its citizens; indeed, even in cases of murder, the deprivation of the life of the murderer is only redoubling the loss already sustained by the Commonwealth. I should therefore propose the abolition of all capital punishments, and in their place substituting some mode of making those whose offences may be deemed of a capital nature, work hard the remainder of their lives, for the benefit of the community they have injured, for society commits SUICIDE every time it deprives itself of the services of any of its members, merely because they have already injured it.

Education.

I have now reached what I conceive to be the most interesting and important of all human objects, since from it springs the only permanent liberty and durable happiness of man, THE CULTURE OF THE HUMAN MIND, and THE EDUCATION OF THE MEMBERS WHO COMPOSE SOCIETY, and this should of course form an institution that ought to be considered of the first consequence to the Commonwealth, and be cordially cherished by all the citizens.

There needs no argument to prove the pains that have been taken by despots, priests, and usurpers, to keep the bulk of the people in a state of the most savage ignorance; almost every page of History, as well ancient as modern, is a strong and irrefragable evidence of their malign and wicked endeavours. They well knew the importance of education; they were not unacquainted that KNOWLEDGE and LIBERTY went hand in hand, and that wherever the first prevailed generally, the latter must be the inevitable consequence; they were perfectly aware that an enlightened people would not consent to that shameful degradation of their species, of becoming the vile slaves and abettors of LAWLESS OPPRESSERS, SANGUINARY TYRANTS, and PECULATING ADVENTURERS; they felt, that man cultivated and educated, would consider his fellow man only as a man, and not as a god, or being of a superior order. To prevent, therefore, this salutary institution from obtaining, which would immediately tend to a total subversion of their usurped power, formed the most prominent and most interesting speculation of every chief. But it was to be done with art and circumspection, with the apparent consent of the citizens, and not by prohibitory laws which would at once have blown up this MINE OF INFAMY, and have opened the eyes of those whom it was necessary, to further their own views, and that they might be enabled to continue with impunity their nefarious practices, to keep in a state of utter blindness; to effectuate this iniquitous scheme, and prevent education from sending forth its irradiating beams amongst the citizens, required Machiavellian skill, and more than common duplicity and adroitness, because it was indispensably requisite for this purpose to have the appearance of encouraging that which they meant most effectually to smother and destroy; we therefore see the greatest despots encouraging men of letters at their courts, and founding universities, but we at the same time have the melancholy spectacle of their fixing the price of labour at so low a rate as completely secludes the labourious citizen, who lives by his industry alone, from any hope of being able to maintain the expence of educating his children; we see them lay heavy imposts on all the necessaries of life, thus rendering it absolutely requisite to employ that time which ought to be dedicated to education in hard labour, to support existence; we see them under every kind of specious pretext, clogging with stamps and other duties the free circulation of knowledge; we see newspapers put under inquisitorial laws, and in most countries we see licencers of publications established, who are careful in rejecting all those works that have any tendency to conduct the people to TRUTH, and REASON, and make them throw off the bandeau of SUPERSTITION, FALSEHOOD and TYRANNY; the theatres are shackled in the same manner; by these practices education, and the means of acquiring information, has been confined to a small circle of citizens, who have always been either bought over by the friends of rapacious government, or hunted down by oppression if they have ever presumed the attempting to illuminate the mind and enlighten the understanding of the mass of mankind; unintelligible and technical terms have been introduced into all the sciences, and thus by a combination of circumstances that have had all the shew of accident and casualty, although in fact they are connected links of the great and heavy chain that has been villain-ously forged to bind man down in the most degrading ignorance, knowledge and instruction, has been ingrossed by the few to the injury of the many, and has been made a lucrative trade in the hands of those, who, seduced by corrupt influence, have, instead of imparting it generally, most scandalously abused it, from a conviction that they were in no fear of detection by the generality of their fellow citizens, and concurred in the great but diabolical plan of maintaining IGNORANCE, CREDULITY and SUPERSTITION, by means of which men have been made SLAVES. Indeed, education has been so very rare and uncommon that those who have possessed this advantage have generally obtained a great degree of credit with the people, who, though not permitted themselves to experience its beneficent effects, have always admired it in others. CORRUPTION saw this with pleasure, besieged and subdued the greater part of the learned; OPPRESSION and TYRANNY putting to flight those few honest men who opposed its attacks; thus turning to its advantage this disposition in the people which they feared to gratify; these venal sons of education thus gained over, readily lent their aid to perpetuate abuses in which they were now become interested, to rivet closely the fetters of a tyranny in which they were permitted to participate and keep man in a state of abject slavery, by rooting him in ignorance and folly, to prevent their own iniquitous measures from being discovered; nay, some of these have even so infamously disgraced themselves, and been such vile tools in the hands of corruption, as to write treatises to prove that man's felicity was considerably diminished and abridged by literary acquirements, and that the more ignorant the man the more com-pletely happy his condition. In consequence, falsehood has every where obtained, systems of error have been established, and men have been left to grope in blindness their way through those dark caverns into which the cunning of priests and tyrants have precipit-ated them, and which their infernal policy has always prevented from being enlightened by the sacred and brilliant rays of EDUCATION, KNOWLEDGE, and TRUTH, which alone can conduct them to the groves of happiness.

To restore then liberty to long insulted man, to draw immortal and immutable TRUTH out of those holes and corners into which falsehood, superstition, and tyranny has driven it, and place it on those altars which are at present occupied by ERROR, and to remove that disgraceful ignorance which debases human nature, rendering it corrupt, venal, and profligate, I intend that EDUCATION shall form a part of the national establishment of the Commonwealth, and be considered as one of the first objects of the legislator's care, because to form good and virtuous citizens for a state, it is absolutely necessary that they should be instructed in their rights, know how to maintain them, and be acquainted with their nature and consequence; I therefore propose, that in each district there shall be erected a sufficient number of PUBLIC SCHOOLS, to educate all the children of the district, and that from the age of four to fourteen, no citizen shall be suffered to withhold his child from receiving an education at one of the public seminaries of the district in which he resides, upon pain of forfeiting his rights as a citizen for ever; and that the rising generation may at all times receive the impulse of the public will, and that each parent may have a due share in and controul over the education of his child, I propose, that every year the MASTERS, MISTRESSES, or TUTORS, shall be elected by ballot, by an absolute majority of the electors of the district, that is to say, by the suffrage of not less than TWELVE THOUSAND FIVE HUNDRED AND ONE; the new election to take place one month previous to the expiration of each year; and each master, mistress, or tutor to receive a salary of FOUR BUSHELS of wheat per diem, or an equivalent in money, taking the average market price of the district, and to live rent free in the national school, which shall always be the property of the Commonwealth, and be fitted up with a library, and with mathematical, astronomical, optical and other scientific apparatus, for the use of the pupils; the children to be cloathed, boarded and lodged during the ten years of their education, at the public expence, and without any distinction whatever; the expence to be borne by the inhabitants of the district by assessment.

And to prevent abuses taking place in these establishments, and to ensure a punctual and steady conduct in the masters, mistresses, or tutors, I propose, that there shall be chosen, in each district, by a majority of the whole electors, FORTY persons who shall form a committee of superintendance, TEN to go out every three months, by rotation, and to be supplied by ten other citizens, who shall also be chosen by an absolute majority of the whole suffrages of the district; these shall be bound to examine once in every month, or as much oftener as they shall think right, all the schools of the district, and make their report to the representative body, and to the district, which report shall be lodged with the register, for public inspection; they shall also audit the accounts of the expenditure attending the public seminaries, and settle the quota of each citizen towards defraying them, every third month, for the ensuing THREE MONTHS; as the members of this committee will be immediately interested in their functions, so I propose, that no salary shall attend the execution of them; and to prevent the affairs of the district ever getting into the hands of a junto, I propose that, no citizen, after having served on the committee, shall be again eligible to be chosen for twelve months; they shall also inspect the conduct of the municipal officers, and report thereon.

The qualification of a master or tutor to be, having attained THIRTY YEARS, having resided in the district for FOUR years, being a father of a family, and having elective franchise.

The qualification for a mistress to be, having attained TWENTY-SIX YEARS, being a mother, and having resided in the district seven years.

The qualification for a member of the committee of inspection to be, having attained TWENTY-ONE YEARS, having been resident twelve months in the district, and having elective franchise, and being father of a family.

I also propose, that no RELIGIOUS DOCTRINE whatever shall be taught in the national schools; and that any master, mistress, or tutor may be displaced, on twelve thousand five hundred and one of the electors of the district signifying to the register that he or she has lost their confidence.

I also propose, that twice in every year the scholars of each district shall assemble at some place, to be previously appointed by the committee of superintendance, to celebrate civic games, and other exercises that may be productive of activity and health amongst the youth; on which days also, they shall elect from amongst themselves, one of the scholars who shall deliver AN ORATION ON LIBERTY, and the benefits accruing from education, which shall be printed and distributed through the Commonwealth and a copy lodged, with the register of the district, signed by the youth who pronounced it.

Military Force and Discipline.

The introduction of what have been termed SOLDIERS, that is to say, men carefully separated from their brother citizens, and exclusively instructed in the art of murdering their fellow-man, has been one of those means of which tyrants have availed themselves to destroy the liberty and independence of man, and subjugate him to that disgraceful state of slavery and oppression under which we at present see him groaning, and languishing in almost every climate; and the evil that has resulted to society from this institution is too glaring and notorious to admit of controversy; yet in a state of association, some kind of defence is absolutely necessary to preserve the citizens from foreign insult, and domestic depredation; now, as every member of the community is equally interested in the preservation of his rights and liberty, and as teaching one man the use of offensive weapons in preference to another, is giving the one a decided superiority and mastery over his fellow-citizen; and as CORRUPTION has been enabled, by artful men, to spread its baleful influence over these military automatons, and thus to enslave nations to the arbitrary caprice of individuals, I propose, as a remedy for these evils, and to maintain amongst all the citizens, that equality of right, from which alone must flow their respective and collective happiness, and security against oppression – That EVERY CITIZEN in the Commonwealth SHALL BE A SOLDIER AND EVERY SOLDIER A CITIZEN. For this purpose, I intend that the science of MILITARY TACTICS shall form a part of the education of youth; thus placing all the citizens upon a level in the use of arms, after which, if they suffer their liberty to be wrested from them, by ambitious and designing knaves, it will be their own fault, and they deserve only to be slaves. The man, who having the means of preserving his LIBERTY, voluntarily gives it up, is unworthy of being a FREEMAN.

I therefore propose, that in every district there shall be erected national military schools, into which the youth, after they have obtained the age of fourteen, shall be sent for one year more to learn the exercise and duty of a soldier, and defender of himself and his country. The MASTERS of these schools to be chosen in the same manner as those of the other seminaries of the Commonwealth, and to be paid in the same manner; the same qualifications to be requisite, and the schools to be under the superintendance of the COMMITTEE OF FORTY; and the expences attending them to be defrayed by the citizens of the district, in the same manner as those incurred by other public schools. I also propose, that one day in every two months, every citizen from the age of fifteen to fifty, shall form himself, with his neighbours, into regiments, and go through the martial exercise, and military evolutions: this will prevent their forgetting the great principle of defence, and render them at all times ready and fit to defend their country in case of attack. I also propose, that every citizen who shall have obtained the age of fourteen, shall be furnished, by his district, with a firelock and bayonet, which he shall be bound to keep in complete repair, and fit for immediate use, if occasion requires, to defend himself and the Commonwealth.

In cases of public emergency, that is to say, of defence, for I would propose, that the citizens should never enter upon offensive war; the force that shall be deemed necessary by the legislature shall be called out by an equal portion from each district, to be chosen by lot, and without distinction of persons. This force to be paid for their services in such manner, and at such rates as the legislative body shall judge fitting and expedient, and to remain on foot only so long as the public danger shall be declared to exist by the national representation.

Thus all being adequate to the defence of themselves, and of their country, it would be impossible to subjugate, as at present, one part of a nation by another, and, at the same time, the society would be preserved from foreign attack, since it would be, in fact, attacking an hornet's nest to attack a nation of armed men, well disciplined, and whose common and natural interest would consist in supporting and protecting each other. Thus those bloody and cruel wars that have so often depopulated the earth, would receive an effectual check; ambition would not know where to rear its head with any probable chance of success; cruel and blood-thirsty chiefs would be abandoned by an enlightened people, and we should no more have the misfortune to see either an ALEXANDER or a CÆSAR; a MAHOMET or a CORTEZ; a CHARLES THE TWELFTH or a LEWIS the FOURTEENTH; a WILLIAM THE CONQUEROR or a CZAR PETER. – Peace would be restored to the blood drenched earth; security would reign in the cottage and the city, and men would no longer be liable to have infamous and oppressive measures insolently crammed down their throats with the point of a bayonet, or to be cruelly and wicked crimped or kidnapped; tyranny would receive its vital blow, and despotism become as obsolete and uncommon as it is now prevalent and fashionable. The necessity of reforming abuses would no where exist, because citizens instructed in their rights, and rendered capable of defending them, would never suffer a set of wretched and cowardly miscreants to usurp an authority over them not warranted by their nature, nor conducive to the felicity and repose of the people; spies and informers would get into disuse and disesteem; gaols would become almost unnecessary, and the science of government really become the art of rendering the Commonwealth happy and flourishing.

Provision for the Poor.

Nothing seems more rational than that society should be obliged to provide for all its members, I therefore propose, that in every district there shall be erected NATIONAL MANUFACTORIES of such articles, that every citizen wanting employment may be able to assist. In these manufactories, I propose, none should be admitted unless they produce a voucher from TWELVE of their neighbouring fellow citizens, to the propriety of their conduct, their industry, and their incapability of procuring employ. To each of those citizens who shall have past the AGE OF FIFTY without having been enabled to provide for their old age, I propose, that upon production of a certificate signed by TWELVE of their neighbours, who are citizens, having elective franchise, of their former good conduct, industry, and of their present incapacity, the register of the district shall regularly pay FOUR bushels of wheat per week, or the value thereof at the average market price of the district.

Constitution.

The first business of the legislative body should be to frame a CONSTITUTION upon the sacred RIGHTS OF MAN, and all LAWS and DECREES should be considered as null and of none effect that deviated from the principles of this constitution; and the proposer, and those concerned, to be at all times answerable to the people for their conduct, a majority of whom shall decide their fate; and in order that the constitution may be such as is convenient and suitable to the people, I propose, that every SEVEN YEARS it shall either receive the sanction of a majority of the people, or undergo such alteration as they shall deem necessary; for this purpose a TREBLE number of representatives shall be chosen, independent of the ordinary representative body, whose function shall be to examine and revise the constitution, and which function shall cease when that business is completed; their sittings not to exceed TWO MONTHS in any case. I propose, that they shall be *paid* in the same manner as the other representatives, and their *qualification* and *mode of election* to be the same.

Calculation of the Expence of a Government upon the Foregoing Plan for a population of Ten Millions of Mouths, Spread over a Territory Comprising Fifty Millions of Acres.

Of the above number I suppose there would be three millions of male citizens having elective franchise, that is, who had obtained their eighteenth year; this divided into districts of TWENTY-FIVE THOUSAND each, would make ONE HUNDRED AND TWENTY.

I reckon, for the sake of clearness, the bushel of wheat at six shillings sterling money.

120 REGISTERS, at 3 *bushels of wheat* per diem each	£39,420
3 CLERKS to each REGISTER, at 2 *bushels of wheat* per diem each	78,840
STATIONARY, &c, for each REGISTER'S OFFICE, suppose *one*	
hundred pounds each per annum	12,000
480 DEPUTIES, at 4 *bushels of wheat* per diem each	210,240
TRAVELLING EXPENCES for each DEPUTY, average at *twenty*	
pounds each	9,600
6 CLERKS to the COMMITTEE OF GOVERNMENT, at 2 *bushels of*	
wheat per diem each	1,314
STATIONARY, &c, for the OFFICE, per annum	250
6 CLERKS to the COMMITTEE OF FINANCE, at 2 *bushels of wheat*	
per diem each	1,314
STATIONARY, &c. for the OFFICE, per annum	250
6 CLERKS to the COMMITTEE OF AGRICULTURE, TRADE AND	
PROVISIONS, at 2 *bushels of wheat* per diem each	1,314
STATIONARY, &c. for the OFFICE, per annum	250
PRINTING and other contingent expences of the REPRESENTATIVE	
BODY, COMMITTEES, REGISTERS, &c.	25,000
120 JUDICIAL ADMINISTRATORS, at 3 *bushels of wheat* per diem	
each	39,420

CLERKS to each JUDICIAL ADMINISTRATOR, at 2 *bushels of wheat* per diem each	78,840
STATIONARY, &c. for each OFFICE, at 25ol. per annum	30,000
	£528,052

This may be amply provided for by a tax amounting to ONE TWEN-TIETH PART OF A BUSHEL OF WHEAT, or about FOUR-PENCE PER ACRE PER ANNUM on the lands of the Commonwealth, which will produce a sum of EIGHT HUNDRED AND THIRTY-THREE THOUSAND THREE HUNDRED AND THIRTY-THREE POUNDS, and may be collected without any expence, by the REGISTERS of the districts, and will greatly over-balance all the necessary expences of an HONEST and RATIONAL GOV-ERNMENT, leaving every year the considerable sum of THREE HUN-DRED AND FIVE THOUSAND TWO HUNDRED AND EIGHTY-ONE POUNDS, to be applied to works of PUBLIC UTILITY, and other casualties, as they may occur.

Taxes, raised by FOUR-PENCE per acre on land	£833,333
Expences of Government	528,052
Balance remaining yearly in the Public Treasury	305,281

Thus every FOURTH year the taxes might be remitted to all the citizens; on such years I would propose that they should celebrate a festival to OECONOMY.

I have purposely avoided mentioning any thing concerning the FEMALE CITIZENS, as should this hasty production be favourably received, I have an intention of publishing my ideas concerning women, in a treatise by itself.[2]

F I N I S.

[2] Hodgson's work on the 'Female Citizen' was never published.

Bruce's Voyage to Naples (1802)

[Anon]

A Voyage to Naples
and Journey up Mount Vesuvius

It is not my intention, as is common among writers of travels, to entertain my readers with an account of my birth, parentage, and education. For what is it to them, whether I was born in the north or south of *England*, whether my father was a fat man or a lean one, a cobler or a person of an independent fortune; or whether I was born on a *Sunday* or a *Monday?* when at the same time, perhaps, it does not signify whether I had ever been born at all. However, it will be necessary to say thus much of myself; that I was born a younger brother, and met with the same fate that those gentry generally do, *viz.* to starve for want; while he that has the good luck to come into the world first, is riding in his coach and six.

'Tis true, I had a small fortune, about the quarter of one year's income of the estate, but it did not last long; and when that was gone, by being burthensome to my relations, they soon grew tired of me; and ill-natured things being told them, such as, that if I had not been extravagant, I might have lived comfortably upon the interest of my fortune; that if a person cannot live within his circumstances, he ought to starve; and many others of the same kind: I say, through these means I was entirely deserted by them, and misery soon followed. But what gave me the greatest uneasiness was, to find that those persons who had helped to run out my fortune, were the very people that did me the worst offices. One in particular, whom I had entirely supported while my money lasted, being now come into affluence by the death of an old aunt, was at the head of those that railed the most against me; and I verily believe that he was the chief instrument of my disgrace; but I shall have further occasion to mention him, before I conclude my history.

Being now without a friend in the world to assist me, I began to think of some method to get my bread, but found it a difficult task, having never been bred to any business. I therefore fixed upon the sea as the easiest way of getting a livelihood. Being able to write a tolerable hand, and understanding something of accounts, I prevailed with an acquaintance of mine, a captain of a man of war, who was shortly to go upon the *Mediterranean* station, to take me with him as his clerk.

My mind was now quite at ease; and among the few of my acquaintance that remained, I was furnished with a little money to supply me with proper necessaries for the voyage. One morning I met the captain, when he told me it would be proper I should set out for *Portsmouth* (his ship then lying at *Spithead*) as soon as possible, having received orders to sail immediately. He was so kind as to order me not to lay in any provisions for my own use, as he intended his table should be mine during the voyage. He was likewise pleased to say that I might have occasion for a little money, and most gener-ously put ten guineas into my hand. I made as proper acknowledg-ments to him for his kindness as I was able, and he left me to go over to the admiralty to receive his last instructions.

I employed the remainder of the day in buying such necessaries as I thought I might have occasion for; and the next morning I set out for *Portsmouth*, where I arrived about five in the afternoon. I had scarcely got a little refreshment after my journey, before I saw the captain (in his post-chaise) enter the yard of the inn I had put up at. I immediately waited upon him, and he expressed his approbation of my having so punctually obeyed his orders. As the wind was then fair, he took me in his barge on board; where being soon furnished with a cabin upon the quarter-deck, I began to get my things into it; before I had completed which, I found the ship was under sail. As nothing material happened in our passage, unless the great civilities I received from the captain, I shall not trouble my reader with any particulars, only that after a short and pleasant voyage, we arrived safely at *Naples*, to which place we were ordered to sail.

I shall not here pretend to describe the beauties of this delightful city, and the country around it, there having been already said, by others, so much concerning them. We now saw the famous mountain *Vesuvius*, and I must confess I had a great inclination to visit the top of it. I mentioned my curiosity to the captain; and he told me he would make a party to go there so soon as he had finished the business he came about, which would be in two or three days. I employed my time till then, in viewing the richness and magnificence of their churches and palaces, and all the other curiosities that the shortness of the time would allow me. At last the day came for our visiting this wonderful volcano. The captain had provided proper guides, who conducted us to the top, at least as far as any ever ventured to go. But as the entrance or mouth of the mountain seemed quite calm, and little or no smoke issued out of it, I had a great desire to venture farther, and if possible, to look into the opening; but the guides advised me against it, as it might be attended with bad consequences. However, my curiosity was so great, that notwithstanding the captain himself endeavoured to persuade me from so rash an attempt, I was determined to proceed in my design. I therefore boldly went forward; but when I came within a few yards of the entrance, I laid down, and crawled on all fours toward the mouth of it; a dreadful gust of smoke issued therefrom, and the ground I was upon sunk under me, so that I went in head foremost.

I was instantly so surrounded with fire and sulphur, that I was almost suffocated. As I continued falling, I at last came to a part of the cavern that was as cold as ice; when I was almost perished with the excessive damp that encompassed me. At last I heard such terrible roarings and bellowings, occasioned by the pent-up air, and every now and then saw such gushes of flame and smoke issue from every part around me, that I expected nothing but instant death.

The precipitancy of the motion with which I continued falling was so great, that I had hardly power to offer up prayers to my creator, and to accuse myself with the rashness of the action I had been guilty of, especially as it was contrary to the advice of one, to whom I lay under the greatest obligations. For I must own, that if the captain had been my brother, he could not have behaved in a more affection-ate manner to me than he did, both before and during our whole voyage.

It is impossible to describe the variety of appearances that struck my eye during my descent. Sometimes I was surrounded with nothing but fire and smoke, and the next minute with a brilliancy that sur-passed any thing I had ever seen, which I imagine proceeded from the great quantities of jewels, with which the sides of this cavern were stored.

If it was possible to conceive how fast I fell, I believe it was about a mile every minute. After I had been about an hour and a half in this situation, to my great surprise I discovered light above me or below me as you please, for my head was downward. At that sight I verily thought I had fell through the whole diameter of the globe, and was arrived at the antipodes; but it proved otherwise. At last I got to the end of this pit, or rather, hole, when I found myself in the open air, but surrounded with a lustre that exceeded any thing I had ever seen.

The resplendent glory was so great, and affected my eyes so much, that I thought I should lose the sight of them. However, I perceived that the longer I continued falling, the less was this prodigious brightness, till at last, and by degrees, it became an agreeable light, such as we have on earth in the middle of a fine summer's day. I then perceived a body at a vast distance, resembling our moon at full, but much larger; and I thought I could discover spots in it, which nearly resembled what we see in that luminary. At this sight I was greatly terrified, for as I still continued falling with an incredible quickness, I began to imagine myself dead, and that the immortal or spiritual part of me was going to that place, to which it was destined by its good or bad actions in this world. I still continued falling; and the body I at first discovered increased greatly, the nearer I approached it. At last I could discover nothing, but this globe below me. I then plainly discerned seas, vast continents, mountains, and islands. As at this time the rapidity with which I fell was prodigious, I soon perceived that it was neither more nor less than a world like ours; for then I saw houses, towns, trees, and fields. And now I expected every moment to have my brains dashed out. But, providence so ordered it, that I fell directly upon a load of hay, which lay heaped up together in a field.

There I lay frightened almost out of my senses, and so fatigued with my fall, which was upward of 3000 miles, that I did not know what to do. However, as where I lay did not seem to be upward of six yards from the ground, so soon as I could recover my breath, I determined to slide down. I therefore placed myself on the edge, and instantly descended with such swiftness that I thought I should break every bone in my skin; and when I got to the bottom, I stuck so fast to the ground that I had not power to lift a joint, and seemed to stick as close as a small key to one of our largest magnets or loadstones.

In this situation I must soon have perished, by having my breath squeezed out of my body, had I not been miraculously preserved.

I had not been long in this situation before a venerable old man came up to me. He looked for some time, lifted up his eyes, joined the hands together, and as I imagined said a short prayer. He then from under his robe took a small box of ointment, with which he anointed my joints, as likewise my back; he then did the same to my feet, which was no sooner done than I jumped up and seemed as light as a feather. I instantly fell upon my knees, and attempted to kiss his hand, but he snatched it from me, and with a most angry countenance raised me from the ground; and looking with infinite disdain and scorn mixed with compassion, made signs for me to follow him; which I immediately did with the utmost submission, not knowing what the consequence of disobedience might be, as I discovered by his looks that he so highly resented what is looked upon in our world as the greatest compliment.

We walked over several delightful fields; and what surprised me greatly was, to see the very ground we trod upon covered with gold-dust instead of sand, and precious stones instead of pebbles. At last we arrived at the house, the walls of which were chiefly composed of gems of various sorts and of prodigious size, which made it shine with a splendour not to be conceived; for here gold and jewels are so plentiful, that they are only used in buildings, &c. being of no other use, as money is unknown among the inhabitants, every thing being in common. As soon as we entered, an agreeable elderly woman met my conductor; he said something to her which I did not understand, and pointed to me. She immediately lifted up her eyes, joined her hands, and repeated what, by her manner and gesture, I took to be a prayer of thanksgiving.

I was then introduced into a very neat and elegant parlour, where the good woman gave me a glass of cordial that far excelled anything I had ever tasted. After I had been about an hour in the old gentleman's house, he made signs to me to follow him; which I did with great submission; and the more so, as I was afraid I had incurred his displeasure. He conducted me into an apartment that I took to be his study. As soon as we were entered, he placed me in an elbow chair, joined his hands together, lifted up his eyes, and repeated some words that I did not understand. He then took down a phial, poured some of the liquid into a small cup, and made a sign for me to put out my tongue, which I did. He anointed the tip of it; which was no sooner done than I began to prattle in a language that was entirely unknown to me; with which he seemed pleased, and again joined his hands, lifted up his eyes, and repeated some words which sounded like those I then could utter, without my knowing the meaning. He also anointed my ears, and lastly my forehead, my temples, and the top of my head. I then found that I instantly understood his language; for upon his joining his hands, lifting up his eyes, and repeating the following words, –

'*Mem Egen! ton testeron egi alip astagenos, aperon didenemos esteron, ag operon estemedoros,*' I immediately knew the English to be,

'Great God! blessed be thy name, a stranger is arrived, and through thy mercies has received knowledge.'

I then fell prostrate before him, and embraced his feet. He flew from me with the utmost indignation, and repeated these words: –

'*Erlios onamos, acceberos erliaton phisteron te andabos nan Egen asteros epanidos.*'

Which is in *English*,

'Earthly mortal, quit the vanities of the earth, and know that none but God is to be worshipped.'

After this my kind host reconducted me into the parlour from whence I came, and where I found his wife, his eldest son, a youth about seventy, and a daughter about fifty, who had been a few days married, with several other sons and daughters of different ages. I was congratulated by them all on my acquiring their language; and after a very good supper, and a most hearty welcome, which made everything the sweeter, I was conducted to my bed.

That the reader may not get impatient to know where I am all this while, I think it necessary to acquaint him that I am in that part of the world which is placed directly in the centre of the earth. The space that I had fallen through was as deep as the crust of our world is thick, which is a little more than a hundred miles. When I got through that, I arrived in the regions peculiar to the central world, which, by its attractive qualities, continued drawing me toward it, till such time as I arrived upon its surface.

I shall now proceed to give an account of the manner of living, &c., of the world I am now in. As to their meals, they have three; the first about eight in the morning, the other about one, and the last at six at night; after which they retire to rest; neither does any of their meals exceed above ten minutes, for they have no notion of bestowing more time than is absolutely necessary to satisfy the calls of nature, which they say is soon accomplished. Their food consists entirely of the productions of the earth, as roots of various sorts, with plenty of the most delicious fruits, which are in season all the year round. They never kill any living creature for food, nor is any vice held in more detestation among them than luxury of any sort. They never lye on any thing better than a sort of mattrass, neither do they use any thing to cover them, but a rugg or quilt. This manner of lying makes them very hardy, and their temperance in eating and drinking renders them so healthy, that a man is only reckoned middle-aged at an hundred and fifty, many living to three hundred and upward. The dress they wear, is a sort of petticoat from their waist downward to their ancles; their shoes are made of leather, but large and easy. They wear their own hair to a great length, and likewise their beards, it being reckoned among them the greatest piece of impiety to destroy or make away with what God has been pleased to give them; for as I have, in the time I stayed with them, often had occasion to mention some particular customs in our world, I never could find that they looked upon any with so much contempt and disdain, as the altering and endeavouring to amend the manner in which it has pleased our creator to form us. For, say they, can God act inconsistently? Can infinite goodness and perfection create us with hair on purpose that we should cut it off? And attempt to mend by art, what is finished by an all-wise hand.

I must own that this kind of reasoning was so strong, that I had no reply to make. To return – upon their heads they have a sort of turban adorned with feathers of various colours. They wear a jacket that reaches three or four inches below their waists, not straight as we wear them in *England*, but the sleeves and body slit and fur-belowed[1] as we see in old *Spanish* pictures; and over the whole they have a robe, not confined to any particular colour, but according to the inclination of the wearer. By this means they are easy, the blood has a free circulation, and various disorders are prevented, which are too often among us occasioned by bracing ourselves up, and as far as in us lies preventing the intent of our exquisite formation. The

---

[1] Furbelowed: plaited together on the petticoats or gowns of women.

women wear almost the same dress as the men, only they have no turbans, and their hair, which is very long, hangs carelessly down their shoulders.

As soon as I was up the next morning, I waited on my kind host, whom I found with his wife, son, and the rest of his family. After a good breakfast, which was greatly heightened by the agreeable manner in which it was conducted, and the cheerfulness that appeared on the faces of the whole family, he addressed me in the following manner: – 'my son, as by the divine permission you have acquired our language, it is highly necessary that you should be acquainted with those wonderful particulars that relate to our world. And be assured I will give you the best account in my power; and far from thinking it a trouble, I shall look upon it as an infinite pleasure. But as it will be more convenient to retire into my study, I flatter myself, that the time between this and dinner, you will not think disagreeably employed.' So saying, he rose and proceeded to his library; and with a pleasing curiosity I followed him.

As soon as my kind conductor had placed himself in his chair, and I was seated by him, he began as follows: – 'Know, O son of earth! that thou art not the first, by many, that chance has thrown upon our globe, neither is it impossible for us to visit your world; that god whom we truly adore has blessed us with those gifts that you are strangers to. We can, when we please, transport ourselves to your regions; and what surpasses even that, we have the gift of knowing the thoughts of those we converse with. By this means we are much better acquainted with your earthly brethren than you are yourselves, who can judge only by appearances. Often do you clasp that man to your bosom as a friend, who at the same time is your greatest enemy, and only professes friendship, while you have wherewithal to make him welcome; but when that fails, he will not only desert you, but leave you to starve in a dungeon, and pretend he never heard your name. These things, and worse, are common in your world; I have often made an excursion thither myself; and having the gifts I before mentioned, have seen things greatly unworthy of those beings that are, like ourselves, made after the image of our creator. Perhaps at a proper time I may tell you some particulars, but for the present we will confine ourselves to what relates to the world we are now upon, and which is in the centre of your globe.' I thanked him, and he thus proceeded: – 'My son, for I will no longer call thee son of earth, which is among us an infamous title; but for the future I will only call thee son, and I am sufficiently assured thou will deserve that name; therefore attend. The world on which we live is the very centre of that globe you call the earth; and as I shall as far as possible confine my description to your ideas, I will call it a vast magnet or loadstone; which by its attractive quality draws every thing in your world toward it; and the nearer you approach its surface, the greater of course must be the power of its attraction. You may remember that when I first saw you, you seemed and felt as if you was fixed to the ground. I relieved you by an ointment which we central inhabitants always carry about us, for the assistance of strangers; your clinging to our globe proceeded from the vast power of attraction that is given to our world; for if it has the power to attract bodies, at the distance of 3000 miles and upward, how much more must the force be, when you are upon its surface? This you have experienced, and I have assisted you; therefore, in case an incident of this sort should ever happen to you while you are among us, and that you should find one of your own brethren in the same situation I did you, take this bottle and assist those that may be in the like distress.' I accepted the phial with many thanks, and he thus proceeded: –

'I am very sensible that you earthly inhabitants think that God has created nothing but your world to be inhabited, and that you are the only great lords thereof; that even the sun, the moon, stars, and planets, were made only to enlighten the grain of sand that you inhabit. But know, vain mortals, that there is no end of creation, and that every pebble, every leaf, nay the most minute thing that can be conceived, is a world to millions. In a drop of water no larger than a pin's point, you may discover, with ordinary glasses, numbers of living creatures of various sizes and different structures. If we see these small parts of the creation so plentifully stocked with inhabitants, how can we imagine that the vast bodies that fill the regions of unlimited space were only formed for us to gaze upon, and not full of beings to glorify the great author of their existence! Every part of creation is absolutely necessary to keep together the whole; and like the wheels in a clock, if the minutest is removed, it puts a stop to the whole movement. For this reason a fly is of as much use in that part of creation which it is ordained to fill, as a monarch is in that in which he is. Our central globe is absolutely requisite for the very being of your world. If there was no attractive power to keep all things in order, how could any thing exist? Your towns, your houses, your very selves, instead of adhering to the surface, would float in the air, and have no resting place. The accident that brought you here, has made you, in one particular, wiser than your greatest men; for they, with all their sagacity, could never find out what the centre was composed of; with the particulars of which you are now made acquainted.'

I told him, that it was true, several weak minds in our world did think that every thing was created for their use only, but that many others were of a much better way of thinking, and well satisfied that the planets were inhabited, and that the fixed stars were suns without end, and all space stored with beings to sing their great creator's praise. That as to what was at the centre of our world, it had been matter of great dispute among the learned.

'Do not think,' says he, 'that when I appear severe upon the inhabitants of your world, I then mean the whole; it is only against the depraved and narrow-minded of them; for I am well convinced, that there are several among you, who have quite a different notion of things, and to them I pay a due respect. As I perceive you are an *Englishman*, I shall, as near as possible, adapt my discourse according to your manners and customs; and particularly when I have occasion to mention time or space, I shall confine myself to your method of calculating. I shall therefore tell you that this globe we are now upon, is one thousand miles diameter, consequently three thousand and upward of miles in circumference. We have no sun, but every thing grows spontaneous, and we are enlightened by the concave part of your world, which is entirely covered with jewels of different sorts and immense sizes. The carbuncles, the rubies, the vast quantity of diamonds, of saphires, of emeralds, topazes, and all the various sorts of precious stones that are known among you, with many others, are there in such quantities, and all of them of such a prodigious size, that the lustre that comes from them gives light to our world. But perhaps you will ask, how these jewels can show so great a lustre, without the assistance of a light body to dart its rays upon them; for that a diamond cannot be seen in the dark, and that it is absolutely necessary, to discover its brilliancy, that it be assisted by the sun, or some other body, to dart its rays upon you. This I will explain. Our world then is itself a luminous body, which casting its rays upon the immense number of jewels with which the concave part of your world is studded, they strike the surface of our world with all their brilliancy; but even this would be only a partial light, were it not for our atmosphere, which is computed at thirty miles high. Their rays meeting with it, are refracted, and by that means occasion an equal and universal light. For the sun itself would be of little service to you were it not for your atmosphere; without that, he would appear as a piece of red hot iron, at an immense distance; and you would only see him (as through a smoked glass) without his being of any service to you. Thus our day is occasioned; and we should have had no night, had not the wise creator provided other means for us to have a proper time for repose. In short, there is an opaque body, exactly the size and shape of half the concave part of your world; the distance of which from the surface of our globe, we reckon at two thousand five hundred and upward of miles. This moving round us once in twenty-four hours, occasions day and night; for at six our day begins, and at six the night takes place. But even our nights are not quite dark; for in the body (before mentioned) are sprinkled, by an omnipotent hand, thousands of precious stones; and of so large a size, that even at that distance they appear as large and bright as the most brilliant of your planets. Thus when day forsakes us, we are comforted by a sky, as glorious as yours on the most starry night. (And indeed so I found it; for nothing can be more beautiful than their nights are.) Our world,' continued he, 'is likewise of a warm nature; and the particles of heat arising from its surface, diffuse a moderate warmth over the whole; and by this means we have never an extremity of heat or cold, but a constant agreeable temperature. We have vast plenty of all sorts of the productions of nature; but to destroy any creature that has life, to feed our luxury, is held the greatest crime, and unknown among us, being well assured that we have no right to take away that life which God has been pleased to give. As we have a long time between this and dinner, if you please we will take a little walk. And as our capital is only 300 miles off, my son shall accompany you there in a day or two; and you may, if you please, return the next; but I fancy you will find wherewithal to entertain you for some time.'

I was greatly surprised at travelling 300 miles, and returning the next day. However, I deferred the satisfying my curiosity till a more convenient time. I therefore waited on my kind host, and we most agreeably spent the time till dinner, in walking and chatting. As soon as we had dined, the good old man presented me with clothes suitable to the fashion of the country. And I do not know that ever I was so pleased in my life. I felt so easy, and so light, that I thought I could jump over the moon.

I got up the next morning earlier than usual, for it was hardly light, and I directed my course to those charming fields that I had traversed the day before with my worthy host. To endeavour to describe their beauties, would be impossible; in short, though they have no assistance but nature, they infinitely surpass anything that was ever produced by art in our world. Here is a continual spring, and the perfume that arises from the beautifully enamelled ground, and the verdure of the trees around, exceed even the most exquisite nosegay that could adorn the cabinet of any of our earthly monarchs.

Being a little fatigued with walking, I laid down on this bed of flowers; where I was enchanted with the melodious warblings of thousands of feathered songsters, which surrounded me. Among the rest, I perceived one; the most beautiful I had ever beheld, the strength and melody of whose voice exceeded any of its companions. As I had laid quite motionless for fear of frightening these heavenly choristers, and almost stupified with pleasure, I now softly ventured to raise my head, that I might the more thoroughly examine the beauties of this charmer. Being greatly apprehensive that the least motion I should make, would scare them away (as is common in our world), I only just raised my head on my right hand, which I had no sooner done, than, to my infinite surprise and joy, instead of flying from me, they came close to me; some perched on my shoulders, some on my head, some on my thighs; and the beautiful little creature seated itself upon my hand, and put its beak to my lips. My surprise was so great, that I really thought myself enchanted, and I began to imagine that they were corporeal beings attending the actions of the inhabitants of the Central World; in the same manner that we are told aerial or incorporeal ones do upon ours on earth. Presently they began a concert that surpassed anything I had ever heard. While I was thus delightfully entertained, I perceived at a distance my generous host, who missing me in my room, was come to tell me that breakfast was ready. I rose and attended him home, our delightful concert accompanying us the whole way.

I found his wife and son, and all the rest of the family, except his married daughter, she being gone to her husband, who lived about a hundred miles off; which being so near, gave her often the opportunity of paying her duty to her dear parents, as she could easily dine with them, and return home to supper. As soon as breakfast was over, my worthy friend conducted me to his study; where, when we were seated, he began as follows: –

'My dear son, as I do not doubt but you will soon have an inclination to visit our capital, I am desirous of giving you what instructions I am able, that you may be the better prepared (in our absence) to account for those things which, to you, may appear wonderful and supernatural. Therefore as you may, perhaps, have met with some things that may have created your surprise, if any such have occurred, freely name them, and as freely as I will explain what to you may have appeared a phenomenon.' I returned him thanks, and acquainted him with my surprise at the freedom of the birds I had observed in the morning, so uncommon among us. He smiled, and thus proceeded:

'You must know, my son, that among us, what you to-day took for a miracle, happens every hour, nay every minute. But as I shall be obliged to be a little severe upon your world, you must excuse me, for nothing that I shall say will be intended to offend, but instruct you. Know then that, with us, not only the various feathered inhabitants of the air, but likewise all the different creatures of our world, are as tame as the most domestic animals among you. And why should they be otherwise? We are, and they know it, their friends. Instead of persecuting and destroying them, as in your world you do for your diversion; next after the worshipping and adoring our creator, it is the principal part of our religion to protect what he has been pleased to give life to. For this reason they are in no fear of us; and as they fly from and avoid you as their enemies, they are pleased in being free with us as their friends. The reason that you never perceived this before, was, that since you have been here, you have wore your earthly garb; for which reason they shunned you. Now, as you appear like one of us, they behaved in the manner you this morning saw them. I must further tell you, that we believe every living creature to be endued with a rational soul. This may not appear so extraordinary to you, as you must undoubtedly have heard of several in your world that have supported this doctrine. However, we are well assured of the truth of it; and what you are pleased to call instinct, we call reason. You allow no animals to have souls; we allow them all to have souls. I have long inhabited your world, and I do not doubt but you may at least remember my name, when I tell you that I am that very *Pacolet*, that was so kind a friend to one of the best writers your world ever produced (Sir *Richard Steel*, in the "Tatlers")[2]; and for this reason I am well acquainted not only with your customs, but your doctrines. You allow none but yourselves to have reason; the more shame for you, when those exceed you so far. Must it not be paying yourselves a bad compliment, to say you are the only rational part of the creation, and at the same time perceive what you call brutes behave with infinite more reason than yourselves, while one of your own species shall behave in a manner inconsistent with all reason? In what manner does that part which you call the brute creation behave inconsistently with reason? Is it shown by the ant, who lays up for winter, while the spendthrift squanders all to-day, and starves to-morrow? Is it in the beaver, whose skill in architecture exceeds the famed *Inigo* himself? Is it in the bee, whose works greatly surpass those of any of your rational beings, and whose armies are better conducted than yours by your most famous generals? The very spider provides itself a house, while your rational beings are starving for want of a covering to their heads. The young of any species as soon as delivered from their dam, have sense to avoid what is hurtful. Is it so with the young of your rational beings? Your children, till they are a year old, or more, are mere idiots, and would as soon grasp a flaming candle as a rattle. It is reason, or is it not, that makes the new-hatched duckling fly to its element the water, and the chick to avoid it? Is it reason that causes your horse, your dog, or any other creature that you treat so well, to be faithful to you; and after years of absence, single you out of hundreds; and immediately, in their dumb way, return you thanks for favours formerly received, and thereby show their gratitude? A quality unknown to you men of reason! Surely this is reason. I remember when I was in your world to hear a gentleman tell the following true story: –

"In a ship", said he, "that brought me here from the *West-Indies*, there was a monkey tied to the shrouds of the quarter-deck. I often took delight in playing with, and making much of him. By this means I became a great favourite; and though he was of a fierce mischievous disposition, yet to me he was as quiet as a lamb. It happened one afternoon, that several of the seamen were teasing and vexing him,

---

[2] *The Tatler* (4 vols., 1743), vol. I, pp. 83–92.

some striking him, others throwing things, and in short using him very ill. I happened to be standing close to one of the men who had used him the worst, and by accident had laid my hand on his shoulder. The creature watching an opportunity to revenge himself for the insult received, suddenly jumped upon his shoulder, seized my hand with his teeth, and made them meet through the fleshy part, between my forefinger and thumb. The wound was so great that I was obliged to retire to get it dressed, and though many years ago, the mark is still visible. I wondered that the creature should be so treacherous to me, who had always used him with so much kindness; but a considerable time after I found my error, and that the compliment was not intended for me, but the person whose shoulder I was leaning upon; in short, we landed in *England*, and I heard no more of the monkey. About two years after, I happened to visit a lady in *London*; and upon coming into her room, I saw a monkey chained in the window. Upon my entrance he fell a jumping and skipping like a mad thing. I was going toward him, but the lady desired me to desist, assuring me that he was the most mischievous creature of the kind ever seen, and that there was only one servant in the house durst go near him, and that was the footman who fed him. As he still jumped and tore excessively, I ventured toward him; when, on a nearer approach, I discovered him to be the identical monkey who had bit me so severely on board the ship. The creature, as soon as it could reach me, snatched up one of my hands, looked at it, and threw it down again; took up the other, and perceived the mark his teeth had occasioned. He then immediately began to kiss and lick it, as an acknowledgement for the injury he had formerly done me through mistake, this being the only method in his power to make me reparation."

'Now,' continued my host, 'that this creature should, after so long a time as three years, know the gentleman, and remember the injury he had done him, and as far as was in his power make him satisfaction, must be reason, or there is no such thing as reason. I could mention many other instances of the reason in beasts, but I do not doubt that many must occur to yourself, and particularly in dogs. Nay, I have heard, when I was in your world that a jury brought in a person guilty of murder, merely upon the evidence of a dog, and he was hanged accordingly. Surely at least that jury allowed the dog to be a rational creature, or they would not have had so great a regard to his evidence. Treachery, deceit, fraud, ingratitude, slander, and backbiting are unknown among what you are pleased to call the brute part of the creation. Strange they should be so universal among the rational part! The brute creation have only two passions, and both natural; being by divine wisdom made most predominant, in order to supply and preserve the creation; I mean hunger and lust. For these they will fight and quarrel; but when these are satisfied, all animosities cease. With your rational beings, the whole study of their lives is to feed upon their fellow-creatures. Deceit, falshood, avarice, cunning, and ingratitude, with a train of other vices, are what they are made up of. How can you boast of being the only creatures blest with reason, when those very beings to which you deny it, act so much more consistently with it? But, my dear son, for the present we will suspend this subject, which I may appear to have handled too roughly; but my chief aim in it was to convince you, that what I mentioned when we first met; of our believing all creatures to have rational souls, is not so unreasonable a tenet as you might at first think it.'

I returned him many thanks for the trouble he had been at; and we parted for the present, but not before he again desired me not to take his free manner of speaking ill, for that he meant no personal affront, and only designed to expose folly, ignorance, and prejudice.

As I was by this time looked upon as one of their family, between meals I strolled about as I pleased, without interruption; and being well acquainted with their hours of eating, it is not to be imagined I was to be looked for at those times.

In this world there are no such things as servants. The inhabitants increase fast; therefore there always remain sufficient children unmarried, to do the family work. So that here they treat not their fellow creatures, those of the same flesh and blood with themselves, as slaves or brutes, as with us. For a great person in our world will treat his dog, or my lady her monkey, with infinitely more tenderness than their domestics; and frequently little *Shock* has got the cholic, or a fever on his nerves, when no expence is spared to procure the best advice and attendance for him, while the poor footman is dying unheeded in the garret through a fever, which he got by waiting in the rain and snow, till four in the morning, upon his lady at a rout, a drum, or perhaps a worse place. In short, in this country there are no degrees of nobility. Every body is equally respected, if they are honest, and a particular regard is shown to nothing but wisdom and old age; these are held in great veneration, and they only meet with a superior respect. That bane to society and humanity, that golden idol which makes the villain respected, and the man of virtue despised who is not in possession of it, is here unknown, any farther than as dirt to trample on. In these happy regions there is no such thing as want; the earth without labour yields an abundance of all necessaries of life, and the industry of the people furnish their own families with clothing; and they are astonished to hear that on earth, almost the whole of what God created alike for the use of every individual, is in the hands of a few; and while they wallow in luxury, those, who have as much right to the productious of their common mother, the earth, are starving for want. Here is never seen that little brat of power, a thing void of every quality but that of being born to undeserved riches, strutting as if the ground was not good enough to bear him, and cocking his impudent nose at merit in rags. The insolence of these creatures of fortune, with whom we are pestered, is here unknown, and nothing but friendship, hospitality, and a brotherly affection to all their fellow-creatures, reigns in this happy world. The equality of fortune runs through the whole empire, and there being no such things as places of profit, prevents numbers of rogueries too common among us. That bit of dirt, for which we would sell our God, our country, and our very souls, they being strangers to (at least the use we put it to), makes them not liable to the like temptations. But I am painting the vices of the inhabitants of our world, when I ought to be acquainting them with the customs of an unknown one.

I had one day strolled a good way from home, musing on my present situation, and happy change from world to world, when I found myself in the middle of a large forest. The most agreeable perfume came from a tuft of trees at a small distance, to which I directed my course. I had hardly entered this little wood, before I perceived a monstrous lion, as I thought, asleep; but upon my approach he instantly arose, shook his mane, and stretched himself as we often see a cat after sleeping. This sight alarmed me greatly, and I attempted to hide myself behind a tree: by this time he saw, and came trotting up to me. I then expected nothing but immediate death; but to my agreeable surprise, as soon as he came near to me, he lay on one side, licked my feet, and played all the fawning tricks that we see a dog do when he wants to be made much of. I now recollected what the good old man had told me, *viz.* 'that all the creatures of this world are as tame as our most domestic animals.' I then took courage, and stooped down and stroked him, as one would do a lap-dog. He seemed greatly pleased, and as soon as he rose, he went and fetched a large stone, came and laid it down at my feet, and looked me full in the face with a sort of impatient pleasure. As I had often seen dogs with us do the same, through a desire to fetch and carry, I had a mind to try the experiment. I accordingly took up the stone, and threw it as far as I could; he pursued with all the quickness he was master of, and returned galloping with it in his mouth, and laid it down at my feet. I repeated it several times with the same success; and having played with him till I was tired, I left him in order to return home. In my way, I discovered a hare on her seat. I then wished I had a gun; but not being so provided, I stooped down for a stone to knock her on the head; she saw me, instantly came running up to me, licked my hands, and played a thousand fawning tricks. I must own my conscience then flew in my face, and I was ashamed I had not yet been able to shake off my cruel and inhuman disposition; but resolved to be more circumspect for the future.

At the beginning of this book I mentioned the husband and wife holding up their hands, and repeating words I did not then understand, also the resentment the old man showed, at my attempting to prostrate myself before him to kiss his hand. There is not one thing that happens to them, for which they do not instantly return thanks to their creator. This they do by raising their hands and addressing a few *extempore* words to him, who is goodness without bounds, and who never fails to hearken to those that properly call upon him. As to the latter part, they hold it as the greatest insult that can be offered to the supreme being, to pay the same respect to his creatures that they do to himself.

To return – After I had passed sometime in the most agreeable manner with this good family; the son, one night, proposed our setting out the next day for the capital. I embraced the proposal with joy; and at our retiring to rest, he told me he would have everything ready for our departure by eight in the morning. 'For,' says he, 'as it is not above 300 miles thither, we may easily accomplish our journey while it is light; so if you please to be ready by that time, I will be prepared to attend you.' I promised him I would, and we retired to our respective apartments. When I got to my room, I could not help wondering how we were to travel 300 miles in so little time, for as yet I had not seen their manner of travelling. In the morning I got up and waited on the family in the parlour, where we breakfasted; the good old lady had made up a basket with sweet cakes and different fruits, and a bottle of excellent cordial, to carry with us on our journey. After taking an affectionate leave of my good old man, his wife, and family, we prepared for our journey.

As soon as we came to the door, I saw a vehicle, something resembling one of our single-horse chaises, but much lighter and neater, for the back and sides was a thin sort of lattice. At each side, instead of wheels, were two enormous bladders, belonging to what beast I did not know, but ten times as large as those of a bullock. These were fastened by a girth, which went under the bottom of the chaise, and making two wings, served to sustain it (while in the air) in a proper equilibrium. Before the chaise were two birds, about twice as big as our largest swans, but of a different colour and make. They resembled the most beautiful green parrots both in colour and shape. To the breasts of these were fastened silken cords, which being introduced into the chaise, served to guide them, as the reins with us do horses.

As soon as we were seated, and my conductor had taken hold of the reins, they spread their wings, and in an instant soared to the heighth of a quarter of a mile; and my companion gently moving the reins, to direct their course, they proceeded at a prodigious rate; and what was very remarkable, they seldom moved their wings, but after a flap kept them extended for a considerable time, as smooth as a hawk hovering for his prey; and it is necessary to observe, that the bladders keep the chaise up in an equal line with the birds. In this manner we travelled at a vast rate; but I must own I was a little frightened when I looked down, and saw the towns and houses so far beneath me.

After we had proceeded on our journey about three hours, my companion showed me at a considerable distance a country-seat; it seemed to be about ten miles a-head of us, and he informed me it was his married sister's house; and if I approved of it, we should call there and take a little refreshment. As I had a great regard for the lady, on account of her amiable disposition, beside a sort of curiosity to see her husband, I readily consented. As soon as we came over the court that led to the house, he stopped the birds, and taking some small cakes about the size of gingerbread nuts from under his robe, he threw them down upon the ground; the birds immediately descended in pursuit of their food, and in an instant we were *landed,* if I may use the expression, before the gate of a genteel and elegant house. He immediately discharged the birds from their fetters, and they flew away, and were presently out of sight. I expressed my surprise at his discharging them till we got to our journey's end; but he desired I would suspend my curiosity, and that I might depend upon it, he would take care to provide for the remainder of our journey.

We had hardly entered the court-yard before the good old lady came to meet us; and in the most affectionate manner returned her brother thanks for the favour he had done her, in paying her a visit, which, she said, gave her more than ordinary pleasure, as he had brought me along with him. As soon as we entered, she acquainted us, that her husband was gone into the garden to fish, but that she would immediately call him; or, if we pleased, conduct us to him. The latter was accepted. After we had entered the garden, and passed through the most delightful walks and groves I ever beheld, we discovered her husband at a small distance, sitting by the side of a large pond. As soon as he saw us, he rose to meet us; and after saluting most affectionately his brother-in-law, he was, by his wife, introduced to me. Having heard my story before, he received me with the utmost complaisance. Then addressing himself to his wife, 'my dear,' says he, 'I have had good sport since I saw you; and if you please to bring our visitors along with you, I will show them the success I have met with; for I verily believe, I have made a thousand fish happy, by filling their bellies.' We followed him to the pond, and found a cistern near it full of clear water, with several fish in it of different sorts, flouncing and playing about; at the side of it was a vessel full of a sort of grain, of which he every now and then threw a handful or two in, to feed the fish he had caught. He then went to the pond-side, and said he would show us what diversion he had. Upon his approach, he stirred the water with a stick, and hundreds of fish, of different sorts, appeared on the surface, and came so near him, that he might take them out with his hand; which having done, he put them into the cistern, and threw several handfuls of grain in, to feed them. After he had for some time entertained us with his dexterity, in first catching the fish, and then filling their bellies, he took the cistern, and delivered the fish again to the pond; though the cistern was three or four hundred weight, he lifted it with all the ease imaginable; for a body on our earth whose weight is one pound, on the surface of this globe would be fifty or sixty, the attractive power being so much greater. This must easily appear to all those who are acquainted in the least degree with the nature and cause of gravity. As soon as he had done fishing, the lady told us she would go and prepare dinner; and insisted upon our staying; which we consented to. During her absence, the master of the house entertained us with showing us his garden. After we had amused ourselves till such time as he thought every thing in the house was ready for our reception, he conducted us in; where we found a dinner, most elegantly prepared after the manner of this country; and if the various productions of the ground can be sufficient to satisfy the demands of nature, we had them in a plentiful degree.

In our passage to the house, I could not help reflecting how much more pleasure it must give one to protect life than to take it away; and how much happier he must be in catching the fish with no other intention than to feed them, than it can be with us, to first torture them with hooks and then throw them on the ground to expire in agonies. Surely, if we were to make it our own case, we should refrain from many barbarities, that we look upon as amusements, and not entertain ourselves by tormenting any thing that has life, when we are sensible how terrible it would be to us to be served in the same manner; for every thing that has life as naturally endeavours to preserve it, and feels pain as severely as we, the great self-conceited lords of the universe. It is necessary to observe, that though the fowls of the air, and the various sort of land creatures, are so tame as has before been mentioned, yet the inhabitants of the watery element are a little more shy, which I imagine must proceed from their not being so often among them, and consequently not so familiar.

I shall next describe the person and dress of our kind entertainers: – The husband was tall and well-shaped, the most amiable and inviting aspect I ever beheld, full of benevolence and humanity; indeed, this is the characteristic of most of the inhabitants of this country. His beard was not very long, he not being above seventy years of age; he wore a turban on his head, of a sort of blue sattin, adorned with plumes of various colours. His jacket was white, his petticoat the same, and his robe (that covered the whole) of crimson;

his person was agreeable; but his behaviour charming. His delightful consort had something exceedingly enchanting in her countenance, though not a complete beauty. Her hair, which was black, hung down in ringlets to her waist; her jacket was of pink; her petticoat, the same. As she wore no robe, the more easily might be perceived the gracefulness of her person; which exceeded any thing I had ever seen in our world, though unassisted by stays, or any other invention made use of by us to render a shape becoming, which generally produces the contrary effect.

By these amiable persons we were entertained in the most agreeable manner during the remainder of the day; and as they pressed us very much to stay all night, we readily consented, intending to pursue our journey the next morning early. After a variety of pleasing conversation, and supper being ended, we retired to rest.

The next morning when I left my chamber, I found none but my companion stirring. He took me into the court-yard; and pulling from under his robe a sort of whistle, he blew three times; when instantly several of the same kind of birds appeared that had brought us to this place. He singled out two; and having fixed them to the harness, and left with them some of the same nuts he made use of the day before, we left the chaise ready prepared for our journey, in order to return to the house, where we found our kind host and his wife preparing breakfast against we made our appearance. As soon as we had finished it, and taken an affectionate leave of our worthy entertainers, we stept into our chaise, and instantly were carried up into the air.

We had now about 200 miles to travel; which, at the rate we proceeded, would be accomplished in about six hours; but before we had gone half our journey, I did not forget to remind my companion of the basket his mother had given us at our setting out; and I believe the hint was as agreeable to him as to myself; for we ate very heartily of the cakes and fruit, and did not neglect to taste the good lady's cordial; the air having given me a prodigious appetite.

About half an hour after one we discovered the capital, which is called *Oudenteminos* – in *English*, the wonder of the world; and soon after we came directly over the principal square; when my conductor throwing down a few nuts, the birds descended immediately. We put up this night at an acquaintance's house of my companion's, where we were entertained with an elegance and hospitality peculiar to these people; and the next morning he conducted me to see the city.

The principal square is in the very centre of the city, and is an octagon, from each square of which proceeds a street of a mile long, and as broad as the *Hay-market*. This forms eight principal streets, and the intervals between them are composed of by-streets and ground for the use of the inhabitants. In the middle of the square is the principal church, much larger than St. *Paul*'s, and quite a plain building. At the extremity of each of these streets is a church, but not near so large as that in the square; and streets being carried from the end of one of the principal to the end of another, and so all round the whole, the city forms a large octagon. Their houses are all of an equal heighth, *viz.* six stories, and in each of them live several families.

As I had a great curiosity to see their king, my companion promised me that satisfaction the next morning. Accordingly, about ten o'clock we sat off for the palace. It was about half a mile out of town; and being so near, we had a pleasant walk.

I asked my conductor the manner in which his majesty was to be addressed, that I might be prepared for the introduction. He burst out laughing, and begged to know if I thought their emperors took upon themselves the state that our earthly kings did? 'No,' said he, 'our kings know they are men as well as their subjects; and so far from attempting to be treated as gods, and looking upon their fellow-creatures as a species beneath them, they think it their duty to be the principal servant of the people. There is no such thing here as an hereditary succession. The reigning prince is always the oldest person in the empire. We are only one people, and there is but one prince; for this reason, there is the age of every person in the empire registered. It is seldom among ourselves, that the prince has any occasion to exert his authority, though sometimes it so happens. But what for these hundred years last past has given the greatest uneasiness to our government, has been a parcel of the inhabitants of your world, who were about that time thrown upon this. But be not offended; they were not of your country, but without exception the wickedest race of mortals that ever existed. By the account they gave, they were for their sins swallowed up by an earthquake; and though numbers perished, above a hundred men and women arrived safe on our world, where they met with the greatest hospitality; but they made so ungrateful a return for favours received, that our emperor was obliged to deal severer with them than is customary among us. In short, they were confined to one spot, which bears the name of the earthly quarter; and I have heard that since their first coming they have increased to thousands.'

This discourse brought us to the habitation of the monarch. Upon our entering the hall, I saw several persons of different ages; but one in particular drew my attention. He was upward of six feet high, his countenance majestic; his beard was as white as snow, and reached down to his waist; he had on his head a turban of white sattin adorned with feathers of the most beautiful colours; his jacket was blue, his petticoat the same, and over the whole was a purple robe. 'That,' says I to my friend, is the king.' – 'You judge right,' says he, 'and I will have the honour of introducing you to him.' He did so; and after mentioning the particulars of my adventures, he received me in the most courteous and obliging manner. He asked me how long I had been in this country, and what part of the earth I belonged to, and several other questions; to which I gave him proper answers. But when I mentioned to him that *Great Britain* gave me birth, he was pleased most heartily to congratulate me on my good fortune, in being born on so happy a spot. 'For,' continued he, 'the *Britons* were always a brave, generous, and free people; and never failed to reward merit whenever they discovered it.'

To have so great a prince talk to me in so familiar a manner, quite charmed me. I must own it so sensibly affected me, that I wanted words to express my gratitude. He made me promise to be his guest at dinner, as long as I stayed in the city. 'And sorry I am,' says he, 'to tell you, that your stay in our world cannot be long; for since the perfidy we met with from the people of yours, we never permit any person belonging to the earth to continue here above twelve months. To-morrow I shall expect you and my old friend's son to dinner. I will likewise give you a more agreeable entertainment than you have met with, since you have been among us. In the meantime, may our great creator preserve you!' So saying, we parted, not without my being filled with a love and veneration that I never felt before; for undoubtedly nothing can create in us more respect to our superiors than a free and benevolent temper.

I had been near seven months in this country, and had not heard, until now, of a countryman of mine, who had lived here about a hundred years; and his company, it seems, was the agreeable entertainment that the emperor was to give me the next day.

'Mr *Thompson* (for that is his name),' said my companion, 'was born of a very good and ancient family in the north of *England*; but being a younger son, he was brought up to the law; the qualifications necessary for that profession he was a stranger to; for he had a heart that always made him feel the distresses of his fellow-creatures, and he was so strictly scrupulous, that he could never bring himself to take a fee to do a dishonest thing; besides, his inclination was always to accommodate matters between parties in a friendly manner, rather than set them together by the ears, for his own advantage and their destruction. He likewise frequently paid debts for those he was employed to send to gaol, when they were not too large; and when they were, he never would be engaged on these occasions, being a great enemy to the imprisoning the body, when the person had it not in his power to pay the debt. By these means, you may imagine he could not think of making an estate, but, on the contrary, was always extremely poor. This profession not suiting his inclination, he soon quitted it, and lived retired upon the little he had left, thinking there was more pleasure in an honest obscurity, than in the greatest splendour, when acquired by villainy and oppression, and the ruin of his fellow-creatures. The accident that brought him among us, was very extraordinary. He had one day dined with a friend in the country, where he stayed very late, and coming home at night he lost his way: at last he discovered a light, which proved to be what is called in your world a Will in the whisp, or Jack in the lantern, a sort of meteor rising out of fenny and marshy places. He followed it for some time, but presently sunk down, and found himself surrounded with mud, which he soon got clear of, and then continued falling as it were down a great precipice. In short, he tumbled through the crust of the upper world, and at last arrived in this; the manner of which, as you have already experienced, I need not enter into particulars concerning.'

The next day at dinner we waited on the emperor. As there were several persons assembled, he asked with great good nature, whether I could distinguish among the company, which was my countryman? I looked round me, and soon pitched upon one who I thought must be Mr *Thompson*. There was a sweetness in his looks that exceeded any thing I had ever beheld. He was above five feet ten inches high, pretty corpulent, and his cheeks resembled the damask rose; there was an exceeding deal of benevolence in his countenance, and his air commanded respect. Though in his 130th year, he did not look older than a healthy person does among us at 40. The emperor introduced me to him, and he received me with great tenderness. He asked me several questions relating to his native world, all which I answered to the best of my power.

During dinner Mr *Thompson* entertained us with his discourse in the most agreeable manner. It chiefly turned upon the wonderful works of God, and how infinitely they surpassed the conceptions or ideas of mortals. After dinner having a plumb, with the blue upon it as fresh as gathered, in his hand, he took notice that it was a world to thousands, and that what we saw and called the blue, was composed of an infinite number of living creatures of different sizes, and no doubt but there were some among them that fed upon the smallest, and were as terrible to them as a lion was to a lamb; 'for,' says he, 'nothing is great or small but by comparison; that is, by comparing the magnitude of one body with that of another, *viz.* a mouse is small in comparison to a cat, a cat to an elephant, and an elephant to a mountain; a mountain to the world, and the world in comparison to the sun. On the contrary, a mouse is a monster, when compared to a flea; a flea to a mite, and a mite to one of those living creatures, which are discovered by the help of glasses, and millions of which a grain of sand would cover. Yet one of these minute bodies must be of a stupendous size, when compared with one of the globules of blood that runs through its veins. But as matter is indivisible, that is, cannot be divided into nothing, one of these globules must be in comparison to minuter parts of matter, as the whole world is to a grain of sand. But how exquisitely fine must be the tendons and fibres that are in the texture of these little creatures! and yet they are large when compared with the parts of which they are composed. What I have said of great and small, may likewise be applied to space. We can only judge of it by comparison. We look upon the distance between us and the sun to be infinite, being 81,000,000 of miles; but the diameter of the space contained in the earth's annual orbit round the sun is upward of 162,000,000 miles; consequently, the orbit itself 416,000,000, is no more in comparison to that contained in the orbit of the nearest fixed star, than the size of a grain of sand is to the whole world; and even this vast space will bear no comparison to infinite and unlimited space. It is the same as to time. We can only judge according to our senses. We look upon 100 years, in the world I came from, as a prodigious age; but what is it in comparison to 10,000? An hour is long in comparison to a minute, and a whole day to an hour. A whole day is short to a year, and a year to a hundred. But these calculations are only according to our ideas. *Cicero* in his *Tusculans* mentions an insect on the river *Hypanis*, whose life never exceeds the time between sun-rising and sun-setting.[3] To these creatures that time must be an age; and one of them that lives till sun-set must be comparatively as old as a man at a hundred. The life of a fly is but a summer; a horse is old at twelve; and if we may believe historians, a raven lives 100 years. And yet this long term is no more in comparison to the raven, than the short one is to *Cicero's Hypanians*. As we see that the lives of different creatures differ so much on that little grain of sand the earth, no doubt but other worlds may be peopled by beings that are young at 1000 or 10,000 years; for he that created the one, is able to create the other; and with him there can be no time. Past, present, and to come, he comprehends at one view. For my own part, till by mere accident I was thrown upon this Central World, I had no idea of there being one, and inhabited, in the bowels of the earth; but as I am now convinced that there is, I can the readier believe that no part of matter is uninhabited; and this plumb that I have now in my hand is, without doubt, a world to millions. In short these things are wonderful to us; yet, though we cannot comprehend, our wonder ceases, when we consider that all this is the work of an omnipotent being. How vain are we then to attempt to search into his ways, and to pronounce those things impossible, that we cannot comprehend?'

This discourse of Mr *Thompson* met with universal approbation, and he was pleased to proceed: –

'Our comprehension is confined to a very narrow sphere; and beyond that we are no more capable of judging, than the fly was when perched on the cupola of St. *Paul's*. "Is this," says he, "that finely polished structure, that is the boast of mankind? For my part, I can see nothing but a rough unfinished piece, full of unequalities." To his microscopic eye the most polished marble or ivory would

---

[3] *M. Tully Cicero's Five Books of Tusculan Disputations* (1715), p. 47.

appear full of rocks and cavities. So it is with man. We can comprehend nothing but what we can see; and it is insolent in us to imagine
that an omnipotent hand can form nothing, but what may be taken
within the narrow limit of our optics. A fish sees not water, their
element; neither can we the air, that is ours; but as it is a liquid as
well as the sea, the same hand that formed it so much finer, can
make an eye of such a structure as to see, and perhaps therein to
discover myriads of living creatures of different sizes and species.
There is no forming an idea of things that are beyond the limit of
our conceptions; but we must, we cannot refuse to allow, that he who
created what we are eye witnesses to, is capable of creating (and
undoubtedly has) what we can form no notion of. As magnitude,
space, and time are only comparative, so is creation. What we see of
it is no more in comparison to the whole, than the time contained in
a second is to eternity; for as his power is infinite, so must be his
works. For this reason, with me, it will not admit of a doubt, but that
there are in the universe beings as much superior to us, as we are to
the most minute and senseless reptile. The inhabitants of a leaf or
flower proudly strut and say, 'we are the lords of the creation; every
thing was made for us; there is no other world than this that we
inhabit, and the whole works of an infinite creator are limited to that
of a leaf.' So it is with silly man. He has the arrogance to say, that
this small grain of sand which we possess, is the whole that God
created to be inhabited. He will likewise say, that those stupendous
bodies which are to be seen from the world I came from, and which
are well known to the inhabitants of this, as *Saturn, Jupiter,* 200 times
larger than the earth, were only made for its use, and that the moon
was only formed to light it. How ridiculous! when every requisite
necessary for living beings is discovered in them. They have their
atmospheres, which can be of no use to us, or any in the universe,
unless they be created for the same use that ours is, *viz.* to be the
great cause of life; and that they are, is evident from this – God
creates nothing in vain. The moon is so near us, that we have every
certainty of its being inhabited, except that of seeing its inhabitants;
for we can very plainly discover seas, continents, islands, peninsulas,
and mountains, and are even able to measure the heighth of the last.
We are certain that the moon is a body in every particular resembling
the earth, a terraqueous globe. Can we then refuse inhabitants to so
large a body, and in every manner provided for their reception, when

we see even a leaf to be a world to millions? No man of reason can. And if we allow this, we must likewise allow that all the planets are inhabited. I imagine we make no doubt but that the planets are worlds, and inhabited, especially as they are of so stupendous a size, and furnished with every necessary for life; when we see that the minutest thing which can be conceived is a world to thousands. It is said that there are more living creatures about the leviathan, which are invisible to the naked eye, than there are visible ones upon the face of the whole earth. Nay, a microscope discovers a louse to be a very lousy creature; a flea has a thousand invisible insects that teaze him as he jumps from place to place; and no doubt but those which teaze him are served in the same manner by thousands of others on their bodies, and so on *ad infinitum*. Beside this, I make no doubt but that the air is inhabited with millions of living beings.'

Mr *Thompson* having finished, the whole company returned him thanks for his entertaining discourse, and we spent together the remainder of the day in agreeable conversation. At parting the emperor insisted on us dining with him the next day; to which we consented. The next day we waited on the emperor at dinner-time, who received us with the utmost civility and complaisance. While we were at dinner, I must own I was quite dejected; and the thoughts of being so soon obliged to leave this happy country affected me greatly. However I endeavoured, as well as I could, to keep up my spirits. But this did not prevent the king, and the rest of the company, from observing my melancholy; and knowing the reason of it, he was most graciously pleased to assure me that my leaving the country could not give me more uneasiness than it did himself. 'But,' says he, 'though we have an inviolable law, that no inhabitant of the earth shall stay here above twelve months, yet there is none to prevent their returning again, after they have left us; and though it is impossible for that to happen, but by our assistance, yet you may depend upon it, if it is your desire, we will find a method to bring you here again.' I returned him many thanks for his goodness, and assured him that, if I had it in my own power to follow my inclinations, I would never quit a country, where I had received so many marks of favour, and whose inhabitants rather resembled angels than men.

Says he, 'it is certain that we are blessed with particular marks of the divine favour; but the greatest blessing we enjoy, and what is the chief cause of our happiness, is the not having occasion for that trash,

which in your world is, by the majority, more revered than the great
creator himself. Indeed we have it in a much greater abundance than
in your world, but we only use it to trample upon. As a proof of what
I have asserted, read your own histories; and you will there find, that
it has been the destruction of the greatest empires. *Rome* never saw
such generals and patriots, as she did when they were, upon any state
emergency, fetched from the plough; and having saved their country,
returned to the plough again. The wise *Lycurgus* was so sensible that
wealth, and its constant attendant luxury, were the greatest enemies
to mankind, that he prohibited the introduction of gold and silver
into his commonwealth. While these regulations continued in vigour,
the *Lacedemonians* were a great and happy people; but afterward,
upon gold and silver being introduced, the people became luxurious,
corrupt, factious, and effeminate. I cannot help observing to you, that
in your world riches is a cloak to all villainies; nay, I may venture to
say there are no villains among you but poor ones. A miserable wretch
who steals a sixpence, to save himself from starving, shall be hanged;
while the great villain, that robs his fellow-subjects of thousands,
shall glory in the theft. What among the great is called superior
talents, and respected accordingly, among the poor is called villainy,
and punished as such. I defy you to mention to me an instance in
your world, where a man, though the greatest rascal that ever existed,
provided he has money, no matter how he came by it, is not respected
and caressed, and even by those who have the reins of government
in their hands, and ought impartially to distribute justice without
favour or affection; and hang the great rogue, as well as the little
one.'

I told him there was so much truth in his observations, that I had
no reply to make, and was sorry that our world gave any one so much
reason to remark them, and especially with so much justice. 'Nay,'
says he, 'look through life, and you will find, in your world, there are
no bad people but poor ones; and that a rich man attains the reputation of a great one, by the very same methods that a poor one gets a
halter; only with this difference, that the poor one steals an halfpenny
role through hunger, and the great one robs thousands through ambition. Thanks to the great God, none of these temptations are among
us, and consequently none of the inconveniences that arise from
them.'

Our discourse afterward was upon various subjects; and he was pleased to tell me, that though he had reigned above sixty years (being then upward of 350 years of age), he had never been obliged to bring any body to public trial for misdemeanours, 'But,' said he, 'to-morrow a man is to be publicly judged for a crime, that with us is held the greatest. But as it appears that his curiosity prevailed with him to visit the earthly quarter, where he continued a considerable time, I am in hopes it will be a means of mitigating his punishment, by considering him as having been corrupted by those people, otherwise it will be no less than death. I do not doubt but you will have a curiosity to hear the trial. If so, you must be there early.' After taking a respectful leave of the emperor and the company, we returned to our habitation, where we spent the remainder of the day agreeably, and then went to rest.

The next morning we sat out sooner than ordinary, as the trial was to come on at eight o'clock. When we arrived at the palace, we found the emperor, and a vast number of persons, already assembled. As soon as he saw us, he accosted us in the most obliging manner; and as soon as he had done speaking, he proceeded to the place of trial, which was a large field; and being seated on an eminence prepared for that purpose, seventy of the oldest persons took their seats on each side of him, and soon after the criminal appeared. He was dressed in a black jacket and petticoat, his robe and turban the same colour, and no feathers. As soon as he was brought before the emperor, he was by him acquainted with the crime laid to his charge, in (as near as I can remember) the following words: –

'It is near 400 years, that our creator, by his unspeakable mercies, has allowed me to enjoy life. In all that time I never felt so uneasy a moment as I at this instant do. What pain must it give every inhabitant of the Central World, to see one of their brethren called before this venerable assembly, to answer for a crime that was hardly ever heard of before among us! You are charged with a crime of the blackest nature, and which, by our laws, is punished with death. It is a crime so detestable in itself, that it ought above all others to be punished with the utmost severity. I most heartily wish, that you may be able so far to clear yourself, as to wipe off that stain which must otherwise be for ever left to posterity, upon this age, in case you are found guilty. The crime alledged against you is that of ingratitude; and it makes my blood run cold to repeat the word. As I intend to detain the assembly as short a time as possible, I shall now order your accusers to appear,* *and acquaint us with what they have to say in regard to the charge, and then you will be allowed to make your defence.'*

There was only one person that appeared against him, and he delivered into court a paper containing the charge; which being read, was to the following effect: –

'*He had known the prisoner from his infancy. That he had always bore the best of characters until this unhappy affair happened. That be (the prisoner), through a silly curiosity, had gone to visit the earthly quarter. That he had stayed there above a month. That upon his return home, he called at his (the deponent's) house, and acquainted him with the excursion he had made; and at the same time told him, he was fearful he had incurred his father's displeasure by staying away so long; and desired him (this deponent) to give him a lodging in his house, and to endeavour to make friends between him and his (the prisoner's) father. That he (this deponent) gave him a very friendly reception, and waited on his father with a view to accommodate matters between them. That finding his father a little refractory, he continued the prisoner in his house for the space of three weeks and more, during which time he endeavoured to do him all the good offices in his power. That at last, he (the deponent) prevailed with the father to be reconciled to the son; and to receive him again into favour. That after the prisoner was received by his father, he told him,* that it was by his *(the deponent's)* instigation, that he had been so long from home; and that he should never have visited the earthly quarter, had it not been by his *(the deponent's)* persuasion. *That this false representation has occasioned great ill-will from the father of the prisoner to him (this deponent). And that likewise upon his (this deponent's) coming home one night from his (the prisoner's) father, during the time of him (the prisoner) being in this deponent's house, he found his youngest daughter, a girl about thirty, all in tears, and upon him (this deponent) asking her the reason, she acquainted him, that the prisoner, during his (the deponent's) absence, had offered violence to her; and said, the old prig, her father, was a scoundrel; and as soon as he had completed the reconciliation between him and his father, he would return him thanks by a kick on the breech,* dem *him, or words to that effect.*'

The prisoner being asked whether he was guilty or not, pleaded guilty, and threw himself on the mercy of the emperor, and the court. He likewise begged leave, in mitigation of his crime, to acquaint them, that he unhappily had heard of the earthly quarter; that his curiosity carried him there; that when he was got among those people, upon his mentioning that he was sure it would disoblige his father, and the great duty that was due from a son to a parent, they laughed at him, and said, his father was an old *prig* (a word that he did not understand), and that no *bloods* ought to have any regard for such old fools. As to the abuse offered the deponent's daughter, he acknowledged it, and that he made use of the words *dem me*, but did not know their meaning; but that they were often made use of by those people. That they likewise told him, that no young fellow ought to be looked on as a *buck*, till such time as he had either debauched his friend's daughter, or his wife. That he was sorry for the errors he had been guilty of, but, as he ingenuously confessed them, he hoped he should meet with mercy.

The emperor observed to the court, that though the young fellow made a frank and open confession of his fault; yet it would be danger-ous to permit him to dwell among them; and, that though he now seemed sensible of his crime, he might again relapse, and how fatal a thing of that sort might be to the whole empire, by debauching the morals of the youth, and, in time, introducing all the vices that were practised in the earthly world. He therefore recommended it to the wisdom of the judges, to endeavour to prevent in time, what at last might be the destruction of the empire. They therefore, in less than a quarter of an hour, resolved upon the following sentence, *viz.*

'*That the prisoner shall be taken to the place from whence he came; that he there shall have his beard and hair cut off; that from thence he shall be conducted to the earthly quarter, and never come out of it upon pain of death.*'

This sentence being confirmed by the emperor, it was immediately put into execution, and the court then broke up.

This affair, I must own, shocked me a good deal. To see the poor young fellow banished from the society of the most amiable set of men I had ever been among to a set of wretches that did not deserve to live, affected me greatly. But his doom was irrevocable; and had he been the emperor's son, it would have been put in full force. For here there is no favour or affection. If a person incurs a penalty by any breach of the constitution, he must submit to it.

How different with us! How many instances have we yearly of poor devils that have no friends suffering for trifles at the gallows; when the person guilty of the most enormous crimes (murder not excepted) shall receive a reprieve; because, perhaps, the person condemned has married a woman that is acquainted with a person, who is intimate with another, that is a great favourite of the stay-maker who works for the lady that is woman to the mistress of some great man in power.

Surely the lives of our fellow-creatures ought not to be held so cheap; and few, very few, should be so hastily launched into eternity, because they have the misfortune to be destitute of money or friends. But to return,

Though (as I said before) this young fellow's unhappy case shocked me greatly, I had soon after a greater cause of grief; for notwithstanding I had been so ill used in the world where I was born, and had so little reason to be affected with the punishments inflicted on those that originally sprung from the loins of my earthly brethren, yet I still had a little natural affection left for my countrymen (for so I call all that belong to our world); and though they brought their punishment upon themselves, I could not help pitying them. I speak of the earthly quarter (of which mention has been made), whose ancestors were formerly part of the inhabitants of our globe, but were thrown by an earthquake, near a hundred years ago, upon the central world; where they and their posterity might have enjoyed all the happiness they could wish for. But their many crimes had obliged the central inhabitants to confine them to a particular district. Even here they might have lived happily; but that mischievous, litigious, and rebellious disposition, that they had acquired from their parents, was eternally giving great uneasiness to the government; and now the time was come that they, and their whole race, were to be extinguished. The occasion of it was as follows: –

About this time, an express arrived from the earthly quarter, which brought an account, that these people (who were now increased to 2000 and upward) were all up in arms, and that they aimed at nothing less than the total destruction of the whole central empire. To kill men, women, and children, was their resolution, and by that method become masters of all that world. For this purpose they provided themselves with all sorts of the destructive implements made use of in our world. They were likewise furnished with a large quantity of gunpowder, and a regular train of artillery; having learned the art of making powder, by a manuscript that belonged to one of their ancestors. This express likewise brought an account, that the day was fixed on which they were to make the attack, by first destroying the emperor, and then assaulting the capital; and that they did not doubt of meeting with success, as the inhabitants could not make any resistance, being strangers to all sorts of arms, they having no occasion for any among themselves.

It must be imagined that this account alarmed the emperor greatly; and as the persons that had assisted at the trial of the young fellow were all on the spot, he acquainted them with the news he had received, and immediately dispatches were sent to the capital, and different parts of the empire. In a few days, two or three thousand vehicles (such as I have described before) arrived at the capital, with two persons in each. The emperor then called a council of 500 of the oldest persons present; and having acquainted them with the dangerous situation the empire was in, and how necessary it was speedily to avert the impending danger, several debates arose. Some were for putting them all to death, which they might easily have done in the night-time; for having the advantage of travelling with such expedition, they might with ease arrive over their town, when they were all asleep, and set it on fire, and by that means entirely destroy them. But this was over-ruled, murder being so contrary to their constitution and religion: beside that, by this means several innocent women and children might suffer; and hard it would be that they should be punished for the crimes of their husbands and parents. It was next proposed that 1500 chariots should set out the next night at six o'clock; and as the earthly quarter was only 150 miles distant, they might arrive there by about twelve, when they would be all asleep: that they should alight near the town, and as soon as they were entered, a certain number should secure each house, and with strong cords tye the men in their beds securely, until the emperor and his council's pleasure should be known. This met with universal approbation; and the emperor giving his consent to it, it was agreed to be put in execution the next night.

The remainder of this day, and all the next, was employed in preparing every thing necessary for the expedition, but particularly cords. The emperor had determined to head the cavalcade; and though he was persuaded against it, as it might endanger his health, yet he persisted in it, alledging, that his health or even life was not worth preserving, when not employed, on every occasion, in the service of his country. I continued, during the time they were absent, at the house of my companion's friend, with his wife and daughters; he, and the father and son, intending to go on the expedition. And now the time being come, they proceeded on their journey, but it was so dark I could not see the cavalcade, which otherwise must have been agreeable and surprising. To have seen 1500 chariots on their march through the open air, must have surpassed any thing we ever saw in our world. This whole night I was troubled with the most anxious thoughts; what between a little love that was still left for my countrymen, and the high veneration I had for the people among whom I then was, my mind was so agitated that I got little or no rest. I rose the next morning as soon as it was light and strolled about the town till breakfast-time; and when I came home, my landlady perceiving the perturbation of my mind, took every method in her power to alleviate my anxiety. About an hour after dinner, as we were sitting together in serious discourse, all on a sudden the sky was darkened, as with an eclipse. I jumped up and ran to the door, where I saw the whole air filled with chariots. I immediately concluded that it was the emperor returned, and so it happened; for shortly after, the nuts fell as thick as hail, and instantly the whole city was filled with chariots.

I soon discovered my companion and his worthy friend and sons; they met me with great affection, and acquainted me that their scheme had met with the desired success. That they found the whole town asleep, and, as was agreed on, had fastened them in their beds. That all their instruments of death, together with their powder, were destroyed; and that after great debates, it had been decided on, in order to prevent their increase, and in time to extirpate the whole race, to castrate all the males; a desperate disease requiring a desperate remedy. That the females had it left to their option, either to live with their husbands, or to marry among the central inhabitants; but that they generally embraced the latter. That the men were to be dispersed in small numbers, so that in a few years the whole race of them would be extinct. 'And thus,' says he, 'we have defeated this barbarous conspiracy, and made a proper provision, to prevent the like for the future. But, my dear friend, do not let this dispirit you; for be assured, no person in the empire is more esteemed than yourself, although you belong to the world they came from.' I made a proper return to his compliments, and we went into the house, where we were received in the most courteous manner by the good lady and her daughters.

I was greatly concerned at the severe operation my countrymen had undergone; but as they had brought it upon themselves, the melancholy which it had occasioned me soon wore off.

I was now desirous to know what was become of the young fellow whose trial I was at, and who had been banished to the earthly quarter; when, upon inquiry, they informed me, that as he had exerted himself greatly on this occasion, and was of very much service, he obtained a pardon from the emperor, and was restored to his liberty. As my companions were a good deal fatigued with their expedition, we went to bed sooner than usual.

I have often mentioned, that here the use of gold is unknown, but it is to be understood the use we put it to; for in this world gold is as common as stones with us, and as such used only in building their houses, paving their streets, &c. and precious stones of all sorts are so extremely plenty, that they are generally made use of for the same purposes, being of a prodigious size. Often have I thought to myself, when I have been walking upon a pavement of diamonds and other valuable jewels how much I exceeded the greatest of our earthly monarchs; who could trample under foot what by them is set so great a price upon, and for the attaining of which so many lives are lost. This always brought me to consider the little value of any thing that is common, and that every thing is prized in our world according to the plenty or scarcity of it.

I must confess that their towns and houses make a most dazzling appearance, which is easier to be conceived than described. For how greatly must the lustre, that every where surrounds one, exceed any thing in our world, when the largest brilliant in it is no more to be compared to the smallest here, than a pebble is to a large paving-stone.

I was one day walking in the fields, enchanted with delights which every way surrounded me, when I perceived in the air a dark spot, about the size of half a crown. I kept my eyes fixed upon it; and as it increased greatly, I could soon perceive that it was something falling from the earth. I observed with great attention where it fell, and instantly flew to the place, which was about three fields from me. When I came there, I found it was a man. But what was my surprise, when I found it to be the person mentioned at the beginning of this book, and who in our world had been to me the most ungrateful wretch that ever existed! One whom at my own expence I had long maintained in his distress; and who, after he came to affluence, had requited my services, by doing me all the injury that lay in his power. One who, instead of acknowledging the favours he had received, not only refused me his assistance, but so effectually did me ill offices with my friends and relations, as to make them likewise forsake me; which occasioned me for a long time to undergo the greatest hardships. But this was not a time to remember injuries. He stood in need of my assistance, and it was my duty to give it him. His ingratitude was no excuse for my behaving contrary to the dictates of humanity. I therefore immediately took out my bottle, which had been given me when I first came here, and applied the ointment in the same manner the good old man had done to me in the like distress. He instantly jumped up, and attempted to embrace my feet. I flew from him, and said in *English*, 'attempt not to worship him to whom you have been the greatest of enemies. I now have had it in my power to show a proper revenge, and the most agreeable one it has been to me, by returning good for bad. In return for the many injuries I have received from you, I have saved your life. Look in my face, for my dress cannot alter that; and there you will see the man, who formerly was your best of friends, and whose friendship you requited, by being his worst of enemies.'

His surprise and astonishment cannot be described; for upon hearing me speak *English*, he instantly knew me; but for a long time could get out no more than, 'Oh! my God, is it you?' As soon as he recovered, he said, 'you have been long dead, and we are both now in that place where we are to be rewarded or punished, according to the manner in which we lived on earth; but the happy lot is yours, and mine the wretched; for of all my crimes, that against you is the greatest.'

I assured him that we were both alive, and still mortal; and that he was arrived in a world that exceeded ours, as much as angels did men. I happened to have a little bottle of cordial in my pocket, of which I gave him some; and it revived him greatly; but I found him bruised very much by his fall, it happening upon the hard ground. He most earnestly begged pardon for his perfidy toward me, and I very readily gave it him. After acquainting him with the particulars of my adventures, and likewise having informed him where we were, and described this world and inhabitants to him, I desired to know what accident had sent him to the Central World.

Mr *Worldly* (for that was his name) acquainted me, that he, and several others, had made a party to visit the wonders of the peak of *Derby*. That in too curiously viewing, and advancing too far into that wonderful chasm called the *Devil's Arse*, his foot had slipped, and he tumbled into a vast hole. That he continued falling for a considerable time, and at last was surrounded with a glory that exceeded any thing he had ever beheld. That the quickness of the motion with which he fell had quite deprived him of his senses; and that he could give no account of any thing farther, till the time that I had found him. He then proceeded to tell me, that upon my being missing, all the search imaginable had been made after me; that my friends hearing nothing of me, it was concluded that I had either been drowned, or some other way destroyed. That then those relations, who had used me with so much cruelty, had relented greatly, and blamed their own too great severity to me. 'And,' says he, 'we often find that death softens the hearts of those who were inexorable to the cries and distresses of the person when living. For my own part, after it was reported that you was dead, my conscience was so stung with the injuries I had done you, that I had not an easy moment, and often thought myself accessary to your death.' I again assured him, that I most heartily forgave him, and he swore to me an inviolable friendship. I then carried him to the house of my friend; where, having told them his story, he was received by them all with the utmost civility.

Soon after he came into the house, the operation was performed upon him (as formerly it had been upon me); by which he acquired their language, to his great surprise and satisfaction. Our discourse till bed-time turned chiefly upon what has already been said, relating to the world we were upon.

Mr *Worldly*, by the bruises he had received in his fall, was the next morning attacked with a violent fever; and as there were no such things as doctors in this country (the inhabitants never having occasion for any of them), I undertook to supply their place. But all was in vain; for the third day after he came among us, he expired. I was most sensibly affected with this disaster, especially as he had appeared so sensible of the injustice he had done me, and as I had promised myself much satisfaction in his future acquaintance. No pains were spared to give him a decent funeral; at which the emperor himself, my companion, his friend and family, and many of the inhabitants, attended.

As Mr *Worldly*, in our discourse together, had told me that my relations would rejoice to hear I was alive, and likewise had mentioned the concern they had shown on my supposed death; I must own it greatly abated the concern I had been under, at the thoughts of leaving this country at the year's end. I therefore determined to propose to my companion, at a proper opportunity, our return to his father's; for I began to long to see the good old man and lady, and stay sometime with them before my departure. But how that was to be performed, I could not conceive; for though I had tumbled down, I had no idea of tumbling up again. I had still two or three months good; so I gave myself no great concern about it, and left the management of my return entirely to them.

We now past our time in the most agreeable manner, in walking and conversation. As to the pleasures of *Vauxhall* and *Ranelagh*, they were exceeded by every common field; and the warbling of the birds far surpassed any concert in our world.

One day, as my friend and I were conversing together upon different subjects, I observed by his discourse that he had a greater inclination to return to his father's than myself; and when I questioned him upon it; 'my friend,' said he, 'I can disguise nothing from you. I have for a long time paid my addresses to a lady in our neighbourhood, whose charms exceed any thing that was ever yet beheld. The only obstacle I met with to accomplish my utmost wishes, was the obtaining her own consent. I have this day received an express, that upon my return she is determined to make me happy.'

I congratulated him upon his good fortune, and assured him that the sooner we sat out, the more agreeable it would be to me. As soon as we had made our intentions known, the whole town vied with one another, which should entertain us in the most friendly manner. This took us up ten or twelve days; at the end of which time, we took our leave of the emperor, and the rest of our friends, and agreed to set out the next morning on our return home. About eight o'clock we began our journey, after having taken leave of our kind host and his family. My companion had a mind to acquaint his sister with his good fortune. Accordingly, we arrived there about noon, and were received with the greatest affection. She pressed us very earnestly to stay dinner, but we excused ourselves, and proceeded on our journey; and reached home about six in the evening.

It is impossible to express the joy, which the old man and lady expressed on seeing us return. After we came into the parlour, we gave them a particular account of our reception by the emperor, &c. and every other particular that had happened during our absence. Now nothing was the topic of our conversation, but the approaching nuptials; and the next day the son proposed making a visit to his intended spouse, and was so kind as to invite me to accompany him. Accordingly, the next morning he sat out for the house that contained the treasure of his soul. It was about three hours journey, and we arrived there before dinner. But to express their transports is impossible.

After the first raptures were a little subsided, I was introduced to the parents, by whom I was received with that unaffected complaisance that is peculiar to these people. When I was introduced to the future bride, and had made her a compliment on her approaching happiness, she was pleased to say, that she had long heard of my being a friend of her intended spouse; and that nothing now gave her concern, but to think that the time of my stay among them would be so short, that I should not have a long proof of that happiness she expected from my friend, and which she was in hopes to afford him. I told her, that though I could not long be an eye-witness of their happiness, yet in the little time I had had the honour of being in her company, I was sufficiently convinced, that whoever had the pleasure of possessing her must be the happiest of mortals. She was pleased to return me thanks for my compliment; when dinner being ready, we retired to the room appointed for that purpose. After we had been very agreeably entertained here the best part of the day, my companion took an affectionate leave of his future bride; and we immediately returned to his father's.

The next morning, my friend's sister and brother-in-law arrived very early; and before eight we had several friends and relations assembled together to be present at the approaching ceremony. The bridegroom was dressed all in white, except his robe, which was sky-colour; and indeed he made a fine appearance. About nine we set out for the place which possessed the treasure of his soul.

We found her beautiful as *Venus*; and the dress she had chosen added to her natural charms. God's command to them is the same as in our world, *viz.* to increase and multiply. Therefore nothing more is required on these occasions, than the consent of the parties to be joined together.

As soon as the parties were met, the father of the bride conducted her into the middle of the assembly, and the father of the bridegroom did the same by him. They were respectively acquainted by their parents, that marriage was an holy institution, ordered by God to keep up the race of mankind. That it was as great a felicity as could befal a man in this world, if the parties agreed as they ought; but if married contrary to their inclinations, a greater misery could not happen. For these reasons, it had ever been the practice of their ancestors, not to interfere in the choice their children had made. Therefore they desired them to declare freely, before the whole company, whether the choice they had made of each other proceeded entirely from their own inclinations, or whether they had been in any degree influenced or directed in it by parents or any other relations. Upon their both declaring, that it proceeded entirely from the love they bore each other, their hands were joined, and they mutually promised to be faithful.

After the ceremony was over, the company were regaled in an elegant manner; and after a great deal of mirth and good humour, the bridegroom conducted his spouse to her father's house, and the rest of the company retired to their respective homes. Notwithstanding I passed my time in the most agreeable manner, my desire to return to my native country increased. I therefore took an opportunity to tell my worthy old friend of it; and I begged that he would be so kind to add to the number of favours I had already received from him, that of putting me in a way of accomplishing my design. He was pleased to say, that it gave him great concern to think that he must part with me; 'but I will not only comply with your request, but likewise accompany you myself.' I returned him many thanks for his goodness, and it gave me great pleasure to think that I should have his company. I employed my time between this and my departure, in taking leave of all my friends and acquaintance; which when done, the old man was as good as his word, and got every thing in readiness. As soon as we came to the door, I perceived two very large birds; to the beak of each of them was fastened a long ribbon, which my kind conductor taking in his hand, he directed me to get upon its back, and himself mounted the other. He kept the ribbon that was fastened to mine in his hand, as we often see a groom hold a rein of his young master's horse, before he is perfected in riding; and upon his giving the signal, they extended their wings, and soared up with us at a

prodigious rate. I believe in about six hours, we had got half way on
our journey. My conductor now desired me to observe the glory that
surrounded me (for we were come so near to the concave part of our
world, that the jewels with which it was studded almost took away
my eye-sight); but this did not last long, for presently we were surrounded with a total darkness. He then told me that we were got into
the crust of our world; and that the passing of it would be much
more difficult than all the former part of our journey. And indeed so
it was, for the space was so much confined, that the birds had hardly
room to move their wings; but in about an hour after we had been
in this darkness, I discovered light, and presently afterward we arrived
safe upon my mother world, but in what part I never knew.

He congratulated me upon our safe arrival; and told me, that we
were within a few miles of *London*, whither he would accompany me,
but that I must submit, for a little while, to have my eyes covered,
that I might not know in what part to find this entrance to their world.
I consented to it; and after being carried through the air a quarter
of an hour, the birds settled on the ground, and I dismounted; but
as soon as my eyes were uncovered, I missed the birds, and what
became of them, I never could learn. The ointment, which had been
used upon me at my first falling on the centre, had rendered my body
of a proper gravity for that world, by taking off the great power of its
attractive quality; but now, as I was arrived in our world, where the
attraction was not near so great, I found much inconvenience from
it, for I could hardly keep my feet on the ground, and got two or
three tumbles upon my nose; but my friend soon relieved me, by
sprinkling me with a certain liquid, which instantly restored me to
my proper weight. As we had both of us our central garbs on, I
recollected an old friend, who lived in *Piccadilly*, that I was in hopes
might supply us with proper dresses, as he dealt in those sorts of
things. We accordingly went to his house; and on the door being
opened, the maid, as soon as she saw us in such odd dresses,
screamed out, 'a ghost a ghost!' The noise brought down the master,
who upon my speaking to him instantly knew me. I told him, that I
and my friend had been upon a frolic a masquerading; and that as
we were a good way from home, I should be greatly obliged to him
if he would furnish us with some other dress; to which he agreed;
but expressed a good deal of surprise at the prodigious length of my
friend's beard. I told him that he was a foreigner, spoke no *English*,

and that it was the custom of the country he came from, to wear their beards to that length. With this his curiosity was satisfied.

I let my acquaintance know that we were without money; he generously lent me a couple of guineas, and insisted on our dining with him the next day. I must own that now the calls of hunger were very strong upon me, which I signified to my old friend; and I found that a little supper would not be disagreeable to him. And it is not to be wondered at that we should be hungry, considering that we had travelled this day no less than 3000 miles; which will be easily seen, if the reader pleases to observe, that the diameter of our world is 7000 miles, the diameter of the central globe 1000; consequently from the surface of one to the surface of the other, must be 3000 miles. We now prepared to seek out a proper house to allay the cravings of nature; and we pitched upon the *Thatched House* tavern. As I knew my friend would touch nothing that had had life, as soon as we entered I ordered a large sallad, some artichoaks to be boiled, with other things of that sort, and a dash of tarts and cream cheese. When we had supped, and drank a bottle of claret, we paid our reckoning, and went to *Piero*'s bagnio, to take up our quarters for the night. Upon my getting up in the morning, I went to my good old friend's chamber, whom I found already risen; and after having breakfasted, we sallied into the streets, where we did not want for crowds of gazers; for his beard was of a prodigious length, and as white as silver.

I now began to think of furnishing myself with a little money by disposing of a diamond, which my friend brought from the Central World. We accordingly took coach, and drove to a jeweller's in the city, who gave me 75 pounds for it, which was about half its value. We then went to a coffee-house near the Royal Exchange, where I met a very old acquaintance (a clergyman), who expressed a surprising pleasure at seeing me, for he said he had heard that I was dead.

As soon as he had taken leave of us and left the room, my friend looked very gravely in my face, and asked me how long I had known that person. I told him many years, that we were school-fellows together, that he was now in a very prosperous situation; and that he owed all he had in the world to my family. Says he, 'at the time you was in distress no doubt but he assisted you.' I told him, that I had often applied to him; even at times that I knew he had it in his power to relieve me; but that he had always excused himself; and that, indeed, he had so pretty a manner in making his excuse, and always accompanied it with so many professions of friendship, that a denial from him was more agreeable than a compliance in others, and that I was sure he was warmly my friend. 'God help you!' says he, 'you little think what deceit those fine protestations are a cloak to; for as you know, we can discover the sentiments of those we converse with, I perceived at the time he was talking to you so much insincerity in every word he said, and I saw into his heart so well, that be assured he is the greatest enemy you have, and at this instant is doing you a disservice, though I have it not in my power to know what; otherwise we would guard against it. But as I must soon leave you, be advised by me, if you intend to avoid falling into such hardships a second time as you have already felt, look henceforward on all mankind as your enemies, and guard against them as such. You have often been deceived. You may be so again; but by this means you must be safe from all such accidents.'

Some time after, as we were crossing *Covent Garden*, two ill-looking ugly fellows made directly up to us, when one of them immediately asked me if my name was not *Bruce*? I replied, 'yes, that is my name.' He then told me he had an action against me for the sum of twenty pounds. I asked him at whose suit? He told me, Mr. *Buckram* the taylor. I remembered that I owed him the sum, but was greatly surprised he should know that I was in the land of the living. However, I told the officer that so small a sum as twenty pounds should not oblige me to go to prison; but that if he would step into a tavern with me, I would discharge the action. He immediately consented. As soon as we came into the house, and had got a room, I paid him the debt and charges, and gave him a guinea for himself, with which he was greatly pleased. I now had a strong curiosity to know by what means Mr. *Buckram* could be informed of my being in *London*. I therefore questioned the officer about it; and upon my promising secrecy, he told me that Mr. *Silvertongue* had seen me in the morning at a coffee-house in the city; that he immediately acquainted Mr. *Buckram* with it, and had persuaded him to take out a writ, and arrest me for that he had seen a good deal of money about me.

I must own, this account filled me with so much rage and indignation, that I was quite uneasy. As soon as the officer had left us, 'well,' says my companion, 'what do you think now of your friend?' – 'Think,' says I, 'I could not have thought there was such a villain in nature.'

We now proceeded to my friend's house in *Piccadilly*. The first thing I did was to repay the two guineas, and purchase the clothes we had borrowed of him; after which he entertained us with great cheerfulness. When dinner was over, we sent our central clothes to *Piero's* with orders to keep the same rooms we had the night before; and after taking our leave, we went into the mall, where we walked till supper time.

As we were going to bed, my companion told me, he was determined to return home the next morning. 'But I enjoin you, by our friendship,' says he, 'not to stir out of your room till your usual hour; nor by any means endeavour to find out the time or manner of my departure, for I shall set out early; and as my return will be much speedier than my journey hither, I shall be at home by dinner. But if your curiosity leads you to pry into the manner of my performing my journey, you will lose my friendship forever. You may depend upon sometime or other seeing me again, or some of my family. In the mean time, may the great creator preserve you! and trust not to mankind.' So saying, he affectionately embraced me. As soon as I got to my chamber, I threw myself upon the bed, but could not get one wink of sleep. However, as my worthy friend had enjoined me to keep my room till my usual hour, I most religiously observed it.

A little after eight I went into his chamber. He had left the clothes which I purchased, and taken his own. The clothes that I brought from the centre I have still by me, and in my will have left them (after my decease) to be lodged with Sir *Hans Sloane's* curiosities in the *British* Museum.

I spent the remainder of the day in the most melancholy manner I ever did in my life; and in the evening I went to Captain *Will's* coffee house, to inquire after my worthy friend the captain that had been so kind to me, and carried me with him to *Italy*; but was informed that he had been dead some months.

The next morning I set out for my relations in the country, who received me with great affection. This indeed greatly alleviated my grief; but it was with much difficulty that I could make them believe the truth of my adventures. After staying with them for some time, they gave me a sum of money, and settled a decent income on me for life. I paid off all my debts, and took a little cottage in *Kent*; where I live now with as much comfort as is possible in this world; for I keep little company, and am daily in the pleasing expectation of seeing some of my central acquaintances.

It is in this retreat that I have collected together the particulars of my adventures; and it is on this spot that I hope to finish my days, unless some happy accident carries me again to the centre.